ANGLERS journal & ALMANAC

TIDE AND FISHING PREDICTIONS FOR 2025 & 2026

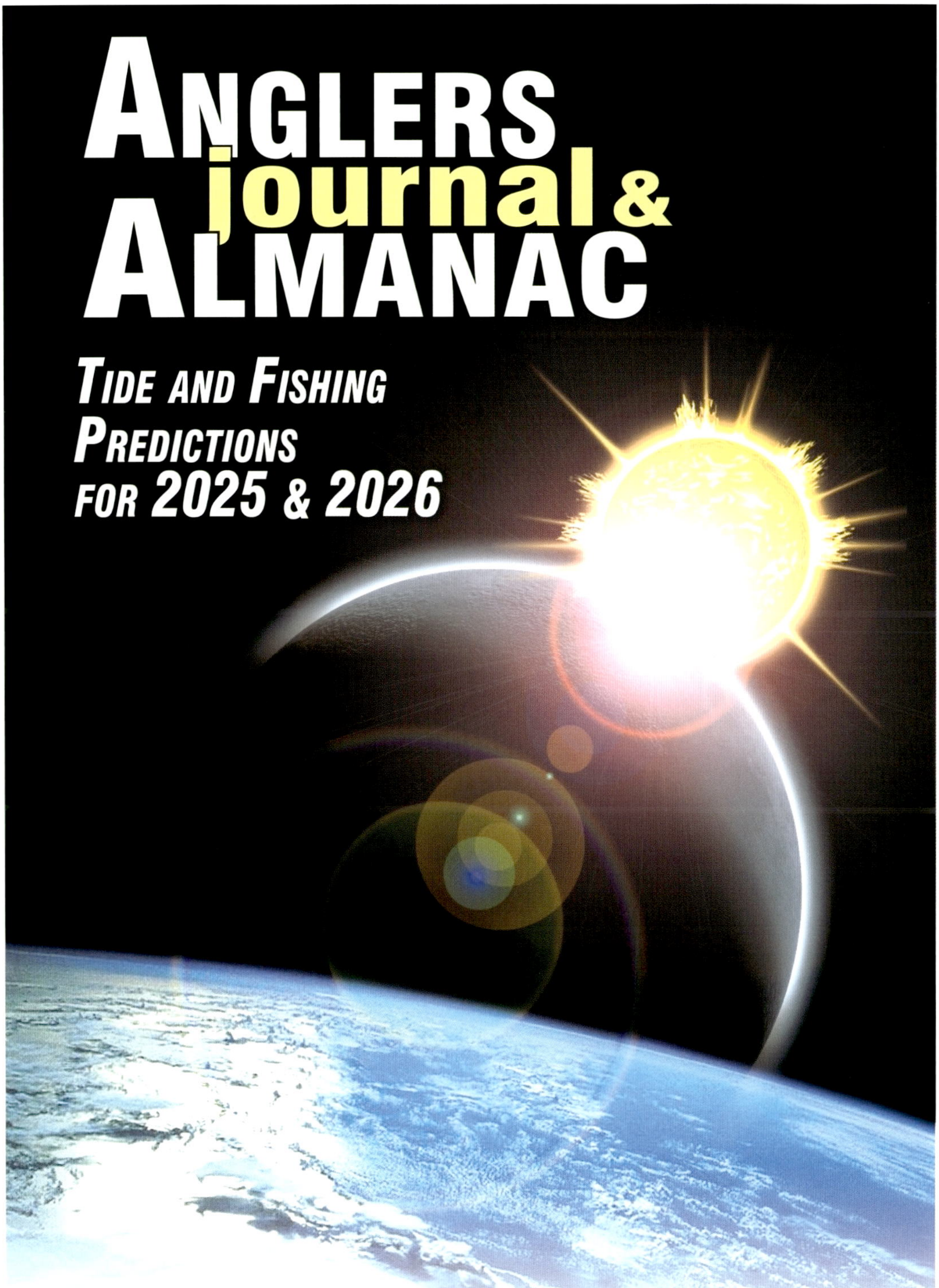

DISCLAIMER

The solar/lunar bite times in this book were derived from the program* WXTide32 *and are predictions. While they are as accurate as possible, they should be used as a guide only. Local conditions and changes can cause variations, so consult a website such as the* Bureau of Meteorology Oceanographic Services, (www.bom.gov.au/oceanography/tides) *as close as possible to the tide date and time before your fishing trip for the most up-to-date information and if you require certified information.
The publisher, Australian Fishing Network, advises that the information in this guide should not be used for navigation and should not be relied on for crucial situations.

"This product is based on Bureau of Meteorology information that has subsequently been modified. The Bureau does not necessarily support or endorse, or have any connection with, the product.
In respect of that part of the information which is sourced from the Bureau, and to the maximum extent permitted by law:
(i) The Bureau makes no representation and gives no warranty of any kind whether express, implied, statutory or otherwise in respect to the availability, accuracy, currency, completeness, quality or reliability of the information or that the information will be fit for any particular purpose or will not infringe any third party Intellectual Property rights; and
(ii) the Bureau's liability for any loss, damage, cost or expense resulting from use of, or reliance on, the information is entirely excluded."
"The Bureau of Meteorology gives no warranty of any kind whether express, implied, statutory or otherwise in respect to the availability, accuracy, currency, completeness, quality or reliability of the information or that the information will be fit for any particular purpose or will not infringe any third party Intellectual Property rights.
The Bureau's liability for any loss, damage, cost or expense resulting from use of, or reliance on, the information is entirely excluded."

Illustrations: Trevor Hawkins
Cover Photo Credits: Ben Godfrey and Ben Scullin

Published in 2025 by
AFN Fishing & Outdoors
PO Box 544, Croydon, VIC 3136
Tel: (03) 9729 8788
Email: sales@afn.com.au
www.afn.com.au

ISBN 9781 8651 3440 6

J1387

CONTENTS

Basic KNOT TYING

Improved Clinch Knot

This simple yet strong knot is very good for attaching hooks and snap swivels to your line.

1. Thread the line in the hook eye and pull to get a few inches of tag end.
2. Take five turns around the standing line.
3. Thread the tag end through the first loop in front of the hook eye.

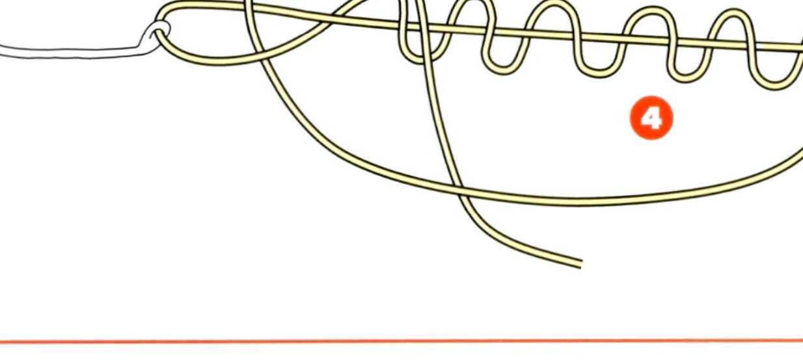

4. Thread the tag end through the large loop just formed. Wet the knot and pull steadily on the standing line to cinch the knot against the hook. Trim the tag and you're done.

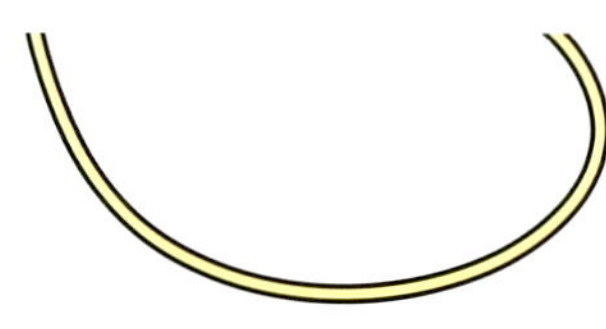

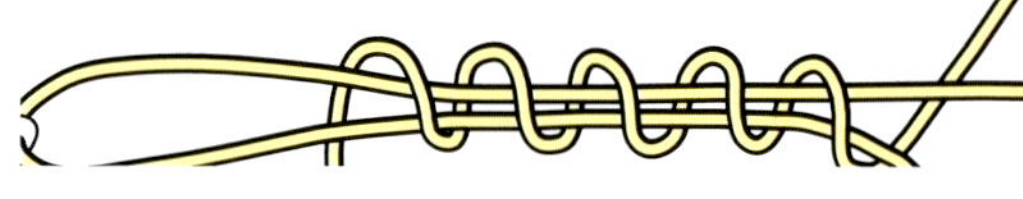

Uni Knot

Another simple, strong knot for attaching terminal tackle.

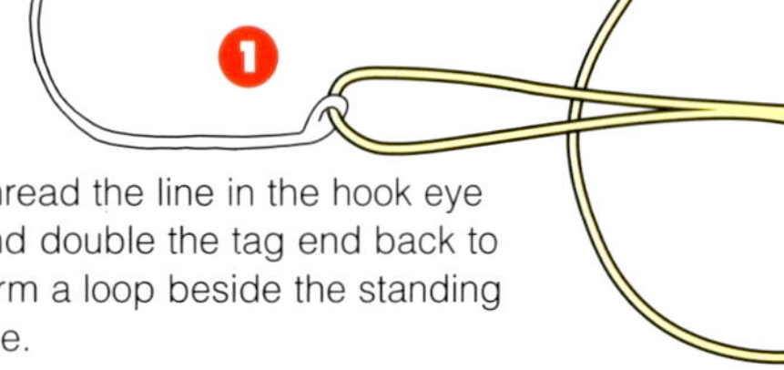

1. Thread the line in the hook eye and double the tag end back to form a loop beside the standing line.

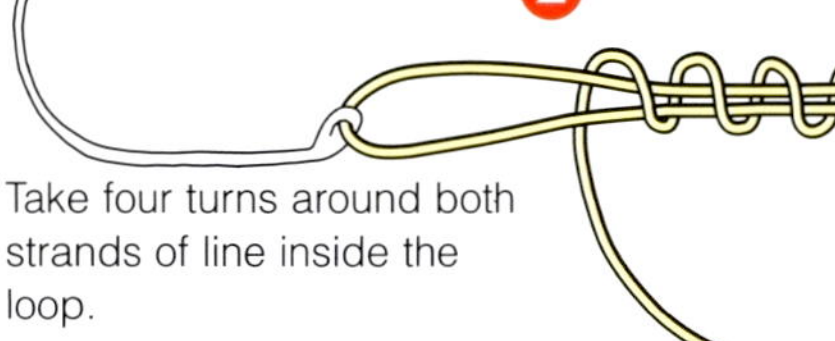

2. Take four turns around both strands of line inside the loop.

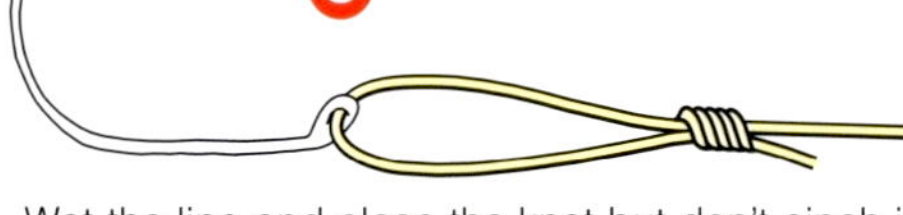

3. Wet the line and close the knot but don't cinch it down completely.

4. Slide the knot against the hook eye, pull it tight and trim the tag.

Blood Bight Dropper Knot

This knot is used to make loops that stand off the main line, to which you can attach your hooks. Additionally you can tie a Blood Bight at the end of the rig and use it to attach your sinkers. This is a very important knot when making rigs to fish off piers, rocks, surf and jetties. It is also used when bottom fishing offshore and in bays.

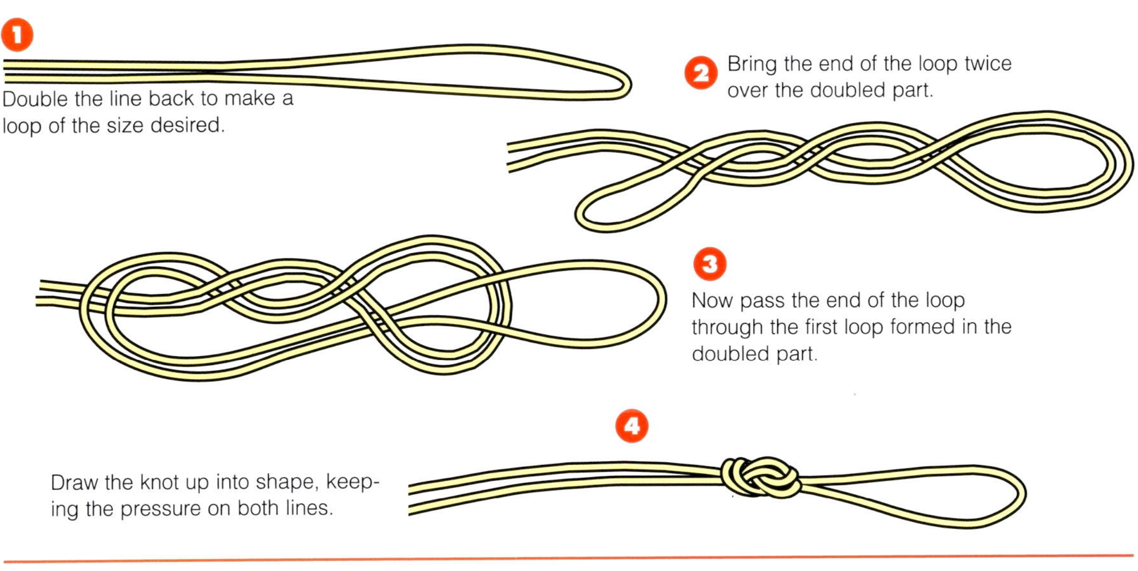

1. Double the line back to make a loop of the size desired.

2. Bring the end of the loop twice over the doubled part.

3. Now pass the end of the loop through the first loop formed in the doubled part.

4. Draw the knot up into shape, keeping the pressure on both lines.

Lefty's Loop

This knot is about the easiest of the lure loop knots to master and is equally effective on light or heavy lines. When locked it doesn't slip and it has a very high knot strength, well over 90 percent, so it can be used with leaders or just straight onto the main line.

1. First make a simple overhand knot.

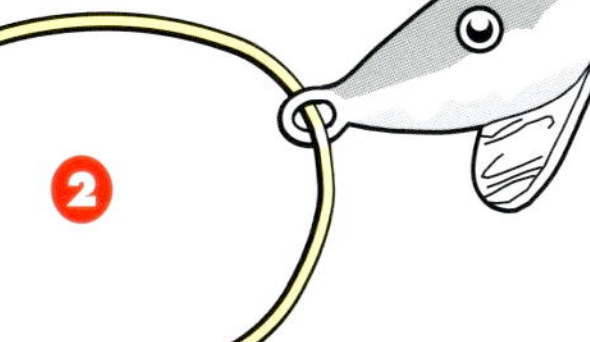

2. Pass the tag end back through the circle after feeding the line through the eye of your lure.

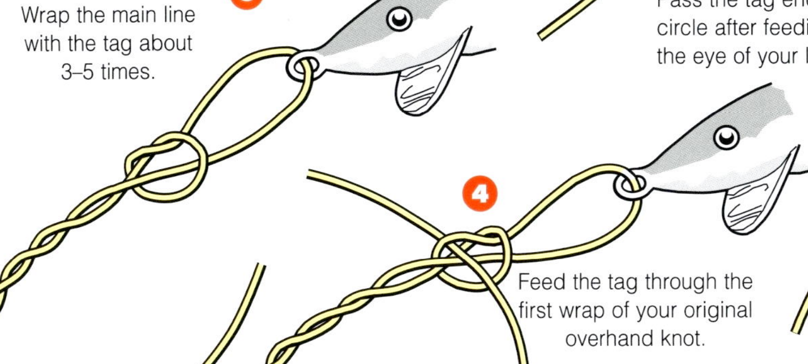

3. Wrap the main line with the tag about 3–5 times.

4. Feed the tag through the first wrap of your original overhand knot.

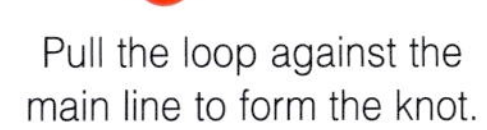

5. Pull the loop against the main line to form the knot.

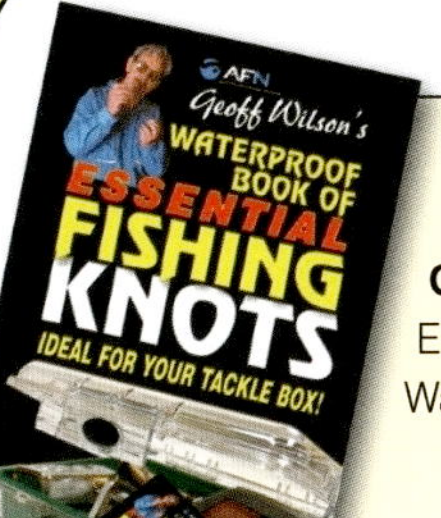

Geoff Wilson
Essential Knots
Waterproof Book

Form a loop in the end of the heavier line by bending back about 5 inches of line. Pass the tag end of the lighter line through this loop.

Pinch the lines about 3 inches from the end of the loop, leaving about 3 inches of tag beyond this point to tie the knot.

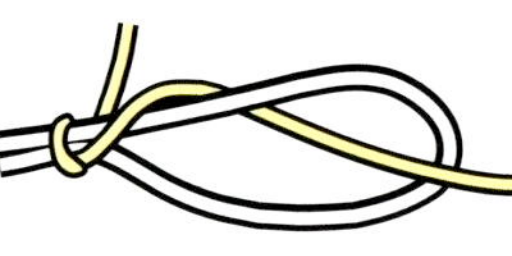

3

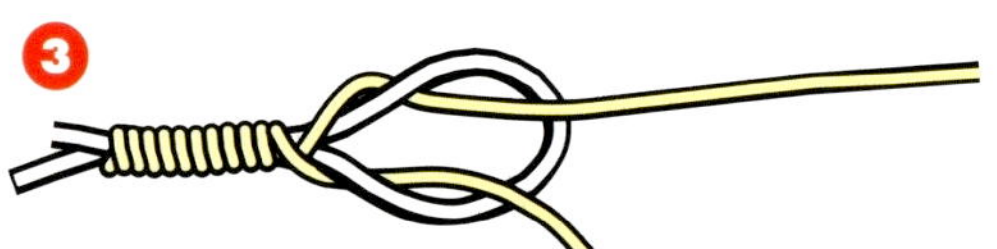

Working down toward the loop, take 10 wraps around all three strands of line. Pass the tag end through the end loop on the same side it originally entered.

Albright Knot

The Albright knot serves to join two monofilament lines of different diameters, such as when attaching a heavier leader to your main line. DO NOT use the Albight to tie a mono leader to superbraid line because the knot may slip!

4 Slowly pull both strands of lighter line while grasping the heavier line and working the knot's coils toward the loop end. Do not let the coils slip off the loop. Tighten, then trim the tag ends.

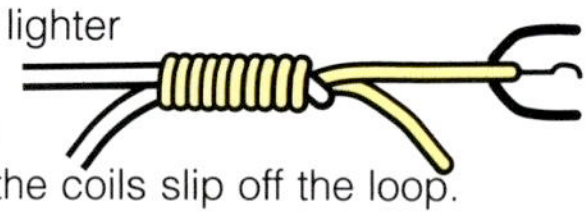

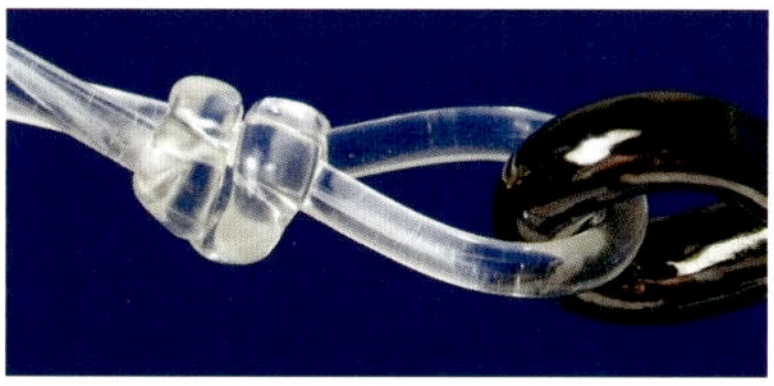

Thumb Knot

This is the knot to use with 60- to 200-pound-test monofilament. It may be that you are live baiting for tuna or grouper or trolling offshore with big lures. With really heavy monofilament you need a knot that allows you to tighten and lock it. The locked half blood and uni knots are not suitable here.

This is an optional knot to learn and only needed if you require a rig in the following section that specifies this knot.

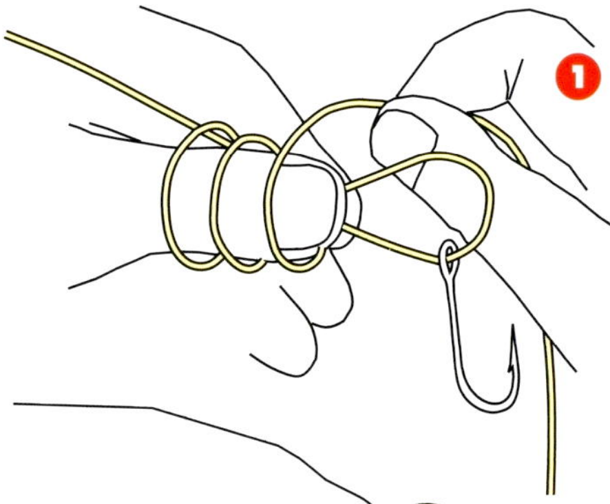

1 Thread your hook with the line and make a loop so that the hook is suspended from the loop. Pinch the crossover between the thumb and finger of your left hand. Start wrapping your left thumb and loop with the tag. Make three wraps in all, working from the base of your thumb toward the thumbnail.

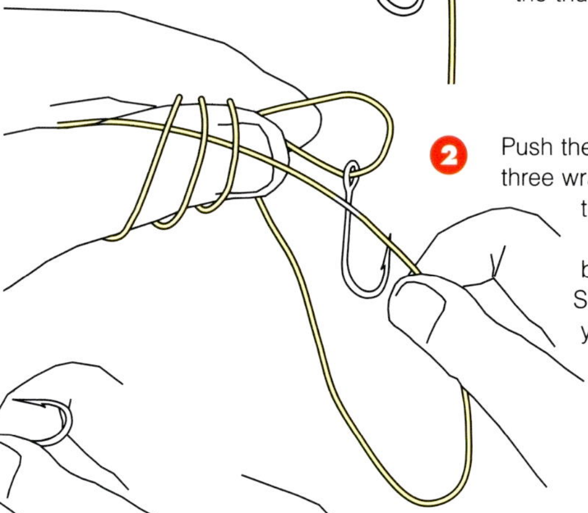

2 Push the tag back under those three wraps alongside your thumb. Push it all the way back toward the base of your thumb. Secure the tag against your left thumb with your middle finger.

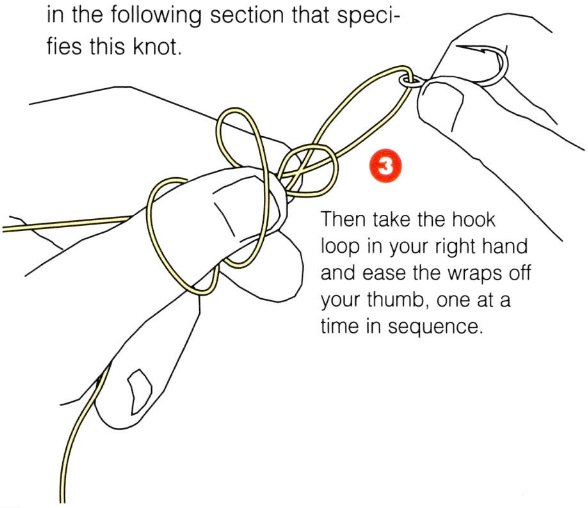

3 Then take the hook loop in your right hand and ease the wraps off your thumb, one at a time in sequence.

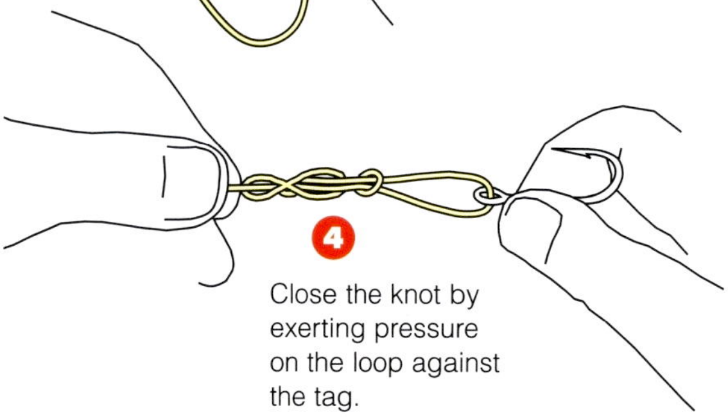

4 Close the knot by exerting pressure on the loop against the tag.

Double Uni Knot

The double uni quickly and effectively joins two lines. It's ideal for attaching a monofilament leader to superbraid line because it won't slip when tied correctly.

1. Run the lines to be joined parallel and then take one tag end and form a loop over the other line.
2. Wrap the tag through the loop and around the lines four or five times.
3. Draw the knot together.
4. Repeat the process with the other tag end.

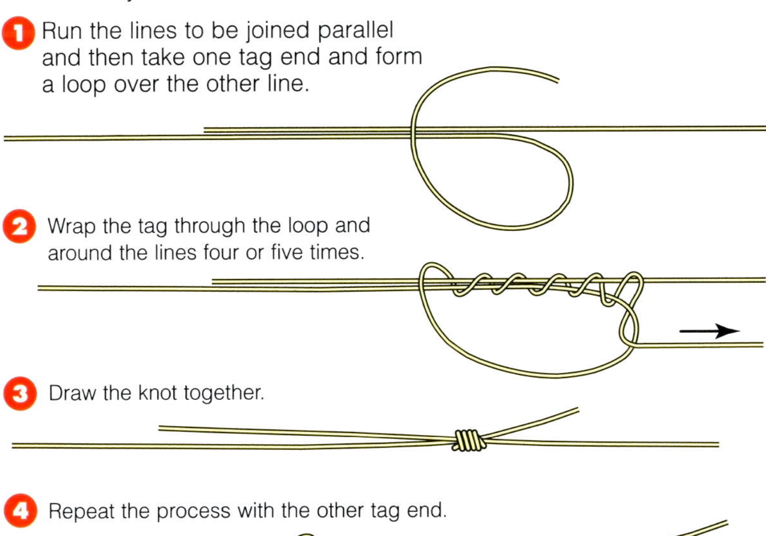

5. Lubricate both knots and then pull them together.

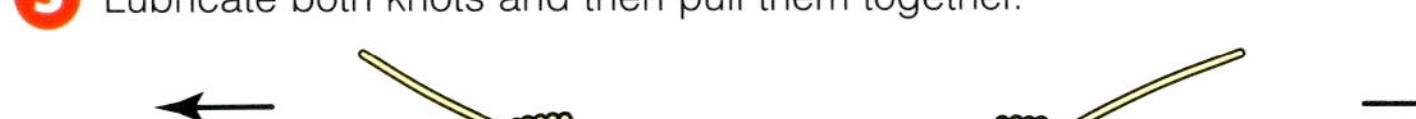

6. Then take the tag ends to clinch the knots tight. Pull on the lines again to ensure that the knots are snug. Trim off the tags.

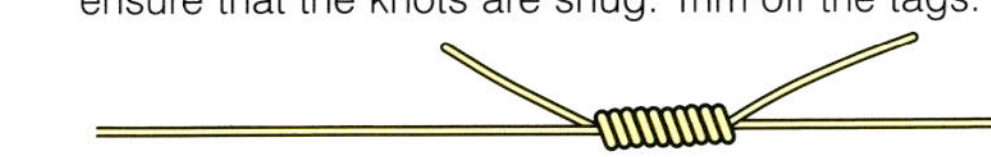

Arbor Knot

This is a very fast and secure knot for attaching line to the reel.

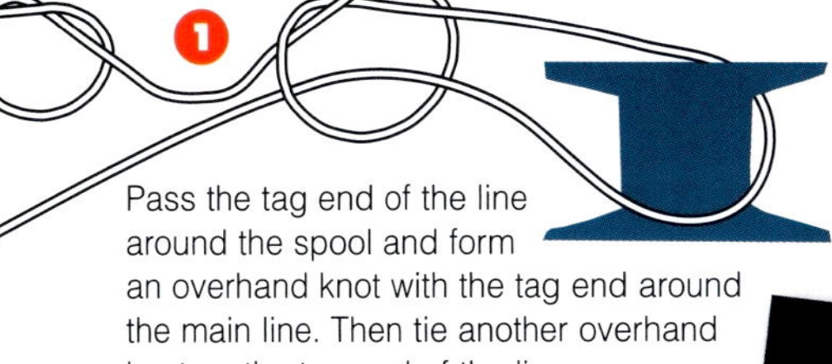

1. Pass the tag end of the line around the spool and form an overhand knot with the tag end around the main line. Then tie another overhand knot on the tag end of the line.

2. Lubricate the knots, tighten down by pulling the main line and trim the tag.

SUPERBRAID LINE

In 1979 Dutch State Mines (Royal DSM N.V.), a company in Holland, invented an incredibly strong synthetic fiber and named it Dyneema. The production process draws a mixture of ultrahigh molecular-weight polyethylene (UHMWPE) into fibers. The extreme length of individual molecules and their capacity to align themselves in the direction of the fiber give Dyneema its phenomenal strength. In a pound-for-pound comparison, Dyneema—a material light enough to float—rates 15 times stronger than steel!

After receiving license from DSM, Allied Signal (now called Honeywell) developed a chemically similar fiber in the United States and named it Spectra. Dyneema and Spectra exhibit nearly identical properties that include good abrasion resistance as well as resistance to UV light, chemicals and water. Both materials find use in products as varied as bulletproof armor, boat sails and really important stuff like fishing lines.

Unlike monofilament, which consists of a single strand of nylon, Spectra/Dyneema lines contain many filaments that are braided together. These lines have earned the nickname "superbraid" because they are very thin yet extremely strong and abrasion-resistant. They have very little stretch, making it easier to detect subtle bites. On the other hand, superbraid's thin diameter and slick surface require extra care when tying knots. It is also very hard to pick out backlashes in baitcasters.

Lure COLOUR SELECTION

Fish & Colour

Fish have eyes that possess a fixed, non-dilating pupil so they cannot adjust to brighter or dimmer light conditions. As a result many fish when feeding will conceal themselves in shaded cover so they can see and pounce on food fishes that are passing in brighter light.

A fish's ability to see a lure is determined by two factors, namely the clarity of the water and its visibility.

CLARITY

This is a measure of the cloudiness of the water or it is often said to be the transparency of the water. The clearer the water the further a fish can see a lure.

VISIBILITY

This is a measure of the available light in the water. Available light decreases with depth and darkening light conditions associated with dusk and night, cloud and low light conditions outside.

The combination of these two factors will affect how fish will see colour and hence your lure!

To understand the balance of the two, realise that fish will be most active at a light level affording them optimum cover from being seen, yet themselves being in an optimum position to see prey. Hence fish may be active in cloudy water (low clarity) in the middle of the day and on another day be most active before dawn (low visibility) in clear water.

Also note that our choices include rattlers, spinners and vibrators as when clarity and visibility are low it is best to add sound to the equation.

What Colours can Fish See?

As far as fish are concerned there are nine basic colours in nature that usually do the job. These are red, purple, orange, yellow, green, blue, silver, white and black.

Red – An all-time proven fish catching colour. Possibly because it is the colour of blood, which excites all predators. It is also the colour of the gills of food fishes, the target area where fish strike to cripple their prey.

Purple – Along with blue this is an outstanding fish catching colour. Purple has enduring colour recognition even at long distances.

Orange – Has good contrasting ability in a subdued and warm fashion. Some food fishes have orange stripes or spots.

Yellow – An all-time, proven fish-catching colour. As it reflects any available light, it contrasts with almost everything: underwater, cover, sky or the bottom. A colour seen by fish at great distances.

Green – A great summertime colour and the colour of life-supporting plants which give off vital oxygen in the fish world. Solid green lures never work well on their own, possibility because they blend in too well to the backgrounds. Green is ideal for scaling and trimming and chartruese (combination of green and yellow) is a hot choice.

Blue – Probably natures truest colour and an all-time best seller in the US. It has enduring recognition even at distance.

White & Silver – A dominant combination of colours in the fish world. Especially in the manner in which fish scales reflect light. Flashing scales attract a predators eye instantly. White and silver reflect all light in all conditions even in muddy water.

Black – Black contrasts against any colour except black itself. It is a great option in muddy water.

FRESHWATER

CLEAR WATER

Depth (m) | Full Sun | Partial Cloud | Overcast | Rain | Sunrise & sunset

1 2 3 4 5 6 7 8 9 10

SALTWATER

CLEAR WATER INSHORE

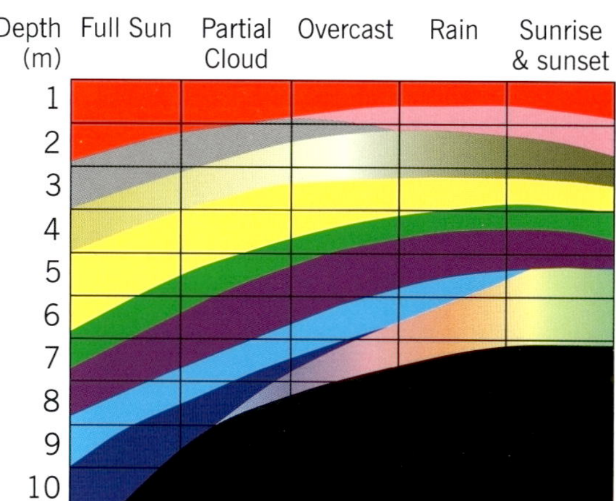

MUDDY OR TANNIN STAINED WATER

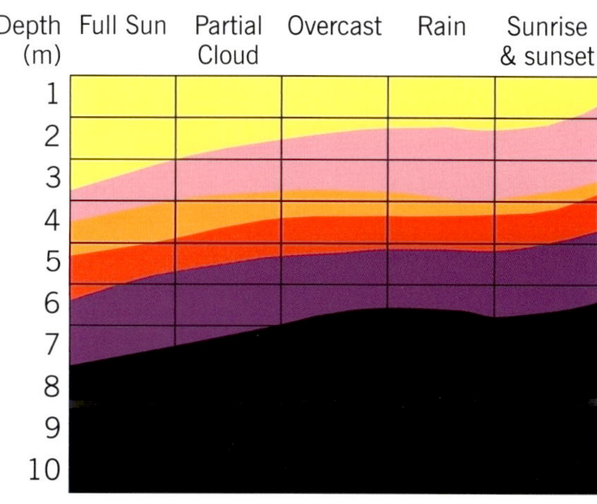

CLEAR WATER OFFSHORE

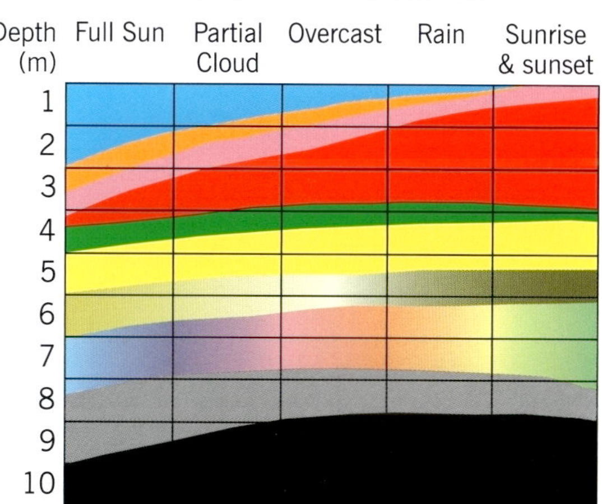

'GREEN' OR ALGAL STAINED WATER

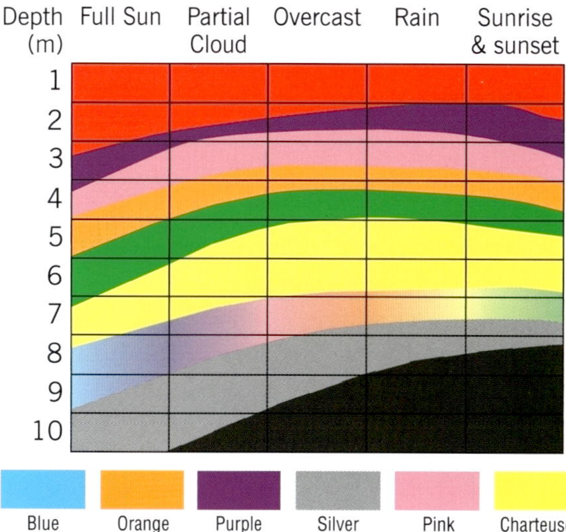

MUDDY WATER

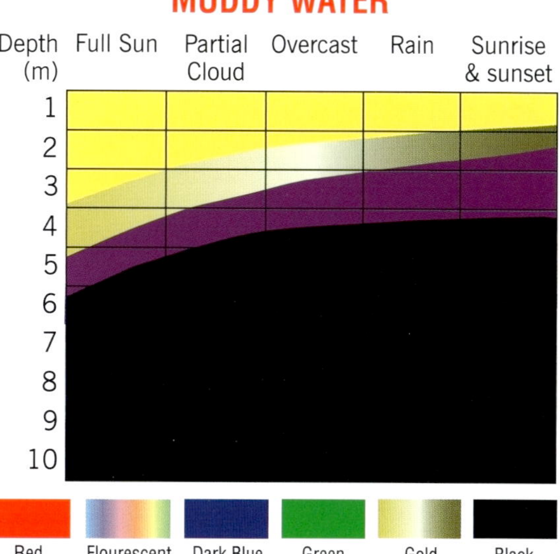

Blue | Orange | Purple | Silver | Pink | Charteuse | Red | Flourescent | Dark Blue | Green | Gold Metallic | Black

1. Overlap of colours at similar depths occurs—both work well
2. Combinations of adjacent colours work well
3. Individual lures differ in appearance at depth. Use experimentation to determine which lures work best.
4. Temperature differences in water cause differing visual results. Experiment.

Basic HOOK GUIDE

The following are some suggested hook sizes for species. Hook size is governed by bait size, not by the size of the fish you are after. You may want to adjust the size or type of hook being used depending on bait. For live baiting the thickness of the shank is important, which is why Tuna Circles are not recommended, however they have a growing following among anglers fishing fillets and those trolling skip baits.

Species	Hook Size	Hook Style	Bait
Whiting	No. 6–8	long shank hooks	squid, pippies
Snapper	3/0–6/0	Suicide or Octopus	pilchards, squid
Flathead	1/0–3/0	Suicide or Octopus	whitebait, squid
Salmon	2/0–4/0	Suicide or long shank	whitebait, pippies
Mulloway	4/0 –6/0	Suicide or Octopus	
Tailor	2/0 –4/0	long shanked and ganged	
Estuary perch	No. 4 No. 10 No. 6 – 8	Baitholder Baitholder Baitholder	shrimp, bass yabbies; smelt/minnow; worms
Trout	No. 14 No. 10	Suicide or long shank Suicide or long shank	mudeyes; straight shanked smelt and minnow;
Murray cod	No. 4 – 2/0	long shank	bardi grubs, worms and yabbies
Yellowbelly	No. 4 – 2/0	long shank	bardi grubs, worms and yabbies
Tuna	6/0 to 9/0	Suicide or Octopus	
Sharks	2X strong; 4/0–8/0 small sharks; 14/0 for big denizens.		
Barracouta	3/0 to 4/0	long shank	
Barramundi	2/0 to 6/0	Suicide or Octopus	
Carp	No. 4 – 6 No. 10 as big as No. 2		corn, worms, shrimp; maggots; dough baits and cheese.
Bream	No. 4– 8	Baitholder pattern	
Elephant fish	2/0–4/0	Suicide or Octopus pattern	
Yellowtail kingfish	6/0–8/0		depending on bait size

Fish LENGTH & WEIGHT

Weigh your fish with a ruler

Fish Biologists have collected vast quantities of length and weight data from a variety of fish species. This has enabled length and weight relationships to be calculated for some fish species which can be used to estimate weight of a fish by measuring its length. Please note that these figures are estimates only and individual fish weight will vary depending on age, sex, season and recent feeding activity.

Measuring length

In some of the conversion tables, fork length measurements have been used. Fork length is measured from the snout to the fork of the tail. Total length is measured from the snout to the tip of the tail.

Remember: Legal lengths (total lengths) are measured from the point of the snout to the tip of the tail.

The data was sourced from:http;//www.fisheries.nsw.gov.au/rec/gen/weigh.htm and is subject to their copyright.

Species: TROUT
Salmo trutta, Oncorhynchus mykiss, Salvelinus fontinalis

Total Length (cm)	Brown Weight (kg)	Rainbow Weight (kg)	Brook Weight (kg)
18	0.06	0.07	0.06
20	0.10	0.10	0.10
23	0.13	0.13	0.13
25	0.18	0.17	0.18
28	0.24	0.23	0.24
30	0.30	0.29	0.31
33	0.38	0.40	0.45
36	0.48	0.50	0.60
38	0.60	0.59	0.85
41	0.75	0.73	0.97
43	0.88	0.86	1.17
46	1.07	0.97	1.45
48	1.28	1.18	
51	1.54	1.56	
53	1.79	1.65	
56	1.93	1.72	
58	2.23		
61	2.59		
64	2.60		
66	2.70		
69	2.81		

Species: MURRAY COD
Maccullochella peelii peelii

Total Length (cm)	Weight (kg)	Total Length (cm)	Weight (kg)
40	1.1	72	7.6
42	1.3	74	8.3
44	1.5	76	9
46	1.8	78	9.8
48	2	80	10.7
50	2.3	82	11.6
52	2.6	84	12.5
54	3	86	13.5
56	3.3	88	14.6
58	3.7	90	15.7
60	4.2	92	16.8
62	4.6	94	18
64	5.2	96	19.3
66	5.7	98	20.7
68	6.3	100	22.1
70	6.9		

Species: AUSTRALIAN BASS
Macquaria novemaculeata

Please note: **The following table has fork length measurements. Legal lengths are total lengths and are measured from the point of the snout to the tip of the tail.**

Fork Length (cm)	Weight (kg)	Fork Length (cm)	Weight (kg)
25	0.3	43	1.6
26	0.3	44	1.7
27	0.4	45	1.8
28	0.4	46	1.9
29	0.5	47	2
30	0.5	48	2.2
31	0.6	49	2.3
32	0.6	50	2.5
33	0.7	51	2.6
34	0.8	52	2.8
35	0.8	53	2.9
36	0.9	54	3.1
37	1	55	3.3
38	1.1	56	3.5
39	1.2	57	3.7
40	1.3	58	3.9
41	1.3	59	4.1

Reference: Harris, J. H. 1987. Growth of Australian bass, Macquaria novemaculeata (Perciformes, Percichthyidae), in the Sydney basin. Australian Journal of Marine and Freshwater Research 38:351-361.

SPECIES: MULLOWAY *Argyrosomus japonicus*

Total Length (cm)	Weight (kg)	Total Length (cm)	Weight (kg)
45	1	145	30.8
46	1.1	150	34
48	1.2	155	37.4
50	1.3	160	41.1
52	1.5	165	45
54	1.7	170	49.1
56	1.9	175	53.5
58	2.1	180	58.1
60	2.3	185	63
64	2.8	190	68.1
68	3.3	195	73.5
72	3.9	140	27.7
76	4.6	200	79.2
80	5.4		
84	6.2		
88	7.1		
92	8.1		
96	9.2		
100	10.3		
104	11.6		
108	12.9		
112	14.4		
116	16		
120	17.6		
124	19.4		
128	21.4		
130	22.3		
135	24.9		

SPECIES: YELLOWTAIL KINGFISH
Seriola lalandi

Please note: **The following table has fork length measurements. Legal lengths are total lengths and are measured from the point of the snout to the tip of the tail.**

Fork Length (cm)	Weight (kg)	Fork Length (cm)	Weight (kg)
60	2.8	94	10.6
61	2.9	96	11.3
62	3	98	12
63	3.2	100	12.8
64	3.4	105	14.8
65	3.5	110	17
66	3.7	115	19.4
67	3.8	120	22
68	4	125	24.9
69	4.2	130	28
70	4.4	135	31.4
71	4.6	140	35
72	4.8	145	38.9
73	5	150	43
74	5.2	155	47.5
76	5.6	160	52
78	6.1	165	57.3
80	6.5	170	62.6
82	7	175	68.3
84	7.6	180	74.3
86	8.1	185	80.7
88	8.7	190	87.4
90	9.3	195	94.5
92	9.9	200	101.9

Reference: Stewart, J., D. J. Ferrell, B. van der Walt, D. Johnson,and M. Lowry. 2002.? Assessment of length and age composition of commercial kingfish landings.
Final report to the Fisheries Research and Development Corporation, Project No. 97/126.
NSW Fisheries, Cronulla.

SPECIES: SNAPPER
Pagrus auratus

Please note: **The following table has fork length measurements. Legal lengths are total lengths and are measured from the point of the snout to the tip of the tail.**

Fork Length (cm)	Weight (kg)	Fork Length (cm)	Weight (kg)
30	0.6	62	4.5
31	0.7	64	4.9
32	0.7	66	5.4
33	0.8	68	5.8
34	0.9	70	6.3
35	0.9	72	6.9
36	1	74	7.4
37	1.1	76	8
38	1.2	78	8.6
39	1.3	80	9.2
40	1.3	82	9.8
42	1.5	84	10.5
44	1.7	86	11.2
46	2	88	12
48	2.2	90	12.7
50	2.5	92	13.5
52	2.8	94	14.4
54	3.1	96	15.2
56	3.4	98	16.1
58	3.8	100	17.1
60	4.1		

Reference: Moran M. J. and C. Burton. 1990. Relationships among partial and whole lengths and weights for Western Australian pink snapper Chrysophys auratus (Sparidae). Fisheries Department of Western Australia, Fisheries Research Report No. 89.

SPECIES: YELLOWFIN BREAM
Acanthopagrus australis

Please note: **The following table has fork length measurements. Legal lengths are total lengths and are measured from the point of the snout to the tip of the tail.**

Fork Length (cm)	Weight (kg)	Fork Length (cm)	Weight (kg)
25	0.4	48	2.7
26	0.4	49	2.9
27	0.5	50	3.1
28	0.5	51	3.2
29	0.6	52	3.4
30	0.7	53	3.6
31	0.7	54	3.8
32	0.8	55	4.1
33	0.9	56	4.3
34	1	57	4.5
35	1	58	4.8
36	1.1	59	5.1
37	1.2	60	5.3
38	1.3	61	5.5
39	1.5	62	5.8
40	1.6	63	6.1
41	1.7	64	6.4
42	1.8	65	6.7
43	1.9	66	7.1
44	2.1	67	7.3
45	2.2	68	7.7
46	2.4	69	8
47	2.5	70	8.4

Reference: Steffe, A.S., Murphy, J.J., Chapman, D.J., Tarlinton, B.E. and Grinberg, A.? 1996. An assessment of the impact of offshore recreational fishing in NSW? waters on the management of commercial fisheries. FRDC Project no. 94/053.? Publishers, Fisheries Research Institute, NSW Fisheries. 139pp.

EFFECTS ON AUSTRALIAN FISH

FRESHWATER FISH

	RANGE		MOST ACTIVE		SPAWNING	
NATIVE FISH	C	F	C	F	C	F
Australian Bass	2–36	36–97	15–25	60–78	14–20	58–69
Barramundi	20–40	69–105	24–29	77–85	25–30	78–86
Estuary Perch	10–25	50–78	15–22	60–72	14.5–16	58–61
Clarence River Cod	Assumed to be the same as Murray Cod					
Golden Perch	4–37	40–100	14–27	58–82	23–26	74–79
Gulf Saratoga	7–40	45–105	24–29	77–85	30	86
Macquarie Perch	4–28	40–83	10–17	50–63	14–20	58–69
Murray Cod	2–34	36–94	16–25	61–78	17–22	63–72
River Blackfish	0–28	32–83	15–23	60–74	16	61
Southern Saratoga	7–40	45–105	25–31	20–88	20–23	63–74
Silver Perch	4–38	40–101	14–26	58–79	24–27	77–82
2-Spined Blackfish	0–25	32–78	15–23	60–74	16	61
Trout Cod	4–28	40–83	13–19	56–67	15–21	60–70
INTRODUCED SPECIES						
Atlantic Salmon	3–25	37–78	10–18	50–65	7–10	45–50
Brook Trout	0–25	32–78	10–15	50–60	7–12	45–55
Brown Trout	3–25	37–78	13–20	56–69	7–10	45–50
Chinook Salmon	3–25	37–78	10–18	50–65	7–10	45–50
European Carp	0–41	32–106	15–32	60–90		
Redfin	0–36	32–98	8–27	47–82	10–20	50–69
Rainbow Trout	3–25	37–78	10–18	50–65	7–10	45–50
Roach	0–38	32–101	8–25	47–78	15	60
Tench	0–39	32–102	20–26	69–79	16	61

SALTWATER FISH

Water temperature has less of an effect on saltwater fish, but is still worth looking at.

	C	F
Atlantic Salmon	10–18	50–85
Barramundi	24–29	77–85
Black Marlin	19–26	67–79
Bonito	16–24	61–77
Cobia	19–29	67–85
Dolphinfish	24–30	77–86
Frigate Mackerel	19–24	67–77
SHARKS		
–Black Whaler	11–31	51–87
–Bronze Whaler	11–31	51–87
–Tiger	17–31	63–87
–Mako	15–31	60–87
–Hammerhead	15–31	60–87
–Blue	15–26	60–79
–Thresher	15–24	60–77
Snapper	12–16	55–61
Spanish Mackerel	23–30	74–86
TUNA		
–Big-eye	15–29	60–85
–Longtail	18–21	65–70
–Mackerel	15–29	60–85
–Southern Bluefin	11–25	51–78
–Striped Tuna	15–27	60–82
–Yellowfin	15–29	60–85
Wahoo	23–30	74–86
Yellowtail Kingfish	13–25	56–78

Basic WIND SPEED GUIDE

When most people hear the weather forecast and it is for moderate to fresh winds, not too many would know how fast the wind speed will be.
The Beaufort Wind Scale is the standard measure and gives you some idea of what conditions will be like on the water.

	Units in km/h	Units in knots	Description on Land.	Description at Sea
CALM	0	0	Smoke rises vertically.	Sea like a mirror.
LIGHT WINDS	19 km/h or less	10 knots or less	Wind felt on face; leaves rustle; ordinary vanes moved by wind.	Small wavelets, ripples formed but do not break: A glassy appearance maintained.
MODERATE WINDS	20–29 km/h	11–16 knots	Raises dust and loose paper; small branches are moved.	Small waves - becoming longer; fairly frequent white horses.
FRESH WINDS	30–39 km/h	17–21 knots	Small trees in leaf begin to sway; crested waveless form on inland water.	Moderate waves, taking a more pronounced long form; many white horses are formed—a chance of some spray.
STRONG WINDS	40–50 km/h	22–27 knots	Large branches in motion; whistling heard in telephone wires; umbrellas used with difficulty.	Large waves begin to form; the white foam crests are more extensive with probably some spray.
	51–62 km/h	28–33 knots	Whole trees in motion; inconvenience felt when walking against wind.	Sea heaps up and white foam from breaking waves begins to be blown in streaks along direction of wind.
GALE	63–75 km/h	34–40 knots	Twigs break off trees; progress generally impeded.	Moderately high waves of greater length; edges of crests begin to break into spindrift; foam is blown in well-marked streaks along the direction of the wind.
	76–87 km/h	41–47 knots	Slight structural damage occurs—roofing dislodged; larger branches break off.	High waves; dense streaks of foam; crests of waves begin to topple, tumble and roll over; spray may affect visibility.
STORM	88–102 km/h	48–55 knots	Seldom experienced inland; trees uprooted; considerable structural damage.	Very high waves with long overhanging crests; the resulting foam in great patches is blown in dense white streaks; the surface of the sea takes on a white appearance; the tumbling of the sea becomes heavy with visibility affected.
	103 km/h or more	56 knots plus	Very rarely experienced—widespread damage.	Exceptionally high waves; small and medium sized ships occasionally lost from view behind waves; the sea is completely covered with long white patches of foam; the edges of wave crests are blown into froth.

Basic LINE OPTIONS GUIDE

The following are suggested line options based on scenario.

SPECIES	SCENARIO	METHOD	LINE
Whiting/flathead	Beach/bay Deep water/current	Bait Bait	Mono 3–5 kg Braid 10 kg
Snapper	Beach/bay Deep water/current	Bait Bait	Mono 8 kg Braid 15 kg
Mulloway	Estuary/surf	Bait	Braid 15 kg Mono 10 kg
Australian Bass **Estuary perch**	River	Bait Spin/troll	Mono 3 kg Braid 10 kg
Salmon/tailor	Beach/bay	Bait Spin/troll	Mono 3–5 kg Braid 10 kg
Murray cod **Yellowbelly**	Lakes/rivers	Trolling Spinning Bait	Braid 10–15 kg Braid 10 kg Mono 8–10 kg
Trout	Lakes Rivers Lakes/rivers	Trolling Bait Bait Spin	Braid 5 kg Mono 3 kg Mono 3 kg Mono 2–3 kg
Barramundi	Beach/estuary	Troll Spin Bait	Braid 10 kg Braid 10 kg Mono/Braid 8–10 kg
Mangrove jack	Estuary Offshore reefs	Spin Bait Bait	Braid 10 kg Mono 8 kg Braid 15 kg
Small tuna	Offshore/Landbased Game	Trolling Spin Bait	Mono 5–10 kg
Big tuna	Offshore Landbased Game	Trolling Cubing Live bait Spinning	Mono 10–15 kg Braid 15 kg Mono 15 kg Mono 10 kg
Marlin	Landbased Game Offshore	Live bait Trolling	Mono 15–24 kg Braid 24 kg Mono/braid 15–6 kg
Sharks	Offshore Landbased Game	Bait Bait	Braid/Mono 15–24 kg Braid/Mono 15–24 kg

Basic GUIDE TO BOATING

It is very easy to own a boat in Australia, but with ownership comes the responsibility for the safety of your passengers and equipment. It is also vital that you know all the boating regulations in the areas that you will be using your boat. While there are many regulations that are similar if not the same for each state, it is still up to you as skipper to know or find out the specific regulations for the areas you intend to go boating.

Remember that you must have a current boating licence.

Getting started

Before you purchase a boat, go out on the water with other boat owners. Try to go boating in as many different types, shapes and sizes and brands of boats as possible. You might want the boat primarily for fishing, but what type of fishing? Open sea, bay, river, dam—the style of fishing you want to do will dictate what type of boat you will need.

Once you have settled on the boat type, the next major purchases will be the motor and the trailer. It is important that you have the right power to suit your boat choice. Boating Industry Association dealers will advise you an a range of power to suit your boat and what you may require it to do.

If you are purchasing a used boat, you will have less legal safeguards than when buying from a registered dealer. You will need to take extra care in assessing the condition of the boat and the motor. As with buying a used car, it will pay to have an expert look at it for you. Even if the motor is a write off, the boat itself may still be worth purchasing.

Housing your boat

You must also consider where you will keep your boat. How much space you have will determine where it is kept, and where it is kept will determine how often you use it. It's not much use having to plan weeks ahead to get to your boat—you might as well not have it.

Planning your trip

The safety and success or any boating trip depends on the amount of preparation before venturing out on the water.

- Get up-to-date nautical charts and study them closely. They will accurately display information about ocean depths, coastal features, lights, piles, beacons and navigation hazards.
- Make sure that your boat is suitable for where you plan to go
- Make sure it is seaworthy when fully loaded
- Check the motor is in good condition
- Check that you have enough fuel for the trip and any unforeseen changes in plans
- Check that you have all the safety equipment required and that it is in good condition
- Make sure that you know how to use the safety equipment
- Make sure that the weather forecast is the most up-to-date that you can get.
- Make sure that you carry the right gear other than what the law insists on. eg: chart, compass, water, food, extra clothing, tools, extra line for the anchor and sun protection.
- Before you take to the water, leave your trip intentions with someone. Make sure that they know when you are leaving, where you are going, when you are returning, vessel details and a contact number.

Loading the boat

The boat you have might be the best model, well constructed with the highest safety standards, well powered by the motor, and be properly equipped, but still have a poor ride and even at times be dangerous. In the end it all comes down to how well the skipper handles the boat, where the passengers are positioned, and how many of them there are. The boat's seaworthiness depends on the complete load it carries and where and how it is placed.

Getting into the water

Before getting anywhere near the water at the end of the ramp, make sure that the trailer lighting is disconnected and the boat is firmly attached to the trailer. Treat all other boat owners with respect, you never know when you might need their help. Make sure the bung is in.

Make sure that there are no hazards on the ramp or in the surrounding water area. Line up your car and trailer so that you can keep backing down the ramp as straight as possible.

When actually launching the boat, keep hold of the bow line, so the boat doesn't float off without you. It is better to get your passengers on board after the boat is launched and the engine started. Park your trailer sensibly, and not in anyone else's way.

Out on the water

The rules and regulations of the road which apply to waters in most states are so long and intricate they are a complete book in themselves. The following points cover most of the encounters you might have with other vessels.

- The whole time you are on the water, you must keep extremely alert and be ready to give way to any other vessels.
- If you are the vessel that must give way, do it in good time.

BASIC BOATING MANOEUVRES

Port: If a power driven vessel approaches in this area, procede with caution, maintaining both course and speed.

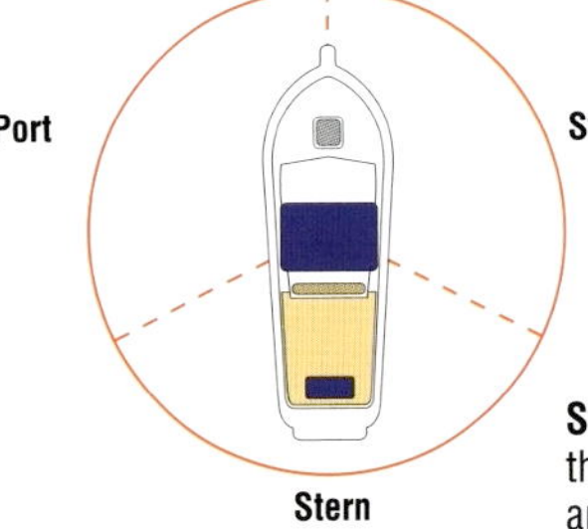

Starboard: When any type of vessel approaches in the area, keep out of its way.

Stern: If any vessels approach this area, maintain both speed and course with caution.

When you make your move, make it so that it will be obvious to the other vessel

- Generally power boats have to keep out of the way of sailing and fishing vessels, and any other vessels that are hampered by dredging, cable laying, etc.
- Always keep to the right in channels. Remember when on the water, look to the right, give way to the right, turn to the right and stay to the right.

Crossing a bar

Conditions on a bar change suddenly without warning. No amount of experience or type of boat makes crossing a bar safe when the conditions are adverse or at least marginal. No situation can warrant taking the risk of trying to cross when conditions are questionable. Once started, you are committed to crossing the bar, so if in any doubt do not even try to cross.

Here are some pointers for going out to sea over a bar:

- Craft not capable of standing up to adverse sea conditions outside the bar should not leave port
- Ensure that there is reserve fuel and provisions if conditions prevent returning over the bar when it is time to go back to port
- Get a weather report for the time of your crossing out to sea and also one for when you are going to return
- Do not venture out if you are in any doubt of your ability to return
- Cross on an incoming tide —vessels are more likely to experience adverse conditions at or near low tide.
- Watch where other vessels are crossing—this will be the most likely spot where you should cross
- Make sure that the vessels ahead are well clear before attempting your own crossing
- Approach at moderate speed, watching for the spot where the waves break least or at best not at all. Wait for a flatter than usual stretch of water and motor through.
- If at all possible, it is best to have the waves slightly on the bow so that your boat gently rolls over the crest of each wave.

Here are some pointers for coming in to shore over a bar:

- Coming in from the open sea, increase the power of your vessel to catch up with the ingoing waves.
- Position your vessel on the back of the wave. Definitely do not surf down the face of the wave.
- Match your vessel's speed to that of the waves but do not try to overtake the waves.

Getting out of the water

Centre your boat to the centre of your trailer and carefully take your boat up to the trailer until the winch or safety chain can be secured.

If you do not have the confidence to drive your boat on to the trailer, secure a line to the bow and stern to control the boat as you use the winch.

Get your trailer and boat off the ramp as quickly as possible to allow other boats to get access to the ramp. Park in the appropriate area and finish securing the boat ready for towing.

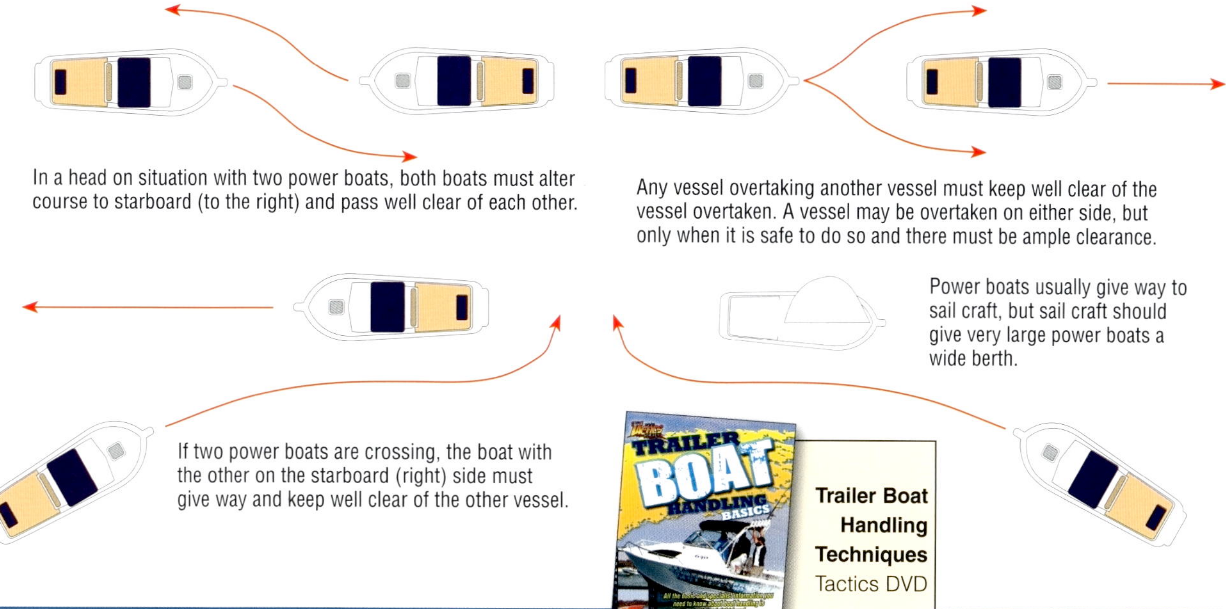

In a head on situation with two power boats, both boats must alter course to starboard (to the right) and pass well clear of each other.

Any vessel overtaking another vessel must keep well clear of the vessel overtaken. A vessel may be overtaken on either side, but only when it is safe to do so and there must be ample clearance.

Power boats usually give way to sail craft, but sail craft should give very large power boats a wide berth.

If two power boats are crossing, the boat with the other on the starboard (right) side must give way and keep well clear of the other vessel.

Basic BOATING KNOTS

ANCHOR BEND

An Anchor Bend is the knot most commonly used to connect a line to an anchor.

1. Make two turns around the shackle, leaving turns open. Take a half turn around the standing line and then feed the free end through the turns and pull tight.

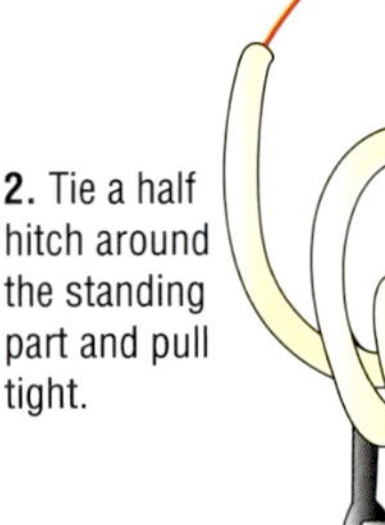

2. Tie a half hitch around the standing part and pull tight.

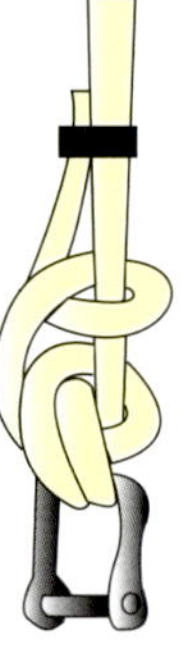

3. Sieze the free end or tie a backup knot with the free end around the standing part.

BOWLINE

One of the most useful knots. It forms a secure loop, is easy to tie and untie and won't jam.

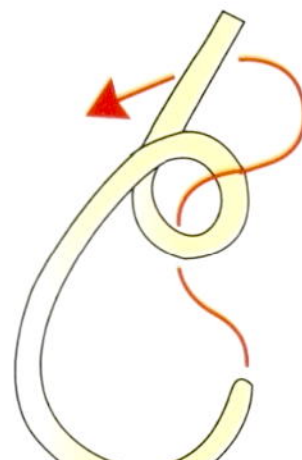

1. Form an eye in the rope with the standing part of the rope running underneath. Run the free end up through the eye making a loop below the eye.

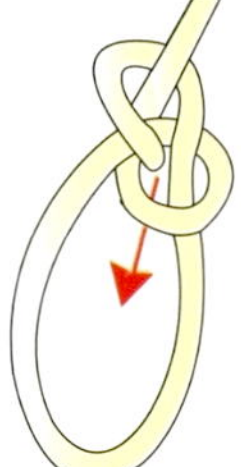

2. Take a turn around the standing part and feed the free end back down into the eye and hold there.

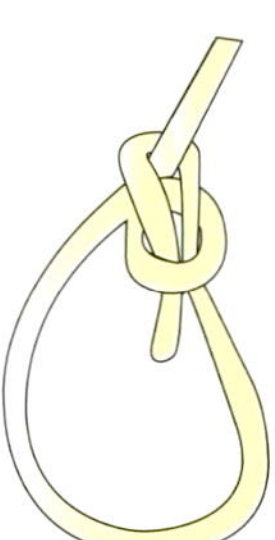

3. Pull standing part to tighten down the knot.

CLEAT HITCH

Take a turn around the base of the cleat and bring the line over the front face of the cleat, below each of the horns in turn in a figure 8 pattern. Then back and underneath the crossing turn as shown in step 4.

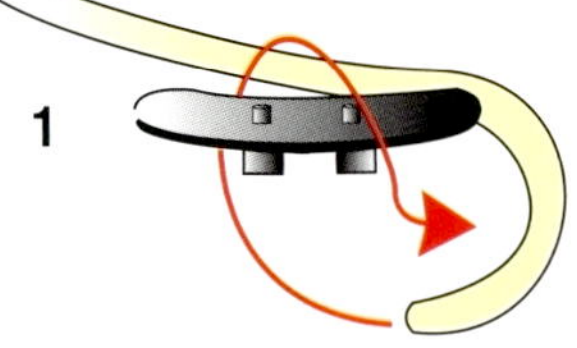

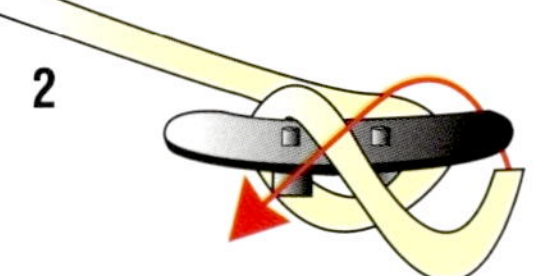

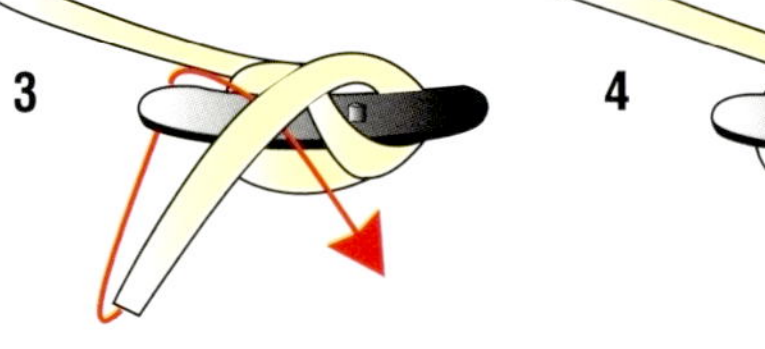

CLOVE HITCH

A simple hitch, it holds firmly but is not totally secure.

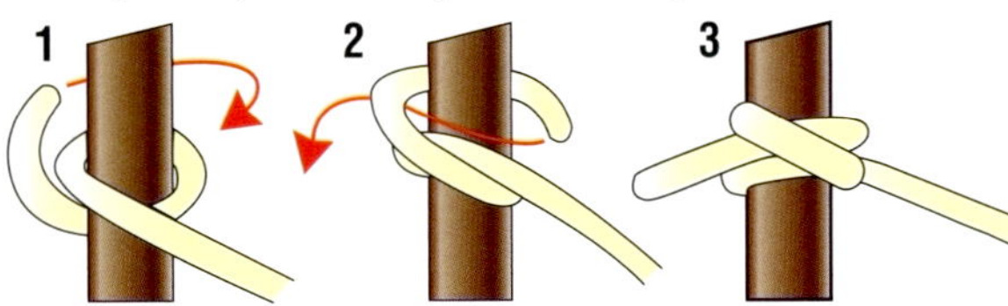

Make a turn around a post with the free end running underneath the standing part. Take a second turn around in the same direction and feed the free end through the eye of the seciond turn. Pull tight.

SHEET BEND

Very good for tying two lines together, especially lines of different sizes. This knot will also hold slippery nylon rope in it's doubled form, but not well enough for climbers.

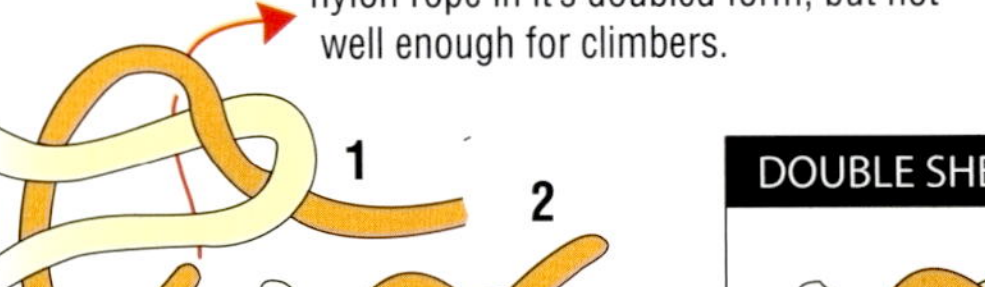

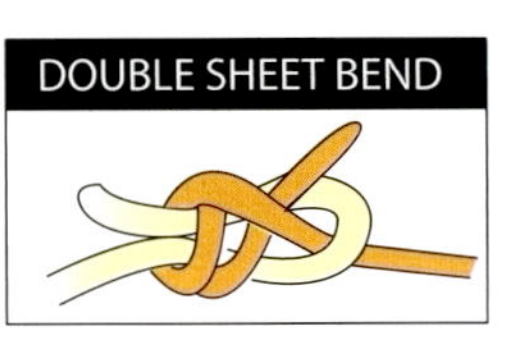

MOORING HITCH

A knot which holds fast while under tension, yet can be quickly released by a tug on the free end. It is only a temporary knot though, and not to be used to moor a boat.

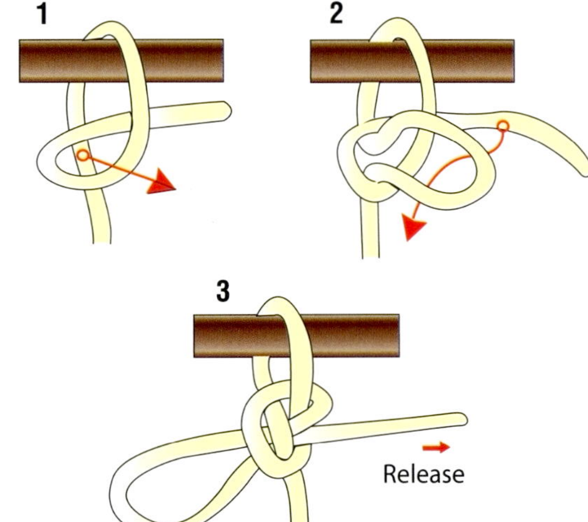

Guide to SOLAR/LUNAR

BEST FISHING TIMES AND TIDES

So much information is available to anglers on a day-to-day basis that it's difficult to know what we should start considering when planning our trips or deciding whether to go fishing. Most anglers make their decisions around three predictable factors. These are the times of sunrise and sunset, the condition and height of the tides, and the position of the moon.

This Almanac provides the tide times and heights for the major station in each Australian State along with time differences for many areas. Additionally, for anglers planning a trip beyond the immediate future, for each month and major station there is a graph showing the variation of the tides during the month so that an easy comparison can be made. Do I go fishing this week or next? Or do I want a large variation between the tides or is it easier to fish if the change is smaller? Are questions that are easier to answer if we can see the big picture. Sunrise and sunset times are standardised at Melbourne and Eastern Standard Time. Latitude, time zone and daylight savings adjustments need to be applied for your local area.

The peak fishing times are presented to simulate the logical progression of the Moon as it orbits the Earth. The first is the minor peak at moonrise, no matter what time of day at which it occurs. The second is the major peak when the moon is directly overhead, the third is the minor peak at moonset and the fourth is the major peak when the moon is directly overhead on the opposite side of the globe.

Where the notation (ND) occurs in this table it indicates that the relevant peak period is actually just after midnight on the next day and is duplicated in the next day's information. This will only occur if the first chronological peak for the day is after 5 a.m.

A list of adjustments to the peak activity times is supplied for major centres in each State and Territory. The adjustments are shown as a positive or negative number. This is the number of minutes to adjust the peak time to your local time. If the adjustment is a negative number then the peak time at your local area is that number of minutes earlier than in the book. If the adjustment is a positive number then it is that number of minutes later than the time in the book.

For example, the adjustment for Sydney is -30. So if fishing in Sydney and the peak time is shown as 08:30 in the book, then that peak time will be 30 minutes earlier, or 08:00.

During Daylight Savings Time, add an hour to the printed peak activity times if the state waters you are fishing are effected by Daylight Savings Time adjustments.

MOON PHASE:	NEW	FIRST QTR.	FULL	LAST QTR.

Solar & Lunar TIME ADJUSTMENTS

Australia
(Minutes)

NEW SOUTH WALES

Albury	-5
Armadale	-30
Batemans Bay	-25
Bega	-25
Bermagui	-20
Bourke	0
Braidwood	-10
Broken Hill	+10
Canberra	-10
Coffs Harbour	-30
Corryong	-10
Dubbo	-10
Eden	-20
Eucumbene	-20
Glen Innes	-30
Goulburn	-10
Grafton	-30
Griffith	0
Hat Head	-30
Jervis Bay	-20
Lithgow	-25
Menindee Lakes	+10
Moree	-15
Narrandara	-5
Newcastle	-30
Nowra	-25
Parkes	-10
Port Macquarie	-30
Port Stephens	-30
Seal Rocks	-30
Snowy Mountains	-20
Sydney	-30
Tweed Heads	-30
Wagga Wagga	-5
Wollongong	-30
Yamba	-30

NORTHERN TERRITORY

Alice Springs	+20
Borroloola	+10
Cape Don	+30
Daly Waters	+15
Darwin	+30
Gove	+10
Groote Eylandt	+10
Jabiru	+25
Kakadu	+40
Katherine	+30
Maningrida	+20
Matananka	+30
Roper Valley	+15
Tennent Creek	+20

QUEENSLAND

Brisbane	-30
Burketown	+30
Cairns	0
Cape York	+10
Cloncurry	+30
Emerald	-10
Gladstone	-25
Gold Coast	-30
Goondawindi	-25
Hervey Bay	-30
Longreach	0
Mackay	-20
Mount Isa	+30
Normanton	+20
Rockhampton	-20
Toowoomba	-30
Townsville	-5
Weipa	+10

SOUTH AUSTRALIA

Adelaide	0
Ardrossin	+5
Black Point	+5
Cape Jervis	0
Cape Jervis	0
Ceduna	+20
Clare Bay	+25
Coffin Bay	+10
Coober Pedy	+20
Cook	+30
Fowlers Bay	+25
Kangaroo Island	+5
Kingston SE	-5
Marion Bay	+5
Mt Gambier	-10
Murray Bridge	0
Outer Harbour	0
Port Augusta	+5
Port Gawler	0
Port Lincoln	+10
Port Vincent	+5
Renmark	-10
Robe	-5
Sceale Bay	+20
Smoky Bay	+20
Streaky Bay	+20
Victor Harbour	0
Whyalla	+5
Yorke Peninsula	+5

TASMANIA

Burnie	-5
Great Lake	-5
Hobart	-10
Launceston	-10
St Marys	-10
Strahan	0
East coast	0
Central	-5
West coast	-10

VICTORIA

Apollo Bay	+5
Ballarat	+5
Bemm River	-15
Bendigo	0
Bendoc	-15
Cann River	-15
Carrum	0
Dargo	-5
Dartmouth	-10
Echuca	0
Eildon	0
Geelong	0
Golden Beach	-5
Halls Gap	+10
Hamilton	+10
Hastings	0
Horsham	+10
Inverloch	0
Lakes Entrance	-10
Mallacoota	-20
Marlo	-15
McLoughlins Beach	-5
Melbourne	0
Mildura	+10
Omeo	-10
Ouyen	+10
Port Albert	-5
Port Fairy	+10
Port Welshpool	-5
Portland	+10
San Semo	0
Shallow Inlet	-5
Swan Hill	+5
Tamboon	-15
Torquay	0
Walhalla	-5
Wangaratta	-5
Warnambool	+10
Wilsons Promontory	-5

WESTERN AUSTRALIA

Albany	-10
Augusta	0
Broome	-30
Busselton	0
Carnarvon	+10
Dampier	-5
Derby	-30
Esperance	-20
Eucla	-50
Exmouth	+5
Gearaldton	+5
Geraldton	+10
Jurien	+5
Kalbarri	+5
Kalgoolie	-20
Kununurra	-50
Mandurah	0
Onslow	0
Pemberton	0
Perth	0
Port Hedland	-10
Rottnest Island	0
Shark Bay	+10
Steep Point	+10
Wyndham	-50

New Zealand

Auckland	0
Blenheim	+5
Cape Farewell	+10
Cape Regina	+10
Chatham Islands	0
Christchurch	+10
Dunedin	+20
East Cape	-15
Gisborne	-15
Greymouth	+15
Halfmoon Bay	+30
Hamilton	0
Invercargill	+30
Kaikoura Peninsula	+5
Kaipara	+5
Milford Sound	+30
Mt. Cook	+20
Napier	-10
New Plymouth	+5
Oamaru	+20
Palmerston North	-5
Queenstown	+25
Rotorua	-5
Whakatane	-10
Taupo	-5
Te Anau	+30
Timaru	+15
Waitangi	+5
Wellington	0
Westport	+10

Tide TIME ADJUSTMENTS

FOR LOW AND HIGH TIDES

Approximate variation times only, taken from various sources.

QUEENSLAND

Ballina	-1hr 10min
Bribie Island	-10min
Brunswick Heads	-1hr 20min
Burleigh Heads	-1hr 30min
Byron Bay	-1hr 20min
Caloundra	-1hr 30min
Cleveland	+15min
Coomera River	+1hr 30min
Donnybrook	+1hr
Fraser Island East	+1hr 20min
Hervey Bay	+1hr
Jumpinpin	-1hr 30 min
Manly	+15min
Nerang River Nerang	+1hr
Noosa	-1hr 30min
Redcliffe	0
Redland Bay	+30min
Runaway Bay	-10min
Sanctuary Cove	+30min
Scarborough	+5min
Southport Broadwater	-35min
Tangalooma	-30min
Tin Can Bay	+5min
Toorbul	+30min
Tweed Heads	-45min
Victoria Pt	+15min

NEW SOUTH WALES

Ballina Boat Dock	+15min
Batemans Bay	-1min
Bermagui	+5min
Blackmans Point	+1hr 15min
Botany Bay	+3min
Broughton Island	-6min
Byron Bay	0
Chinderah	+1hr 15min
Clyde River Bridge	+15min
Coffs Harbour	-2min
Como	+30min
Coraki	+4hrs
Crookhaven Jetty	+15min
Crowdy Head	0
Danger Island	+18min
Dolls Point	+15min
Ettalong	+30min
Evans Head Bridge	0
Fig Tree Bridge	+15min
Forster	+1minute
Gabo Island	-9min
Gladesville Bridge	+15min
Gladstone	+2hrs 10min
Gosford	+2hrs 21min
Grafton	+4hrs 1 min
Greenwell Point	+45min
Harrington	+1 min
Harrington Inlet	+16min
Hexham	+1hr 10min
Huskisson	+3min
Iluka	0
Jervis Bay	-3min
Kempsey	+3hrs 15min
Kendall	+3hrs 30min
Kiama	0
Kurnell	0
Lismore	+1hr 15min
Liverpool+	+2hrs 30min
Lower Portland Ferry	+3hrs 5min
Lugarno	+1hr
Maclean	+2hrs 15min
Merimbula Lake Bridge	+1hr 30min
Milperra	+2hrs 10min
Morpeth	+3hrs 10min
Moruya	+30min
Murwillumbah	+2hrs 30min
Narooma	+40min
Nelson Bay	+30min
Peats Ferry Bridge	+1hr
Pindimar	+45min
Pittwater Entrance	0
Port Hacking	+2min
Port Hacking Audley	+ 30min
Port Hacking Burraneer	+15min
Port Hacking Lilli Pilli	+30min
Port Macquarie	+21min
Port Stephens (Entrance or Nelson head)	0
Queens Lake	+2hrs
Raleigh	+1hr
Raymond Terrace	+1hr 55min
Salamander Bay	+45min
Sandon	+30min
Shoalhaven River Nowra	+2hrs 10min
Shoalhaven River O'Keefes Point	+2hrs
Silverwater Bridge	+15min
Soldiers Point	+1hr
South West Rocks	+1hr 2min
Swansea	-3min
Taree	+2hrs
Tea Gardens	+1hr
Terranora Inlet	+2hrs 10min
The Spit Bridge	0
Trial Bay	0
Tweed Heads	+4min
Ulladulla Harbour	0
Ulmarra	+4hrs 30min
Wardell	+1 hr 30 min
Watson Taylors Lake	+2hrs
Watts Creek	Fort Denison plus 1 hr
Wauchope	+1hr 30min
Windsor	+5hrs 50min
Wingham	+3hrs 15min
Wisemans Ferry	+2hrs 15min
Wollomba River mouth	+1hr 50min
Wollongong	0
Wooli	+1hr 5min

VICTORIA

Port Phillip	0
Altona	+3hrs 25min
Apollo Bay	-25min
Barwon Heads	+15 min
Cape Otway	-30 min
Cowes	+1hr 15min
Dromana	+3hrs 20min
Flinders	+48min
Frankston	+3hrs 20min
Geelong	+3hrs 30min
Hastings	+1hr 15min
Hovell Pile	+3hrs 20min
Lorne	-20min
Maribyrnong River	+3hrs 15min
McLoughinns	+2hrs 25min
Mornington	+3hrs 20min
New Haven	+1hr 25min
Point Cook	+3hrs 10min
Portarlington	+3hrs 15min
Portsea	+1hr 20min
Queenscliff	+35min
Rosebud	+3hrs 20min
Rye	+3hrs
Sandringham	+3hrs 20min
Sorrento	+2hrs 15min
St Kilda	+3hrs 20min
St Leonards	+3hrs 15min
Stony Point	+1hr
Tooradin	+1hr 45min
Venus Bay	0
Warratah Bay	0
Werribee River	+3hrs 15min
Williamstown	+3hrs 25min
Woolamai	0

TASMANIA

Tidal adjustments for the Southern and South East coast of Tasmania do not vary significantly from Hobart times, except for:

Denison	+2hrs 25min
Granville Harbour	+20min
Recherche Bay	-30min
St Helens	+1hr 30min

SOUTH AUSTRALIA

Glenelg	-10min
Port Noarlunga	-15min
Ardrossan	-5min

WESTERN AUSTRALIA

Hillarys	-15min
Rottnest Island	-10min
Swan River Causeway	+1hr

USING THIS BOOK

These amendments are approximations only. They should not be used for navigation, especially when intending to cross bars, navigate channels or undertake any activity for which the tide time must be accurate.

If accurate times are required for navigation consult an official source such as the Bureau of Meteorology website at www.bom.gov.au/oceanography/tides

Example of use: If the adjustment is +30min for an area and the time is shown as 08:30AM in the book, then the adjusted time for that area will be 30 minutes later (09:00AM).

Important Daylight Savings Note:

During Daylight Savings Time add an hour to the printed tide times to state waters effected by Daylight Savings Time adjustments.

TIDE TIMES

Adelaide Outer Harbour - SA

DAY/DATE	TIDE 1	TIDE 2	TIDE 3	TIDE 4
Mon 1	1:22 AM (0.63) L	8:08 AM (2.32) H	2:31 PM (1.02) L	7:36 PM (1.65) H
Tue 2	1:26 AM (0.80) L	8:32 AM (2.09) H	3:12 PM (1.31) L	6:41 PM (1.42) H
Wed 3	12:38 AM (0.97) L	8:41 AM (1.78) H	10:56 PM (0.86) L	
Thu 4	5:42 AM (1.64) H	9:46 AM (1.42) L	3:41 PM (2.04) H	10:41 PM (0.59) L
Fri 5	5:05 AM (1.81) H	10:06 AM (1.09) L	4:12 PM (2.34) H	10:54 PM (0.39) L
Sat 6	5:07 AM (1.96) H	10:28 AM (0.83) L	4:37 PM (2.53) H	11:09 PM (0.29) L
Sun 7	5:15 AM (2.07) H	10:48 AM (0.64) L	4:58 PM (2.61) H	11:22 PM (0.28) L
Mon 8	5:23 AM (2.17) H	11:08 AM (0.50) L	5:16 PM (2.60) H	11:35 PM (0.31) L
Tue 9	5:34 AM (2.29) H	11:32 AM (0.41) L	5:35 PM (2.52) H	11:48 PM (0.35) L
Wed 10	5:50 AM (2.41) H	12:00 PM (0.39) L	5:56 PM (2.38) H	
Thu 11	12:00 AM (0.41) L	6:09 AM (2.50) H	12:28 PM (0.44) L	6:15 PM (2.18) H
Fri 12	12:08 AM (0.47) L	6:28 AM (2.56) H	12:52 PM (0.55) L	6:28 PM (1.99) H
Sat 13	12:11 AM (0.49) L	6:45 AM (2.58) H	1:09 PM (0.67) L	6:35 PM (1.85) H
Sun 14	12:14 AM (0.46) L	7:02 AM (2.55) H	1:21 PM (0.81) L	6:40 PM (1.76) H
Mon 15	12:24 AM (0.45) L	7:19 AM (2.45) H	1:33 PM (0.98) L	6:36 PM (1.66) H
Tue 16	12:31 AM (0.53) L	7:32 AM (2.23) H	1:36 PM (1.22) L	6:00 PM (1.58) H
Wed 17	12:16 AM (0.67) L	7:15 AM (1.91) H	11:26 PM (0.73) L	
Thu 18	5:57 AM (1.72) H	10:42 AM (1.34) L	4:11 PM (1.96) H	10:49 PM (0.61) L
Fri 19	5:07 AM (1.81) H	10:20 AM (1.00) L	4:20 PM (2.22) H	10:47 PM (0.47) L
Sat 20	4:53 AM (1.99) H	10:30 AM (0.71) L	4:35 PM (2.38) H	10:54 PM (0.39) L
Sun 21	4:54 AM (2.16) H	10:44 AM (0.53) L	4:49 PM (2.44) H	11:01 PM (0.38) L
Mon 22	4:59 AM (2.29) H	10:58 AM (0.42) L	5:01 PM (2.43) H	11:06 PM (0.38) L
Tue 23	5:07 AM (2.41) H	11:14 AM (0.36) L	5:14 PM (2.38) H	11:14 PM (0.38) L
Wed 24	5:21 AM (2.51) H	11:34 AM (0.34) L	5:31 PM (2.31) H	11:27 PM (0.38) L
Thu 25	5:41 AM (2.57) H	11:58 AM (0.37) L	5:51 PM (2.22) H	11:41 PM (0.41) L
Fri 26	6:02 AM (2.59) H	12:22 PM (0.44) L	6:09 PM (2.10) H	11:56 PM (0.46) L
Sat 27	6:22 AM (2.57) H	12:43 PM (0.52) L	6:26 PM (2.00) H	
Sun 28	12:09 AM (0.50) L	6:40 AM (2.53) H	1:02 PM (0.61) L	6:40 PM (1.90) H
Mon 29	12:23 AM (0.54) L	6:58 AM (2.46) H	1:22 PM (0.72) L	6:54 PM (1.80) H
Tue 30	12:37 AM (0.62) L	7:18 AM (2.33) H	1:45 PM (0.89) L	7:04 PM (1.62) H

Brisbane Bar - QLD

DAY/DATE	TIDE 1	TIDE 2	TIDE 3	TIDE 4
Mon 1	2:47 AM (1.43) H	9:03 AM (0.77) L	4:22 PM (1.90) H	11:21 PM (0.99) L
Tue 2	4:25 AM (1.40) H	10:24 AM (0.78) L	5:39 PM (2.00) H	
Wed 3	12:33 AM (0.87) L	5:48 AM (1.48) H	11:39 AM (0.70) L	6:36 PM (2.14) H
Thu 4	1:23 AM (0.73) L	6:46 AM (1.62) H	12:41 PM (0.58) L	7:24 PM (2.28) H
Fri 5	2:07 AM (0.60) L	7:34 AM (1.76) H	1:34 PM (0.46) L	8:07 PM (2.41) H
Sat 6	2:47 AM (0.49) L	8:18 AM (1.89) H	2:23 PM (0.36) L	8:47 PM (2.49) H
Sun 7	3:26 AM (0.40) L	9:02 AM (2.01) H	3:10 PM (0.30) L	9:26 PM (2.53) H
Mon 8	4:03 AM (0.32) L	9:45 AM (2.12) H	3:55 PM (0.28) L	10:03 PM (2.51) H
Tue 9	4:40 AM (0.27) L	10:29 AM (2.21) H	4:41 PM (0.31) L	10:41 PM (2.43) H
Wed 10	5:15 AM (0.26) L	11:13 AM (2.27) H	5:26 PM (0.39) L	11:18 PM (2.27) H
Thu 11	5:48 AM (0.29) L	11:58 AM (2.29) H	6:14 PM (0.52) L	11:59 PM (2.07) H
Fri 12	6:23 AM (0.35) L	12:46 PM (2.27) H	7:07 PM (0.66) L	
Sat 13	12:43 AM (1.84) H	7:01 AM (0.44) L	1:41 PM (2.22) H	8:13 PM (0.79) L
Sun 14	1:39 AM (1.62) H	7:52 AM (0.56) L	2:49 PM (2.17) H	9:43 PM (0.86) L
Mon 15	3:04 AM (1.46) H	9:03 AM (0.65) L	4:10 PM (2.15) H	11:19 PM (0.81) L
Tue 16	4:48 AM (1.46) H	10:32 AM (0.67) L	5:30 PM (2.21) H	
Wed 17	12:33 AM (0.68) L	6:08 AM (1.58) H	11:55 AM (0.61) L	6:35 PM (2.29) H
Thu 18	1:29 AM (0.56) L	7:07 AM (1.74) H	1:01 PM (0.51) L	7:28 PM (2.36) H
Fri 19	2:13 AM (0.47) L	7:55 AM (1.87) H	1:54 PM (0.44) L	8:11 PM (2.39) H
Sat 20	2:50 AM (0.42) L	8:35 AM (1.97) H	2:39 PM (0.40) L	8:48 PM (2.37) H
Sun 21	3:23 AM (0.40) L	9:11 AM (2.05) H	3:18 PM (0.41) L	9:21 PM (2.32) H
Mon 22	3:51 AM (0.39) L	9:45 AM (2.11) H	3:55 PM (0.44) L	9:52 PM (2.25) H
Tue 23	4:16 AM (0.37) L	10:17 AM (2.15) H	4:30 PM (0.50) L	10:20 PM (2.16) H
Wed 24	4:41 AM (0.37) L	10:49 AM (2.17) H	5:03 PM (0.57) L	10:47 PM (2.04) H
Thu 25	5:04 AM (0.39) L	11:22 AM (2.17) H	5:37 PM (0.65) L	11:16 PM (1.91) H
Fri 26	5:30 AM (0.43) L	11:56 AM (2.14) H	6:13 PM (0.74) L	11:46 PM (1.77) H
Sat 27	5:59 AM (0.51) L	12:32 PM (2.08) H	6:53 PM (0.84) L	
Sun 28	12:20 AM (1.62) H	6:30 AM (0.61) L	1:15 PM (2.01) H	7:44 PM (0.93) L
Mon 29	1:03 AM (1.49) H	7:11 AM (0.71) L	2:10 PM (1.94) H	8:57 PM (0.99) L
Tue 30	2:10 AM (1.39) H	8:12 AM (0.80) L	3:25 PM (1.92) H	10:35 PM (0.95) L

Darwin - NT

DAY/DATE	TIDE 1	TIDE 2	TIDE 3	TIDE 4
Mon 1	4:11 AM (3.91) L	9:33 AM (5.16) H	5:40 PM (2.70) L	
Tue 2	12:17 AM (5.05) H	6:14 AM (4.34) L	9:31 AM (4.68) H	7:00 PM (2.97) L
Wed 3	3:06 AM (5.00) H	11:49 AM (4.15) L	2:09 PM (4.20) H	8:56 PM (2.89) L
Thu 4	4:33 AM (5.50) H	11:15 AM (3.74) L	3:54 PM (4.72) H	10:20 PM (2.47) L
Fri 5	5:09 AM (6.01) H	11:30 AM (3.27) L	4:38 PM (5.34) H	11:11 PM (1.96) L
Sat 6	5:43 AM (6.51) H	11:54 AM (2.75) L	5:19 PM (5.98) H	11:52 PM (1.52) L
Sun 7	6:16 AM (6.97) H	12:25 PM (2.19) L	6:00 PM (6.56) H	
Mon 8	12:29 AM (1.19) L	6:47 AM (7.33) H	12:57 PM (1.62) L	6:42 PM (7.05) H
Tue 9	1:01 AM (1.05) L	7:15 AM (7.55) H	1:30 PM (1.11) L	7:23 PM (7.39) H
Wed 10	1:31 AM (1.11) L	7:40 AM (7.61) H	2:03 PM (0.73) L	8:02 PM (7.53) H
Thu 11	2:01 AM (1.37) L	8:01 AM (7.52) H	2:37 PM (0.56) L	8:43 PM (7.46) H
Fri 12	2:32 AM (1.80) L	8:25 AM (7.28) H	3:13 PM (0.63) L	9:24 PM (7.16) H
Sat 13	3:05 AM (2.36) L	8:49 AM (6.87) H	3:51 PM (0.97) L	10:09 PM (6.68) H
Sun 14	3:41 AM (3.01) L	9:15 AM (6.31) H	4:33 PM (1.52) L	11:01 PM (6.08) H
Mon 15	4:26 AM (3.67) L	9:42 AM (5.63) H	5:29 PM (2.16) L	
Tue 16	12:14 AM (5.52) H	6:00 AM (4.22) L	10:19 AM (4.88) H	7:03 PM (2.68) L
Wed 17	2:23 AM (5.38) H	9:38 AM (4.07) L	2:37 PM (4.50) H	9:12 PM (2.66) L
Thu 18	4:07 AM (5.82) H	10:49 AM (3.36) L	4:06 PM (5.15) H	10:30 PM (2.29) L
Fri 19	4:59 AM (6.31) H	11:27 AM (2.72) L	4:58 PM (5.81) H	11:21 PM (1.94) L
Sat 20	5:38 AM (6.71) H	12:00 PM (2.19) L	5:40 PM (6.36) H	
Sun 21	12:00 AM (1.69) L	6:11 AM (6.99) H	12:29 PM (1.76) L	6:17 PM (6.77) H
Mon 22	12:30 AM (1.58) L	6:38 AM (7.15) H	12:55 PM (1.43) L	6:52 PM (7.03) H
Tue 23	12:59 AM (1.60) L	7:00 AM (7.20) H	1:20 PM (1.19) L	7:24 PM (7.16) H
Wed 24	1:23 AM (1.74) L	7:18 AM (7.15) H	1:45 PM (1.06) L	7:54 PM (7.15) H
Thu 25	1:45 AM (1.97) L	7:35 AM (7.02) H	2:08 PM (1.05) L	8:22 PM (7.03) H
Fri 26	2:05 AM (2.26) L	7:53 AM (6.81) H	2:33 PM (1.17) L	8:50 PM (6.82) H
Sat 27	2:26 AM (2.61) L	8:12 AM (6.49) H	3:00 PM (1.44) L	9:20 PM (6.51) H
Sun 28	2:47 AM (3.00) L	8:30 AM (6.08) H	3:29 PM (1.83) L	9:54 PM (6.13) H
Mon 29	3:11 AM (3.43) L	8:43 AM (5.62) H	4:03 PM (2.30) L	10:35 PM (5.70) H
Tue 30	3:43 AM (3.89) L	8:53 AM (5.14) H	4:55 PM (2.79) L	11:35 PM (5.29) H

Fremantle - WA

DAY/DATE	TIDE 1	TIDE 2	TIDE 3	TIDE 4
Mon 1	1:33 AM (1.02) H	3:02 PM (0.59) L		
Tue 2	4:15 AM (1.02) H	3:25 PM (0.56) L		
Wed 3	5:43 AM (1.05) H	3:46 PM (0.54) L		
Thu 4	6:58 AM (1.08) H	4:03 PM (0.53) L		
Fri 5	7:46 AM (1.11) H	4:16 PM (0.54) L	11:35 PM (0.77) H	
Sat 6	12:45 AM (0.77) L	8:30 AM (1.12) H	4:30 PM (0.56) L	10:50 PM (0.78) H
Sun 7	1:52 AM (0.73) L	9:13 AM (1.09) H	4:45 PM (0.60) L	10:57 PM (0.82) H
Mon 8	2:49 AM (0.70) L	9:59 AM (1.03) H	4:56 PM (0.65) L	11:15 PM (0.87) H
Tue 9	3:54 AM (0.68) L	11:07 AM (0.94) H	4:47 PM (0.70) L	11:32 PM (0.93) H
Wed 10	5:09 AM (0.66) L	12:25 PM (0.84) H	4:12 PM (0.72) L	11:14 PM (0.99) H
Thu 11	6:27 AM (0.66) L	1:28 PM (0.73) H	3:53 PM (0.70) L	11:20 PM (1.04) H
Fri 12	9:52 AM (0.61) L	10:47 AM (0.61) L	12:17 PM (0.60) L	11:42 PM (1.07) H
Sat 13	1:02 PM (0.52) L			
Sun 14	12:10 AM (1.07) H	1:45 PM (0.47) L		
Mon 15	12:45 AM (1.04) H	1:43 AM (1.04) L	3:00 AM (1.05) H	2:26 PM (0.45) L
Tue 16	4:04 AM (1.03) H	3:04 PM (0.46) L		
Wed 17	6:29 AM (1.02) H	3:38 PM (0.50) L		
Thu 18	7:30 AM (1.02) H	4:02 PM (0.54) L	11:53 PM (0.77) H	
Fri 19	12:09 AM (0.77) L	8:13 AM (1.01) H	3:59 PM (0.60) L	10:19 PM (0.78) H
Sat 20	1:45 AM (0.73) L	8:50 AM (0.98) H	3:54 PM (0.64) L	10:20 PM (0.82) H
Sun 21	3:00 AM (0.70) L	9:25 AM (0.94) H	3:55 PM (0.67) L	10:18 PM (0.86) H
Mon 22	3:45 AM (0.68) L	9:58 AM (0.89) H	3:19 PM (0.69) L	10:01 PM (0.91) H
Tue 23	4:20 AM (0.66) L	10:30 AM (0.83) H	3:18 PM (0.68) L	9:59 PM (0.96) H
Wed 24	4:56 AM (0.64) L	10:42 AM (0.77) H	3:31 PM (0.68) L	10:14 PM (1.00) H
Thu 25	5:34 AM (0.63) L	10:44 AM (0.71) H	3:31 PM (0.67) L	10:36 PM (1.03) H
Fri 26	6:16 AM (0.63) L	10:58 AM (0.67) H	2:59 PM (0.65) L	11:02 PM (1.04) H
Sat 27	9:49 AM (0.62) L	11:13 AM (0.63) H	12:45 PM (0.62) L	11:31 PM (1.04) H
Sun 28	10:57 AM (0.60) L	11:11 AM (0.60) L	1:15 PM (0.58) L	
Mon 29	12:02 AM (1.02) H	1:45 PM (0.56) L		
Tue 30	12:38 AM (1.00) H	2:11 PM (0.54) L		

Sun Rise & Sun Set Times:

Darwin, NT: Rise: 06:40am Set: 06:40pm

Melbourne, VIC: Rise: 06:20am Set: 06:10pm

Adelaide, SA: Rise: 06:10am Set: 06:00pm

Perth, WA: Rise: 06:10am Set: 06:00pm

Sydney, NSW: Rise: 05:50am Set: 05:40pm

Brisbane, QLD: Rise: 05:40am Set: 05:40pm

Hobart, TAS: Rise: 06:10am Set: 05:50pm

(Note: These times are averages for the month)

Hobart - TAS

DAY/DATE	TIDE 1	TIDE 2	TIDE 3	TIDE 4
Mon 1	4:41 AM (1.03) H	8:00 AM (1.00) L	2:17 PM (1.40) H	10:10 PM (0.57) L
Tue 2	5:31 AM (1.04) H	8:41 AM (0.99) L	3:00 PM (1.42) H	10:54 PM (0.53) L
Wed 3	6:02 AM (1.05) H	9:17 AM (0.97) L	3:46 PM (1.45) H	11:36 PM (0.50) L
Thu 4	6:30 AM (1.05) H	9:53 AM (0.95) L	4:37 PM (1.48) H	
Fri 5	12:17 AM (0.47) L	6:57 AM (1.05) H	10:32 AM (0.92) L	5:27 PM (1.49) H
Sat 6	12:58 AM (0.45) L	7:27 AM (1.06) H	11:21 AM (0.89) L	6:16 PM (1.49) H
Sun 7	1:37 AM (0.46) L	8:00 AM (1.09) H	12:22 PM (0.86) L	7:07 PM (1.46) H
Mon 8	2:17 AM (0.48) L	8:39 AM (1.14) H	1:38 PM (0.81) L	8:04 PM (1.39) H
Tue 9	2:59 AM (0.54) L	9:22 AM (1.21) H	3:10 PM (0.74) L	9:15 PM (1.30) H
Wed 10	3:42 AM (0.62) L	10:09 AM (1.29) H	4:36 PM (0.64) L	10:41 PM (1.23) H
Thu 11	4:29 AM (0.72) L	10:57 AM (1.38) H	5:49 PM (0.52) L	
Fri 12	12:00 AM (1.18) H	5:22 AM (0.82) L	11:44 AM (1.46) H	6:54 PM (0.42) L
Sat 13	1:11 AM (1.14) H	6:19 AM (0.91) L	12:30 PM (1.51) H	7:54 PM (0.35) L
Sun 14	2:29 AM (1.12) H	7:15 AM (0.96) L	1:18 PM (1.54) H	8:53 PM (0.32) L
Mon 15	3:58 AM (1.11) H	8:08 AM (0.97) L	2:09 PM (1.54) H	9:50 PM (0.32) L
Tue 16	4:59 AM (1.11) H	8:56 AM (0.96) L	3:06 PM (1.53) H	10:45 PM (0.34) L
Wed 17	5:42 AM (1.10) H	9:43 AM (0.93) L	4:08 PM (1.50) H	11:37 PM (0.38) L
Thu 18	6:18 AM (1.10) H	10:30 AM (0.89) L	5:08 PM (1.46) H	
Fri 19	12:25 AM (0.44) L	6:53 AM (1.10) H	11:20 AM (0.87) L	6:00 PM (1.41) H
Sat 20	1:09 AM (0.50) L	7:28 AM (1.11) H	12:18 PM (0.84) L	6:50 PM (1.33) H
Sun 21	1:48 AM (0.57) L	8:02 AM (1.13) H	1:30 PM (0.82) L	7:40 PM (1.24) H
Mon 22	2:22 AM (0.65) L	8:38 AM (1.15) H	2:49 PM (0.79) L	8:38 PM (1.16) H
Tue 23	2:49 AM (0.73) L	9:12 AM (1.19) H	4:00 PM (0.74) L	9:52 PM (1.10) H
Wed 24	3:10 AM (0.82) L	9:44 AM (1.23) H	4:56 PM (0.68) L	11:03 PM (1.07) H
Thu 25	3:26 AM (0.89) L	10:15 AM (1.26) H	5:43 PM (0.63) L	
Fri 26	12:02 AM (1.06) H	3:44 AM (0.95) L	10:46 AM (1.30) H	6:26 PM (0.59) L
Sat 27	12:56 AM (1.06) H	4:13 AM (1.00) L	11:22 AM (1.32) H	7:08 PM (0.56) L
Sun 28	1:51 AM (1.06) H	5:23 AM (1.03) L	12:01 PM (1.34) H	7:51 PM (0.54) L
Mon 29	2:57 AM (1.06) H	6:48 AM (1.03) L	12:45 PM (1.35) H	8:35 PM (0.53) L
Tue 30	4:03 AM (1.07) H	7:39 AM (1.02) L	1:30 PM (1.35) H	9:19 PM (0.51) L

Port Phillip Heads - VIC

DAY/DATE	TIDE 1	TIDE 2	TIDE 3	TIDE 4
Mon 1	5:40 AM (1.49) H	11:12 AM (0.74) L	5:16 PM (1.46) H	11:33 PM (0.42) L
Tue 2	6:22 AM (1.44) H	11:47 AM (0.80) L	5:51 PM (1.41) H	
Wed 3	12:09 AM (0.44) L	7:13 AM (1.38) H	12:26 PM (0.87) L	6:30 PM (1.35) H
Thu 4	12:48 AM (0.48) L	8:12 AM (1.34) H	1:11 PM (0.93) L	7:22 PM (1.29) H
Fri 5	1:38 AM (0.51) L	9:18 AM (1.32) H	2:11 PM (0.97) L	8:30 PM (1.24) H
Sat 6	2:41 AM (0.53) L	10:27 AM (1.34) H	3:29 PM (0.95) L	9:53 PM (1.24) H
Sun 7	3:56 AM (0.54) L	11:27 AM (1.39) H	4:54 PM (0.86) L	11:14 PM (1.30) H
Mon 8	5:10 AM (0.52) L	12:18 PM (1.46) H	5:58 PM (0.72) L	
Tue 9	12:22 AM (1.41) H	6:12 AM (0.50) L	1:02 PM (1.53) H	6:45 PM (0.57) L
Wed 10	1:19 AM (1.54) H	7:02 AM (0.49) L	1:44 PM (1.58) H	7:28 PM (0.42) L
Thu 11	2:11 AM (1.65) H	7:49 AM (0.50) L	2:22 PM (1.62) H	8:11 PM (0.30) L
Fri 12	2:59 AM (1.72) H	8:33 AM (0.53) L	2:59 PM (1.63) H	8:54 PM (0.22) L
Sat 13	3:45 AM (1.75) H	9:17 AM (0.56) L	3:36 PM (1.62) H	9:39 PM (0.18) L
Sun 14	4:32 AM (1.72) H	10:00 AM (0.61) L	4:14 PM (1.59) H	10:23 PM (0.19) L
Mon 15	5:20 AM (1.65) H	10:43 AM (0.66) L	4:55 PM (1.55) H	11:09 PM (0.23) L
Tue 16	6:14 AM (1.55) H	11:26 AM (0.72) L	5:39 PM (1.48) H	11:56 PM (0.31) L
Wed 17	7:14 AM (1.46) H	12:13 PM (0.78) L	6:32 PM (1.40) H	
Thu 18	12:48 AM (0.40) L	8:21 AM (1.38) H	1:08 PM (0.83) L	7:41 PM (1.32) H
Fri 19	1:53 AM (0.49) L	9:30 AM (1.35) H	2:26 PM (0.85) L	9:09 PM (1.27) H
Sat 20	3:15 AM (0.55) L	10:34 AM (1.36) H	4:05 PM (0.81) L	10:34 PM (1.29) H
Sun 21	4:36 AM (0.57) L	11:33 AM (1.39) H	5:24 PM (0.70) L	11:46 PM (1.36) H
Mon 22	5:43 AM (0.56) L	12:24 PM (1.44) H	6:18 PM (0.58) L	
Tue 23	12:47 AM (1.46) H	6:36 AM (0.55) L	1:06 PM (1.48) H	7:00 PM (0.48) L
Wed 24	1:37 AM (1.54) H	7:19 AM (0.55) L	1:42 PM (1.50) H	7:37 PM (0.40) L
Thu 25	2:18 AM (1.61) H	7:56 AM (0.56) L	2:12 PM (1.51) H	8:10 PM (0.35) L
Fri 26	2:54 AM (1.64) H	8:30 AM (0.58) L	2:41 PM (1.51) H	8:43 PM (0.32) L
Sat 27	3:26 AM (1.65) H	9:02 AM (0.60) L	3:09 PM (1.51) H	9:15 PM (0.32) L
Sun 28	3:55 AM (1.63) H	9:35 AM (0.62) L	3:39 PM (1.49) H	9:47 PM (0.33) L
Mon 29	4:27 AM (1.59) H	10:08 AM (0.66) L	4:11 PM (1.46) H	10:20 PM (0.35) L
Tue 30	5:02 AM (1.54) H	10:42 AM (0.70) L	4:45 PM (1.41) H	10:53 PM (0.38) L

Fort Denison - NSW

DAY/DATE	TIDE 1	TIDE 2	TIDE 3	TIDE 4
Mon 1	2:14 AM (1.08) H	7:47 AM (0.74) L	2:45 PM (1.44) H	9:58 PM (0.69) L
Tue 2	3:40 AM (1.07) H	9:02 AM (0.75) L	3:56 PM (1.47) H	11:04 PM (0.62) L
Wed 3	4:53 AM (1.12) H	10:13 AM (0.72) L	4:57 PM (1.55) H	11:54 PM (0.53) L
Thu 4	5:45 AM (1.19) H	11:11 AM (0.64) L	5:47 PM (1.65) H	
Fri 5	12:35 AM (0.43) L	6:28 AM (1.28) H	12:00 PM (0.55) L	6:30 PM (1.74) H
Sat 6	1:12 AM (0.33) L	7:07 AM (1.37) H	12:45 PM (0.45) L	7:12 PM (1.82) H
Sun 7	1:46 AM (0.26) L	7:45 AM (1.47) H	1:30 PM (0.37) L	7:53 PM (1.87) H
Mon 8	2:22 AM (0.21) L	8:25 AM (1.57) H	2:17 PM (0.31) L	8:36 PM (1.86) H
Tue 9	2:59 AM (0.19) L	9:07 AM (1.66) H	3:06 PM (0.29) L	9:20 PM (1.79) H
Wed 10	3:37 AM (0.22) L	9:50 AM (1.72) H	3:58 PM (0.29) L	10:07 PM (1.68) H
Thu 11	4:16 AM (0.29) L	10:36 AM (1.75) H	4:53 PM (0.33) L	10:58 PM (1.53) H
Fri 12	4:59 AM (0.38) L	11:25 AM (1.75) H	5:54 PM (0.40) L	11:53 PM (1.37) H
Sat 13	5:45 AM (0.49) L	12:19 PM (1.71) H	7:03 PM (0.47) L	
Sun 14	12:59 AM (1.23) H	6:40 AM (0.60) L	1:22 PM (1.66) H	8:25 PM (0.51) L
Mon 15	2:20 AM (1.14) H	7:49 AM (0.67) L	2:36 PM (1.63) H	9:48 PM (0.50) L
Tue 16	3:50 AM (1.14) H	9:10 AM (0.68) L	3:54 PM (1.63) H	10:59 PM (0.46) L
Wed 17	5:01 AM (1.20) H	10:26 AM (0.64) L	5:01 PM (1.67) H	11:54 PM (0.40) L
Thu 18	5:54 AM (1.28) H	11:28 AM (0.56) L	5:56 PM (1.71) H	
Fri 19	12:37 AM (0.36) L	6:38 AM (1.37) H	12:20 PM (0.49) L	6:42 PM (1.72) H
Sat 20	1:15 AM (0.33) L	7:16 AM (1.44) H	1:05 PM (0.44) L	7:22 PM (1.71) H
Sun 21	1:47 AM (0.33) L	7:53 AM (1.51) H	1:47 PM (0.42) L	8:00 PM (1.67) H
Mon 22	2:17 AM (0.34) L	8:27 AM (1.55) H	2:26 PM (0.41) L	8:34 PM (1.61) H
Tue 23	2:45 AM (0.37) L	8:59 AM (1.58) H	3:04 PM (0.42) L	9:08 PM (1.53) H
Wed 24	3:11 AM (0.42) L	9:30 AM (1.61) H	3:43 PM (0.45) L	9:43 PM (1.45) H
Thu 25	3:37 AM (0.47) L	10:02 AM (1.61) H	4:22 PM (0.49) L	10:19 PM (1.36) H
Fri 26	4:05 AM (0.53) L	10:36 AM (1.59) H	5:04 PM (0.53) L	10:58 PM (1.28) H
Sat 27	4:37 AM (0.59) L	11:14 AM (1.56) H	5:51 PM (0.59) L	11:42 PM (1.19) H
Sun 28	5:15 AM (0.66) L	11:57 AM (1.51) H	6:47 PM (0.64) L	
Mon 29	12:35 AM (1.12) H	6:01 AM (0.73) L	12:49 PM (1.46) H	7:57 PM (0.67) L
Tue 30	1:44 AM (1.08) H	7:05 AM (0.77) L	1:56 PM (1.44) H	9:14 PM (0.65) L

BITE TIMES

Apogee moon phase on Friday 26th
Perigee moon phase on Wednesday 10th

New moon on Monday 22nd
First quarter moon on Tuesday 30th
Full moon on Monday 8th
Last quarter moon phase on Sunday 14th

DAY	MINOR BITE	MAJOR BITE	MINOR BITE	MAJOR BITE	SALT WATER RATING	FRESH WATER RATING
MON 1	10:05 AM	5:58 PM	12:57 AM	5:32 AM	5	6
TUE 2	10:55 AM	6:52 PM	1:55 AM	6:25 AM	4	5
WED 3	11:54 AM	7:46 PM	2:47 AM	7:18 AM	3	5
THUR 4	12:59 PM	8:40 PM	3:32 AM	8:13 AM	6	6
FRI 5	2:08 PM	9:32 PM	4:10 AM	9:05 AM	5	7
SAT 6	3:19 PM	10:22 PM	4:44 AM	9:56 AM	5	7
SUN 7	4:30 PM	11:11 PM	5:13 AM	10:46 AM	3	8
MON 8	5:42 PM	11:59 PM	5:39 AM	11:35 AM	5	7
TUE 9	6:54 PM		6:05 AM	12:23 PM	7	6
WED 10	8:08 PM	12:48 AM	6:32 AM	1:13 PM	7	6
THUR 11	9:24 PM	1:39 AM	7:01 AM	2:05 PM	5	5
FRI 12	10:40 PM	2:33 AM	7:34 AM	3:01 PM	3	6
SAT 13	11:55 PM	3:31 AM	8:15 AM	4:00 PM	4	4
SUN 14		4:31 AM	9:05 AM	5:02 PM	5	5
MON 15	1:03 AM	5:33 AM	10:03 AM	6:03 PM	6	6

DAY	MINOR BITE	MAJOR BITE	MINOR BITE	MAJOR BITE	SALT WATER RATING	FRESH WATER RATING
TUE 16	2:02 AM	6:34 AM	11:10 AM	7:03 PM	7	7
WED 17	2:50 AM	7:32 AM	12:20 PM	7:58 PM	7	8
THUR 18	3:28 AM	8:25 AM	1:29 PM	8:49 PM	7	8
FRI 19	3:59 AM	9:14 AM	2:37 PM	9:36 PM	5	8
SAT 20	4:26 AM	9:59 AM	3:41 PM	10:19 PM	6	7
SUN 21	4:49 AM	10:41 AM	4:43 PM	11:01 PM	8	8
MON 22	5:11 AM	11:22 AM	5:44 PM	11:42 PM	8	8
TUE 23	5:32 AM	12:03 PM	6:44 PM		8	6
WED 24	5:55 AM	12:44 PM	7:44 PM	12:23 AM	7	6
THUR 25	6:19 AM	1:27 PM	8:45 PM	1:05 AM	6	7
FRI 26	6:47 AM	2:12 PM	9:46 PM	1:49 AM	5	5
SAT 27	7:20 AM	2:59 PM	10:46 PM	2:35 AM	4	6
SUN 28	7:59 AM	3:50 PM	11:44 PM	3:24 AM	4	6
MON 29	8:46 AM	4:42 PM		4:15 AM	3	5
TUE 30	9:40 AM	5:35 PM	12:38 AM	5:08 AM	4	6

TIDE TIMES

Adelaide Outer Harbour - SA

DAY/DATE	TIDE 1	TIDE 2	TIDE 3	TIDE 4
Wed 1	12:43 AM (0.77) L	7:37 AM (2.10) H	2:09 PM (1.17) L	6:33 PM (1.40) H
Thu 2	12:03 AM (0.95) L	7:23 AM (1.77) H	10:19 PM (0.88) L	
Fri 3	5:00 AM (1.66) H	9:40 AM (1.32) L	3:23 PM (1.92) H	10:02 PM (0.61) L
Sat 4	4:23 AM (1.88) H	9:49 AM (0.94) L	3:50 PM (2.23) H	10:14 PM (0.40) L
Sun 5	5:27 AM (2.10) H	11:11 AM (0.63) L	5:16 PM (2.41) H	11:30 PM (0.33) L
Mon 6	5:37 AM (2.27) H	11:33 AM (0.42) L	5:39 PM (2.44) H	11:44 PM (0.34) L
Tue 7	5:47 AM (2.40) H	11:56 AM (0.30) L	5:58 PM (2.37) H	11:55 PM (0.40) L
Wed 8	5:57 AM (2.53) H	12:20 PM (0.25) L	6:15 PM (2.24) H	
Thu 9	12:04 AM (0.46) L	6:13 AM (2.64) H	12:46 PM (0.27) L	6:34 PM (2.07) H
Fri 10	12:13 AM (0.50) L	6:33 AM (2.69) H	1:13 PM (0.37) L	6:49 PM (1.88) H
Sat 11	12:19 AM (0.53) L	6:53 AM (2.68) H	1:34 PM (0.52) L	6:59 PM (1.73) H
Sun 12	12:23 AM (0.52) L	7:11 AM (2.62) H	1:46 PM (0.67) L	7:05 PM (1.66) H
Mon 13	12:32 AM (0.49) L	7:27 AM (2.53) H	1:52 PM (0.80) L	7:09 PM (1.64) H
Tue 14	12:47 AM (0.49) L	7:43 AM (2.37) H	2:01 PM (0.93) L	7:12 PM (1.60) H
Wed 15	1:02 AM (0.61) L	7:55 AM (2.12) H		
Thu 16	12:52 AM (0.82) L	7:36 AM (1.81) H	1:25 PM (1.33) L	5:32 PM (1.53) H
Fri 17	6:04 AM (1.65) H	11:06 AM (1.24) L	4:40 PM (1.75) H	10:51 PM (0.81) L
Sat 18	5:04 AM (1.84) H	10:48 AM (0.88) L	4:46 PM (2.00) H	10:52 PM (0.62) L
Sun 19	4:58 AM (2.12) H	11:03 AM (0.59) L	5:04 PM (2.17) H	11:04 PM (0.50) L
Mon 20	5:08 AM (2.34) H	11:21 AM (0.40) L	5:22 PM (2.23) H	11:15 PM (0.46) L
Tue 21	5:21 AM (2.49) H	11:39 AM (0.29) L	5:39 PM (2.23) H	11:25 PM (0.45) L
Wed 22	5:35 AM (2.60) H	11:59 AM (0.25) L	5:55 PM (2.19) H	11:38 PM (0.45) L
Thu 23	5:52 AM (2.67) H	12:20 PM (0.25) L	6:14 PM (2.12) H	11:54 PM (0.47) L
Fri 24	6:13 AM (2.69) H	12:45 PM (0.30) L	6:36 PM (2.04) H	
Sat 25	12:12 AM (0.51) L	6:36 AM (2.66) H	1:09 PM (0.37) L	6:56 PM (1.94) H
Sun 26	12:29 AM (0.56) L	6:58 AM (2.60) H	1:31 PM (0.47) L	7:14 PM (1.85) H
Mon 27	12:45 AM (0.60) L	7:17 AM (2.53) H	1:51 PM (0.56) L	7:30 PM (1.78) H
Tue 28	1:01 AM (0.64) L	7:37 AM (2.44) H	2:12 PM (0.66) L	7:48 PM (1.70) H
Wed 29	1:19 AM (0.72) L	8:02 AM (2.30) H	2:42 PM (0.81) L	8:11 PM (1.55) H
Thu 30	1:36 AM (0.89) L	8:30 AM (2.06) H	3:31 PM (1.04) L	8:36 PM (1.33) H
Fri 31	1:13 AM (1.13) L	9:03 AM (1.71) H	9:27 PM (1.04) L	

Brisbane Bar - QLD

DAY/DATE	TIDE 1	TIDE 2	TIDE 3	TIDE 4
Wed 1	3:52 AM (1.39) H	9:37 AM (0.82) L	4:45 PM (1.99) H	11:48 PM (0.83) L
Thu 2	5:18 AM (1.51) H	11:00 AM (0.74) L	5:50 PM (2.11) H	
Fri 3	12:42 AM (0.68) L	6:17 AM (1.68) H	12:09 PM (0.61) L	6:43 PM (2.25) H
Sat 4	1:28 AM (0.53) L	7:08 AM (1.86) H	1:07 PM (0.49) L	7:28 PM (2.36) H
Sun 5	2:09 AM (0.40) L	7:54 AM (2.03) H	2:00 PM (0.40) L	8:11 PM (2.42) H
Mon 6	2:49 AM (0.30) L	8:39 AM (2.18) H	2:52 PM (0.34) L	8:52 PM (2.41) H
Tue 7	3:27 AM (0.23) L	9:23 AM (2.32) H	3:41 PM (0.32) L	9:33 PM (2.35) H
Wed 8	4:03 AM (0.19) L	10:08 AM (2.42) H	4:30 PM (0.35) L	10:15 PM (2.22) H
Thu 9	4:39 AM (0.20) L	10:53 AM (2.48) H	5:20 PM (0.42) L	10:58 PM (2.05) H
Fri 10	5:15 AM (0.25) L	11:41 AM (2.48) H	6:13 PM (0.53) L	11:43 PM (1.85) H
Sat 11	5:52 AM (0.35) L	12:30 PM (2.42) H	7:12 PM (0.65) L	
Sun 12	12:35 AM (1.66) H	6:35 AM (0.47) L	1:27 PM (2.33) H	8:24 PM (0.74) L
Mon 13	1:43 AM (1.50) H	7:31 AM (0.61) L	2:32 PM (2.23) H	9:45 PM (0.77) L
Tue 14	3:14 AM (1.44) H	8:49 AM (0.72) L	3:47 PM (2.17) H	11:01 PM (0.72) L
Wed 15	4:44 AM (1.52) H	10:21 AM (0.73) L	5:01 PM (2.17) H	
Thu 16	12:03 AM (0.63) L	5:52 AM (1.67) H	11:39 AM (0.67) L	6:03 PM (2.20) H
Fri 17	12:53 AM (0.54) L	6:45 AM (1.84) H	12:41 PM (0.60) L	6:54 PM (2.22) H
Sat 18	1:34 AM (0.46) L	7:30 AM (1.98) H	1:32 PM (0.54) L	7:36 PM (2.21) H
Sun 19	2:10 AM (0.41) L	8:09 AM (2.09) H	2:16 PM (0.52) L	8:13 PM (2.18) H
Mon 20	2:40 AM (0.38) L	8:45 AM (2.18) H	2:58 PM (0.52) L	8:46 PM (2.12) H
Tue 21	3:08 AM (0.35) L	9:18 AM (2.24) H	3:35 PM (0.54) L	9:17 PM (2.05) H
Wed 22	3:34 AM (0.34) L	9:50 AM (2.29) H	4:12 PM (0.57) L	9:47 PM (1.97) H
Thu 23	4:00 AM (0.35) L	10:23 AM (2.30) H	4:47 PM (0.61) L	10:17 PM (1.88) H
Fri 24	4:26 AM (0.38) L	10:55 AM (2.29) H	5:21 PM (0.66) L	10:48 PM (1.78) H
Sat 25	4:54 AM (0.43) L	11:29 AM (2.25) H	5:57 PM (0.73) L	11:21 PM (1.68) H
Sun 26	5:24 AM (0.51) L	12:04 PM (2.19) H	6:36 PM (0.80) L	11:59 PM (1.59) H
Mon 27	5:59 AM (0.60) L	12:45 PM (2.12) H	7:25 PM (0.87) L	
Tue 28	12:45 AM (1.50) H	6:41 AM (0.69) L	1:35 PM (2.06) H	8:29 PM (0.90) L
Wed 29	1:48 AM (1.45) H	7:39 AM (0.77) L	2:38 PM (2.03) H	9:45 PM (0.86) L
Thu 30	3:16 AM (1.47) H	8:57 AM (0.80) L	3:49 PM (2.06) H	10:54 PM (0.76) L
Fri 31	4:39 AM (1.59) H	10:19 AM (0.76) L	4:55 PM (2.13) H	11:50 PM (0.62) L

Darwin - NT

DAY/DATE	TIDE 1	TIDE 2	TIDE 3	TIDE 4
Wed 1	5:29 AM (4.32) L	9:00 AM (4.67) H	6:15 PM (3.15) L	
Thu 2	1:17 AM (5.10) H	11:03 AM (4.13) L	1:35 PM (4.18) H	8:12 PM (3.15) L
Fri 3	3:36 AM (5.46) H	10:29 AM (3.62) L	3:39 PM (4.82) H	9:45 PM (2.75) L
Sat 4	4:21 AM (5.98) H	10:50 AM (3.02) L	4:22 PM (5.55) H	10:39 PM (2.27) L
Sun 5	4:57 AM (6.48) H	11:20 AM (2.36) L	5:04 PM (6.28) H	11:21 PM (1.87) L
Mon 6	5:30 AM (6.92) H	11:53 AM (1.67) L	5:47 PM (6.95) H	
Tue 7	12:00 AM (1.60) L	6:00 AM (7.25) H	12:26 PM (1.02) L	6:30 PM (7.48) H
Wed 8	12:33 AM (1.52) L	6:28 AM (7.45) H	1:00 PM (0.50) L	7:11 PM (7.81) H
Thu 9	1:06 AM (1.61) L	6:54 AM (7.50) H	1:34 PM (0.20) L	7:51 PM (7.90) H
Fri 10	1:39 AM (1.86) L	7:20 AM (7.40) H	2:10 PM (0.17) L	8:31 PM (7.73) H
Sat 11	2:13 AM (2.25) L	7:49 AM (7.12) H	2:46 PM (0.44) L	9:13 PM (7.35) H
Sun 12	2:50 AM (2.74) L	8:19 AM (6.66) H	3:27 PM (0.99) L	9:58 PM (6.80) H
Mon 13	3:31 AM (3.28) L	8:52 AM (6.03) H	4:13 PM (1.71) L	10:52 PM (6.18) H
Tue 14	4:30 AM (3.81) L	9:30 AM (5.29) H	5:15 PM (2.47) L	
Wed 15	12:03 AM (5.68) H	6:37 AM (4.08) L	11:00 AM (4.56) H	6:54 PM (3.00) L
Thu 16	1:47 AM (5.53) H	9:14 AM (3.63) L	2:49 PM (4.77) H	8:50 PM (3.02) L
Fri 17	3:20 AM (5.80) H	10:15 AM (2.97) L	3:56 PM (5.43) H	10:05 PM (2.77) L
Sat 18	4:15 AM (6.14) H	10:54 AM (2.39) L	4:43 PM (6.02) H	10:53 PM (2.52) L
Sun 19	4:54 AM (6.43) H	11:27 AM (1.92) L	5:23 PM (6.51) H	11:30 PM (2.35) L
Mon 20	5:24 AM (6.64) H	11:55 AM (1.55) L	6:00 PM (6.89) H	
Tue 21	12:01 AM (2.26) L	5:49 AM (6.76) H	12:20 PM (1.26) L	6:34 PM (7.14) H
Wed 22	12:30 AM (2.25) L	6:11 AM (6.81) H	12:45 PM (1.05) L	7:06 PM (7.27) H
Thu 23	12:55 AM (2.31) L	6:31 AM (6.81) H	1:08 PM (0.94) L	7:35 PM (7.27) H
Fri 24	1:18 AM (2.43) L	6:54 AM (6.73) H	1:33 PM (0.95) L	8:02 PM (7.18) H
Sat 25	1:42 AM (2.61) L	7:17 AM (6.57) H	2:00 PM (1.11) L	8:30 PM (6.99) H
Sun 26	2:08 AM (2.84) L	7:42 AM (6.31) H	2:30 PM (1.41) L	9:00 PM (6.72) H
Mon 27	2:36 AM (3.12) L	8:05 AM (5.97) H	3:00 PM (1.81) L	9:33 PM (6.39) H
Tue 28	3:08 AM (3.45) L	8:29 AM (5.57) H	3:34 PM (2.28) L	10:15 PM (6.02) H
Wed 29	3:53 AM (3.81) L	8:56 AM (5.14) H	4:23 PM (2.74) L	11:09 PM (5.68) H
Thu 30	5:18 AM (4.09) L	9:45 AM (4.68) H	5:35 PM (3.12) L	
Fri 31	12:25 AM (5.49) H	7:43 AM (3.98) L	12:34 PM (4.42) H	7:12 PM (3.27) L

Fremantle - WA

DAY/DATE	TIDE 1	TIDE 2	TIDE 3	TIDE 4
Wed 1	1:26 AM (0.97) H	2:33 PM (0.53) L		
Thu 2	4:42 AM (0.96) H	2:50 PM (0.53) L		
Fri 3	6:24 AM (0.98) H	3:00 PM (0.54) L	10:27 PM (0.79) H	
Sat 4	12:28 AM (0.78) L	7:30 AM (0.99) H	3:09 PM (0.57) L	9:23 PM (0.81) H
Sun 5	1:37 AM (0.72) L	8:26 AM (0.97) H	3:19 PM (0.61) L	9:23 PM (0.86) H
Mon 6	2:52 AM (0.66) L	9:32 AM (0.92) H	3:24 PM (0.66) L	9:31 PM (0.93) H
Tue 7	4:00 AM (0.59) L	10:48 AM (0.85) H	3:01 PM (0.70) L	9:40 PM (1.00) H
Wed 8	5:01 AM (0.54) L	11:53 AM (0.77) H	2:40 PM (0.71) L	9:54 PM (1.06) H
Thu 9	6:30 AM (0.51) L	1:00 PM (0.68) H	2:13 PM (0.68) L	10:14 PM (1.11) H
Fri 10	8:29 AM (0.47) L	10:38 PM (1.12) H		
Sat 11	9:45 AM (0.45) L	10:23 AM (0.45) L	11:30 AM (0.45) L	11:04 PM (1.11) H
Sun 12	12:27 PM (0.42) L	11:34 PM (1.06) H		
Mon 13	1:13 PM (0.42) L			
Tue 14	12:06 AM (1.00) H	1:34 AM (0.98) L	2:27 AM (0.99) H	1:53 PM (0.46) L
Wed 15	12:43 AM (0.93) H	1:52 AM (0.92) L	3:29 AM (0.94) H	2:27 PM (0.51) L
Thu 16	6:15 AM (0.89) H	2:49 PM (0.57) L	10:16 PM (0.80) H	
Fri 17	12:41 AM (0.78) L	7:18 AM (0.87) H	2:44 PM (0.63) L	8:57 PM (0.83) H
Sat 18	2:14 AM (0.73) L	8:11 AM (0.85) H	2:29 PM (0.66) L	8:52 PM (0.88) H
Sun 19	2:58 AM (0.68) L	9:05 AM (0.82) H	2:13 PM (0.69) L	8:43 PM (0.93) H
Mon 20	3:37 AM (0.63) L	9:59 AM (0.79) H	1:41 PM (0.69) L	8:43 PM (0.98) H
Tue 21	4:15 AM (0.59) L	10:47 AM (0.75) H	1:56 PM (0.68) L	8:54 PM (1.03) H
Wed 22	4:52 AM (0.56) L	11:32 AM (0.72) H	2:12 PM (0.68) L	9:12 PM (1.06) H
Thu 23	5:30 AM (0.54) L	12:18 PM (0.68) H	2:12 PM (0.67) L	9:34 PM (1.08) H
Fri 24	6:17 AM (0.53) L	10:00 PM (1.09) H		
Sat 25	8:17 AM (0.52) L	10:28 PM (1.08) H		
Sun 26	9:07 AM (0.53) L	10:58 PM (1.06) H		
Mon 27	9:56 AM (0.54) L	11:46 AM (0.55) H	12:03 PM (0.55) L	11:29 PM (1.03) H
Tue 28	10:55 AM (0.55) L	11:34 AM (0.55) L	12:48 PM (0.54) L	
Wed 29	12:04 AM (1.00) H	1:16 PM (0.54) L		
Thu 30	12:45 AM (0.96) H	1:34 PM (0.55) L		
Fri 31	3:28 AM (0.91) H	1:34 PM (0.57) L	9:38 PM (0.83) H	11:56 PM (0.82) L

Sun Rise & Sun Set Times:

*__Adelaide, SA:__ Rise: 06:30am Set: 07:20pm
Brisbane, QLD: Rise: 05:10am Set: 05:50pm
Darwin, NT: Rise: 06:20am Set: 06:40pm
Perth, WA: Rise: 05:30am Set: 06:20pm
Hobart, TAS: Rise: 06:20am Set: 07:30pm
*__Melbourne, VIC:__ Rise: 06:30am Set: 07:30pm
*__Sydney, NSW:__ Rise: 06:13am Set: 07:08pm

(Note: These times are averages for the month)

*Note: Daylight Savings start (clocks turn forward 1 hour) on Sunday, October 1st at 2:00 AM for states marked * Subtract1 hour from rise/set time for days before Oct 1st*

Hobart - TAS

DAY/DATE	TIDE 1	TIDE 2	TIDE 3	TIDE 4
Wed 1	4:41 AM (1.07) H	8:21 AM (0.99) L	2:17 PM (1.36) H	10:00 PM (0.49) L
Thu 2	5:08 AM (1.07) H	9:02 AM (0.95) L	3:09 PM (1.37) H	10:41 PM (0.48) L
Fri 3	5:33 AM (1.08) H	9:45 AM (0.91) L	4:04 PM (1.38) H	11:19 PM (0.47) L
Sat 4	6:00 AM (1.10) H	10:35 AM (0.85) L	5:00 PM (1.37) H	11:58 PM (0.48) L
Sun 5	7:31 AM (1.15) H	12:34 PM (0.79) L	6:59 PM (1.34) H	
Mon 6	1:36 AM (0.53) L	8:05 AM (1.21) H	1:45 PM (0.71) L	8:00 PM (1.29) H
Tue 7	2:16 AM (0.60) L	8:43 AM (1.29) H	3:04 PM (0.61) L	9:14 PM (1.23) H
Wed 8	3:00 AM (0.70) L	9:25 AM (1.37) H	4:23 PM (0.48) L	10:42 PM (1.18) H
Thu 9	3:51 AM (0.81) L	10:14 AM (1.45) H	5:33 PM (0.36) L	
Fri 10	12:04 AM (1.17) H	4:53 AM (0.91) L	11:06 AM (1.51) H	6:37 PM (0.26) L
Sat 11	1:16 AM (1.17) H	6:02 AM (0.98) L	12:02 PM (1.54) H	7:36 PM (0.21) L
Sun 12	2:29 AM (1.17) H	7:08 AM (1.01) L	12:57 PM (1.55) H	8:33 PM (0.21) L
Mon 13	3:42 AM (1.17) H	8:07 AM (1.01) L	1:52 PM (1.52) H	9:30 PM (0.25) L
Tue 14	4:42 AM (1.16) H	9:02 AM (0.98) L	2:51 PM (1.47) H	10:25 PM (0.31) L
Wed 15	5:27 AM (1.15) H	9:58 AM (0.93) L	3:54 PM (1.41) H	11:15 PM (0.39) L
Thu 16	6:04 AM (1.15) H	10:53 AM (0.88) L	5:00 PM (1.34) H	
Fri 17	12:00 AM (0.47) L	6:37 AM (1.15) H	11:52 AM (0.83) L	5:59 PM (1.26) H
Sat 18	12:37 AM (0.55) L	7:09 AM (1.17) H	12:53 PM (0.79) L	6:52 PM (1.19) H
Sun 19	1:07 AM (0.64) L	7:38 AM (1.19) H	1:56 PM (0.74) L	7:45 PM (1.12) H
Mon 20	1:30 AM (0.72) L	8:05 AM (1.22) H	2:59 PM (0.69) L	8:45 PM (1.06) H
Tue 21	1:45 AM (0.80) L	8:30 AM (1.25) H	3:54 PM (0.64) L	10:00 PM (1.02) H
Wed 22	2:00 AM (0.88) L	8:55 AM (1.29) H	4:42 PM (0.58) L	11:15 PM (1.03) H
Thu 23	2:20 AM (0.95) L	9:20 AM (1.32) H	5:24 PM (0.53) L	
Fri 24	12:17 AM (1.05) H	2:45 AM (1.01) L	9:50 AM (1.34) H	6:04 PM (0.49) L
Sat 25	1:13 AM (1.07) H	3:18 AM (1.05) L	10:28 AM (1.35) H	6:44 PM (0.47) L
Sun 26	2:04 AM (1.09) H	4:06 AM (1.08) L	11:12 AM (1.35) H	7:26 PM (0.47) L
Mon 27	2:54 AM (1.10) H	6:10 AM (1.08) L	12:00 PM (1.35) H	8:08 PM (0.46) L
Tue 28	3:39 AM (1.10) H	7:19 AM (1.06) L	12:52 PM (1.33) H	8:51 PM (0.46) L
Wed 29	4:13 AM (1.10) H	8:10 AM (1.03) L	1:43 PM (1.32) H	9:32 PM (0.46) L
Thu 30	4:41 AM (1.11) H	8:59 AM (0.99) L	2:34 PM (1.30) H	10:11 PM (0.46) L
Fri 31	5:07 AM (1.12) H	9:49 AM (0.94) L	3:31 PM (1.28) H	10:47 PM (0.47) L

Port Phillip Heads - VIC

DAY/DATE	TIDE 1	TIDE 2	TIDE 3	TIDE 4
Wed 1	5:43 AM (1.47) H	11:15 AM (0.75) L	5:19 PM (1.36) H	11:26 PM (0.42) L
Thu 2	6:30 AM (1.40) H	11:51 AM (0.80) L	6:01 PM (1.30) H	
Fri 3	12:03 AM (0.46) L	7:25 AM (1.34) H	12:33 PM (0.83) L	6:56 PM (1.24) H
Sat 4	12:51 AM (0.52) L	8:29 AM (1.30) H	1:29 PM (0.85) L	8:09 PM (1.21) H
Sun 5	1:54 AM (0.58) L	10:35 AM (1.30) H	3:43 PM (0.81) L	10:38 PM (1.25) H
Mon 6	4:11 AM (0.62) L	11:36 AM (1.34) H	5:03 PM (0.70) L	
Tue 7	12:00 AM (1.35) H	5:35 AM (0.64) L	12:30 PM (1.40) H	6:12 PM (0.54) L
Wed 8	1:08 AM (1.50) H	6:47 AM (0.62) L	1:19 PM (1.46) H	7:05 PM (0.38) L
Thu 9	2:05 AM (1.65) H	7:43 AM (0.60) L	2:04 PM (1.51) H	7:53 PM (0.24) L
Fri 10	2:56 AM (1.77) H	8:30 AM (0.59) L	2:46 PM (1.56) H	8:40 PM (0.15) L
Sat 11	3:44 AM (1.82) H	9:15 AM (0.59) L	3:29 PM (1.58) H	9:27 PM (0.11) L
Sun 12	4:30 AM (1.81) H	9:58 AM (0.59) L	4:10 PM (1.58) H	10:14 PM (0.11) L
Mon 13	5:16 AM (1.75) H	10:41 AM (0.61) L	4:53 PM (1.55) H	11:01 PM (0.17) L
Tue 14	6:04 AM (1.65) H	11:25 AM (0.63) L	5:38 PM (1.49) H	11:48 PM (0.25) L
Wed 15	6:56 AM (1.55) H	12:10 PM (0.67) L	6:28 PM (1.42) H	
Thu 16	12:37 AM (0.36) L	7:54 AM (1.45) H	1:00 PM (0.70) L	7:28 PM (1.33) H
Fri 17	1:30 AM (0.47) L	8:56 AM (1.37) H	2:00 PM (0.73) L	8:48 PM (1.26) H
Sat 18	2:32 AM (0.59) L	9:58 AM (1.33) H	3:22 PM (0.73) L	10:18 PM (1.25) H
Sun 19	3:49 AM (0.67) L	10:57 AM (1.32) H	4:48 PM (0.67) L	11:35 PM (1.30) H
Mon 20	5:11 AM (0.71) L	11:52 AM (1.33) H	5:56 PM (0.58) L	
Tue 21	12:41 AM (1.40) H	6:22 AM (0.71) L	12:41 PM (1.36) H	6:45 PM (0.48) L
Wed 22	1:35 AM (1.50) H	7:16 AM (0.69) L	1:23 PM (1.38) H	7:24 PM (0.40) L
Thu 23	2:18 AM (1.59) H	7:57 AM (0.67) L	1:59 PM (1.41) H	8:00 PM (0.34) L
Fri 24	2:56 AM (1.65) H	8:31 AM (0.66) L	2:31 PM (1.43) H	8:33 PM (0.30) L
Sat 25	3:27 AM (1.68) H	9:04 AM (0.64) L	3:03 PM (1.44) H	9:07 PM (0.29) L
Sun 26	3:57 AM (1.69) H	9:36 AM (0.64) L	3:36 PM (1.45) H	9:41 PM (0.29) L
Mon 27	4:28 AM (1.67) H	10:10 AM (0.64) L	4:10 PM (1.44) H	10:14 PM (0.31) L
Tue 28	5:00 AM (1.63) H	10:43 AM (0.66) L	4:45 PM (1.41) H	10:45 PM (0.34) L
Wed 29	5:36 AM (1.57) H	11:15 AM (0.68) L	5:19 PM (1.37) H	11:15 PM (0.37) L
Thu 30	6:15 AM (1.51) H	11:49 AM (0.71) L	5:58 PM (1.32) H	11:48 PM (0.42) L
Fri 31	6:58 AM (1.45) H	12:24 PM (0.72) L	6:43 PM (1.28) H	

Fort Denison - NSW

DAY/DATE	TIDE 1	TIDE 2	TIDE 3	TIDE 4
Wed 1	3:07 AM (1.09) H	8:25 AM (0.78) L	3:10 PM (1.46) H	10:19 PM (0.59) L
Thu 2	4:18 AM (1.15) H	9:40 AM (0.73) L	4:16 PM (1.52) H	11:09 PM (0.49) L
Fri 3	5:10 AM (1.24) H	10:43 AM (0.64) L	5:10 PM (1.61) H	11:51 PM (0.40) L
Sat 4	5:53 AM (1.36) H	11:36 AM (0.53) L	5:57 PM (1.70) H	
Sun 5	12:29 AM (0.31) L	7:33 AM (1.49) H	1:25 PM (0.42) L	7:42 PM (1.76) H
Mon 6	2:05 AM (0.24) L	8:14 AM (1.63) H	2:14 PM (0.32) L	8:27 PM (1.77) H
Tue 7	2:43 AM (0.21) L	8:55 AM (1.75) H	3:04 PM (0.25) L	9:14 PM (1.74) H
Wed 8	3:22 AM (0.22) L	9:39 AM (1.85) H	3:56 PM (0.21) L	10:02 PM (1.66) H
Thu 9	4:02 AM (0.27) L	10:24 AM (1.90) H	4:50 PM (0.21) L	10:55 PM (1.54) H
Fri 10	4:45 AM (0.36) L	11:13 AM (1.91) H	5:47 PM (0.25) L	11:50 PM (1.41) H
Sat 11	5:32 AM (0.46) L	12:03 PM (1.86) H	6:50 PM (0.33) L	
Sun 12	12:51 AM (1.29) H	6:25 AM (0.57) L	1:00 PM (1.78) H	8:00 PM (0.40) L
Mon 13	2:00 AM (1.20) H	7:28 AM (0.66) L	2:05 PM (1.69) H	9:17 PM (0.46) L
Tue 14	3:22 AM (1.16) H	8:42 AM (0.71) L	3:19 PM (1.62) H	10:30 PM (0.47) L
Wed 15	4:39 AM (1.20) H	10:02 AM (0.71) L	4:35 PM (1.59) H	11:31 PM (0.46) L
Thu 16	5:41 AM (1.27) H	11:15 AM (0.66) L	5:39 PM (1.58) H	
Fri 17	12:20 AM (0.44) L	6:29 AM (1.36) H	12:15 PM (0.59) L	6:31 PM (1.58) H
Sat 18	1:00 AM (0.42) L	7:11 AM (1.45) H	1:07 PM (0.53) L	7:15 PM (1.57) H
Sun 19	1:34 AM (0.41) L	7:47 AM (1.53) H	1:51 PM (0.49) L	7:54 PM (1.54) H
Mon 20	2:04 AM (0.41) L	8:21 AM (1.59) H	2:32 PM (0.45) L	8:30 PM (1.50) H
Tue 21	2:32 AM (0.43) L	8:53 AM (1.65) H	3:10 PM (0.43) L	9:07 PM (1.46) H
Wed 22	3:00 AM (0.45) L	9:24 AM (1.68) H	3:47 PM (0.42) L	9:43 PM (1.41) H
Thu 23	3:28 AM (0.49) L	9:56 AM (1.70) H	4:24 PM (0.43) L	10:19 PM (1.36) H
Fri 24	3:57 AM (0.54) L	10:29 AM (1.70) H	5:02 PM (0.45) L	10:58 PM (1.30) H
Sat 25	4:29 AM (0.59) L	11:03 AM (1.68) H	5:44 PM (0.49) L	11:39 PM (1.25) H
Sun 26	5:04 AM (0.64) L	11:41 AM (1.64) H	6:29 PM (0.53) L	
Mon 27	12:24 AM (1.19) H	5:45 AM (0.69) L	12:24 PM (1.59) H	7:20 PM (0.58) L
Tue 28	1:15 AM (1.15) H	6:33 AM (0.74) L	1:14 PM (1.53) H	8:20 PM (0.60) L
Wed 29	2:17 AM (1.13) H	7:34 AM (0.78) L	2:13 PM (1.50) H	9:26 PM (0.59) L
Thu 30	3:29 AM (1.15) H	8:47 AM (0.78) L	3:20 PM (1.49) H	10:25 PM (0.54) L
Fri 31	4:34 AM (1.23) H	10:01 AM (0.74) L	4:28 PM (1.52) H	11:16 PM (0.47) L

BITE TIMES

Apogee moon phase on Friday 24th
Perigee moon phase on Wednesday 8th

New moon on Tuesday 21st
First quarter moon on Thursday 30th
Full moon on Tuesday 7th
Last quarter moon phase on Tuesday 14th

DAY	MINOR BITE	MAJOR BITE	MINOR BITE	MAJOR BITE	SALT WATER RATING	FRESH WATER RATING
WED 1	10:42 AM	6:28 PM	1:24 AM	6:01 AM	5	6
THUR 2	11:48 AM	7:19 PM	2:05 AM	6:53 AM	4	5
FRI 3	12:57 PM	8:09 PM	2:40 AM	7:44 AM	3	5
SAT 4	2:07 PM	8:58 PM	3:10 AM	8:33 AM	6	6
SUN 5	3:17 PM	9:47 PM	3:38 AM	9:22 AM	5	7
MON 6	4:30 PM	10:36 PM	4:04 AM	10:11 AM	3	8
TUE 7	5:44 PM	11:27 PM	4:30 AM	11:01 AM	5	7
WED 8	7:01 PM		4:59 AM	11:54 AM	7	6
THUR 9	8:21 PM	12:21 AM	5:31 AM	12:50 PM	7	6
FRI 10	9:39 PM	1:19 AM	6:10 AM	1:50 PM	5	5
SAT 11	10:53 PM	2:21 AM	6:58 AM	2:52 PM	4	4
SUN 12	11:57 PM	3:25 AM	7:55 AM	3:56 PM	3	6
MON 13		4:28 AM	9:01 AM	4:57 PM	4	4
TUE 14	12:48 AM	5:27 AM	10:11 AM	5:54 PM	5	5
WED 15	1:30 AM	6:22 AM	11:21 AM	6:47 PM	6	6

DAY	MINOR BITE	MAJOR BITE	MINOR BITE	MAJOR BITE	SALT WATER RATING	FRESH WATER RATING
THUR 16	2:03 AM	7:12 AM	12:29 PM	7:34 PM	7	7
FRI 17	2:30 AM	7:58 AM	1:34 PM	8:18 PM	7	8
SAT 18	2:54 AM	8:40 AM	2:35 PM	9:00 PM	5	8
SUN 19	3:16 AM	9:21 AM	3:36 PM	9:41 PM	6	7
MON 20	3:37 AM	10:01 AM	4:35 PM	10:21 PM	8	8
TUE 21	3:59 AM	10:42 AM	5:35 PM	11:03 PM	8	8
WED 22	4:23 AM	11:24 AM	6:35 PM	11:45 PM	8	8
THUR 23	4:49 AM	12:08 PM	7:36 PM		8	6
FRI 24	5:20 AM	12:55 PM	8:37 PM	12:31 AM	7	6
SAT 25	5:57 AM	1:44 PM	9:36 PM	1:19 AM	6	7
SUN 26	6:41 AM	2:35 PM	10:31 PM	2:09 AM	5	5
MON 27	7:32 AM	3:27 PM	11:19 PM	3:00 AM	4	6
TUE 28	8:30 AM	4:19 PM		3:53 AM	3	5
WED 29	9:33 AM	5:10 PM	12:01 AM	4:44 AM	3	5
THUR 30	10:39 AM	5:59 PM	12:37 AM	5:34 AM	4	6
FRI 31	11:46 AM	6:47 PM	1:08 AM	6:23 AM	5	6

TIDE TIMES

Adelaide Outer Harbour - SA

DAY/DATE	TIDE 1	TIDE 2	TIDE 3	TIDE 4
Sat 1	4:38 AM (1.58) H	9:36 AM (1.29) L	3:17 PM (1.74) H	9:50 PM (0.77) L
Sun 2	4:17 AM (1.90) H	10:10 AM (0.87) L	4:11 PM (2.01) H	10:17 PM (0.59) L
Mon 3	4:32 AM (2.20) H	10:43 AM (0.53) L	4:48 PM (2.15) H	10:42 PM (0.52) L
Tue 4	4:51 AM (2.41) H	11:14 AM (0.31) L	5:18 PM (2.15) H	11:01 PM (0.55) L
Wed 5	5:09 AM (2.57) H	11:43 AM (0.19) L	5:44 PM (2.06) H	11:16 PM (0.60) L
Thu 6	5:26 AM (2.69) H	12:12 PM (0.18) L	6:05 PM (1.91) H	11:28 PM (0.63) L
Fri 7	5:47 AM (2.76) H	12:41 PM (0.24) L	6:24 PM (1.76) H	11:39 PM (0.65) L
Sat 8	6:12 AM (2.76) H	1:09 PM (0.36) L	6:41 PM (1.63) H	11:51 PM (0.65) L
Sun 9	6:36 AM (2.69) H	1:33 PM (0.52) L	6:55 PM (1.55) H	
Mon 10	12:04 AM (0.64) L	7:00 AM (2.58) H	1:49 PM (0.68) L	7:07 PM (1.54) H
Tue 11	12:22 AM (0.63) L	7:21 AM (2.43) H	1:59 PM (0.78) L	7:24 PM (1.56) H
Wed 12	12:48 AM (0.68) L	7:45 AM (2.25) H	2:13 PM (0.87) L	7:49 PM (1.55) H
Thu 13	1:19 AM (0.83) L	8:11 AM (2.01) H	2:42 PM (0.98) L	8:26 PM (1.47) H
Fri 14	1:50 AM (1.09) L	8:33 AM (1.69) H	3:36 PM (1.17) L	
Sat 15	4:26 AM (1.46) H	9:46 AM (1.32) L	2:15 PM (1.43) H	8:52 PM (1.06) L
Sun 16	3:24 AM (1.82) H	10:00 AM (0.95) L	3:46 PM (1.66) H	9:34 PM (0.86) L
Mon 17	3:52 AM (2.15) H	10:28 AM (0.64) L	4:24 PM (1.85) H	10:05 PM (0.72) L
Tue 18	4:20 AM (2.40) H	10:57 AM (0.42) L	4:56 PM (1.96) H	10:31 PM (0.65) L
Wed 19	4:45 AM (2.56) H	11:24 AM (0.29) L	5:23 PM (1.99) H	10:53 PM (0.62) L
Thu 20	5:09 AM (2.65) H	11:49 AM (0.24) L	5:47 PM (1.98) H	11:14 PM (0.62) L
Fri 21	5:33 AM (2.69) H	12:15 PM (0.24) L	6:11 PM (1.94) H	11:36 PM (0.62) L
Sat 22	5:59 AM (2.70) H	12:41 PM (0.27) L	6:35 PM (1.89) H	11:59 PM (0.63) L
Sun 23	6:25 AM (2.66) H	1:08 PM (0.33) L	6:59 PM (1.84) H	
Mon 24	12:23 AM (0.65) L	6:51 AM (2.60) H	1:34 PM (0.41) L	7:21 PM (1.79) H
Tue 25	12:46 AM (0.69) L	7:17 AM (2.52) H	1:59 PM (0.48) L	7:45 PM (1.74) H
Wed 26	1:09 AM (0.74) L	7:42 AM (2.42) H	2:27 PM (0.56) L	8:13 PM (1.70) H
Thu 27	1:38 AM (0.82) L	8:13 AM (2.29) H	3:02 PM (0.65) L	8:56 PM (1.64) H
Fri 28	2:18 AM (0.96) L	8:53 AM (2.08) H	3:53 PM (0.79) L	10:12 PM (1.56) H
Sat 29	3:29 AM (1.17) L	10:02 AM (1.80) H	5:27 PM (0.94) L	
Sun 30	12:44 AM (1.62) H	7:06 AM (1.23) L	12:48 PM (1.58) H	7:41 PM (0.96) L

Brisbane Bar - QLD

DAY/DATE	TIDE 1	TIDE 2	TIDE 3	TIDE 4
Sat 1	5:44 AM (1.77) H	11:31 AM (0.68) L	5:53 PM (2.21) H	
Sun 2	12:40 AM (0.48) L	6:38 AM (1.98) H	12:37 PM (0.58) L	6:44 PM (2.26) H
Mon 3	1:26 AM (0.35) L	7:28 AM (2.18) H	1:38 PM (0.50) L	7:32 PM (2.26) H
Tue 4	2:09 AM (0.26) L	8:15 AM (2.36) H	2:35 PM (0.44) L	8:19 PM (2.21) H
Wed 5	2:49 AM (0.20) L	9:02 AM (2.50) H	3:30 PM (0.41) L	9:06 PM (2.12) H
Thu 6	3:29 AM (0.18) L	9:49 AM (2.60) H	4:23 PM (0.41) L	9:55 PM (2.00) H
Fri 7	4:08 AM (0.20) L	10:37 AM (2.64) H	5:17 PM (0.45) L	10:45 PM (1.87) H
Sat 8	4:48 AM (0.26) L	11:27 AM (2.62) H	6:14 PM (0.52) L	11:37 PM (1.73) H
Sun 9	5:31 AM (0.36) L	12:17 PM (2.54) H	7:15 PM (0.60) L	
Mon 10	12:34 AM (1.62) H	6:20 AM (0.50) L	1:12 PM (2.42) H	8:17 PM (0.66) L
Tue 11	1:41 AM (1.54) H	7:18 AM (0.63) L	2:10 PM (2.30) H	9:21 PM (0.69) L
Wed 12	2:56 AM (1.54) H	8:30 AM (0.74) L	3:13 PM (2.20) H	10:20 PM (0.67) L
Thu 13	4:13 AM (1.62) H	9:51 AM (0.79) L	4:16 PM (2.13) H	11:15 PM (0.63) L
Fri 14	5:18 AM (1.75) H	11:04 AM (0.78) L	5:15 PM (2.08) H	
Sat 15	12:03 AM (0.56) L	6:13 AM (1.91) H	12:09 PM (0.75) L	6:07 PM (2.05) H
Sun 16	12:45 AM (0.50) L	7:00 AM (2.05) H	1:03 PM (0.71) L	6:52 PM (2.01) H
Mon 17	1:22 AM (0.44) L	7:40 AM (2.17) H	1:52 PM (0.68) L	7:33 PM (1.97) H
Tue 18	1:55 AM (0.40) L	8:17 AM (2.27) H	2:37 PM (0.65) L	8:11 PM (1.92) H
Wed 19	2:27 AM (0.37) L	8:53 AM (2.34) H	3:18 PM (0.63) L	8:46 PM (1.87) H
Thu 20	2:57 AM (0.36) L	9:28 AM (2.38) H	3:58 PM (0.63) L	9:21 PM (1.82) H
Fri 21	3:27 AM (0.37) L	10:01 AM (2.39) H	4:35 PM (0.65) L	9:55 PM (1.77) H
Sat 22	3:57 AM (0.40) L	10:35 AM (2.37) H	5:11 PM (0.68) L	10:30 PM (1.72) H
Sun 23	4:29 AM (0.44) L	11:10 AM (2.34) H	5:48 PM (0.72) L	11:06 PM (1.68) H
Mon 24	5:02 AM (0.50) L	11:46 AM (2.30) H	6:28 PM (0.76) L	11:47 PM (1.64) H
Tue 25	5:40 AM (0.56) L	12:27 PM (2.25) H	7:13 PM (0.78) L	
Wed 26	12:34 AM (1.60) H	6:24 AM (0.63) L	1:11 PM (2.21) H	8:03 PM (0.79) L
Thu 27	1:31 AM (1.59) H	7:17 AM (0.71) L	2:02 PM (2.18) H	9:00 PM (0.75) L
Fri 28	2:42 AM (1.61) H	8:25 AM (0.77) L	3:00 PM (2.16) H	10:00 PM (0.67) L
Sat 29	3:57 AM (1.71) H	9:40 AM (0.79) L	4:01 PM (2.15) H	10:56 PM (0.57) L
Sun 30	5:06 AM (1.88) H	10:56 AM (0.76) L	5:02 PM (2.13) H	11:50 PM (0.47) L

Darwin - NT

DAY/DATE	TIDE 1	TIDE 2	TIDE 3	TIDE 4
Sat 1	1:57 AM (5.58) H	9:13 AM (3.43) L	2:52 PM (4.95) H	8:46 PM (3.10) L
Sun 2	3:07 AM (5.92) H	9:58 AM (2.75) L	3:52 PM (5.69) H	9:53 PM (2.79) L
Mon 3	3:55 AM (6.30) H	10:37 AM (2.01) L	4:42 PM (6.45) H	10:43 PM (2.51) L
Tue 4	4:34 AM (6.66) H	11:15 AM (1.29) L	5:29 PM (7.12) H	11:27 PM (2.31) L
Wed 5	5:09 AM (6.94) H	11:53 AM (0.67) L	6:15 PM (7.63) H	
Thu 6	12:06 AM (2.23) L	5:42 AM (7.12) H	12:30 PM (0.24) L	6:59 PM (7.92) H
Fri 7	12:44 AM (2.27) L	6:15 AM (7.19) H	1:08 PM (0.05) L	7:41 PM (7.97) H
Sat 8	1:21 AM (2.41) L	6:49 AM (7.10) H	1:47 PM (0.16) L	8:23 PM (7.78) H
Sun 9	2:01 AM (2.65) L	7:27 AM (6.84) H	2:29 PM (0.54) L	9:06 PM (7.41) H
Mon 10	2:45 AM (2.96) L	8:07 AM (6.41) H	3:13 PM (1.15) L	9:53 PM (6.95) H
Tue 11	3:38 AM (3.30) L	8:52 AM (5.84) H	4:01 PM (1.88) L	10:44 PM (6.46) H
Wed 12	4:53 AM (3.57) L	9:52 AM (5.21) H	5:03 PM (2.59) L	11:43 PM (6.05) H
Thu 13	6:30 AM (3.59) L	11:50 AM (4.75) H	6:23 PM (3.14) L	
Fri 14	12:52 AM (5.81) H	8:06 AM (3.27) L	2:02 PM (4.92) H	7:52 PM (3.39) L
Sat 15	2:03 AM (5.77) H	9:18 AM (2.80) L	3:21 PM (5.40) H	9:11 PM (3.39) L
Sun 16	3:05 AM (5.86) H	10:08 AM (2.34) L	4:16 PM (5.91) H	10:11 PM (3.27) L
Mon 17	3:53 AM (6.00) H	10:45 AM (1.95) L	5:00 PM (6.36) H	10:56 PM (3.14) L
Tue 18	4:29 AM (6.12) H	11:17 AM (1.62) L	5:40 PM (6.74) H	11:33 PM (3.01) L
Wed 19	5:00 AM (6.23) H	11:45 AM (1.36) L	6:16 PM (7.02) H	
Thu 20	12:04 AM (2.93) L	5:28 AM (6.32) H	12:12 PM (1.16) L	6:49 PM (7.18) H
Fri 21	12:32 AM (2.88) L	5:56 AM (6.37) H	12:40 PM (1.06) L	7:19 PM (7.22) H
Sat 22	1:00 AM (2.87) L	6:25 AM (6.38) H	1:09 PM (1.07) L	7:49 PM (7.18) H
Sun 23	1:27 AM (2.91) L	6:55 AM (6.32) H	1:39 PM (1.19) L	8:18 PM (7.06) H
Mon 24	1:56 AM (3.00) L	7:26 AM (6.18) H	2:10 PM (1.41) L	8:50 PM (6.88) H
Tue 25	2:30 AM (3.15) L	7:58 AM (5.97) H	2:43 PM (1.73) L	9:24 PM (6.66) H
Wed 26	3:09 AM (3.34) L	8:32 AM (5.69) H	3:17 PM (2.10) L	10:02 PM (6.43) H
Thu 27	4:00 AM (3.52) L	9:15 AM (5.36) H	3:59 PM (2.50) L	10:46 PM (6.20) H
Fri 28	5:10 AM (3.61) L	10:18 AM (5.04) H	4:55 PM (2.91) L	11:39 PM (6.01) H
Sat 29	6:34 AM (3.47) L	11:57 AM (4.89) H	6:10 PM (3.24) L	
Sun 30	12:40 AM (5.91) H	7:53 AM (3.08) L	1:44 PM (5.13) H	7:34 PM (3.42) L

Fremantle - WA

DAY/DATE	TIDE 1	TIDE 2	TIDE 3	TIDE 4
Sat 1	5:15 AM (0.88) H	1:34 PM (0.60) L	8:05 PM (0.86) H	
Sun 2	1:17 AM (0.74) L	7:15 AM (0.84) H	1:41 PM (0.65) L	8:01 PM (0.93) H
Mon 3	2:39 AM (0.65) L	9:00 AM (0.81) H	1:44 PM (0.69) L	8:11 PM (1.01) H
Tue 4	3:41 AM (0.55) L	10:22 AM (0.77) H	1:27 PM (0.72) L	8:29 PM (1.08) H
Wed 5	4:45 AM (0.47) L	11:31 AM (0.72) H	12:51 PM (0.72) L	8:51 PM (1.15) H
Thu 6	6:10 AM (0.40) L	9:16 PM (1.19) H		
Fri 7	7:22 AM (0.36) L	9:45 PM (1.20) H		
Sat 8	8:20 AM (0.35) L	10:13 PM (1.17) H		
Sun 9	9:25 AM (0.39) L	10:40 PM (1.11) H		
Mon 10	11:46 AM (0.42) L	11:06 PM (1.04) H		
Tue 11	12:37 PM (0.47) L	11:33 PM (0.96) H		
Wed 12	1:16 PM (0.54) L	9:57 PM (0.88) H	10:10 PM (0.88) L	11:57 PM (0.89) H
Thu 13	1:44 PM (0.61) L	9:30 PM (0.85) H		
Fri 14	1:17 PM (0.68) L	7:51 PM (0.88) H		
Sat 15	5:34 AM (0.73) L	6:33 AM (0.73) L	12:20 PM (0.70) L	7:44 PM (0.93) H
Sun 16	4:26 AM (0.68) L	9:05 AM (0.71) H	11:07 AM (0.70) L	7:41 PM (0.99) H
Mon 17	4:41 AM (0.62) L	10:06 AM (0.71) H	11:37 AM (0.70) L	7:45 PM (1.04) H
Tue 18	4:26 AM (0.57) L	10:56 AM (0.70) H	12:07 PM (0.70) L	7:59 PM (1.09) H
Wed 19	4:59 AM (0.52) L	11:54 AM (0.69) H	12:22 PM (0.69) L	8:17 PM (1.12) H
Thu 20	5:41 AM (0.48) L	8:40 PM (1.14) H		
Fri 21	6:23 AM (0.46) L	9:07 PM (1.15) H		
Sat 22	7:05 AM (0.45) L	9:36 PM (1.14) H		
Sun 23	7:45 AM (0.46) L	10:06 PM (1.12) H		
Mon 24	8:25 AM (0.48) L	10:36 PM (1.09) H		
Tue 25	9:06 AM (0.50) L	11:08 PM (1.05) H		
Wed 26	9:46 AM (0.53) L	11:41 PM (1.01) H		
Thu 27	10:26 AM (0.57) L			
Fri 28	12:14 AM (0.95) H	11:00 AM (0.60) L	9:42 PM (0.88) H	11:14 PM (0.87) L
Sat 29	12:44 AM (0.88) H	11:25 AM (0.64) L	7:05 PM (0.90) H	
Sun 30	11:35 AM (0.69) L	6:55 PM (0.97) H		

Sun Rise & Sun Set Times:

Darwin, NT: Rise: 06:10am Set: 06:50pm

Melbourne, VIC: Rise: 06:00am Set: 08:10pm

Adelaide, SA: Rise: 06:00am Set: 07:50pm

Perth, WA: Rise: 05:00am Set: 06:50pm

Sydney, NSW: Rise: 05:40am Set: 07:30pm

Brisbane, QLD: Rise: 04:40am Set: 06:10pm

Hobart, TAS: Rise: 05:30am Set: 08:10pm

(Note: These times are averages for the month)

Hobart - TAS

DAY/DATE	TIDE 1	TIDE 2	TIDE 3	TIDE 4
Sat 1	5:34 AM (1.16) H	10:45 AM (0.86) L	4:34 PM (1.25) H	11:22 PM (0.50) L
Sun 2	6:04 AM (1.21) H	11:45 AM (0.77) L	5:42 PM (1.22) H	11:57 PM (0.56) L
Mon 3	6:38 AM (1.29) H	12:51 PM (0.66) L	6:52 PM (1.18) H	
Tue 4	12:32 AM (0.65) L	7:14 AM (1.37) H	2:01 PM (0.52) L	8:09 PM (1.14) H
Wed 5	1:11 AM (0.76) L	7:54 AM (1.46) H	3:12 PM (0.38) L	9:36 PM (1.12) H
Thu 6	1:54 AM (0.87) L	8:39 AM (1.53) H	4:18 PM (0.25) L	11:01 PM (1.13) H
Fri 7	2:48 AM (0.98) L	9:30 AM (1.59) H	5:20 PM (0.16) L	
Sat 8	12:17 AM (1.16) H	4:13 AM (1.05) L	10:29 AM (1.61) H	6:18 PM (0.11) L
Sun 9	1:27 AM (1.18) H	5:43 AM (1.07) L	11:29 AM (1.59) H	7:15 PM (0.12) L
Mon 10	2:30 AM (1.20) H	6:52 AM (1.04) L	12:30 PM (1.55) H	8:11 PM (0.17) L
Tue 11	3:24 AM (1.20) H	7:54 AM (1.00) L	1:30 PM (1.47) H	9:05 PM (0.26) L
Wed 12	4:08 AM (1.19) H	8:56 AM (0.95) L	2:32 PM (1.37) H	9:55 PM (0.36) L
Thu 13	4:46 AM (1.20) H	10:00 AM (0.89) L	3:39 PM (1.26) H	10:38 PM (0.46) L
Fri 14	5:20 AM (1.21) H	11:08 AM (0.83) L	4:45 PM (1.16) H	11:12 PM (0.56) L
Sat 15	5:51 AM (1.24) H	12:14 PM (0.76) L	5:46 PM (1.07) H	11:36 PM (0.66) L
Sun 16	6:18 AM (1.27) H	1:15 PM (0.69) L	6:47 PM (1.01) H	11:50 PM (0.74) L
Mon 17	6:44 AM (1.30) H	2:08 PM (0.63) L	7:53 PM (0.97) H	
Tue 18	12:00 AM (0.82) L	7:07 AM (1.33) H	2:55 PM (0.57) L	9:08 PM (0.96) H
Wed 19	12:12 AM (0.89) L	7:30 AM (1.36) H	3:35 PM (0.52) L	10:23 PM (0.98) H
Thu 20	12:30 AM (0.95) L	7:57 AM (1.39) H	4:14 PM (0.47) L	11:31 PM (1.02) H
Fri 21	12:51 AM (1.01) L	8:29 AM (1.41) H	4:51 PM (0.44) L	
Sat 22	12:39 AM (1.05) H	1:14 AM (1.05) L	9:05 AM (1.41) H	5:30 PM (0.42) L
Sun 23	9:47 AM (1.41) H	6:10 PM (0.41) L		
Mon 24	10:32 AM (1.39) H	6:50 PM (0.41) L		
Tue 25	2:48 AM (1.10) H	5:18 AM (1.09) L	11:19 AM (1.37) H	7:31 PM (0.41) L
Wed 26	3:07 AM (1.11) H	6:40 AM (1.06) L	12:09 PM (1.33) H	8:11 PM (0.42) L
Thu 27	3:27 AM (1.12) H	7:42 AM (1.02) L	1:01 PM (1.29) H	8:48 PM (0.44) L
Fri 28	3:50 AM (1.15) H	8:44 AM (0.97) L	2:00 PM (1.23) H	9:23 PM (0.46) L
Sat 29	4:15 AM (1.20) H	9:47 AM (0.89) L	3:06 PM (1.17) H	9:57 PM (0.51) L
Sun 30	4:44 AM (1.26) H	10:52 AM (0.78) L	4:19 PM (1.12) H	10:30 PM (0.57) L

Port Phillip Heads - VIC

DAY/DATE	TIDE 1	TIDE 2	TIDE 3	TIDE 4
Sat 1	12:27 AM (0.48) L	7:45 AM (1.39) H	1:06 PM (0.72) L	7:42 PM (1.24) H
Sun 2	1:16 AM (0.56) L	8:40 AM (1.35) H	2:00 PM (0.69) L	8:57 PM (1.24) H
Mon 3	2:19 AM (0.65) L	9:39 AM (1.33) H	3:06 PM (0.63) L	10:25 PM (1.31) H
Tue 4	3:35 AM (0.74) L	10:39 AM (1.33) H	4:18 PM (0.52) L	11:43 PM (1.44) H
Wed 5	5:00 AM (0.78) L	11:37 AM (1.36) H	5:28 PM (0.39) L	
Thu 6	12:49 AM (1.59) H	6:18 AM (0.77) L	12:33 PM (1.41) H	6:28 PM (0.25) L
Fri 7	1:46 AM (1.73) H	7:18 AM (0.73) L	1:26 PM (1.46) H	7:22 PM (0.15) L
Sat 8	2:39 AM (1.81) H	8:08 AM (0.69) L	2:15 PM (1.51) H	8:15 PM (0.09) L
Sun 9	3:28 AM (1.84) H	8:55 AM (0.66) L	3:03 PM (1.54) H	9:04 PM (0.08) L
Mon 10	4:15 AM (1.82) H	9:40 AM (0.63) L	3:51 PM (1.54) H	9:54 PM (0.12) L
Tue 11	5:02 AM (1.75) H	10:26 AM (0.61) L	4:38 PM (1.51) H	10:44 PM (0.20) L
Wed 12	5:50 AM (1.66) H	11:12 AM (0.60) L	5:28 PM (1.46) H	11:31 PM (0.30) L
Thu 13	6:39 AM (1.57) H	12:01 PM (0.60) L	6:22 PM (1.38) H	
Fri 14	12:20 AM (0.42) L	7:30 AM (1.49) H	12:55 PM (0.61) L	7:30 PM (1.30) H
Sat 15	1:10 AM (0.55) L	8:22 AM (1.41) H	1:55 PM (0.61) L	8:54 PM (1.27) H
Sun 16	2:05 AM (0.67) L	9:15 AM (1.36) H	3:01 PM (0.60) L	10:11 PM (1.28) H
Mon 17	3:09 AM (0.77) L	10:07 AM (1.32) H	4:09 PM (0.56) L	11:18 PM (1.34) H
Tue 18	4:24 AM (0.84) L	10:58 AM (1.29) H	5:09 PM (0.51) L	
Wed 19	12:19 AM (1.43) H	5:41 AM (0.85) L	11:47 AM (1.29) H	6:00 PM (0.44) L
Thu 20	1:10 AM (1.51) H	6:42 AM (0.83) L	12:32 PM (1.30) H	6:44 PM (0.38) L
Fri 21	1:53 AM (1.59) H	7:27 AM (0.80) L	1:14 PM (1.33) H	7:24 PM (0.33) L
Sat 22	2:29 AM (1.64) H	8:04 AM (0.76) L	1:53 PM (1.36) H	8:01 PM (0.30) L
Sun 23	3:01 AM (1.67) H	8:40 AM (0.72) L	2:31 PM (1.38) H	8:39 PM (0.29) L
Mon 24	3:33 AM (1.68) H	9:15 AM (0.69) L	3:09 PM (1.40) H	9:14 PM (0.29) L
Tue 25	4:07 AM (1.67) H	9:48 AM (0.68) L	3:47 PM (1.40) H	9:46 PM (0.31) L
Wed 26	4:42 AM (1.64) H	10:22 AM (0.67) L	4:25 PM (1.38) H	10:17 PM (0.33) L
Thu 27	5:16 AM (1.61) H	10:56 AM (0.66) L	5:03 PM (1.35) H	10:47 PM (0.38) L
Fri 28	5:53 AM (1.56) H	11:30 AM (0.64) L	5:45 PM (1.33) H	11:22 PM (0.43) L
Sat 29	6:30 AM (1.51) H	12:07 PM (0.62) L	6:33 PM (1.30) H	
Sun 30	12:04 AM (0.51) L	7:11 AM (1.46) H	12:48 PM (0.58) L	7:32 PM (1.30) H

Fort Denison - NSW

DAY/DATE	TIDE 1	TIDE 2	TIDE 3	TIDE 4
Sat 1	5:28 AM (1.34) H	11:09 AM (0.66) L	5:27 PM (1.57) H	
Sun 2	12:00 AM (0.39) L	6:15 AM (1.48) H	12:10 PM (0.55) L	6:20 PM (1.62) H
Mon 3	12:42 AM (0.33) L	6:59 AM (1.63) H	1:06 PM (0.42) L	7:12 PM (1.64) H
Tue 4	1:23 AM (0.29) L	7:42 AM (1.78) H	2:00 PM (0.31) L	8:02 PM (1.63) H
Wed 5	2:04 AM (0.29) L	8:28 AM (1.90) H	2:54 PM (0.22) L	8:56 PM (1.59) H
Thu 6	2:47 AM (0.32) L	9:15 AM (1.99) H	3:48 PM (0.18) L	9:50 PM (1.52) H
Fri 7	3:33 AM (0.37) L	10:03 AM (2.03) H	4:45 PM (0.17) L	10:46 PM (1.44) H
Sat 8	4:22 AM (0.44) L	10:54 AM (2.01) H	5:42 PM (0.21) L	11:45 PM (1.35) H
Sun 9	5:15 AM (0.52) L	11:48 AM (1.95) H	6:44 PM (0.28) L	
Mon 10	12:45 AM (1.28) H	6:12 AM (0.60) L	12:45 PM (1.84) H	7:47 PM (0.36) L
Tue 11	1:51 AM (1.24) H	7:15 AM (0.67) L	1:45 PM (1.73) H	8:52 PM (0.43) L
Wed 12	3:00 AM (1.24) H	8:25 AM (0.71) L	2:52 PM (1.62) H	9:53 PM (0.48) L
Thu 13	4:06 AM (1.28) H	9:38 AM (0.72) L	3:59 PM (1.53) H	10:46 PM (0.50) L
Fri 14	5:03 AM (1.34) H	10:49 AM (0.71) L	5:00 PM (1.47) H	11:31 PM (0.51) L
Sat 15	5:52 AM (1.42) H	11:53 AM (0.66) L	5:54 PM (1.43) H	

DAY/DATE	TIDE 1	TIDE 2	TIDE 3	TIDE 4
Sun 16	12:11 AM (0.51) L	6:35 AM (1.51) H	12:48 PM (0.61) L	6:41 PM (1.40) H
Mon 17	12:45 AM (0.51) L	7:13 AM (1.59) H	1:35 PM (0.56) L	7:24 PM (1.38) H
Tue 18	1:17 AM (0.51) L	7:48 AM (1.65) H	2:16 PM (0.51) L	8:04 PM (1.36) H
Wed 19	1:49 AM (0.52) L	8:21 AM (1.71) H	2:55 PM (0.46) L	8:44 PM (1.34) H
Thu 20	2:21 AM (0.54) L	8:55 AM (1.74) H	3:32 PM (0.43) L	9:23 PM (1.32) H
Fri 21	2:53 AM (0.56) L	9:29 AM (1.76) H	4:10 PM (0.42) L	10:02 PM (1.30) H
Sat 22	3:28 AM (0.59) L	10:04 AM (1.77) H	4:47 PM (0.43) L	10:42 PM (1.28) H
Sun 23	4:04 AM (0.62) L	10:41 AM (1.75) H	5:28 PM (0.45) L	11:23 PM (1.25) H
Mon 24	4:44 AM (0.65) L	11:20 AM (1.72) H	6:10 PM (0.49) L	
Tue 25	12:06 AM (1.23) H	5:26 AM (0.68) L	12:01 PM (1.68) H	6:56 PM (0.51) L
Wed 26	12:55 AM (1.21) H	6:14 AM (0.71) L	12:47 PM (1.63) H	7:46 PM (0.53) L
Thu 27	1:48 AM (1.22) H	7:10 AM (0.74) L	1:38 PM (1.58) H	8:38 PM (0.52) L
Fri 28	2:48 AM (1.25) H	8:15 AM (0.75) L	2:35 PM (1.54) H	9:30 PM (0.50) L
Sat 29	3:48 AM (1.33) H	9:25 AM (0.73) L	3:39 PM (1.51) H	10:21 PM (0.46) L
Sun 30	4:44 AM (1.44) H	10:37 AM (0.67) L	4:45 PM (1.50) H	11:10 PM (0.43) L

BITE TIMES

Apogee moon phase on Thursday 20th
Perigee moon phase on Thursday 6th

● New moon on Thursday 20th
First quarter moon on Friday 28th
○ Full moon on Thursday 6th
Last quarter moon phase on Wednesday 12th

DAY	MINOR BITE	MAJOR BITE	MINOR BITE	MAJOR BITE	SALT WATER RATING	FRESH WATER RATING
SAT 1	12:54 PM	7:34 PM	1:36 AM	7:10 AM	4	5
SUN 2	2:04 PM	8:21 PM	2:02 AM	7:57 AM	3	5
MON 3	3:16 PM	9:11 PM	2:28 AM	8:46 AM	6	6
TUE 4	4:31 PM	10:03 PM	2:55 AM	9:37 AM	3	8
WED 5	5:50 PM	11:00 PM	3:25 AM	10:31 AM	5	7
THUR 6	7:12 PM		4:01 AM	11:31 AM	7 ○	6
FRI 7	8:31 PM	12:02 AM	4:46 AM	12:34 PM	7	6
SAT 8	9:42 PM	1:07 AM	5:41 AM	1:39 PM	5	5
SUN 9	10:41 PM	2:13 AM	6:46 AM	2:45 PM	4	4
MON 10	11:27 PM	3:17 AM	7:57 AM	3:46 PM	3	6
TUE 11		4:16 AM	9:10 AM	4:41 PM	4	4
WED 12	12:04 AM	5:08 AM	10:20 AM	5:32 PM	5	5
THUR 13	12:33 AM	5:56 AM	11:27 AM	6:18 PM	6	6
FRI 14	12:59 AM	6:40 AM	12:29 PM	7:00 PM	7	7
SAT 15	1:21 AM	7:21 AM	1:30 PM	7:41 PM	7	7

DAY	MINOR BITE	MAJOR BITE	MINOR BITE	MAJOR BITE	SALT WATER RATING	FRESH WATER RATING
SUN 16	1:42 AM	8:01 AM	2:29 PM	8:21 PM	7	8
MON 17	2:04 AM	8:41 AM	3:28 PM	9:01 PM	5	8
TUE 18	2:27 AM	9:22 AM	4:28 PM	9:44 PM	6	7
WED 19	2:53 AM	10:06 AM	5:29 PM	10:29 PM	8	8
THUR 20	3:22 AM	10:52 AM	6:30 PM	11:15 PM	8 ●	8
FRI 21	3:57 AM	11:40 AM	7:29 PM		8	6
SAT 22	4:39 AM	12:31 PM	8:25 PM	12:05 AM	7	6
SUN 23	5:28 AM	1:23 PM	9:16 PM	12:57 AM	7	6
MON 24	6:24 AM	2:15 PM	10:00 PM	1:49 AM	6	7
TUE 25	7:25 AM	3:05 PM	10:37 PM	2:39 AM	5	5
WED 26	8:29 AM	3:54 PM	11:09 PM	3:29 AM	4	6
THUR 27	9:34 AM	4:41 PM	11:37 PM	4:17 AM	3	5
FRI 28	10:39 AM	5:26 PM		5:03 AM	4	6
SAT 29	11:46 AM	6:12 PM	12:02 AM	5:48 AM	5	6
SUN 30	12:54 PM	6:58 PM	12:27 AM	6:34 AM	4	5

DECEMBER 2025

TIDE TIMES

Adelaide Outer Harbour - SA

DAY/DATE	TIDE 1	TIDE 2	TIDE 3	TIDE 4
Mon 1	2:31 AM (1.89) H	9:15 AM (0.92) L	3:12 PM (1.66) H	9:00 PM (0.89) L
Tue 2	3:27 AM (2.17) H	10:16 AM (0.58) L	4:24 PM (1.76) H	9:48 PM (0.86) L
Wed 3	4:07 AM (2.40) H	11:02 AM (0.35) L	5:12 PM (1.79) H	10:23 PM (0.86) L
Thu 4	4:40 AM (2.56) H	11:42 AM (0.23) L	5:49 PM (1.73) H	10:49 PM (0.87) L
Fri 5	5:11 AM (2.66) H	12:18 PM (0.21) L	6:17 PM (1.64) H	11:11 PM (0.85) L
Sat 6	5:40 AM (2.70) H	12:51 PM (0.26) L	6:38 PM (1.57) H	11:33 PM (0.81) L
Sun 7	6:10 AM (2.69) H	1:21 PM (0.36) L	6:57 PM (1.54) H	11:57 PM (0.76) L
Mon 8	6:41 AM (2.62) H	1:45 PM (0.47) L	7:15 PM (1.56) H	
Tue 9	12:24 AM (0.73) L	7:09 AM (2.51) H	2:03 PM (0.57) L	7:36 PM (1.62) H
Wed 10	12:54 AM (0.73) L	7:36 AM (2.38) H	2:18 PM (0.62) L	8:04 PM (1.71) H
Thu 11	1:31 AM (0.77) L	8:04 AM (2.23) H	2:37 PM (0.64) L	8:42 PM (1.78) H
Fri 12	2:16 AM (0.87) L	8:38 AM (2.05) H	3:06 PM (0.67) L	9:36 PM (1.82) H
Sat 13	3:20 AM (1.02) L	9:22 AM (1.81) H	3:49 PM (0.77) L	10:55 PM (1.83) H
Sun 14	5:05 AM (1.18) L	10:36 AM (1.54) H	4:56 PM (0.92) L	
Mon 15	12:44 AM (1.89) H	8:16 AM (1.11) L	1:17 PM (1.37) H	7:04 PM (1.04) L
Tue 16	2:25 AM (2.05) H	9:54 AM (0.83) L	3:43 PM (1.48) H	8:54 PM (1.02) L
Wed 17	3:33 AM (2.25) H	10:43 AM (0.58) L	4:46 PM (1.64) H	9:54 PM (0.94) L
Thu 18	4:20 AM (2.41) H	11:21 AM (0.41) L	5:26 PM (1.75) H	10:36 PM (0.88) L
Fri 19	4:57 AM (2.51) H	11:53 AM (0.31) L	5:57 PM (1.80) H	11:08 PM (0.82) L
Sat 20	5:30 AM (2.58) H	12:22 PM (0.27) L	6:23 PM (1.82) H	11:36 PM (0.76) L
Sun 21	5:59 AM (2.62) H	12:48 PM (0.27) L	6:46 PM (1.83) H	
Mon 22	12:03 AM (0.70) L	6:27 AM (2.63) H	1:14 PM (0.28) L	7:09 PM (1.84) H
Tue 23	12:32 AM (0.67) L	6:55 AM (2.61) H	1:40 PM (0.30) L	7:35 PM (1.85) H
Wed 24	1:02 AM (0.67) L	7:24 AM (2.55) H	2:06 PM (0.33) L	8:02 PM (1.87) H
Thu 25	1:33 AM (0.69) L	7:52 AM (2.46) H	2:32 PM (0.37) L	8:32 PM (1.89) H
Fri 26	2:09 AM (0.74) L	8:22 AM (2.34) H	2:59 PM (0.43) L	9:08 PM (1.93) H
Sat 27	2:52 AM (0.81) L	8:57 AM (2.16) H	3:29 PM (0.52) L	9:53 PM (1.96) H
Sun 28	3:49 AM (0.91) L	9:41 AM (1.91) H	4:05 PM (0.67) L	10:50 PM (1.97) H
Mon 29	5:11 AM (1.03) L	10:41 AM (1.60) H	4:45 PM (0.87) L	
Tue 30	12:03 AM (1.98) H	7:44 AM (1.03) L	12:44 PM (1.28) H	5:45 PM (1.11) L
Wed 31	1:55 AM (2.03) H	10:13 AM (0.77) L	5:07 PM (1.35) H	8:37 PM (1.24) L

Brisbane Bar - QLD

DAY/DATE	TIDE 1	TIDE 2	TIDE 3	TIDE 4
Mon 1	6:07 AM (2.08) H	12:09 PM (0.71) L	6:01 PM (2.10) H	
Tue 2	12:41 AM (0.37) L	7:02 AM (2.29) H	1:19 PM (0.64) L	6:59 PM (2.05) H
Wed 3	1:30 AM (0.29) L	7:55 AM (2.47) H	2:24 PM (0.56) L	7:54 PM (1.98) H
Thu 4	2:17 AM (0.25) L	8:46 AM (2.61) H	3:24 PM (0.51) L	8:49 PM (1.92) H
Fri 5	3:03 AM (0.22) L	9:36 AM (2.70) H	4:21 PM (0.47) L	9:45 PM (1.86) H
Sat 6	3:48 AM (0.24) L	10:26 AM (2.73) H	5:16 PM (0.47) L	10:38 PM (1.80) H
Sun 7	4:34 AM (0.28) L	11:15 AM (2.70) H	6:10 PM (0.50) L	11:31 PM (1.75) H
Mon 8	5:21 AM (0.37) L	12:03 PM (2.61) H	7:01 PM (0.55) L	
Tue 9	12:25 AM (1.71) H	6:10 AM (0.48) L	12:51 PM (2.50) H	7:51 PM (0.60) L
Wed 10	1:19 AM (1.69) H	7:01 AM (0.61) L	1:39 PM (2.36) H	8:39 PM (0.64) L
Thu 11	2:18 AM (1.69) H	8:00 AM (0.74) L	2:28 PM (2.21) H	9:26 PM (0.66) L
Fri 12	3:23 AM (1.72) H	9:05 AM (0.85) L	3:19 PM (2.08) H	10:13 PM (0.65) L
Sat 13	4:30 AM (1.80) H	10:16 AM (0.91) L	4:14 PM (1.96) H	11:00 PM (0.62) L
Sun 14	5:31 AM (1.92) H	11:28 AM (0.92) L	5:10 PM (1.87) H	11:46 PM (0.58) L
Mon 15	6:24 AM (2.06) H	12:33 PM (0.89) L	6:04 PM (1.82) H	
Tue 16	12:31 AM (0.53) L	7:10 AM (2.18) H	1:30 PM (0.82) L	6:55 PM (1.78) H
Wed 17	1:13 AM (0.49) L	7:52 AM (2.29) H	2:19 PM (0.76) L	7:42 PM (1.76) H
Thu 18	1:51 AM (0.45) L	8:31 AM (2.36) H	3:04 PM (0.71) L	8:24 PM (1.75) H
Fri 19	2:29 AM (0.43) L	9:09 AM (2.41) H	3:45 PM (0.68) L	9:03 PM (1.75) H
Sat 20	3:04 AM (0.42) L	9:45 AM (2.43) H	4:25 PM (0.67) L	9:41 PM (1.76) H
Sun 21	3:39 AM (0.42) L	10:21 AM (2.43) H	5:01 PM (0.67) L	10:17 PM (1.76) H
Mon 22	4:15 AM (0.43) L	10:57 AM (2.43) H	5:38 PM (0.68) L	10:57 PM (1.77) H
Tue 23	4:51 AM (0.45) L	11:32 AM (2.42) H	6:15 PM (0.68) L	11:38 PM (1.77) H
Wed 24	5:30 AM (0.50) L	12:09 PM (2.40) H	6:55 PM (0.68) L	
Thu 25	12:22 AM (1.77) H	6:13 AM (0.57) L	12:47 PM (2.36) H	7:35 PM (0.67) L
Fri 26	1:13 AM (1.77) H	7:01 AM (0.65) L	1:30 PM (2.30) H	8:19 PM (0.64) L
Sat 27	2:10 AM (1.80) H	7:59 AM (0.74) L	2:17 PM (2.21) H	9:09 PM (0.60) L
Sun 28	3:16 AM (1.86) H	9:08 AM (0.82) L	3:14 PM (2.10) H	10:03 PM (0.56) L
Mon 29	4:29 AM (1.99) H	10:26 AM (0.86) L	4:19 PM (1.98) H	11:01 PM (0.51) L
Tue 30	5:38 AM (2.15) H	11:49 AM (0.84) L	5:29 PM (1.89) H	
Wed 31	12:01 AM (0.46) L	6:43 AM (2.33) H	1:11 PM (0.76) L	6:37 PM (1.83) H

Darwin - NT

DAY/DATE	TIDE 1	TIDE 2	TIDE 3	TIDE 4
Mon 1	1:44 AM (5.92) H	8:58 AM (2.50) L	3:10 PM (5.70) H	8:55 PM (3.40) L
Tue 2	2:44 AM (6.04) H	9:52 AM (1.85) L	4:15 PM (6.37) H	10:01 PM (3.27) L
Wed 3	3:36 AM (6.24) H	10:40 AM (1.23) L	5:12 PM (6.99) H	10:57 PM (3.11) L
Thu 4	4:23 AM (6.45) H	11:25 AM (0.72) L	6:03 PM (7.47) H	11:45 PM (2.97) L
Fri 5	5:07 AM (6.65) H	12:09 PM (0.38) L	6:51 PM (7.76) H	
Sat 6	12:30 AM (2.86) L	5:50 AM (6.77) H	12:52 PM (0.26) L	7:37 PM (7.85) H
Sun 7	1:14 AM (2.80) L	6:34 AM (6.78) H	1:36 PM (0.38) L	8:20 PM (7.76) H
Mon 8	2:00 AM (2.80) L	7:20 AM (6.65) H	2:19 PM (0.71) L	9:03 PM (7.55) H
Tue 9	2:51 AM (2.86) L	8:09 AM (6.37) H	3:04 PM (1.23) L	9:45 PM (7.24) H
Wed 10	3:47 AM (2.94) L	9:01 AM (5.98) H	3:50 PM (1.85) L	10:27 PM (6.89) H
Thu 11	4:48 AM (3.01) L	10:04 AM (5.55) H	4:38 PM (2.51) L	11:08 PM (6.52) H
Fri 12	5:52 AM (3.02) L	11:21 AM (5.19) H	5:31 PM (3.12) L	11:51 PM (6.16) H
Sat 13	6:57 AM (2.95) L	12:48 PM (5.04) H	6:34 PM (3.62) L	
Sun 14	12:39 AM (5.85) H	8:02 AM (2.79) L	2:19 PM (5.16) H	7:48 PM (3.92) L
Mon 15	1:34 AM (5.62) H	9:04 AM (2.54) L	3:41 PM (5.53) H	9:10 PM (3.99) L
Tue 16	2:37 AM (5.51) H	9:57 AM (2.26) L	4:39 PM (5.98) H	10:21 PM (3.87) L
Wed 17	3:34 AM (5.54) H	10:39 AM (1.98) L	5:23 PM (6.39) H	11:14 PM (3.67) L
Thu 18	4:19 AM (5.65) H	11:15 AM (1.71) L	6:02 PM (6.72) H	11:52 PM (3.48) L
Fri 19	4:59 AM (5.81) H	11:50 AM (1.49) L	6:38 PM (6.95) H	
Sat 20	12:23 AM (3.31) L	5:34 AM (5.98) H	12:23 PM (1.33) L	7:11 PM (7.08) H
Sun 21	12:51 AM (3.18) L	6:09 AM (6.13) H	12:56 PM (1.24) L	7:43 PM (7.15) H
Mon 22	1:20 AM (3.08) L	6:44 AM (6.23) H	1:29 PM (1.24) L	8:14 PM (7.17) H
Tue 23	1:53 AM (3.01) L	7:19 AM (6.26) H	2:00 PM (1.34) L	8:45 PM (7.14) H
Wed 24	2:30 AM (2.97) L	7:56 AM (6.21) H	2:31 PM (1.52) L	9:15 PM (7.06) H
Thu 25	3:12 AM (2.95) L	8:35 AM (6.07) H	3:03 PM (1.80) L	9:46 PM (6.94) H
Fri 26	3:59 AM (2.93) L	9:22 AM (5.88) H	3:37 PM (2.17) L	10:18 PM (6.76) H
Sat 27	4:49 AM (2.89) L	10:17 AM (5.66) H	4:18 PM (2.64) L	10:53 PM (6.53) H
Sun 28	5:45 AM (2.78) L	11:27 AM (5.47) H	5:12 PM (3.15) L	11:33 PM (6.26) H
Mon 29	6:44 AM (2.60) L	12:46 PM (5.43) H	6:23 PM (3.64) L	
Tue 30	12:20 AM (5.99) H	7:52 AM (2.33) L	2:21 PM (5.62) H	7:54 PM (3.95) L
Wed 31	1:24 AM (5.79) H	9:05 AM (1.96) L	3:54 PM (6.10) H	9:25 PM (3.97) L

Fremantle - WA

DAY/DATE	TIDE 1	TIDE 2	TIDE 3	TIDE 4
Mon 1	3:35 AM (0.67) L	7:03 PM (1.05) H		
Tue 2	4:09 AM (0.55) L	7:25 PM (1.14) H		
Wed 3	4:56 AM (0.44) L	7:54 PM (1.21) H		
Thu 4	5:45 AM (0.35) L	8:27 PM (1.25) H		
Fri 5	6:32 AM (0.30) L	9:02 PM (1.25) H		
Sat 6	7:19 AM (0.30) L	9:38 PM (1.22) H		
Sun 7	8:05 AM (0.33) L	10:09 PM (1.17) H		
Mon 8	8:50 AM (0.40) L	10:30 PM (1.09) H		
Tue 9	9:30 AM (0.48) L	10:45 PM (1.01) H		
Wed 10	9:47 AM (0.57) L	11:00 PM (0.94) H		
Thu 11	9:52 AM (0.64) L	9:04 PM (0.89) H		
Fri 12	7:38 AM (0.65) L	7:11 PM (0.89) H		
Sat 13	7:38 AM (0.64) L	6:45 PM (0.95) H		
Sun 14	6:51 AM (0.62) L	6:46 PM (1.01) H		
Mon 15	5:35 AM (0.59) L	6:53 PM (1.06) H		
Tue 16	5:14 AM (0.55) L	7:08 PM (1.11) H		
Wed 17	5:21 AM (0.50) L	7:30 PM (1.14) H		
Thu 18	5:33 AM (0.46) L	7:55 PM (1.16) H		
Fri 19	5:54 AM (0.44) L	8:25 PM (1.17) H		
Sat 20	6:20 AM (0.42) L	8:57 PM (1.17) H		
Sun 21	6:49 AM (0.42) L	9:30 PM (1.16) H		
Mon 22	7:16 AM (0.44) L	10:01 PM (1.14) H		
Tue 23	7:41 AM (0.47) L	10:31 PM (1.10) H		
Wed 24	7:58 AM (0.50) L	11:00 PM (1.05) H		
Thu 25	8:03 AM (0.54) L	11:26 PM (0.99) H		
Fri 26	8:00 AM (0.58) L	11:45 PM (0.91) H		
Sat 27	7:51 AM (0.62) L	5:57 PM (0.89) H		
Sun 28	7:40 AM (0.64) L	5:35 PM (0.96) H		
Mon 29	6:25 AM (0.63) L	5:45 PM (1.05) H		
Tue 30	4:07 AM (0.54) L	6:17 PM (1.13) H		
Wed 31	4:32 AM (0.44) L	6:57 PM (1.20) H		

Sun Rise & Sun Set Times:

Darwin, NT: Rise: 06:10am Set: 07:00pm

Melbourne, VIC: Rise: 05:50am Set: 08:30pm

Adelaide, SA: Rise: 05:50am Set: 08:20pm

Perth, WA: Rise: 05:00am Set: 07:10pm

Sydney, NSW: Rise: 05:30am Set: 08:00pm

Brisbane, QLD: Rise: 04:40am Set: 06:30pm

Hobart, TAS: Rise: 05:20am Set: 08:40pm

(Note: These times are averages for the month)

Hobart - TAS

DAY/DATE	TIDE 1	TIDE 2	TIDE 3	TIDE 4
Mon 1	5:15 AM (1.35) H	11:56 AM (0.65) L	5:38 PM (1.07) H	11:02 PM (0.66) L
Tue 2	5:50 AM (1.44) H	1:00 PM (0.50) L	7:01 PM (1.04) H	11:36 PM (0.76) L
Wed 3	6:30 AM (1.52) H	2:03 PM (0.35) L	8:28 PM (1.04) H	
Thu 4	12:14 AM (0.87) L	7:16 AM (1.60) H	3:05 PM (0.22) L	9:50 PM (1.07) H
Fri 5	12:57 AM (0.96) L	8:08 AM (1.65) H	4:06 PM (0.13) L	11:05 PM (1.10) H
Sat 6	1:51 AM (1.03) L	9:04 AM (1.67) H	5:03 PM (0.08) L	
Sun 7	12:15 AM (1.13) H	3:23 AM (1.07) L	10:04 AM (1.65) H	6:00 PM (0.09) L
Mon 8	1:16 AM (1.15) H	5:16 AM (1.06) L	11:05 AM (1.59) H	6:54 PM (0.14) L
Tue 9	2:07 AM (1.17) H	6:31 AM (1.01) L	12:07 PM (1.50) H	7:47 PM (0.22) L
Wed 10	2:50 AM (1.19) H	7:41 AM (0.96) L	1:11 PM (1.37) H	8:36 PM (0.33) L
Thu 11	3:28 AM (1.21) H	8:51 AM (0.90) L	2:15 PM (1.24) H	9:20 PM (0.44) L
Fri 12	4:01 AM (1.24) H	10:04 AM (0.83) L	3:20 PM (1.11) H	9:56 PM (0.55) L
Sat 13	4:32 AM (1.28) H	11:14 AM (0.75) L	4:28 PM (1.01) H	10:21 PM (0.66) L
Sun 14	5:00 AM (1.31) H	12:15 PM (0.68) L	5:38 PM (0.94) H	10:35 PM (0.74) L
Mon 15	5:27 AM (1.35) H	1:07 PM (0.61) L	6:54 PM (0.91) H	10:42 PM (0.81) L
Tue 16	5:51 AM (1.38) H	1:50 PM (0.55) L	8:10 PM (0.92) H	10:52 PM (0.87) L
Wed 17	6:16 AM (1.40) H	2:29 PM (0.50) L	9:16 PM (0.94) H	11:12 PM (0.92) L
Thu 18	6:45 AM (1.43) H	3:05 PM (0.46) L	10:16 PM (0.97) H	11:36 PM (0.97) L
Fri 19	7:20 AM (1.44) H	3:43 PM (0.42) L	11:18 PM (1.00) H	
Sat 20	12:00 AM (1.00) L	8:00 AM (1.45) H	4:22 PM (0.40) L	
Sun 21	8:42 AM (1.45) H	5:01 PM (0.39) L		
Mon 22	9:26 AM (1.44) H	5:40 PM (0.38) L		
Tue 23	1:49 AM (1.05) H	2:31 AM (1.05) L	10:09 AM (1.41) H	6:18 PM (0.38) L
Wed 24	2:00 AM (1.07) H	4:33 AM (1.05) L	10:55 AM (1.37) H	6:56 PM (0.40) L
Thu 25	2:17 AM (1.10) H	6:10 AM (1.02) L	11:44 AM (1.30) H	7:31 PM (0.42) L
Fri 26	2:40 AM (1.14) H	7:30 AM (0.97) L	12:41 PM (1.23) H	8:06 PM (0.47) L
Sat 27	3:04 AM (1.20) H	8:45 AM (0.89) L	1:51 PM (1.14) H	8:40 PM (0.53) L
Sun 28	3:31 AM (1.28) H	9:53 AM (0.78) L	3:06 PM (1.07) H	9:13 PM (0.60) L
Mon 29	4:01 AM (1.36) H	10:56 AM (0.64) L	4:26 PM (1.01) H	9:46 PM (0.69) L
Tue 30	4:35 AM (1.45) H	11:56 AM (0.49) L	5:54 PM (0.98) H	10:23 PM (0.77) L
Wed 31	5:15 AM (1.53) H	12:55 PM (0.36) L	7:23 PM (0.99) H	11:01 PM (0.85) L

Port Phillip Heads - VIC

DAY/DATE	TIDE 1	TIDE 2	TIDE 3	TIDE 4
Mon 1	12:55 AM (0.61) L	7:56 AM (1.42) H	1:38 PM (0.52) L	8:45 PM (1.32) H
Tue 2	1:55 AM (0.73) L	8:46 AM (1.38) H	2:35 PM (0.46) L	10:05 PM (1.39) H
Wed 3	3:05 AM (0.83) L	9:44 AM (1.36) H	3:40 PM (0.37) L	11:19 PM (1.50) H
Thu 4	4:24 AM (0.88) L	10:45 AM (1.35) H	4:49 PM (0.29) L	
Fri 5	12:26 AM (1.61) H	5:44 AM (0.88) L	11:48 AM (1.38) H	5:57 PM (0.20) L
Sat 6	1:27 AM (1.70) H	6:51 AM (0.84) L	12:52 PM (1.42) H	7:00 PM (0.14) L
Sun 7	2:22 AM (1.76) H	7:46 AM (0.77) L	1:51 PM (1.46) H	7:56 PM (0.11) L
Mon 8	3:14 AM (1.79) H	8:38 AM (0.70) L	2:46 PM (1.50) H	8:50 PM (0.12) L
Tue 9	4:03 AM (1.77) H	9:28 AM (0.63) L	3:38 PM (1.51) H	9:42 PM (0.17) L
Wed 10	4:50 AM (1.73) H	10:17 AM (0.58) L	4:30 PM (1.49) H	10:30 PM (0.25) L
Thu 11	5:35 AM (1.68) H	11:08 AM (0.53) L	5:23 PM (1.44) H	11:18 PM (0.35) L
Fri 12	6:17 AM (1.61) H	11:58 AM (0.50) L	6:20 PM (1.39) H	
Sat 13	12:03 AM (0.47) L	7:00 AM (1.54) H	12:46 PM (0.49) L	7:27 PM (1.34) H
Sun 14	12:47 AM (0.59) L	7:40 AM (1.47) H	1:34 PM (0.48) L	8:36 PM (1.31) H
Mon 15	1:33 AM (0.71) L	8:20 AM (1.40) H	2:23 PM (0.48) L	9:40 PM (1.32) H
Tue 16	2:24 AM (0.81) L	9:03 AM (1.33) H	3:14 PM (0.48) L	10:41 PM (1.35) H
Wed 17	3:24 AM (0.89) L	9:49 AM (1.28) H	4:10 PM (0.46) L	11:39 PM (1.40) H
Thu 18	4:35 AM (0.94) L	10:41 AM (1.25) H	5:07 PM (0.44) L	
Fri 19	12:33 AM (1.46) H	5:48 AM (0.93) L	11:35 AM (1.25) H	6:01 PM (0.40) L
Sat 20	1:20 AM (1.51) H	6:47 AM (0.89) L	12:28 PM (1.26) H	6:50 PM (0.36) L
Sun 21	2:01 AM (1.56) H	7:35 AM (0.84) L	1:17 PM (1.29) H	7:35 PM (0.33) L
Mon 22	2:39 AM (1.60) H	8:16 AM (0.79) L	2:04 PM (1.32) H	8:15 PM (0.30) L
Tue 23	3:15 AM (1.63) H	8:56 AM (0.73) L	2:48 PM (1.35) H	8:52 PM (0.30) L
Wed 24	3:51 AM (1.64) H	9:32 AM (0.68) L	3:30 PM (1.37) H	9:27 PM (0.31) L
Thu 25	4:26 AM (1.64) H	10:09 AM (0.63) L	4:12 PM (1.38) H	9:59 PM (0.34) L
Fri 26	5:00 AM (1.63) H	10:44 AM (0.58) L	4:53 PM (1.38) H	10:33 PM (0.39) L
Sat 27	5:33 AM (1.60) H	11:19 AM (0.53) L	5:37 PM (1.38) H	11:12 PM (0.45) L
Sun 28	6:07 AM (1.57) H	11:56 AM (0.47) L	6:27 PM (1.39) H	11:57 PM (0.54) L
Mon 29	6:42 AM (1.52) H	12:35 PM (0.41) L	7:23 PM (1.39) H	
Tue 30	12:45 AM (0.65) L	7:20 AM (1.48) H	1:20 PM (0.36) L	8:29 PM (1.41) H
Wed 31	1:38 AM (0.76) L	8:04 AM (1.43) H	2:10 PM (0.31) L	9:40 PM (1.44) H

Fort Denison - NSW

DAY/DATE	TIDE 1	TIDE 2	TIDE 3	TIDE 4
Mon 1	5:35 AM (1.58) H	11:46 AM (0.57) L	5:47 PM (1.49) H	11:57 PM (0.40) L
Tue 2	6:25 AM (1.73) H	12:50 PM (0.45) L	6:47 PM (1.48) H	
Wed 3	12:45 AM (0.39) L	7:15 AM (1.87) H	1:50 PM (0.33) L	7:46 PM (1.47) H
Thu 4	1:32 AM (0.39) L	8:05 AM (1.98) H	2:47 PM (0.24) L	8:45 PM (1.45) H
Fri 5	2:23 AM (0.41) L	8:57 AM (2.05) H	3:44 PM (0.18) L	9:42 PM (1.42) H
Sat 6	3:14 AM (0.44) L	9:49 AM (2.08) H	4:38 PM (0.17) L	10:38 PM (1.39) H
Sun 7	4:07 AM (0.47) L	10:42 AM (2.06) H	5:32 PM (0.20) L	11:33 PM (1.36) H
Mon 8	5:02 AM (0.52) L	11:34 AM (1.98) H	6:27 PM (0.27) L	
Tue 9	12:29 AM (1.33) H	5:59 AM (0.57) L	12:27 PM (1.87) H	7:20 PM (0.35) L
Wed 10	1:26 AM (1.32) H	6:56 AM (0.63) L	1:19 PM (1.73) H	8:13 PM (0.43) L
Thu 11	2:23 AM (1.32) H	7:57 AM (0.69) L	2:13 PM (1.59) H	9:01 PM (0.50) L
Fri 12	3:19 AM (1.34) H	9:01 AM (0.74) L	3:09 PM (1.46) H	9:47 PM (0.55) L
Sat 13	4:15 AM (1.39) H	10:12 AM (0.75) L	4:08 PM (1.35) H	10:31 PM (0.58) L
Sun 14	5:06 AM (1.46) H	11:20 AM (0.74) L	5:07 PM (1.28) H	11:14 PM (0.59) L
Mon 15	5:53 AM (1.52) H	12:24 PM (0.69) L	6:03 PM (1.25) H	11:55 PM (0.60) L
Tue 16	6:36 AM (1.59) H	1:16 PM (0.62) L	6:56 PM (1.24) H	
Wed 17	12:35 AM (0.60) L	7:16 AM (1.65) H	2:01 PM (0.55) L	7:44 PM (1.25) H
Thu 18	1:15 AM (0.60) L	7:55 AM (1.71) H	2:41 PM (0.49) L	8:27 PM (1.27) H
Fri 19	1:53 AM (0.60) L	8:32 AM (1.75) H	3:19 PM (0.45) L	9:07 PM (1.28) H
Sat 20	2:31 AM (0.60) L	9:10 AM (1.78) H	3:56 PM (0.42) L	9:46 PM (1.29) H
Sun 21	3:10 AM (0.59) L	9:47 AM (1.80) H	4:32 PM (0.41) L	10:25 PM (1.29) H
Mon 22	3:49 AM (0.59) L	10:25 AM (1.81) H	5:11 PM (0.41) L	11:04 PM (1.29) H
Tue 23	4:30 AM (0.60) L	11:03 AM (1.79) H	5:49 PM (0.42) L	11:45 PM (1.29) H
Wed 24	5:12 AM (0.61) L	11:43 AM (1.76) H	6:30 PM (0.43) L	
Thu 25	12:30 AM (1.31) H	5:58 AM (0.64) L	12:24 PM (1.71) H	7:11 PM (0.44) L
Fri 26	1:18 AM (1.33) H	6:50 AM (0.66) L	1:09 PM (1.64) H	7:55 PM (0.45) L
Sat 27	2:10 AM (1.37) H	7:48 AM (0.69) L	2:00 PM (1.55) H	8:41 PM (0.46) L
Sun 28	3:05 AM (1.44) H	8:56 AM (0.69) L	3:00 PM (1.46) H	9:30 PM (0.48) L
Mon 29	4:02 AM (1.53) H	10:12 AM (0.66) L	4:09 PM (1.39) H	10:24 PM (0.49) L
Tue 30	5:00 AM (1.64) H	11:30 AM (0.58) L	5:23 PM (1.34) H	11:20 PM (0.50) L
Wed 31	5:59 AM (1.76) H	12:43 PM (0.47) L	6:34 PM (1.33) H	

BITE TIMES

Apogee moon phase on Wednesday 17th
Perigee moon phase on Thursday 4th

● **New moon on Saturday 20th**
First quarter moon on Sunday 28th
○ **Full moon on Friday 5th**
Last quarter moon phase on Friday 12th

DAY	MINOR BITE	MAJOR BITE	MINOR BITE	MAJOR BITE	SALT WATER RATING	FRESH WATER RATING
MON 1	2:04 PM	7:47 PM	12:52 AM	7:22 AM	5	6
TUE 2	3:19 PM	8:40 PM	1:20 AM	8:13 AM	4	5
WED 3	4:38 PM	9:39 PM	1:52 AM	9:09 AM	3	5
THUR 4	5:59 PM	10:43 PM	2:31 AM	10:11 AM	6	6
FRI 5	7:16 PM	11:50 PM	3:21 AM	11:16 AM	5	7
SAT 6	8:23 PM		4:22 AM	12:23 PM	3	8
SUN 7	9:17 PM	12:57 AM	5:33 AM	1:28 PM	5	7
MON 8	10:00 PM	2:00 AM	6:49 AM	2:28 PM	7	6
TUE 9	10:33 PM	2:58 AM	8:03 AM	3:23 PM	7	6
WED 10	11:01 PM	3:49 AM	9:13 AM	4:12 PM	5	5
THUR 11	11:25 PM	4:36 AM	10:19 AM	4:57 PM	4	4
FRI 12	11:47 PM	5:19 AM	11:22 AM	5:39 PM	3	6
SAT 13		6:00 AM	12:22 PM	6:19 PM	4	4
SUN 14	12:08 AM	6:40 AM	1:21 PM	7:00 PM	5	5
MON 15	12:31 AM	7:21 AM	2:21 PM	7:42 PM	6	6
TUE 16	12:56 AM	8:04 AM	3:21 PM	8:26 PM	7	7
WED 17	1:24 AM	8:49 AM	4:22 PM	9:12 PM	7	8
THUR 18	1:57 AM	9:36 AM	5:22 PM	10:01 PM	5	8
FRI 19	2:37 AM	10:27 AM	6:20 PM	10:52 PM	6	7
SAT 20	3:24 AM	11:19 AM	7:13 PM	11:45 PM	8	8
SUN 21	4:19 AM	12:11 PM	7:59 PM		8	8
MON 22	5:19 AM	1:02 PM	8:38 PM	12:36 AM	8	8
TUE 23	6:22 AM	1:52 PM	9:11 PM	1:26 AM	8	6
WED 24	7:27 AM	2:39 PM	9:40 PM	2:15 AM	7	6
THUR 25	8:32 AM	3:24 PM	10:06 PM	3:01 AM	6	7
FRI 26	9:37 AM	4:09 PM	10:30 PM	3:46 AM	5	5
SAT 27	10:42 AM	4:53 PM	10:54 PM	4:30 AM	4	6
SUN 28	11:49 AM	5:39 PM	11:19 PM	5:15 AM	3	5
MON 29	12:59 PM	6:28 PM	11:48 PM	6:03 AM	3	5
TUE 30	2:14 PM	7:22 PM		6:55 AM	4	6
WED 31	3:31 PM	8:21 PM	12:23 AM	7:51 AM	5	6

TIDE TIMES

Adelaide Outer Harbour - SA

DAY/DATE	TIDE 1	TIDE 2	TIDE 3	TIDE 4
Thu 1	3:34 AM (2.19) H	11:19 AM (0.48) L	6:02 PM (1.50) H	10:06 PM (1.20) L
Fri 2	4:37 AM (2.36) H	12:04 PM (0.30) L	6:34 PM (1.57) H	10:57 PM (1.10) L
Sat 3	5:22 AM (2.48) H	12:40 PM (0.23) L	6:55 PM (1.59) H	11:30 PM (0.99) L
Sun 4	5:57 AM (2.56) H	1:07 PM (0.25) L	7:06 PM (1.60) H	11:59 PM (0.86) L
Mon 5	6:26 AM (2.58) H	1:29 PM (0.30) L	7:16 PM (1.66) H	
Tue 6	12:26 AM (0.74) L	6:52 AM (2.55) H	1:44 PM (0.36) L	7:29 PM (1.76) H
Wed 7	12:55 AM (0.66) L	7:17 AM (2.49) H	1:57 PM (0.39) L	7:48 PM (1.90) H
Thu 8	1:26 AM (0.62) L	7:41 AM (2.40) H	2:10 PM (0.39) L	8:13 PM (2.04) H
Fri 9	2:00 AM (0.63) L	8:06 AM (2.29) H	2:26 PM (0.37) L	8:44 PM (2.15) H
Sat 10	2:37 AM (0.68) L	8:33 AM (2.15) H	2:47 PM (0.38) L	9:18 PM (2.22) H
Sun 11	3:19 AM (0.77) L	9:04 AM (1.97) H	3:13 PM (0.45) L	10:00 PM (2.20) H
Mon 12	4:09 AM (0.91) L	9:38 AM (1.73) H	3:40 PM (0.61) L	10:47 PM (2.12) H
Tue 13	5:19 AM (1.08) L	10:17 AM (1.43) H	4:05 PM (0.85) L	11:58 PM (1.98) H
Wed 14	9:48 AM (1.10) L	12:41 PM (1.12) H	2:53 PM (1.12) L	
Thu 15	2:35 AM (1.94) H	11:05 AM (0.79) L	5:53 PM (1.41) H	9:36 PM (1.27) L
Fri 16	4:15 AM (2.12) H	11:40 AM (0.53) L	6:04 PM (1.62) H	10:47 PM (1.10) L
Sat 17	5:05 AM (2.30) H	12:09 PM (0.36) L	6:24 PM (1.75) H	11:25 PM (0.94) L
Sun 18	5:40 AM (2.44) H	12:33 PM (0.27) L	6:42 PM (1.82) H	11:52 PM (0.81) L
Mon 19	6:07 AM (2.54) H	12:54 PM (0.22) L	6:57 PM (1.87) H	
Tue 20	12:15 AM (0.69) L	6:31 AM (2.60) H	1:13 PM (0.20) L	7:13 PM (1.94) H
Wed 21	12:42 AM (0.59) L	6:56 AM (2.61) H	1:33 PM (0.19) L	7:33 PM (2.02) H
Thu 22	1:11 AM (0.54) L	7:22 AM (2.57) H	1:54 PM (0.20) L	7:57 PM (2.10) H
Fri 23	1:43 AM (0.53) L	7:47 AM (2.48) H	2:14 PM (0.23) L	8:21 PM (2.18) H
Sat 24	2:15 AM (0.55) L	8:13 AM (2.34) H	2:31 PM (0.29) L	8:46 PM (2.26) H
Sun 25	2:47 AM (0.59) L	8:37 AM (2.16) H	2:47 PM (0.36) L	9:13 PM (2.32) H
Mon 26	3:24 AM (0.68) L	9:02 AM (1.94) H	3:01 PM (0.46) L	9:43 PM (2.31) H
Tue 27	4:06 AM (0.83) L	9:24 AM (1.64) H	3:10 PM (0.61) L	10:17 PM (2.21) H
Wed 28	5:09 AM (1.07) L	9:20 AM (1.30) H	2:53 PM (0.78) L	11:02 PM (1.99) H
Thu 29	1:03 PM (0.78) L			
Fri 30	3:55 AM (1.88) H	12:16 PM (0.50) L	7:22 PM (1.60) H	11:08 PM (1.37) L
Sat 31	5:11 AM (2.16) H	12:30 PM (0.28) L	7:07 PM (1.70) H	11:44 PM (1.11) L

Brisbane Bar - QLD

DAY/DATE	TIDE 1	TIDE 2	TIDE 3	TIDE 4
Thu 1	1:00 AM (0.40) L	7:41 AM (2.50) H	2:22 PM (0.65) L	7:44 PM (1.81) H
Fri 2	1:57 AM (0.34) L	8:36 AM (2.63) H	3:23 PM (0.56) L	8:45 PM (1.82) H
Sat 3	2:50 AM (0.30) L	9:27 AM (2.72) H	4:18 PM (0.50) L	9:41 PM (1.84) H
Sun 4	3:40 AM (0.28) L	10:15 AM (2.74) H	5:08 PM (0.48) L	10:31 PM (1.86) H
Mon 5	4:27 AM (0.30) L	11:00 AM (2.72) H	5:53 PM (0.49) L	11:18 PM (1.88) H
Tue 6	5:12 AM (0.36) L	11:44 AM (2.64) H	6:33 PM (0.52) L	
Wed 7	12:03 AM (1.88) H	5:56 AM (0.46) L	12:23 PM (2.51) H	7:11 PM (0.56) L
Thu 8	12:48 AM (1.87) H	6:40 AM (0.59) L	1:01 PM (2.36) H	7:46 PM (0.60) L
Fri 9	1:34 AM (1.86) H	7:26 AM (0.74) L	1:40 PM (2.19) H	8:23 PM (0.64) L
Sat 10	2:26 AM (1.85) H	8:17 AM (0.89) L	2:20 PM (2.02) H	9:01 PM (0.66) L
Sun 11	3:27 AM (1.87) H	9:22 AM (1.00) L	3:08 PM (1.85) H	9:48 PM (0.68) L
Mon 12	4:37 AM (1.92) H	10:41 AM (1.05) L	4:08 PM (1.72) H	10:43 PM (0.69) L
Tue 13	5:43 AM (2.02) H	12:02 PM (1.02) L	5:18 PM (1.64) H	11:40 PM (0.67) L
Wed 14	6:39 AM (2.13) H	1:11 PM (0.93) L	6:25 PM (1.64) H	
Thu 15	12:35 AM (0.63) L	7:28 AM (2.24) H	2:04 PM (0.83) L	7:22 PM (1.67) H
Fri 16	1:25 AM (0.58) L	8:11 AM (2.33) H	2:49 PM (0.75) L	8:09 PM (1.72) H
Sat 17	2:09 AM (0.52) L	8:51 AM (2.40) H	3:30 PM (0.70) L	8:49 PM (1.78) H
Sun 18	2:49 AM (0.46) L	9:29 AM (2.45) H	4:08 PM (0.66) L	9:28 PM (1.83) H
Mon 19	3:28 AM (0.42) L	10:04 AM (2.49) H	4:45 PM (0.63) L	10:06 PM (1.88) H
Tue 20	4:06 AM (0.40) L	10:39 AM (2.52) H	5:19 PM (0.60) L	10:45 PM (1.93) H
Wed 21	4:44 AM (0.41) L	11:13 AM (2.52) H	5:54 PM (0.58) L	11:25 PM (1.96) H
Thu 22	5:23 AM (0.45) L	11:46 AM (2.49) H	6:28 PM (0.56) L	
Fri 23	12:07 AM (1.98) H	6:03 AM (0.53) L	12:21 PM (2.41) H	7:01 PM (0.55) L
Sat 24	12:51 AM (2.00) H	6:48 AM (0.63) L	12:59 PM (2.29) H	7:38 PM (0.56) L
Sun 25	1:42 AM (2.01) H	7:41 AM (0.75) L	1:42 PM (2.14) H	8:20 PM (0.57) L
Mon 26	2:42 AM (2.03) H	8:45 AM (0.87) L	2:35 PM (1.96) H	9:14 PM (0.60) L
Tue 27	3:55 AM (2.09) H	10:09 AM (0.94) L	3:47 PM (1.79) H	10:19 PM (0.61) L
Wed 28	5:15 AM (2.19) H	11:45 AM (0.92) L	5:13 PM (1.70) H	11:32 PM (0.59) L
Thu 29	6:28 AM (2.34) H	1:14 PM (0.81) L	6:35 PM (1.70) H	
Fri 30	12:45 AM (0.52) L	7:32 AM (2.49) H	2:22 PM (0.67) L	7:46 PM (1.76) H
Sat 31	1:49 AM (0.44) L	8:27 AM (2.61) H	3:17 PM (0.57) L	8:45 PM (1.85) H

Darwin - NT

DAY/DATE	TIDE 1	TIDE 2	TIDE 3	TIDE 4
Thu 1	2:42 AM (5.76) H	10:12 AM (1.54) L	5:02 PM (6.67) H	10:39 PM (3.78) L
Fri 2	3:53 AM (5.92) H	11:10 AM (1.11) L	6:00 PM (7.17) H	11:39 PM (3.47) L
Sat 3	4:52 AM (6.19) H	12:01 PM (0.79) L	6:49 PM (7.54) H	
Sun 4	12:31 AM (3.15) L	5:45 AM (6.46) H	12:49 PM (0.61) L	7:34 PM (7.77) H
Mon 5	1:19 AM (2.84) L	6:35 AM (6.66) H	1:33 PM (0.62) L	8:15 PM (7.85) H
Tue 6	2:07 AM (2.59) L	7:26 AM (6.72) H	2:15 PM (0.82) L	8:52 PM (7.78) H
Wed 7	2:52 AM (2.42) L	8:15 AM (6.64) H	2:54 PM (1.22) L	9:26 PM (7.59) H
Thu 8	3:37 AM (2.34) L	9:04 AM (6.42) H	3:29 PM (1.76) L	9:56 PM (7.30) H
Fri 9	4:21 AM (2.37) L	9:52 AM (6.10) H	3:59 PM (2.38) L	10:23 PM (6.92) H
Sat 10	5:03 AM (2.47) L	10:41 AM (5.72) H	4:22 PM (3.01) L	10:46 PM (6.49) H
Sun 11	5:46 AM (2.61) L	11:35 AM (5.36) H	4:53 PM (3.61) L	11:12 PM (6.04) H
Mon 12	6:33 AM (2.73) L	12:45 PM (5.10) H	6:02 PM (4.14) L	11:47 PM (5.57) H
Tue 13	7:31 AM (2.79) L	2:36 PM (5.12) H	7:42 PM (4.46) L	
Wed 14	12:51 AM (5.16) H	8:45 AM (2.74) L	4:24 PM (5.54) H	9:56 PM (4.41) L
Thu 15	2:39 AM (4.99) H	10:00 AM (2.52) L	5:15 PM (6.00) H	11:21 PM (4.09) L
Fri 16	3:55 AM (5.15) H	10:56 AM (2.21) L	5:54 PM (6.41) H	
Sat 17	12:00 AM (3.78) L	4:45 AM (5.44) H	11:40 AM (1.89) L	6:29 PM (6.74) H
Sun 18	12:29 AM (3.50) L	5:25 AM (5.78) H	12:17 PM (1.59) L	7:01 PM (7.02) H
Mon 19	12:55 AM (3.24) L	6:03 AM (6.10) H	12:52 PM (1.36) L	7:33 PM (7.25) H
Tue 20	1:24 AM (2.97) L	6:41 AM (6.38) H	1:24 PM (1.22) L	8:03 PM (7.41) H
Wed 21	1:56 AM (2.71) L	7:18 AM (6.57) H	1:53 PM (1.21) L	8:30 PM (7.51) H
Thu 22	2:30 AM (2.47) L	7:57 AM (6.67) H	2:21 PM (1.32) L	8:56 PM (7.50) H
Fri 23	3:05 AM (2.27) L	8:37 AM (6.67) H	2:48 PM (1.58) L	9:18 PM (7.40) H
Sat 24	3:43 AM (2.13) L	9:20 AM (6.57) H	3:16 PM (1.99) L	9:42 PM (7.20) H
Sun 25	4:21 AM (2.06) L	10:07 AM (6.35) H	3:48 PM (2.52) L	10:06 PM (6.89) H
Mon 26	5:02 AM (2.08) L	11:00 AM (6.05) H	4:26 PM (3.15) L	10:33 PM (6.50) H
Tue 27	5:49 AM (2.18) L	12:04 PM (5.73) H	5:22 PM (3.81) L	11:08 PM (6.05) H
Wed 28	6:49 AM (2.30) L	1:36 PM (5.52) H	6:59 PM (4.35) L	
Thu 29	12:03 AM (5.57) H	8:24 AM (2.31) L	3:45 PM (5.81) H	9:09 PM (4.43) L
Fri 30	2:05 AM (5.26) H	10:00 AM (2.03) L	5:03 PM (6.39) H	10:51 PM (4.04) L
Sat 31	3:55 AM (5.50) H	11:10 AM (1.60) L	5:59 PM (6.96) H	11:55 PM (3.50) L

Fremantle - WA

DAY/DATE	TIDE 1	TIDE 2	TIDE 3	TIDE 4
Thu 1	5:09 AM (0.36) L	7:39 PM (1.25) H		
Fri 2	5:48 AM (0.31) L	8:24 PM (1.27) H		
Sat 3	6:29 AM (0.30) L	9:09 PM (1.25) H		
Sun 4	7:07 AM (0.33) L	9:53 PM (1.21) H		
Mon 5	7:41 AM (0.39) L	10:29 PM (1.13) H		
Tue 6	8:02 AM (0.47) L	10:37 PM (1.05) H		
Wed 7	8:04 AM (0.56) L	10:31 PM (0.97) H		
Thu 8	7:08 AM (0.61) L	10:21 PM (0.90) H		
Fri 9	6:36 AM (0.61) L	8:37 PM (0.88) H		
Sat 10	6:38 AM (0.60) L	5:18 PM (0.92) H		
Sun 11	6:30 AM (0.58) L	5:23 PM (0.98) H		
Mon 12	5:52 AM (0.57) L	5:40 PM (1.03) H		
Tue 13	5:28 AM (0.54) L	6:07 PM (1.07) H		
Wed 14	5:00 AM (0.51) L	6:38 PM (1.11) H		
Thu 15	5:06 AM (0.48) L	7:12 PM (1.14) H		
Fri 16	5:21 AM (0.45) L	7:46 PM (1.16) H		
Sat 17	5:42 AM (0.44) L	8:22 PM (1.18) H		
Sun 18	6:03 AM (0.43) L	8:58 PM (1.18) H		
Mon 19	6:21 AM (0.44) L	9:31 PM (1.16) H		
Tue 20	6:34 AM (0.47) L	10:03 PM (1.13) H		
Wed 21	6:44 AM (0.50) L	1:28 PM (0.74) H	3:03 PM (0.74) L	10:31 PM (1.07) H
Thu 22	6:49 AM (0.54) L	1:44 PM (0.78) H	4:01 PM (0.76) L	10:56 PM (1.00) H
Fri 23	6:48 AM (0.58) L	2:10 PM (0.83) H	5:07 PM (0.80) L	11:15 PM (0.91) H
Sat 24	6:38 AM (0.61) L	2:40 PM (0.89) H	6:59 PM (0.83) L	8:49 PM (0.84) H
Sun 25	6:28 AM (0.62) L	3:15 PM (0.96) H		
Mon 26	5:37 AM (0.60) L	3:56 PM (1.03) H		
Tue 27	5:00 AM (0.55) L	4:45 PM (1.09) H		
Wed 28	3:48 AM (0.46) L	5:43 PM (1.15) H		
Thu 29	4:20 AM (0.39) L	6:44 PM (1.20) H		
Fri 30	4:57 AM (0.35) L	7:41 PM (1.23) H		
Sat 31	5:34 AM (0.35) L	8:31 PM (1.23) H		

Sun Rise & Sun Set Times:

Darwin, NT: Rise: 06:30am Set: 07:10pm
Melbourne, VIC: Rise: 06:10am Set: 08:40pm
Adelaide, SA: Rise: 05:50am Set: 08:20pm
Perth, WA: Rise: 05:20am Set: 07:20pm
Sydney, NSW: Rise: 05:50am Set: 08:00pm
Brisbane, QLD: Rise: 05:00am Set: 06:40pm
Hobart, TAS: Rise: 05:50am Set: 08:50pm

(Note: These times are averages for the month)

Hobart - TAS

DAY/DATE	TIDE 1	TIDE 2	TIDE 3	TIDE 4
Thu 1	6:00 AM (1.61) H	1:54 PM (0.24) L	8:38 PM (1.02) H	11:45 PM (0.91) L
Fri 2	6:54 AM (1.66) H	2:53 PM (0.16) L	9:42 PM (1.03) H	
Sat 3	12:30 AM (0.96) L	7:51 AM (1.68) H	3:50 PM (0.11) L	10:44 PM (1.05) H
Sun 4	1:30 AM (0.99) L	8:50 AM (1.66) H	4:45 PM (0.11) L	11:45 PM (1.06) H
Mon 5	2:59 AM (1.00) L	9:48 AM (1.60) H	5:39 PM (0.16) L	
Tue 6	12:42 AM (1.09) H	4:51 AM (0.98) L	10:48 AM (1.51) H	6:30 PM (0.23) L
Wed 7	1:28 AM (1.13) H	6:16 AM (0.93) L	11:52 AM (1.38) H	7:18 PM (0.33) L
Thu 8	2:07 AM (1.17) H	7:33 AM (0.87) L	12:59 PM (1.24) H	8:02 PM (0.45) L
Fri 9	2:42 AM (1.22) H	8:46 AM (0.80) L	2:04 PM (1.11) H	8:40 PM (0.56) L
Sat 10	3:14 AM (1.27) H	9:55 AM (0.73) L	3:08 PM (1.00) H	9:11 PM (0.67) L
Sun 11	3:43 AM (1.31) H	10:55 AM (0.66) L	4:15 PM (0.93) H	9:31 PM (0.75) L
Mon 12	4:10 AM (1.35) H	11:47 AM (0.60) L	5:41 PM (0.90) H	9:46 PM (0.82) L
Tue 13	4:37 AM (1.38) H	12:32 PM (0.55) L	7:07 PM (0.91) H	10:03 PM (0.87) L
Wed 14	5:06 AM (1.40) H	1:12 PM (0.50) L	8:05 PM (0.94) H	10:30 PM (0.91) L
Thu 15	5:40 AM (1.42) H	1:51 PM (0.46) L	8:49 PM (0.96) H	11:00 PM (0.93) L
Fri 16	6:18 AM (1.44) H	2:30 PM (0.43) L	9:29 PM (0.97) H	11:33 PM (0.95) L
Sat 17	7:00 AM (1.45) H	3:11 PM (0.41) L	10:11 PM (0.97) H	
Sun 18	12:08 AM (0.95) L	7:44 AM (1.46) H	3:50 PM (0.39) L	10:56 PM (0.97) H
Mon 19	12:47 AM (0.96) L	8:26 AM (1.46) H	4:29 PM (0.38) L	11:41 PM (0.98) H
Tue 20	1:43 AM (0.96) L	9:08 AM (1.43) H	5:06 PM (0.39) L	
Wed 21	12:18 AM (1.01) H	3:01 AM (0.97) L	9:53 AM (1.39) H	5:41 PM (0.40) L
Thu 22	12:49 AM (1.05) H	4:36 AM (0.95) L	10:42 AM (1.32) H	6:15 PM (0.44) L
Fri 23	1:18 AM (1.11) H	6:13 AM (0.90) L	11:42 AM (1.23) H	6:50 PM (0.50) L
Sat 24	1:48 AM (1.19) H	7:37 AM (0.82) L	12:58 PM (1.14) H	7:27 PM (0.57) L
Sun 25	2:18 AM (1.27) H	8:48 AM (0.72) L	2:14 PM (1.06) H	8:05 PM (0.66) L
Mon 26	2:51 AM (1.35) H	9:50 AM (0.60) L	3:27 PM (1.00) H	8:46 PM (0.75) L
Tue 27	3:26 AM (1.43) H	10:48 AM (0.47) L	4:51 PM (0.97) H	9:29 PM (0.82) L
Wed 28	4:05 AM (1.50) H	11:45 AM (0.36) L	6:27 PM (0.98) H	10:12 PM (0.86) L
Thu 29	4:52 AM (1.56) H	12:42 PM (0.27) L	7:34 PM (1.00) H	10:55 PM (0.89) L
Fri 30	5:46 AM (1.60) H	1:39 PM (0.22) L	8:26 PM (1.01) H	11:41 PM (0.90) L
Sat 31	6:45 AM (1.62) H	2:35 PM (0.19) L	9:15 PM (1.01) H	

Port Phillip Heads - VIC

DAY/DATE	TIDE 1	TIDE 2	TIDE 3	TIDE 4
Thu 1	2:38 AM (0.86) L	8:58 AM (1.39) H	3:09 PM (0.28) L	10:52 PM (1.48) H
Fri 2	3:47 AM (0.92) L	10:00 AM (1.36) H	4:17 PM (0.25) L	
Sat 3	12:02 AM (1.54) H	5:07 AM (0.94) L	11:12 AM (1.35) H	5:33 PM (0.22) L
Sun 4	1:08 AM (1.59) H	6:24 AM (0.88) L	12:28 PM (1.37) H	6:45 PM (0.19) L
Mon 5	2:07 AM (1.65) H	7:30 AM (0.79) L	1:36 PM (1.41) H	7:46 PM (0.18) L
Tue 6	3:01 AM (1.69) H	8:30 AM (0.69) L	2:36 PM (1.46) H	8:42 PM (0.19) L
Wed 7	3:49 AM (1.71) H	9:24 AM (0.59) L	3:32 PM (1.48) H	9:33 PM (0.24) L
Thu 8	4:33 AM (1.70) H	10:15 AM (0.50) L	4:27 PM (1.49) H	10:20 PM (0.31) L
Fri 9	5:14 AM (1.68) H	11:01 AM (0.43) L	5:20 PM (1.47) H	11:03 PM (0.40) L
Sat 10	5:49 AM (1.63) H	11:45 AM (0.39) L	6:13 PM (1.44) H	11:44 PM (0.50) L
Sun 11	6:23 AM (1.57) H	12:24 PM (0.37) L	7:06 PM (1.41) H	
Mon 12	12:22 AM (0.60) L	6:55 AM (1.50) H	1:01 PM (0.37) L	8:00 PM (1.38) H
Tue 13	1:01 AM (0.69) L	7:26 AM (1.43) H	1:39 PM (0.39) L	8:52 PM (1.35) H
Wed 14	1:44 AM (0.79) L	8:00 AM (1.37) H	2:20 PM (0.41) L	9:46 PM (1.34) H
Thu 15	2:31 AM (0.87) L	8:42 AM (1.30) H	3:07 PM (0.43) L	10:43 PM (1.34) H
Fri 16	3:30 AM (0.94) L	9:32 AM (1.25) H	4:05 PM (0.44) L	11:42 PM (1.36) H
Sat 17	4:41 AM (0.97) L	10:34 AM (1.22) H	5:12 PM (0.44) L	
Sun 18	12:40 AM (1.39) H	5:59 AM (0.95) L	11:41 AM (1.21) H	6:15 PM (0.41) L
Mon 19	1:31 AM (1.44) H	7:05 AM (0.89) L	12:45 PM (1.23) H	7:09 PM (0.37) L
Tue 20	2:15 AM (1.50) H	7:57 AM (0.81) L	1:42 PM (1.27) H	7:55 PM (0.35) L
Wed 21	2:55 AM (1.56) H	8:40 AM (0.72) L	2:32 PM (1.33) H	8:35 PM (0.34) L
Thu 22	3:31 AM (1.60) H	9:18 AM (0.63) L	3:19 PM (1.38) H	9:12 PM (0.35) L
Fri 23	4:05 AM (1.63) H	9:55 AM (0.54) L	4:03 PM (1.43) H	9:48 PM (0.37) L
Sat 24	4:39 AM (1.63) H	10:30 AM (0.46) L	4:47 PM (1.47) H	10:28 PM (0.42) L
Sun 25	5:11 AM (1.62) H	11:05 AM (0.38) L	5:32 PM (1.50) H	11:09 PM (0.49) L
Mon 26	5:43 AM (1.59) H	11:42 AM (0.31) L	6:19 PM (1.51) H	11:51 PM (0.57) L
Tue 27	6:15 AM (1.55) H	12:21 PM (0.26) L	7:11 PM (1.50) H	
Wed 28	12:35 AM (0.66) L	6:52 AM (1.51) H	1:02 PM (0.24) L	8:09 PM (1.47) H
Thu 29	1:21 AM (0.75) L	7:34 AM (1.45) H	1:49 PM (0.24) L	9:15 PM (1.44) H
Fri 30	2:13 AM (0.84) L	8:25 AM (1.39) H	2:44 PM (0.26) L	10:26 PM (1.42) H
Sat 31	3:15 AM (0.90) L	9:30 AM (1.34) H	3:53 PM (0.29) L	11:40 PM (1.43) H

Fort Denison - NSW

DAY/DATE	TIDE 1	TIDE 2	TIDE 3	TIDE 4
Thu 1	12:17 AM (0.50) L	6:56 AM (1.88) H	1:46 PM (0.36) L	7:40 PM (1.35) H
Fri 2	1:15 AM (0.49) L	7:52 AM (1.97) H	2:45 PM (0.26) L	8:39 PM (1.37) H
Sat 3	2:10 AM (0.46) L	8:46 AM (2.04) H	3:37 PM (0.20) L	9:33 PM (1.39) H
Sun 4	3:04 AM (0.45) L	9:39 AM (2.07) H	4:27 PM (0.18) L	10:25 PM (1.41) H
Mon 5	3:57 AM (0.44) L	10:30 AM (2.05) H	5:15 PM (0.21) L	11:14 PM (1.41) H
Tue 6	4:48 AM (0.47) L	11:17 AM (1.97) H	6:00 PM (0.27) L	
Wed 7	12:01 AM (1.41) H	5:40 AM (0.51) L	12:03 PM (1.84) H	6:43 PM (0.35) L
Thu 8	12:49 AM (1.41) H	6:30 AM (0.58) L	12:46 PM (1.69) H	7:23 PM (0.44) L
Fri 9	1:37 AM (1.40) H	7:24 AM (0.66) L	1:30 PM (1.53) H	8:01 PM (0.52) L
Sat 10	2:26 AM (1.41) H	8:21 AM (0.73) L	2:15 PM (1.38) H	8:41 PM (0.59) L
Sun 11	3:16 AM (1.43) H	9:27 AM (0.77) L	3:09 PM (1.26) H	9:23 PM (0.64) L
Mon 12	4:10 AM (1.46) H	10:40 AM (0.77) L	4:15 PM (1.18) H	10:13 PM (0.68) L
Tue 13	5:05 AM (1.50) H	11:53 AM (0.73) L	5:27 PM (1.15) H	11:07 PM (0.69) L
Wed 14	5:59 AM (1.55) H	12:55 PM (0.66) L	6:33 PM (1.16) H	
Thu 15	12:00 AM (0.69) L	6:47 AM (1.61) H	1:44 PM (0.58) L	7:28 PM (1.20) H
Fri 16	12:50 AM (0.67) L	7:32 AM (1.67) H	2:25 PM (0.51) L	8:12 PM (1.24) H
Sat 17	1:35 AM (0.63) L	8:15 AM (1.73) H	3:02 PM (0.45) L	8:51 PM (1.28) H
Sun 18	2:16 AM (0.59) L	8:53 AM (1.79) H	3:38 PM (0.41) L	9:28 PM (1.32) H
Mon 19	2:56 AM (0.55) L	9:30 AM (1.83) H	4:13 PM (0.37) L	10:04 PM (1.35) H
Tue 20	3:35 AM (0.52) L	10:08 AM (1.85) H	4:46 PM (0.35) L	10:42 PM (1.38) H
Wed 21	4:15 AM (0.51) L	10:45 AM (1.84) H	5:22 PM (0.34) L	11:20 PM (1.42) H
Thu 22	4:59 AM (0.51) L	11:23 AM (1.80) H	5:57 PM (0.35) L	
Fri 23	12:02 AM (1.45) H	5:45 AM (0.53) L	12:03 PM (1.73) H	6:34 PM (0.38) L
Sat 24	12:46 AM (1.48) H	6:35 AM (0.57) L	12:46 PM (1.62) H	7:14 PM (0.42) L
Sun 25	1:34 AM (1.52) H	7:32 AM (0.61) L	1:35 PM (1.50) H	7:57 PM (0.48) L
Mon 26	2:27 AM (1.55) H	8:39 AM (0.64) L	2:34 PM (1.37) H	8:46 PM (0.55) L
Tue 27	3:27 AM (1.60) H	9:59 AM (0.64) L	3:49 PM (1.26) H	9:47 PM (0.60) L
Wed 28	4:33 AM (1.65) H	11:25 AM (0.58) L	5:15 PM (1.22) H	10:57 PM (0.61) L
Thu 29	5:42 AM (1.74) H	12:42 PM (0.48) L	6:35 PM (1.24) H	
Fri 30	12:05 AM (0.59) L	6:46 AM (1.83) H	1:45 PM (0.37) L	7:39 PM (1.30) H
Sat 31	1:08 AM (0.53) L	7:45 AM (1.92) H	2:38 PM (0.28) L	8:32 PM (1.37) H

BITE TIMES

Apogee moon phase on Wednesday 14th
Perigee moon phase on Friday 2nd and Friday 30th

New moon on Monday 19th
First quarter moon on Monday 26th
Full moon on Saturday 3rd
Last quarter moon phase on Sunday 11th

DAY	MINOR BITE	MAJOR BITE	MINOR BITE	MAJOR BITE	SALT WATER RATING	FRESH WATER RATING
THUR 1	4:48 PM	9:26 PM	1:06 AM	8:53 AM	5	7
FRI 2	6:00 PM	10:32 PM	2:00 AM	9:58 AM	3	8
SAT 3	7:01 PM	11:38 PM	3:06 AM	11:05 AM	5	7
SUN 4	7:50 PM		4:20 AM	12:09 PM	7	6
MON 5	8:28 PM	12:40 AM	5:37 AM	1:07 PM	7	6
TUE 6	8:59 PM	1:35 AM	6:51 AM	2:00 PM	5	5
WED 7	9:25 PM	2:26 AM	8:01 AM	2:48 PM	4	4
THUR 8	9:49 PM	3:11 AM	9:07 AM	3:32 PM	3	6
FRI 9	10:11 PM	3:54 AM	10:10 AM	4:15 PM	3	6
SAT 10	10:33 PM	4:36 AM	11:11 AM	4:56 PM	4	4
SUN 11	10:57 PM	5:17 AM	12:12 PM	5:38 PM	5	5
MON 12	11:24 PM	6:00 AM	1:12 PM	6:22 PM	6	6
TUE 13	11:56 PM	6:44 AM	2:13 PM	7:07 PM	7	7
WED 14		7:31 AM	3:14 PM	7:55 PM	7	8
THUR 15	12:33 AM	8:20 AM	4:12 PM	8:45 PM	5	8
FRI 16	1:18 AM	9:12 AM	5:07 PM	9:38 PM	6	7
SAT 17	2:10 AM	10:05 AM	5:55 PM	10:30 PM	8	8
SUN 18	3:09 AM	10:57 AM	6:37 PM	11:22 PM	8	8
MON 19	4:13 AM	11:48 AM	7:13 PM		8	8
TUE 20	5:18 AM	12:36 PM	7:43 PM	12:12 AM	8	6
WED 21	6:24 AM	1:23 PM	8:10 PM	12:59 AM	7	6
THUR 22	7:30 AM	2:08 PM	8:35 PM	1:45 AM	6	7
FRI 23	8:35 AM	2:52 PM	8:58 PM	2:30 AM	5	5
SAT 24	9:41 AM	3:37 PM	9:23 PM	3:14 AM	4	6
SUN 25	10:50 AM	4:24 PM	9:50 PM	4:00 AM	3	5
MON 26	12:01 PM	5:15 PM	10:21 PM	4:49 AM	4	6
TUE 27	1:15 PM	6:10 PM	10:59 PM	5:42 AM	5	6
WED 28	2:30 PM	7:10 PM	11:47 PM	6:40 AM	4	5
THUR 29	3:42 PM	8:14 PM		7:42 AM	3	5
FRI 30	4:46 PM	9:19 PM	12:46 AM	8:46 AM	6	6
SAT 31	5:39 PM	10:21 PM	1:55 AM	9:50 AM	5	7

FEBRUARY 2026

TIDE TIMES

* Additional Tide 5 - See Additional Tide 5

Adelaide Outer Harbour - SA

DAY/DATE	TIDE 5
Sat 28	11:55 PM (1.23) L

DAY/DATE	TIDE 1	TIDE 2	TIDE 3	TIDE 4
Sun 1	5:49 AM (2.37) H	12:49 PM (0.20) L	7:07 PM (1.75) H	
Mon 2	12:06 AM (0.90) L	6:15 AM (2.48) H	1:04 PM (0.21) L	7:08 PM (1.81) H
Tue 3	12:24 AM (0.72) L	6:35 AM (2.50) H	1:15 PM (0.26) L	7:09 PM (1.91) H
Wed 4	12:42 AM (0.59) L	6:51 AM (2.49) H	1:22 PM (0.28) L	7:17 PM (2.06) H
Thu 5	1:03 AM (0.50) L	7:09 AM (2.44) H	1:30 PM (0.27) L	7:32 PM (2.22) H
Fri 6	1:29 AM (0.45) L	7:28 AM (2.37) H	1:42 PM (0.25) L	7:55 PM (2.36) H
Sat 7	1:56 AM (0.46) L	7:49 AM (2.27) H	1:56 PM (0.23) L	8:18 PM (2.45) H
Sun 8	2:24 AM (0.50) L	8:11 AM (2.16) H	2:13 PM (0.24) L	8:44 PM (2.48) H
Mon 9	2:53 AM (0.58) L	8:32 AM (2.02) H	2:30 PM (0.30) L	9:09 PM (2.45) H
Tue 10	3:24 AM (0.70) L	8:53 AM (1.84) H	2:47 PM (0.44) L	9:35 PM (2.33) H
Wed 11	3:59 AM (0.90) L	9:05 AM (1.60) H	2:57 PM (0.64) L	10:02 PM (2.10) H
Thu 12	4:48 AM (1.17) L	8:34 AM (1.33) H	2:25 PM (0.86) L	10:30 PM (1.80) H
Fri 13	12:28 PM (0.82) L	7:37 PM (1.57) H	10:59 PM (1.47) L	
Sat 14	4:39 AM (1.88) H	12:01 PM (0.56) L	6:37 PM (1.70) H	11:23 PM (1.16) L
Sun 15	5:20 AM (2.17) H	12:13 PM (0.35) L	6:33 PM (1.85) H	11:44 PM (0.92) L
Mon 16	5:47 AM (2.37) H	12:29 PM (0.24) L	6:41 PM (1.95) H	
Tue 17	12:02 AM (0.73) L	6:09 AM (2.49) H	12:42 PM (0.19) L	6:48 PM (2.03) H
Wed 18	12:20 AM (0.59) L	6:27 AM (2.54) H	12:55 PM (0.18) L	6:58 PM (2.13) H
Thu 19	12:41 AM (0.47) L	6:46 AM (2.55) H	1:09 PM (0.17) L	7:13 PM (2.25) H
Fri 20	1:07 AM (0.39) L	7:08 AM (2.49) H	1:25 PM (0.19) L	7:32 PM (2.37) H
Sat 21	1:35 AM (0.37) L	7:30 AM (2.36) H	1:40 PM (0.24) L	7:52 PM (2.46) H
Sun 22	2:03 AM (0.40) L	7:50 AM (2.20) H	1:50 PM (0.29) L	8:11 PM (2.53) H
Mon 23	2:28 AM (0.47) L	8:06 AM (2.03) H	1:57 PM (0.32) L	8:30 PM (2.57) H
Tue 24	2:50 AM (0.57) L	8:19 AM (1.86) H	2:03 PM (0.36) L	8:48 PM (2.54) H
Wed 25	3:13 AM (0.74) L	8:27 AM (1.66) H	2:09 PM (0.43) L	9:07 PM (2.38) H
Thu 26	3:34 AM (1.01) L	8:09 AM (1.45) H	1:59 PM (0.55) L	9:14 PM (2.10) H
Fri 27	3:26 AM (1.36) L	6:24 AM (1.45) H	1:10 PM (0.60) L	8:15 PM (1.81) H
Sat 28*	1:04 AM (1.51) L	5:22 AM (1.78) H	12:28 PM (0.47) L	7:06 PM (1.78) H

Brisbane Bar - QLD

DAY/DATE	TIDE 1	TIDE 2	TIDE 3	TIDE 4
Sun 1	2:45 AM (0.36) L	9:15 AM (2.68) H	4:05 PM (0.50) L	9:33 PM (1.93) H
Mon 2	3:34 AM (0.32) L	10:00 AM (2.69) H	4:46 PM (0.48) L	10:17 PM (2.00) H
Tue 3	4:18 AM (0.32) L	10:40 AM (2.66) H	5:23 PM (0.48) L	10:58 PM (2.04) H
Wed 4	4:59 AM (0.38) L	11:16 AM (2.57) H	5:55 PM (0.50) L	11:36 PM (2.06) H
Thu 5	5:37 AM (0.48) L	11:50 AM (2.44) H	6:24 PM (0.53) L	
Fri 6	12:14 AM (2.06) H	6:15 AM (0.61) L	12:22 PM (2.29) H	6:51 PM (0.56) L
Sat 7	12:52 AM (2.05) H	6:54 AM (0.75) L	12:53 PM (2.11) H	7:19 PM (0.60) L
Sun 8	1:33 AM (2.01) H	7:38 AM (0.90) L	1:27 PM (1.93) H	7:52 PM (0.67) L
Mon 9	2:23 AM (1.97) H	8:33 AM (1.03) L	2:09 PM (1.74) H	8:34 PM (0.74) L
Tue 10	3:28 AM (1.94) H	9:52 AM (1.10) L	3:11 PM (1.59) H	9:32 PM (0.81) L
Wed 11	4:49 AM (1.96) H	11:30 AM (1.08) L	4:37 PM (1.52) H	10:46 PM (0.84) L
Thu 12	6:02 AM (2.05) H	12:48 PM (0.98) L	6:02 PM (1.55) H	
Fri 13	12:00 AM (0.79) L	6:59 AM (2.16) H	1:42 PM (0.86) L	7:03 PM (1.65) H
Sat 14	1:00 AM (0.69) L	7:45 AM (2.28) H	2:25 PM (0.77) L	7:49 PM (1.75) H
Sun 15	1:49 AM (0.59) L	8:26 AM (2.38) H	3:04 PM (0.69) L	8:30 PM (1.86) H
Mon 16	2:33 AM (0.50) L	9:03 AM (2.46) H	3:41 PM (0.62) L	9:09 PM (1.96) H
Tue 17	3:15 AM (0.43) L	9:39 AM (2.52) H	4:16 PM (0.56) L	9:48 PM (2.04) H
Wed 18	3:54 AM (0.39) L	10:14 AM (2.55) H	4:50 PM (0.50) L	10:28 PM (2.12) H
Thu 19	4:34 AM (0.40) L	10:47 AM (2.53) H	5:23 PM (0.47) L	11:08 PM (2.18) H
Fri 20	5:15 AM (0.44) L	11:21 AM (2.46) H	5:55 PM (0.46) L	11:48 PM (2.22) H
Sat 21	5:56 AM (0.53) L	11:56 AM (2.33) H	6:26 PM (0.47) L	
Sun 22	12:31 AM (2.23) H	6:40 AM (0.65) L	12:32 PM (2.16) H	7:00 PM (0.52) L
Mon 23	1:18 AM (2.22) H	7:32 AM (0.79) L	1:15 PM (1.96) H	7:40 PM (0.58) L
Tue 24	2:16 AM (2.19) H	8:40 AM (0.91) L	2:15 PM (1.76) H	8:34 PM (0.67) L
Wed 25	3:31 AM (2.17) H	10:13 AM (0.96) L	3:41 PM (1.61) H	9:51 PM (0.73) L
Thu 26	4:58 AM (2.22) H	11:54 AM (0.90) L	5:21 PM (1.60) H	11:20 PM (0.71) L
Fri 27	6:16 AM (2.33) H	1:13 PM (0.76) L	6:44 PM (1.71) H	
Sat 28	12:41 AM (0.62) L	7:19 AM (2.45) H	2:11 PM (0.63) L	7:45 PM (1.85) H

Darwin - NT

DAY/DATE	TIDE 5
Fri 13	11:47 PM (4.15) L

DAY/DATE	TIDE 1	TIDE 2	TIDE 3	TIDE 4
Sun 1	5:01 AM (5.97) H	12:04 PM (1.19) L	6:44 PM (7.43) H	
Mon 2	12:43 AM (2.97) L	5:57 AM (6.44) H	12:49 PM (0.92) L	7:24 PM (7.76) H
Tue 3	1:24 AM (2.48) L	6:47 AM (6.81) H	1:29 PM (0.84) L	7:58 PM (7.92) H
Wed 4	2:01 AM (2.09) L	7:33 AM (7.02) H	2:02 PM (0.98) L	8:28 PM (7.91) H
Thu 5	2:37 AM (1.84) L	8:15 AM (7.05) H	2:33 PM (1.31) L	8:53 PM (7.75) H
Fri 6	3:12 AM (1.74) L	8:54 AM (6.90) H	2:59 PM (1.79) L	9:14 PM (7.47) H
Sat 7	3:44 AM (1.79) L	9:30 AM (6.62) H	3:16 PM (2.34) L	9:30 PM (7.10) H
Sun 8	4:13 AM (1.96) L	10:05 AM (6.25) H	3:27 PM (2.90) L	9:46 PM (6.67) H
Mon 9	4:43 AM (2.21) L	10:44 AM (5.84) H	3:43 PM (3.46) L	10:02 PM (6.16) H
Tue 10	5:16 AM (2.52) L	11:30 AM (5.41) H	4:10 PM (4.03) L	10:19 PM (5.62) H
Wed 11	6:04 AM (2.84) L	12:40 PM (5.06) H	6:02 PM (4.58) L	10:21 PM (5.08) H
Thu 12	7:18 AM (3.08) L	4:30 PM (5.18) H		
Fri 13*	12:01 AM (4.57) L	1:20 AM (4.58) H	9:15 AM (3.04) L	5:09 PM (5.69) H
Sat 14	3:50 AM (4.83) H	10:42 AM (2.66) L	5:41 PM (6.16) H	
Sun 15	12:02 AM (3.78) L	4:43 AM (5.30) H	11:30 AM (2.20) L	6:11 PM (6.60) H
Mon 16	12:21 AM (3.40) L	5:24 AM (5.80) H	12:09 PM (1.78) L	6:41 PM (7.01) H
Tue 17	12:45 AM (2.99) L	6:02 AM (6.28) H	12:42 PM (1.44) L	7:10 PM (7.36) H
Wed 18	1:13 AM (2.55) L	6:41 AM (6.70) H	1:12 PM (1.24) L	7:37 PM (7.61) H
Thu 19	1:43 AM (2.12) L	7:19 AM (7.03) H	1:39 PM (1.19) L	8:01 PM (7.74) H
Fri 20	2:14 AM (1.73) L	7:56 AM (7.24) H	2:04 PM (1.32) L	8:22 PM (7.74) H
Sat 21	2:45 AM (1.44) L	8:33 AM (7.30) H	2:30 PM (1.61) L	8:42 PM (7.62) H
Sun 22	3:18 AM (1.31) L	9:12 AM (7.19) H	2:58 PM (2.06) L	9:02 PM (7.37) H
Mon 23	3:53 AM (1.35) L	9:54 AM (6.90) H	3:27 PM (2.64) L	9:24 PM (6.98) H
Tue 24	4:30 AM (1.59) L	10:40 AM (6.45) H	4:00 PM (3.30) L	9:48 PM (6.48) H
Wed 25	5:11 AM (1.98) L	11:37 AM (5.90) H	4:45 PM (4.00) L	10:18 PM (5.88) H
Thu 26	6:09 AM (2.43) L	1:08 PM (5.46) H	6:37 PM (4.57) L	11:07 PM (5.22) H
Fri 27	8:01 AM (2.72) L	3:46 PM (5.67) H	9:53 PM (4.41) L	
Sat 28	2:46 AM (4.92) H	10:02 AM (2.47) L	4:59 PM (6.28) H	11:15 PM (3.74) L

Fremantle - WA

DAY/DATE	TIDE 1	TIDE 2	TIDE 3	TIDE 4
Sun 1	6:09 AM (0.38) L	9:16 PM (1.20) H		
Mon 2	6:36 AM (0.43) L	9:55 PM (1.14) H		
Tue 3	6:39 AM (0.51) L	1:04 PM (0.74) H	2:36 PM (0.73) L	10:23 PM (1.06) H
Wed 4	6:28 AM (0.58) L	1:11 PM (0.79) H	3:30 PM (0.75) L	10:26 PM (0.97) H
Thu 5	6:05 AM (0.62) L	1:15 PM (0.84) H	4:26 PM (0.78) L	10:20 PM (0.90) H
Fri 6	5:34 AM (0.63) L	1:30 PM (0.89) H	5:34 PM (0.81) L	8:20 PM (0.85) H
Sat 7	5:37 AM (0.61) L	1:54 PM (0.94) H	7:01 PM (0.84) L	8:15 PM (0.84) L
Sun 8	5:37 AM (0.60) L	2:24 PM (0.98) H		
Mon 9	5:06 AM (0.58) L	3:02 PM (1.01) H		
Tue 10	4:58 AM (0.56) L	3:53 PM (1.03) H		
Wed 11	4:40 AM (0.54) L	4:55 PM (1.06) H		
Thu 12	4:18 AM (0.52) L	6:04 PM (1.08) H		
Fri 13	4:31 AM (0.50) L	7:00 PM (1.12) H		
Sat 14	4:48 AM (0.48) L	7:44 PM (1.14) H		
Sun 15	5:05 AM (0.48) L	8:21 PM (1.16) H		
Mon 16	5:16 AM (0.49) L	8:57 PM (1.15) H		
Tue 17	5:24 AM (0.52) L	12:00 PM (0.78) H	2:13 PM (0.75) L	9:30 PM (1.12) H
Wed 18	5:33 AM (0.55) L	12:01 PM (0.81) H	3:04 PM (0.74) L	10:01 PM (1.07) H
Thu 19	5:42 AM (0.59) L	12:18 PM (0.86) H	3:58 PM (0.75) L	10:28 PM (0.99) H
Fri 20	5:39 AM (0.63) L	12:41 PM (0.92) H	5:00 PM (0.75) L	10:48 PM (0.89) H
Sat 21	5:21 AM (0.66) L	1:04 PM (0.97) H	6:22 PM (0.76) L	11:00 PM (0.79) H
Sun 22	5:11 AM (0.66) L	1:30 PM (1.02) H		
Mon 23	4:20 AM (0.63) L	2:09 PM (1.07) H		
Tue 24	2:07 AM (0.56) L	3:01 PM (1.10) H		
Wed 25	2:40 AM (0.49) L	4:00 PM (1.12) H		
Thu 26	3:15 AM (0.44) L	5:13 PM (1.14) H		
Fri 27	3:52 AM (0.43) L	6:51 PM (1.16) H		
Sat 28	4:28 AM (0.44) L	7:49 PM (1.17) H		

* Additional Tide 5 - See Additional Tide 5

Sun Rise & Sun Set Times:

Darwin, NT: Rise: 06:40am Set: 07:10pm

Melbourne, VIC: Rise: 06:40am Set: 08:20pm

Adelaide, SA: Rise: 06:40am Set: 08:10pm

Perth, WA: Rise: 05:50am Set: 07:00pm

Sydney, NSW: Rise: 06:20am Set: 07:40pm

Brisbane, QLD: Rise: 05:30am Set: 06:30pm

Hobart, TAS: Rise: 06:30am Set: 08:20pm

(Note: These times are averages for the month)

Hobart - TAS

DAY/DATE	TIDE 1	TIDE 2	TIDE 3	TIDE 4
Sun 1	12:31 AM (0.90) L	7:44 AM (1.61) H	3:30 PM (0.20) L	10:04 PM (1.02) H
Mon 2	1:34 AM (0.90) L	8:40 AM (1.56) H	4:22 PM (0.24) L	10:57 PM (1.04) H
Tue 3	3:01 AM (0.89) L	9:36 AM (1.47) H	5:12 PM (0.30) L	11:49 PM (1.07) H
Wed 4	4:45 AM (0.87) L	10:37 AM (1.35) H	5:59 PM (0.40) L	
Thu 5	12:34 AM (1.12) H	6:12 AM (0.82) L	11:46 AM (1.22) H	6:41 PM (0.50) L
Fri 6	1:14 AM (1.18) H	7:27 AM (0.75) L	12:57 PM (1.11) H	7:19 PM (0.61) L
Sat 7	1:48 AM (1.23) H	8:30 AM (0.69) L	2:00 PM (1.02) H	7:52 PM (0.71) L
Sun 8	2:19 AM (1.27) H	9:27 AM (0.63) L	3:01 PM (0.96) H	8:20 PM (0.80) L
Mon 9	2:47 AM (1.31) H	10:17 AM (0.58) L	4:15 PM (0.93) H	8:46 PM (0.86) L
Tue 10	3:16 AM (1.33) H	11:01 AM (0.54) L	5:56 PM (0.93) H	9:17 PM (0.90) L
Wed 11	3:48 AM (1.35) H	11:44 AM (0.51) L	6:59 PM (0.96) H	9:53 PM (0.92) L
Thu 12	4:26 AM (1.37) H	12:25 PM (0.48) L	7:35 PM (0.98) H	10:29 PM (0.93) L
Fri 13	5:08 AM (1.39) H	1:06 PM (0.46) L	8:06 PM (0.98) H	11:02 PM (0.92) L
Sat 14	5:54 AM (1.40) H	1:47 PM (0.44) L	8:36 PM (0.98) H	11:36 PM (0.91) L
Sun 15	6:40 AM (1.42) H	2:29 PM (0.43) L	9:07 PM (0.97) H	
Mon 16	12:15 AM (0.89) L	7:23 AM (1.43) H	3:07 PM (0.42) L	9:40 PM (0.98) H
Tue 17	1:03 AM (0.88) L	8:06 AM (1.41) H	3:44 PM (0.42) L	10:15 PM (1.00) H
Wed 18	2:04 AM (0.87) L	8:52 AM (1.37) H	4:19 PM (0.45) L	10:55 PM (1.05) H
Thu 19	3:24 AM (0.85) L	9:44 AM (1.30) H	4:55 PM (0.49) L	11:35 PM (1.11) H
Fri 20	4:59 AM (0.80) L	10:49 AM (1.21) H	5:31 PM (0.56) L	
Sat 21	12:15 AM (1.19) H	6:26 AM (0.71) L	12:13 PM (1.14) H	6:11 PM (0.65) L
Sun 22	12:53 AM (1.27) H	7:37 AM (0.60) L	1:30 PM (1.08) H	6:56 PM (0.74) L
Mon 23	1:32 AM (1.35) H	8:39 AM (0.49) L	2:39 PM (1.04) H	7:47 PM (0.83) L
Tue 24	2:13 AM (1.41) H	9:37 AM (0.40) L	3:57 PM (1.02) H	8:41 PM (0.88) L
Wed 25	2:57 AM (1.46) H	10:33 AM (0.33) L	5:33 PM (1.02) H	9:30 PM (0.91) L
Thu 26	3:45 AM (1.50) H	11:29 AM (0.28) L	6:36 PM (1.03) H	10:16 PM (0.91) L
Fri 27	4:41 AM (1.52) H	12:24 PM (0.26) L	7:20 PM (1.03) H	11:03 PM (0.88) L
Sat 28	5:42 AM (1.53) H	1:18 PM (0.26) L	7:59 PM (1.04) H	11:52 PM (0.85) L

Port Phillip Heads - VIC

DAY/DATE	TIDE 1	TIDE 2	TIDE 3	TIDE 4
Sun 1	4:36 AM (0.92) L	10:51 AM (1.30) H	5:17 PM (0.31) L	
Mon 2	12:49 AM (1.47) H	6:05 AM (0.86) L	12:16 PM (1.32) H	6:36 PM (0.29) L
Tue 3	1:51 AM (1.53) H	7:22 AM (0.75) L	1:30 PM (1.37) H	7:40 PM (0.28) L
Wed 4	2:44 AM (1.59) H	8:25 AM (0.61) L	2:33 PM (1.44) H	8:34 PM (0.29) L
Thu 5	3:29 AM (1.64) H	9:16 AM (0.49) L	3:30 PM (1.50) H	9:23 PM (0.33) L
Fri 6	4:09 AM (1.65) H	10:01 AM (0.40) L	4:22 PM (1.53) H	10:05 PM (0.38) L
Sat 7	4:44 AM (1.64) H	10:41 AM (0.33) L	5:10 PM (1.54) H	10:44 PM (0.45) L
Sun 8	5:15 AM (1.60) H	11:17 AM (0.30) L	5:53 PM (1.53) H	11:20 PM (0.52) L
Mon 9	5:44 AM (1.56) H	11:51 AM (0.29) L	6:33 PM (1.49) H	11:55 PM (0.59) L
Tue 10	6:12 AM (1.50) H	12:24 PM (0.30) L	7:14 PM (1.45) H	
Wed 11	12:30 AM (0.66) L	6:42 AM (1.45) H	12:58 PM (0.33) L	7:56 PM (1.40) H
Thu 12	1:07 AM (0.74) L	7:14 AM (1.39) H	1:34 PM (0.36) L	8:43 PM (1.35) H
Fri 13	1:47 AM (0.81) L	7:51 AM (1.32) H	2:15 PM (0.41) L	9:38 PM (1.31) H
Sat 14	2:34 AM (0.89) L	8:38 AM (1.26) H	3:04 PM (0.45) L	10:42 PM (1.29) H
Sun 15	3:35 AM (0.94) L	9:40 AM (1.20) H	4:08 PM (0.48) L	11:49 PM (1.30) H
Mon 16	4:57 AM (0.95) L	10:57 AM (1.17) H	5:25 PM (0.48) L	
Tue 17	12:51 AM (1.35) H	6:30 AM (0.89) L	12:15 PM (1.19) H	6:37 PM (0.46) L
Wed 18	1:42 AM (1.42) H	7:34 AM (0.78) L	1:23 PM (1.26) H	7:32 PM (0.44) L
Thu 19	2:23 AM (1.49) H	8:16 AM (0.66) L	2:19 PM (1.36) H	8:16 PM (0.42) L
Fri 20	3:01 AM (1.55) H	8:54 AM (0.53) L	3:10 PM (1.46) H	8:58 PM (0.43) L
Sat 21	3:36 AM (1.59) H	9:30 AM (0.41) L	3:56 PM (1.55) H	9:38 PM (0.45) L
Sun 22	4:10 AM (1.60) H	10:05 AM (0.31) L	4:40 PM (1.61) H	10:18 PM (0.48) L
Mon 23	4:44 AM (1.60) H	10:44 AM (0.23) L	5:24 PM (1.63) H	10:59 PM (0.53) L
Tue 24	5:17 AM (1.58) H	11:22 AM (0.19) L	6:09 PM (1.62) H	11:40 PM (0.59) L
Wed 25	5:52 AM (1.55) H	12:02 PM (0.18) L	6:57 PM (1.57) H	
Thu 26	12:20 AM (0.66) L	6:30 AM (1.50) H	12:45 PM (0.20) L	7:50 PM (1.49) H
Fri 27	1:03 AM (0.73) L	7:14 AM (1.44) H	1:30 PM (0.25) L	8:53 PM (1.42) H
Sat 28	1:51 AM (0.80) L	8:07 AM (1.37) H	2:25 PM (0.32) L	10:05 PM (1.37) H

Fort Denison - NSW

DAY/DATE	TIDE 1	TIDE 2	TIDE 3	TIDE 4
Sun 1	2:04 AM (0.47) L	8:38 AM (1.98) H	3:25 PM (0.23) L	9:21 PM (1.43) H
Mon 2	2:57 AM (0.42) L	9:27 AM (2.00) H	4:08 PM (0.22) L	10:05 PM (1.47) H
Tue 3	3:45 AM (0.40) L	10:13 AM (1.96) H	4:47 PM (0.25) L	10:48 PM (1.50) H
Wed 4	4:32 AM (0.42) L	10:55 AM (1.87) H	5:25 PM (0.31) L	11:30 PM (1.51) H
Thu 5	5:18 AM (0.47) L	11:35 AM (1.75) H	5:59 PM (0.38) L	
Fri 6	12:09 AM (1.51) H	6:04 AM (0.54) L	12:13 PM (1.60) H	6:30 PM (0.47) L
Sat 7	12:49 AM (1.50) H	6:51 AM (0.62) L	12:50 PM (1.45) H	7:00 PM (0.55) L
Sun 8	1:30 AM (1.49) H	7:43 AM (0.69) L	1:30 PM (1.32) H	7:33 PM (0.63) L
Mon 9	2:15 AM (1.47) H	8:42 AM (0.75) L	2:19 PM (1.20) H	8:15 PM (0.70) L
Tue 10	3:08 AM (1.46) H	9:55 AM (0.77) L	3:27 PM (1.12) H	9:10 PM (0.75) L
Wed 11	4:11 AM (1.46) H	11:15 AM (0.75) L	4:52 PM (1.10) H	10:21 PM (0.78) L
Thu 12	5:18 AM (1.49) H	12:25 PM (0.68) L	6:13 PM (1.13) H	11:31 PM (0.76) L
Fri 13	6:18 AM (1.55) H	1:18 PM (0.61) L	7:09 PM (1.19) H	
Sat 14	12:30 AM (0.71) L	7:08 AM (1.63) H	2:00 PM (0.53) L	7:51 PM (1.25) H
Sun 15	1:17 AM (0.64) L	7:51 AM (1.71) H	2:36 PM (0.45) L	8:28 PM (1.32) H
Mon 16	2:00 AM (0.57) L	8:30 AM (1.78) H	3:10 PM (0.39) L	9:03 PM (1.39) H
Tue 17	2:39 AM (0.50) L	9:07 AM (1.83) H	3:43 PM (0.34) L	9:38 PM (1.46) H
Wed 18	3:19 AM (0.45) L	9:45 AM (1.85) H	4:15 PM (0.30) L	10:15 PM (1.53) H
Thu 19	4:01 AM (0.42) L	10:23 AM (1.84) H	4:48 PM (0.30) L	10:53 PM (1.59) H
Fri 20	4:46 AM (0.42) L	11:03 AM (1.77) H	5:23 PM (0.32) L	11:33 PM (1.64) H
Sat 21	5:34 AM (0.44) L	11:45 AM (1.67) H	5:59 PM (0.38) L	
Sun 22	12:17 AM (1.67) H	6:27 AM (0.48) L	12:31 PM (1.54) H	6:38 PM (0.46) L
Mon 23	1:04 AM (1.67) H	7:26 AM (0.53) L	1:24 PM (1.40) H	7:22 PM (0.55) L
Tue 24	1:58 AM (1.66) H	8:35 AM (0.58) L	2:28 PM (1.26) H	8:16 PM (0.64) L
Wed 25	3:02 AM (1.64) H	10:00 AM (0.60) L	3:52 PM (1.18) H	9:28 PM (0.70) L
Thu 26	4:18 AM (1.65) H	11:26 AM (0.56) L	5:25 PM (1.18) H	10:50 PM (0.70) L
Fri 27	5:34 AM (1.71) H	12:37 PM (0.48) L	6:38 PM (1.25) H	
Sat 28	12:04 AM (0.64) L	6:40 AM (1.78) H	1:34 PM (0.39) L	7:33 PM (1.35) H

BITE TIMES

Apogee moon phase on Wednesday 11th
Perigee moon phase on Wednesday 25th

New moon on Tuesday 17th
First quarter moon on Tuesday 24th
Full moon on Monday 2nd
Last quarter moon phase on Monday 9th

DAY	MINOR BITE	MAJOR BITE	MINOR BITE	MAJOR BITE	SALT WATER RATING	FRESH WATER RATING
SUN 1	6:21 PM	11:19 PM	3:10 AM	10:50 AM	3	8
MON 2	6:55 PM		4:25 AM	11:45 AM	5	7
TUE 3	7:24 PM	12:12 AM	5:38 AM	12:36 PM	7	6
WED 4	7:49 PM	1:01 AM	6:47 AM	1:23 PM	7	6
THUR 5	8:12 PM	1:46 AM	7:53 AM	2:07 PM	5	5
FRI 6	8:35 PM	2:29 AM	8:56 AM	2:50 PM	4	4
SAT 7	8:58 PM	3:11 AM	9:58 AM	3:32 PM	3	6
SUN 8	9:24 PM	3:54 AM	10:59 AM	4:15 PM	4	4
MON 9	9:54 PM	4:38 AM	12:01 PM	5:00 PM	5	5
TUE 10	10:29 PM	5:24 AM	1:02 PM	5:48 PM	5	5
WED 11	11:11 PM	6:12 AM	2:02 PM	6:37 PM	6	6
THUR 12		7:03 AM	2:58 PM	7:29 PM	7	7
FRI 13		7:55 AM	3:49 PM	8:21 PM	7	8
SAT 14	12:56 AM	8:48 AM	4:33 PM	9:13 PM	5	8

DAY	MINOR BITE	MAJOR BITE	MINOR BITE	MAJOR BITE	SALT WATER RATING	FRESH WATER RATING
SUN 15	1:59 AM	9:39 AM	5:11 PM	10:03 PM	6	7
MON 16	3:04 AM	10:29 AM	5:44 PM	10:52 PM	8	8
TUE 17	4:11 AM	11:17 AM	6:12 PM	11:40 PM	8	8
WED 18	5:18 AM	12:03 PM	6:38 PM		8	6
THUR 19	6:25 AM	12:49 PM	7:02 PM	12:26 AM	7	6
FRI 20	7:32 AM	1:35 PM	7:27 PM	1:11 AM	6	7
SAT 21	8:41 AM	2:22 PM	7:54 PM	1:58 AM	5	5
SUN 22	9:52 AM	3:12 PM	8:24 PM	2:46 AM	4	6
MON 23	11:05 AM	4:06 PM	8:59 PM	3:38 AM	3	5
TUE 24	12:20 PM	5:04 PM	9:43 PM	4:34 AM	4	6
WED 25	1:32 PM	6:05 PM	10:37 PM	5:34 AM	5	6
THUR 26	2:37 PM	7:08 PM	11:41 PM	6:36 AM	4	5
FRI 27	3:32 PM	8:10 PM		7:39 AM	3	5
SAT 28	4:17 PM	9:08 PM	12:52 AM	8:39 AM	6	6

TIDE TIMES

* Additional Tide 5 - See Additional Tide 5

Adelaide Outer Harbour - SA

DAY/DATE	TIDE 5
Sun 15	11:23 PM (1.13) L
Sun 29	11:34 PM (1.12) L

DAY/DATE	TIDE 1	TIDE 2	TIDE 3	TIDE 4
Sun 1	5:35 AM (2.11) H	12:21 PM (0.31) L	6:45 PM (1.88) H	11:57 PM (0.92) L
Mon 2	5:55 AM (2.32) H	12:29 PM (0.25) L	6:41 PM (1.98) H	
Tue 3	12:09 AM (0.70) L	6:12 AM (2.41) H	12:37 PM (0.27) L	6:40 PM (2.07) H
Wed 4	12:21 AM (0.55) L	6:24 AM (2.41) H	12:41 PM (0.30) L	6:41 PM (2.20) H
Thu 5	12:34 AM (0.44) L	6:34 AM (2.38) H	12:45 PM (0.30) L	6:48 PM (2.35) H
Fri 6	12:52 AM (0.38) L	6:48 AM (2.33) H	12:53 PM (0.28) L	7:04 PM (2.50) H
Sat 7	1:15 AM (0.35) L	7:06 AM (2.26) H	1:05 PM (0.26) L	7:25 PM (2.60) H
Sun 8	1:39 AM (0.38) L	7:26 AM (2.18) H	1:20 PM (0.27) L	7:46 PM (2.64) H
Mon 9	2:03 AM (0.43) L	7:45 AM (2.08) H	1:34 PM (0.30) L	8:07 PM (2.63) H
Tue 10	2:25 AM (0.50) L	8:02 AM (1.98) H	1:50 PM (0.34) L	8:26 PM (2.58) H
Wed 11	2:46 AM (0.61) L	8:18 AM (1.86) H	2:04 PM (0.44) L	8:45 PM (2.46) H
Thu 12	3:10 AM (0.78) L	8:29 AM (1.68) H	2:13 PM (0.60) L	9:01 PM (2.24) H
Fri 13	3:33 AM (1.04) L	8:16 AM (1.46) H	1:55 PM (0.80) L	9:01 PM (1.93) H
Sat 14	3:29 AM (1.39) L	5:46 AM (1.41) H	12:32 PM (0.85) L	7:24 PM (1.70) H
Sun 15*	12:01 AM (1.46) L	4:48 AM (1.77) H	11:44 AM (0.63) L	6:17 PM (1.80) H
Mon 16	5:11 AM (2.10) H	11:46 AM (0.41) L	6:07 PM (1.98) H	11:35 PM (0.84) L
Tue 17	5:34 AM (2.32) H	11:59 AM (0.30) L	6:12 PM (2.12) H	11:51 PM (0.63) L
Wed 18	5:53 AM (2.42) H	12:11 PM (0.26) L	6:18 PM (2.24) H	
Thu 19	12:09 AM (0.47) L	6:11 AM (2.44) H	12:21 PM (0.27) L	6:27 PM (2.38) H
Fri 20	12:30 AM (0.36) L	6:28 AM (2.39) H	12:32 PM (0.29) L	6:40 PM (2.52) H
Sat 21	12:54 AM (0.30) L	6:47 AM (2.29) H	12:45 PM (0.33) L	6:59 PM (2.63) H
Sun 22	1:22 AM (0.30) L	7:08 AM (2.14) H	12:57 PM (0.38) L	7:18 PM (2.70) H
Mon 23	1:47 AM (0.38) L	7:25 AM (1.97) H	1:04 PM (0.42) L	7:36 PM (2.72) H
Tue 24	2:08 AM (0.49) L	7:35 AM (1.83) H	1:08 PM (0.41) L	7:51 PM (2.70) H
Wed 25	2:22 AM (0.63) L	7:43 AM (1.73) H	1:16 PM (0.40) L	8:08 PM (2.61) H
Thu 26	2:34 AM (0.79) L	7:45 AM (1.63) H	1:25 PM (0.45) L	8:22 PM (2.42) H
Fri 27	2:44 AM (1.01) L	7:30 AM (1.53) H	1:22 PM (0.59) L	8:21 PM (2.12) H
Sat 28	2:28 AM (1.28) L	6:21 AM (1.51) H	12:43 PM (0.72) L	7:26 PM (1.84) H
Sun 29*	12:42 AM (1.39) L	5:19 AM (1.74) H	11:52 AM (0.67) L	6:21 PM (1.83) H
Mon 30	5:17 AM (2.02) H	11:39 AM (0.53) L	5:57 PM (2.01) H	11:34 PM (0.80) L
Tue 31	5:30 AM (2.20) H	11:44 AM (0.45) L	5:53 PM (2.19) H	11:47 PM (0.58) L

Brisbane Bar - QLD

DAY/DATE	TIDE 1	TIDE 2	TIDE 3	TIDE 4
Sun 1	1:45 AM (0.51) L	8:12 AM (2.54) H	2:58 PM (0.54) L	8:35 PM (1.98) H
Mon 2	2:38 AM (0.42) L	8:57 AM (2.58) H	3:38 PM (0.50) L	9:17 PM (2.08) H
Tue 3	3:24 AM (0.39) L	9:36 AM (2.56) H	4:14 PM (0.48) L	9:57 PM (2.15) H
Wed 4	4:04 AM (0.40) L	10:11 AM (2.50) H	4:44 PM (0.47) L	10:32 PM (2.20) H
Thu 5	4:42 AM (0.46) L	10:44 AM (2.41) H	5:11 PM (0.48) L	11:07 PM (2.24) H
Fri 6	5:17 AM (0.54) L	11:14 AM (2.29) H	5:35 PM (0.49) L	11:41 PM (2.24) H
Sat 7	5:52 AM (0.65) L	11:43 AM (2.14) H	6:00 PM (0.52) L	
Sun 8	12:15 AM (2.22) H	6:28 AM (0.77) L	12:12 PM (1.98) H	6:26 PM (0.58) L
Mon 9	12:50 AM (2.17) H	7:07 AM (0.89) L	12:44 PM (1.81) H	6:56 PM (0.68) L
Tue 10	1:32 AM (2.09) H	7:56 AM (1.00) L	1:25 PM (1.65) H	7:33 PM (0.79) L
Wed 11	2:26 AM (2.01) H	9:06 AM (1.08) L	2:24 PM (1.52) H	8:28 PM (0.89) L
Thu 12	3:42 AM (1.96) H	10:48 AM (1.08) L	3:59 PM (1.47) H	9:49 PM (0.95) L
Fri 13	5:10 AM (2.00) H	12:09 PM (0.99) L	5:33 PM (1.54) H	11:17 PM (0.90) L
Sat 14	6:15 AM (2.11) H	1:03 PM (0.87) L	6:34 PM (1.68) H	
Sun 15	12:27 AM (0.78) L	7:06 AM (2.23) H	1:47 PM (0.75) L	7:21 PM (1.83) H
Mon 16	1:21 AM (0.66) L	7:48 AM (2.35) H	2:27 PM (0.65) L	8:03 PM (1.97) H
Tue 17	2:09 AM (0.55) L	8:28 AM (2.43) H	3:04 PM (0.55) L	8:45 PM (2.11) H
Wed 18	2:55 AM (0.47) L	9:05 AM (2.48) H	3:40 PM (0.47) L	9:26 PM (2.23) H
Thu 19	3:38 AM (0.43) L	9:42 AM (2.47) H	4:15 PM (0.41) L	10:07 PM (2.34) H
Fri 20	4:22 AM (0.43) L	10:17 AM (2.42) H	4:48 PM (0.38) L	10:48 PM (2.42) H
Sat 21	5:05 AM (0.47) L	10:55 AM (2.31) H	5:20 PM (0.39) L	11:30 PM (2.46) H
Sun 22	5:50 AM (0.56) L	11:33 AM (2.15) H	5:52 PM (0.44) L	
Mon 23	12:15 AM (2.45) H	6:39 AM (0.67) L	12:15 PM (1.96) H	6:28 PM (0.52) L
Tue 24	1:03 AM (2.40) H	7:36 AM (0.80) L	1:07 PM (1.77) H	7:12 PM (0.63) L
Wed 25	2:02 AM (2.32) H	8:53 AM (0.89) L	2:18 PM (1.61) H	8:14 PM (0.75) L
Thu 26	3:16 AM (2.25) H	10:25 AM (0.89) L	3:57 PM (1.56) H	9:41 PM (0.82) L
Fri 27	4:41 AM (2.25) H	11:48 AM (0.81) L	5:29 PM (1.66) H	11:15 PM (0.78) L
Sat 28	5:56 AM (2.31) H	12:52 PM (0.70) L	6:37 PM (1.82) H	
Sun 29	12:31 AM (0.68) L	6:56 AM (2.38) H	1:43 PM (0.59) L	7:30 PM (1.99) H
Mon 30	1:32 AM (0.58) L	7:45 AM (2.42) H	2:25 PM (0.53) L	8:15 PM (2.12) H
Tue 31	2:22 AM (0.52) L	8:27 AM (2.41) H	3:01 PM (0.49) L	8:55 PM (2.22) H

Darwin - NT

DAY/DATE	TIDE 1	TIDE 2	TIDE 3	TIDE 4
Sun 1	4:21 AM (5.49) H	11:12 AM (1.98) L	5:45 PM (6.85) H	11:59 PM (3.07) L
Mon 2	5:20 AM (6.12) H	12:00 PM (1.56) L	6:25 PM (7.31) H	
Tue 3	12:35 AM (2.48) L	6:10 AM (6.68) H	12:39 PM (1.30) L	6:58 PM (7.62) H
Wed 4	1:08 AM (1.98) L	6:52 AM (7.08) H	1:12 PM (1.24) L	7:27 PM (7.76) H
Thu 5	1:40 AM (1.60) L	7:30 AM (7.31) H	1:41 PM (1.36) L	7:50 PM (7.75) H
Fri 6	2:09 AM (1.37) L	8:04 AM (7.35) H	2:06 PM (1.64) L	8:10 PM (7.60) H
Sat 7	2:37 AM (1.30) L	8:36 AM (7.24) H	2:27 PM (2.03) L	8:26 PM (7.36) H
Sun 8	3:03 AM (1.37) L	9:06 AM (6.99) H	2:44 PM (2.46) L	8:42 PM (7.03) H
Mon 9	3:29 AM (1.59) L	9:36 AM (6.66) H	2:59 PM (2.93) L	8:59 PM (6.60) H
Tue 10	3:56 AM (1.92) L	10:08 AM (6.25) H	3:14 PM (3.41) L	9:14 PM (6.10) H
Wed 11	4:28 AM (2.35) L	10:46 AM (5.78) H	3:32 PM (3.92) L	9:23 PM (5.57) H
Thu 12	5:11 AM (2.81) L	11:40 AM (5.31) H	3:51 PM (4.44) L	9:19 PM (5.07) H
Fri 13	6:17 AM (3.23) L	1:22 PM (5.00) H	3:17 PM (4.94) L	4:17 PM (4.95) H
Sat 14	8:12 AM (3.36) L	4:40 PM (5.45) H	11:26 PM (4.07) L	
Sun 15	3:47 AM (4.74) H	10:12 AM (3.00) L	5:05 PM (5.95) H	11:30 PM (3.63) L
Mon 16	4:33 AM (5.33) H	11:04 AM (2.50) L	5:33 PM (6.44) H	11:48 PM (3.13) L
Tue 17	5:14 AM (5.94) H	11:44 AM (2.04) L	6:01 PM (6.90) H	
Wed 18	12:15 AM (2.57) L	5:53 AM (6.53) H	12:17 PM (1.69) L	6:30 PM (7.29) H
Thu 19	12:44 AM (1.99) L	6:32 AM (7.05) H	12:48 PM (1.49) L	6:56 PM (7.56) H
Fri 20	1:15 AM (1.45) L	7:11 AM (7.46) H	1:16 PM (1.46) L	7:18 PM (7.69) H
Sat 21	1:46 AM (1.01) L	7:47 AM (7.69) H	1:44 PM (1.60) L	7:40 PM (7.68) H
Sun 22	2:18 AM (0.75) L	8:24 AM (7.73) H	2:12 PM (1.90) L	8:02 PM (7.54) H
Mon 23	2:51 AM (0.72) L	9:01 AM (7.55) H	2:42 PM (2.34) L	8:27 PM (7.24) H
Tue 24	3:27 AM (0.95) L	9:42 AM (7.15) H	3:15 PM (2.89) L	8:54 PM (6.78) H
Wed 25	4:05 AM (1.41) L	10:28 AM (6.59) H	3:52 PM (3.51) L	9:22 PM (6.18) H
Thu 26	4:51 AM (2.03) L	11:26 AM (5.97) H	4:47 PM (4.12) L	9:59 PM (5.48) H
Fri 27	5:58 AM (2.66) L	12:58 PM (5.51) H	7:22 PM (4.43) L	11:42 PM (4.77) H
Sat 28	7:57 AM (3.00) L	3:17 PM (5.68) H	10:04 PM (3.89) L	
Sun 29	3:19 AM (5.07) H	9:53 AM (2.76) L	4:28 PM (6.18) H	10:57 PM (3.18) L
Mon 30	4:27 AM (5.74) H	10:56 AM (2.37) L	5:13 PM (6.64) H	11:35 PM (2.55) L
Tue 31	5:18 AM (6.35) H	11:40 AM (2.06) L	5:48 PM (6.99) H	

Fremantle - WA

DAY/DATE	TIDE 1	TIDE 2	TIDE 3	TIDE 4
Sun 1	4:59 AM (0.48) L	8:35 PM (1.15) H		
Mon 2	5:13 AM (0.53) L	11:39 AM (0.80) H	1:21 PM (0.79) L	9:15 PM (1.11) H
Tue 3	5:01 AM (0.59) L	11:36 AM (0.83) H	2:28 PM (0.77) L	9:47 PM (1.05) H
Wed 4	5:03 AM (0.65) L	11:45 AM (0.88) H	3:31 PM (0.76) L	10:10 PM (0.97) H
Thu 5	4:50 AM (0.69) L	11:53 AM (0.93) H	4:35 PM (0.76) L	10:13 PM (0.89) H
Fri 6	4:17 AM (0.69) L	12:00 PM (0.98) H	5:25 PM (0.77) L	10:15 PM (0.82) H
Sat 7	4:24 AM (0.67) L	11:30 AM (1.03) H	6:13 PM (0.77) L	7:42 PM (0.79) H
Sun 8	4:25 AM (0.66) L	11:35 AM (1.07) H		
Mon 9	3:55 AM (0.64) L	12:00 PM (1.09) H		
Tue 10	3:55 AM (0.62) L	12:31 PM (1.09) H		
Wed 11	2:44 AM (0.61) L	1:08 PM (1.08) H		
Thu 12	2:58 AM (0.59) L	3:36 PM (1.06) H		
Fri 13	3:17 AM (0.57) L	5:00 PM (1.07) H		
Sat 14	3:37 AM (0.56) L	6:32 PM (1.10) H		
Sun 15	3:51 AM (0.57) L	7:27 PM (1.12) H		
Mon 16	4:00 AM (0.58) L	11:34 AM (0.85) H	12:43 PM (0.85) L	8:09 PM (1.12) H
Tue 17	4:07 AM (0.60) L	10:47 AM (0.87) H	1:53 PM (0.81) L	8:50 PM (1.10) H
Wed 18	4:16 AM (0.64) L	10:45 AM (0.91) H	2:56 PM (0.78) L	9:32 PM (1.05) H
Thu 19	4:23 AM (0.68) L	10:58 AM (0.97) H	4:04 PM (0.75) L	10:23 PM (0.97) H
Fri 20	4:11 AM (0.72) L	11:14 AM (1.04) H	5:10 PM (0.72) L	11:54 PM (0.87) H
Sat 21	3:52 AM (0.74) L	11:19 AM (1.10) H	6:24 PM (0.70) L	
Sun 22	12:59 AM (0.78) H	3:39 AM (0.73) L	11:17 AM (1.15) H	11:55 PM (0.66) L
Mon 23	11:36 AM (1.18) H			
Tue 24	12:40 AM (0.58) L	12:01 PM (1.19) H		
Wed 25	1:22 AM (0.53) L	12:33 PM (1.16) H	1:31 PM (1.16) L	2:21 PM (1.16) L
Thu 26	2:02 AM (0.50) L	3:26 PM (1.14) H		
Fri 27	2:40 AM (0.51) L	4:39 PM (1.12) H		
Sat 28	3:15 AM (0.55) L	6:53 PM (1.10) H		
Sun 29	3:40 AM (0.60) L	7:46 PM (1.09) H		
Mon 30	3:44 AM (0.66) L	10:23 AM (0.90) H	2:18 PM (0.86) L	8:30 PM (1.05) H
Tue 31	3:35 AM (0.71) L	10:17 AM (0.95) H	3:17 PM (0.82) L	9:13 PM (1.00) H

Sun Rise & Sun Set Times:

Darwin, NT: Rise: 06:50am Set: 07:00pm

Melbourne, VIC: Rise: 07:10am Set: 07:40pm

Adelaide, SA: Rise: 07:10am Set: 07:30pm

Perth, WA: Rise: 06:10am Set: 06:30pm

Sydney, NSW: Rise: 06:50am Set: 07:10pm

Brisbane, QLD: Rise: 05:40am Set: 06:00pm

Hobart, TAS: Rise: 07:00am Set: 07:30pm

(Note: These times are averages for the month

Hobart - TAS

DAY/DATE	TIDE 1	TIDE 2	TIDE 3	TIDE 4
Sun 1	6:42 AM (1.51) H	2:11 PM (0.29) L	8:39 PM (1.04) H	
Mon 2	12:48 AM (0.83) L	7:37 AM (1.47) H	3:00 PM (0.35) L	9:20 PM (1.05) H
Tue 3	1:58 AM (0.81) L	8:31 AM (1.38) H	3:48 PM (0.42) L	10:05 PM (1.08) H
Wed 4	3:24 AM (0.79) L	9:30 AM (1.28) H	4:32 PM (0.51) L	10:50 PM (1.12) H
Thu 5	4:53 AM (0.74) L	10:39 AM (1.17) H	5:13 PM (0.61) L	11:32 PM (1.17) H
Fri 6	6:07 AM (0.68) L	11:56 AM (1.09) H	5:48 PM (0.71) L	
Sat 7	12:10 AM (1.21) H	7:08 AM (0.62) L	1:02 PM (1.03) H	6:18 PM (0.81) L
Sun 8	12:43 AM (1.25) H	8:00 AM (0.57) L	2:01 PM (1.00) H	6:46 PM (0.88) L
Mon 9	1:14 AM (1.28) H	8:45 AM (0.54) L	3:03 PM (0.99) H	7:22 PM (0.94) L
Tue 10	1:45 AM (1.29) H	9:29 AM (0.51) L	4:29 PM (0.99) H	8:13 PM (0.97) L
Wed 11	2:19 AM (1.31) H	10:11 AM (0.50) L	5:51 PM (1.01) H	9:00 PM (0.98) L
Thu 12	3:00 AM (1.31) H	10:52 AM (0.49) L	6:27 PM (1.02) H	9:43 PM (0.96) L
Fri 13	3:45 AM (1.32) H	11:34 AM (0.48) L	6:53 PM (1.02) H	10:20 PM (0.94) L
Sat 14	4:34 AM (1.34) H	12:15 PM (0.47) L	7:18 PM (1.02) H	10:57 PM (0.91) L
Sun 15	5:24 AM (1.35) H	12:53 PM (0.46) L	7:43 PM (1.03) H	11:36 PM (0.88) L
Mon 16	6:13 AM (1.36) H	1:30 PM (0.46) L	8:08 PM (1.04) H	
Tue 17	12:23 AM (0.85) L	7:00 AM (1.35) H	2:06 PM (0.48) L	8:36 PM (1.07) H
Wed 18	1:19 AM (0.81) L	7:48 AM (1.31) H	2:43 PM (0.52) L	9:09 PM (1.12) H
Thu 19	2:29 AM (0.76) L	8:43 AM (1.26) H	3:20 PM (0.58) L	9:45 PM (1.19) H
Fri 20	3:51 AM (0.69) L	9:52 AM (1.19) H	4:00 PM (0.66) L	10:27 PM (1.26) H
Sat 21	5:12 AM (0.58) L	11:22 AM (1.13) H	4:44 PM (0.76) L	11:13 PM (1.34) H
Sun 22	6:22 AM (0.47) L	12:42 PM (1.11) H	5:37 PM (0.85) L	
Mon 23	12:00 AM (1.41) H	7:24 AM (0.37) L	1:52 PM (1.10) H	6:40 PM (0.92) L
Tue 24	12:50 AM (1.45) H	8:22 AM (0.29) L	3:05 PM (1.10) H	7:43 PM (0.97) L
Wed 25	1:41 AM (1.48) H	9:19 AM (0.26) L	4:29 PM (1.10) H	8:40 PM (0.97) L
Thu 26	2:34 AM (1.48) H	10:15 AM (0.25) L	5:31 PM (1.10) H	9:33 PM (0.95) L
Fri 27	3:32 AM (1.47) H	11:09 AM (0.27) L	6:14 PM (1.10) H	10:25 PM (0.91) L
Sat 28	4:36 AM (1.44) H	12:00 PM (0.32) L	6:50 PM (1.10) H	11:18 PM (0.86) L
Sun 29	5:40 AM (1.41) H	12:48 PM (0.38) L	7:25 PM (1.11) H	
Mon 30	12:16 AM (0.81) L	6:38 AM (1.35) H	1:32 PM (0.45) L	8:00 PM (1.13) H
Tue 31	1:22 AM (0.77) L	7:32 AM (1.28) H	2:14 PM (0.54) L	8:35 PM (1.16) H

Port Phillip Heads - VIC

DAY/DATE	TIDE 1	TIDE 2	TIDE 3	TIDE 4
Sun 1	2:52 AM (0.86) L	9:18 AM (1.30) H	3:36 PM (0.40) L	11:18 PM (1.36) H
Mon 2	4:20 AM (0.86) L	10:50 AM (1.26) H	5:05 PM (0.44) L	
Tue 3	12:27 AM (1.39) H	5:58 AM (0.79) L	12:17 PM (1.30) H	6:26 PM (0.44) L
Wed 4	1:27 AM (1.45) H	7:14 AM (0.66) L	1:30 PM (1.38) H	7:30 PM (0.44) L
Thu 5	2:16 AM (1.52) H	8:10 AM (0.52) L	2:32 PM (1.48) H	8:23 PM (0.44) L
Fri 6	2:59 AM (1.56) H	8:55 AM (0.41) L	3:25 PM (1.56) H	9:08 PM (0.46) L
Sat 7	3:35 AM (1.58) H	9:33 AM (0.33) L	4:10 PM (1.61) H	9:45 PM (0.49) L
Sun 8	4:07 AM (1.57) H	10:08 AM (0.29) L	4:49 PM (1.63) H	10:20 PM (0.53) L
Mon 9	4:36 AM (1.55) H	10:42 AM (0.27) L	5:24 PM (1.61) H	10:54 PM (0.57) L
Tue 10	5:04 AM (1.52) H	11:15 AM (0.27) L	5:57 PM (1.58) H	11:27 PM (0.61) L
Wed 11	5:34 AM (1.49) H	11:46 AM (0.29) L	6:30 PM (1.52) H	
Thu 12	12:00 AM (0.66) L	6:05 AM (1.44) H	12:20 PM (0.33) L	7:07 PM (1.46) H
Fri 13	12:35 AM (0.72) L	6:39 AM (1.39) H	12:54 PM (0.37) L	7:50 PM (1.39) H
Sat 14	1:12 AM (0.78) L	7:15 AM (1.33) H	1:30 PM (0.42) L	8:43 PM (1.33) H
Sun 15	1:52 AM (0.85) L	8:01 AM (1.26) H	2:13 PM (0.48) L	9:45 PM (1.29) H
Mon 16	2:45 AM (0.90) L	9:03 AM (1.20) H	3:07 PM (0.54) L	10:53 PM (1.28) H
Tue 17	3:56 AM (0.90) L	10:25 AM (1.17) H	4:18 PM (0.59) L	11:58 PM (1.31) H
Wed 18	5:30 AM (0.84) L	11:53 AM (1.22) H	5:44 PM (0.60) L	
Thu 19	12:53 AM (1.37) H	6:48 AM (0.71) L	1:06 PM (1.33) H	7:00 PM (0.59) L
Fri 20	1:39 AM (1.44) H	7:34 AM (0.57) L	2:05 PM (1.47) H	7:53 PM (0.57) L
Sat 21	2:21 AM (1.50) H	8:14 AM (0.42) L	2:57 PM (1.60) H	8:37 PM (0.57) L
Sun 22	3:00 AM (1.54) H	8:54 AM (0.30) L	3:43 PM (1.70) H	9:19 PM (0.57) L
Mon 23	3:38 AM (1.57) H	9:34 AM (0.21) L	4:28 PM (1.75) H	10:00 PM (0.58) L
Tue 24	4:15 AM (1.58) H	10:16 AM (0.16) L	5:11 PM (1.75) H	10:42 PM (0.61) L
Wed 25	4:52 AM (1.57) H	11:00 AM (0.16) L	5:56 PM (1.70) H	11:23 PM (0.64) L
Thu 26	5:31 AM (1.54) H	11:44 AM (0.19) L	6:44 PM (1.61) H	
Fri 27	12:04 AM (0.68) L	6:15 AM (1.49) H	12:28 PM (0.25) L	7:36 PM (1.52) H
Sat 28	12:48 AM (0.73) L	7:03 AM (1.42) H	1:15 PM (0.34) L	8:38 PM (1.43) H
Sun 29	1:39 AM (0.78) L	8:04 AM (1.34) H	2:11 PM (0.45) L	9:45 PM (1.38) H
Mon 30	2:45 AM (0.81) L	9:28 AM (1.28) H	3:22 PM (0.55) L	10:52 PM (1.36) H
Tue 31	4:18 AM (0.78) L	11:00 AM (1.28) H	4:48 PM (0.62) L	11:55 PM (1.38) H

Fort Denison - NSW

DAY/DATE	TIDE 1	TIDE 2	TIDE 3	TIDE 4
Sun 1	1:06 AM (0.55) L	7:36 AM (1.85) H	2:21 PM (0.33) L	8:19 PM (1.43) H
Mon 2	2:00 AM (0.47) L	8:25 AM (1.89) H	3:01 PM (0.30) L	9:01 PM (1.51) H
Tue 3	2:47 AM (0.42) L	9:09 AM (1.87) H	3:39 PM (0.30) L	9:41 PM (1.57) H
Wed 4	3:32 AM (0.41) L	9:50 AM (1.82) H	4:12 PM (0.33) L	10:18 PM (1.61) H
Thu 5	4:15 AM (0.42) L	10:29 AM (1.73) H	4:43 PM (0.39) L	10:54 PM (1.63) H
Fri 6	4:58 AM (0.47) L	11:05 AM (1.61) H	5:12 PM (0.46) L	11:29 PM (1.63) H
Sat 7	5:40 AM (0.52) L	11:42 AM (1.49) H	5:39 PM (0.53) L	
Sun 8	12:03 AM (1.62) H	6:23 AM (0.59) L	12:18 PM (1.38) H	6:06 PM (0.61) L
Mon 9	12:40 AM (1.59) H	7:10 AM (0.65) L	12:58 PM (1.28) H	6:38 PM (0.68) L
Tue 10	1:20 AM (1.54) H	8:04 AM (0.71) L	1:46 PM (1.19) H	7:18 PM (0.76) L
Wed 11	2:11 AM (1.49) H	9:12 AM (0.74) L	2:51 PM (1.12) H	8:17 PM (0.82) L
Thu 12	3:15 AM (1.46) H	10:30 AM (0.74) L	4:17 PM (1.11) H	9:37 PM (0.85) L
Fri 13	4:31 AM (1.47) H	11:44 AM (0.70) L	5:42 PM (1.15) H	10:58 PM (0.82) L
Sat 14	5:40 AM (1.52) H	12:39 PM (0.62) L	6:38 PM (1.22) H	
Sun 15	12:02 AM (0.75) L	6:33 AM (1.60) H	1:21 PM (0.54) L	7:19 PM (1.31) H
Mon 16	12:52 AM (0.66) L	7:17 AM (1.68) H	1:57 PM (0.46) L	7:56 PM (1.41) H
Tue 17	1:36 AM (0.57) L	7:57 AM (1.75) H	2:30 PM (0.39) L	8:30 PM (1.51) H
Wed 18	2:19 AM (0.48) L	8:37 AM (1.80) H	3:02 PM (0.34) L	9:07 PM (1.62) H
Thu 19	3:02 AM (0.41) L	9:17 AM (1.80) H	3:36 PM (0.31) L	9:45 PM (1.72) H
Fri 20	3:47 AM (0.37) L	10:00 AM (1.77) H	4:11 PM (0.32) L	10:25 PM (1.80) H
Sat 21	4:36 AM (0.35) L	10:45 AM (1.69) H	4:48 PM (0.37) L	11:07 PM (1.84) H
Sun 22	5:28 AM (0.37) L	11:33 AM (1.58) H	5:28 PM (0.45) L	11:52 PM (1.84) H
Mon 23	6:23 AM (0.42) L	12:25 PM (1.45) H	6:11 PM (0.55) L	
Tue 24	12:43 AM (1.81) H	7:27 AM (0.48) L	1:24 PM (1.32) H	7:01 PM (0.65) L
Wed 25	1:40 AM (1.75) H	8:39 AM (0.54) L	2:35 PM (1.23) H	8:04 PM (0.73) L
Thu 26	2:49 AM (1.70) H	10:00 AM (0.56) L	4:03 PM (1.20) H	9:25 PM (0.77) L
Fri 27	4:09 AM (1.67) H	11:16 AM (0.53) L	5:25 PM (1.25) H	10:49 PM (0.74) L
Sat 28	5:24 AM (1.70) H	12:19 PM (0.49) L	6:27 PM (1.34) H	
Sun 29	12:00 AM (0.67) L	6:26 AM (1.73) H	1:09 PM (0.44) L	7:15 PM (1.44) H
Mon 30	12:59 AM (0.58) L	7:17 AM (1.75) H	1:50 PM (0.41) L	7:57 PM (1.53) H
Tue 31	1:49 AM (0.52) L	8:02 AM (1.74) H	2:27 PM (0.40) L	8:35 PM (1.61) H

BITE TIMES

Apogee moon phase on Tuesday 10th
Perigee moon phase on Sunday 22nd

● **New moon on Thursday 19th**
First quarter moon on Thursday 26th
○ **Full moon on Tuesday 3rd**
Last quarter moon phase on Wednesday 11th

DAY	MINOR BITE	MAJOR BITE	MINOR BITE	MAJOR BITE	SALT WATER RATING	FRESH WATER RATING
SUN 1	4:53 PM	10:02 PM	2:06 AM	9:35 AM	5	7
MON 2	5:23 PM	10:51 PM	3:18 AM	10:26 AM	3	8
TUE 3	5:49 PM	11:37 PM	4:28 AM	11:13 AM	5	7
WED 4	6:13 PM		5:34 AM	11:58 AM	7	6
THUR 5	6:36 PM	12:21 AM	6:39 AM	12:42 PM	7	6
FRI 6	6:59 PM	1:04 AM	7:42 AM	1:24 PM	7	6
SAT 7	7:25 PM	1:46 AM	8:44 AM	2:07 PM	5	5
SUN 8	7:53 PM	2:30 AM	9:46 AM	2:52 PM	4	4
MON 9	8:26 PM	3:16 AM	10:49 AM	3:39 PM	3	6
TUE 10	9:05 PM	4:04 AM	11:50 AM	4:29 PM	4	4
WED 11	9:51 PM	4:54 AM	12:47 PM	5:19 PM	5	5
THUR 12	10:44 PM	5:45 AM	1:40 PM	6:11 PM	6	6
FRI 13	11:43 PM	6:37 AM	2:27 PM	7:03 PM	7	7
SAT 14		7:29 AM	3:07 PM	7:53 PM	7	7
SUN 15	12:47 AM	8:19 AM	3:42 PM	8:43 PM	7	8

DAY	MINOR BITE	MAJOR BITE	MINOR BITE	MAJOR BITE	SALT WATER RATING	FRESH WATER RATING
MON 16	1:52 AM	9:08 AM	4:12 PM	9:31 PM	5	8
TUE 17	2:59 AM	9:55 AM	4:39 PM	10:18 PM	6	7
WED 18	4:07 AM	10:41 AM	5:04 PM	11:03 PM	8	8
THUR 19	5:15 AM	11:27 AM	5:29 PM	11:51 PM	8	8
FRI 20	6:25 AM	12:15 PM	5:55 PM		8	6
SAT 21	7:37 AM	1:06 PM	6:25 PM	12:40 AM	7	6
SUN 22	8:52 AM	2:00 PM	6:59 PM	1:33 AM	6	7
MON 23	10:08 AM	2:58 PM	7:41 PM	2:29 AM	5	5
TUE 24	11:23 AM	3:59 PM	8:33 PM	3:28 AM	4	6
WED 25	12:31 PM	5:02 PM	9:34 PM	4:30 AM	3	5
THUR 26	1:29 PM	6:04 PM	10:43 PM	5:32 AM	4	6
FRI 27	2:16 PM	7:03 PM	11:55 PM	6:33 AM	5	6
SAT 28	2:54 PM	7:57 PM		7:30 AM	4	5
SUN 29	3:26 PM	8:46 PM	1:06 AM	8:21 AM	3	5
MON 30	3:52 PM	9:32 PM	2:15 AM	9:09 AM	6	6
TUE 31	4:16 PM	10:16 PM	3:21 AM	9:54 AM	5	7

TIDE TIMES

* Additional Tide 5 - See Additional Tide 5

Adelaide Outer Harbour - SA

DAY/DATE	TIDE 5
Sun 26	11:33 PM (1.47) L

DAY/DATE	TIDE 1	TIDE 2	TIDE 3	TIDE 4
Wed 1	5:45 AM (2.27) H	11:50 AM (0.43) L	5:56 PM (2.34) H	
Thu 2	12:00 AM (0.45) L	5:58 AM (2.27) H	11:55 AM (0.43) L	6:02 PM (2.48) H
Fri 3	12:15 AM (0.38) L	6:09 AM (2.24) H	12:01 PM (0.41) L	6:14 PM (2.62) H
Sat 4	12:34 AM (0.33) L	6:24 AM (2.20) H	12:13 PM (0.39) L	6:32 PM (2.72) H
Sun 5	12:57 AM (0.33) L	5:45 AM (2.14) H	11:30 AM (0.40) L	5:55 PM (2.75) H
Mon 6	12:22 AM (0.37) L	6:06 AM (2.06) H	11:46 AM (0.43) L	6:17 PM (2.74) H
Tue 7	12:45 AM (0.44) L	6:26 AM (1.97) H	12:03 PM (0.47) L	6:37 PM (2.69) H
Wed 8	1:05 AM (0.53) L	6:43 AM (1.90) H	12:19 PM (0.52) L	6:56 PM (2.62) H
Thu 9	1:25 AM (0.62) L	7:00 AM (1.82) H	12:36 PM (0.59) L	7:15 PM (2.50) H
Fri 10	1:48 AM (0.76) L	7:15 AM (1.69) H	12:50 PM (0.74) L	7:36 PM (2.29) H
Sat 11	2:17 AM (0.99) L	7:24 AM (1.48) H	12:45 PM (0.96) L	7:49 PM (1.98) H
Sun 12	10:48 AM (1.08) L	5:59 PM (1.67) H	10:22 PM (1.54) L	
Mon 13	2:45 AM (1.68) H	9:42 AM (0.84) L	4:21 PM (1.83) H	9:43 PM (1.16) L
Tue 14	3:29 AM (2.00) H	9:52 AM (0.61) L	4:15 PM (2.09) H	10:02 PM (0.82) L
Wed 15	4:00 AM (2.21) H	10:09 AM (0.49) L	4:24 PM (2.31) H	10:26 PM (0.57) L
Thu 16	4:25 AM (2.29) H	10:25 AM (0.46) L	4:35 PM (2.48) H	10:49 PM (0.40) L
Fri 17	4:46 AM (2.26) H	10:37 AM (0.49) L	4:47 PM (2.63) H	11:14 PM (0.31) L
Sat 18	5:07 AM (2.18) H	10:50 AM (0.52) L	5:05 PM (2.76) H	11:41 PM (0.28) L
Sun 19	5:29 AM (2.05) H	11:03 AM (0.55) L	5:27 PM (2.84) H	
Mon 20	12:11 AM (0.33) L	5:50 AM (1.90) H	11:15 AM (0.59) L	5:50 PM (2.84) H
Tue 21	12:38 AM (0.45) L	6:07 AM (1.75) H	11:25 AM (0.61) L	6:11 PM (2.79) H
Wed 22	12:59 AM (0.61) L	6:17 AM (1.65) H	11:34 AM (0.60) L	6:30 PM (2.69) H
Thu 23	1:12 AM (0.76) L	6:27 AM (1.61) H	11:48 AM (0.61) L	6:48 PM (2.55) H
Fri 24	1:22 AM (0.90) L	6:37 AM (1.59) H	12:06 PM (0.69) L	7:07 PM (2.33) H
Sat 25	1:38 AM (1.05) L	6:42 AM (1.51) H	12:16 PM (0.89) L	7:16 PM (2.02) H
Sun 26*	1:53 AM (1.27) L	5:39 AM (1.40) H	11:15 AM (1.12) L	6:03 PM (1.71) H
Mon 27	3:16 AM (1.55) H	9:26 AM (1.05) L	4:05 PM (1.78) H	9:42 PM (1.17) L
Tue 28	3:21 AM (1.80) H	9:25 AM (0.86) L	3:44 PM (2.09) H	9:53 PM (0.84) L
Wed 29	3:45 AM (1.98) H	9:38 AM (0.72) L	3:52 PM (2.36) H	10:14 PM (0.61) L
Thu 30	4:06 AM (2.08) H	9:53 AM (0.65) L	4:07 PM (2.56) H	10:34 PM (0.47) L

Brisbane Bar - QLD

DAY/DATE	TIDE 1	TIDE 2	TIDE 3	TIDE 4
Wed 1	3:05 AM (0.51) L	9:03 AM (2.36) H	3:32 PM (0.47) L	9:30 PM (2.30) H
Thu 2	3:45 AM (0.52) L	9:37 AM (2.29) H	4:00 PM (0.46) L	10:05 PM (2.35) H
Fri 3	4:22 AM (0.57) L	10:08 AM (2.20) H	4:25 PM (0.46) L	10:38 PM (2.38) H
Sat 4	4:58 AM (0.63) L	10:38 AM (2.09) H	4:49 PM (0.48) L	11:10 PM (2.38) H
Sun 5	5:32 AM (0.70) L	11:08 AM (1.97) H	5:15 PM (0.52) L	11:42 PM (2.35) H
Mon 6	6:07 AM (0.78) L	11:39 AM (1.84) H	5:43 PM (0.59) L	
Tue 7	12:16 AM (2.28) H	6:45 AM (0.87) L	12:14 PM (1.72) H	6:14 PM (0.69) L
Wed 8	12:55 AM (2.19) H	7:30 AM (0.96) L	12:55 PM (1.61) H	6:51 PM (0.80) L
Thu 9	1:42 AM (2.10) H	8:31 AM (1.02) L	1:52 PM (1.52) H	7:43 PM (0.90) L
Fri 10	2:45 AM (2.03) H	9:55 AM (1.02) L	3:18 PM (1.51) H	8:58 PM (0.97) L
Sat 11	4:05 AM (2.03) H	11:12 AM (0.95) L	4:49 PM (1.59) H	10:28 PM (0.94) L
Sun 12	5:16 AM (2.10) H	12:09 PM (0.83) L	5:54 PM (1.75) H	11:43 PM (0.84) L
Mon 13	6:13 AM (2.20) H	12:58 PM (0.71) L	6:45 PM (1.93) H	
Tue 14	12:45 AM (0.73) L	7:00 AM (2.29) H	1:41 PM (0.58) L	7:32 PM (2.10) H
Wed 15	1:40 AM (0.62) L	7:44 AM (2.35) H	2:21 PM (0.48) L	8:17 PM (2.27) H
Thu 16	2:31 AM (0.55) L	8:26 AM (2.35) H	3:00 PM (0.40) L	9:00 PM (2.42) H
Fri 17	3:21 AM (0.50) L	9:07 AM (2.31) H	3:36 PM (0.35) L	9:45 PM (2.54) H
Sat 18	4:10 AM (0.48) L	9:50 AM (2.23) H	4:13 PM (0.33) L	10:29 PM (2.62) H
Sun 19	4:59 AM (0.51) L	10:33 AM (2.10) H	4:48 PM (0.36) L	11:14 PM (2.65) H
Mon 20	5:49 AM (0.57) L	11:20 AM (1.96) H	5:26 PM (0.43) L	
Tue 21	12:01 AM (2.61) H	6:45 AM (0.66) L	12:12 PM (1.80) H	6:08 PM (0.53) L
Wed 22	12:54 AM (2.53) H	7:48 AM (0.74) L	1:13 PM (1.68) H	7:00 PM (0.66) L
Thu 23	1:53 AM (2.42) H	9:01 AM (0.79) L	2:30 PM (1.61) H	8:07 PM (0.78) L
Fri 24	3:01 AM (2.33) H	10:13 AM (0.78) L	3:56 PM (1.65) H	9:32 PM (0.84) L
Sat 25	4:15 AM (2.28) H	11:18 AM (0.72) L	5:12 PM (1.78) H	10:58 PM (0.81) L
Sun 26	5:22 AM (2.27) H	12:15 PM (0.64) L	6:14 PM (1.94) H	
Mon 27	12:10 AM (0.75) L	6:19 AM (2.26) H	1:01 PM (0.58) L	7:04 PM (2.10) H
Tue 28	1:09 AM (0.69) L	7:08 AM (2.24) H	1:42 PM (0.52) L	7:48 PM (2.23) H
Wed 29	1:59 AM (0.66) L	7:49 AM (2.19) H	2:16 PM (0.49) L	8:28 PM (2.33) H
Thu 30	2:44 AM (0.64) L	8:27 AM (2.13) H	2:47 PM (0.47) L	9:03 PM (2.40) H

Darwin - NT

DAY/DATE	TIDE 1	TIDE 2	TIDE 3	TIDE 4
Wed 1	12:09 AM (2.02) L	6:01 AM (6.85) H	12:15 PM (1.88) L	6:18 PM (7.22) H
Thu 2	12:39 AM (1.59) L	6:40 AM (7.20) H	12:45 PM (1.84) L	6:42 PM (7.32) H
Fri 3	1:07 AM (1.29) L	7:15 AM (7.39) H	1:13 PM (1.92) L	7:02 PM (7.31) H
Sat 4	1:34 AM (1.11) L	7:46 AM (7.43) H	1:37 PM (2.11) L	7:22 PM (7.21) H
Sun 5	2:00 AM (1.08) L	8:16 AM (7.33) H	2:00 PM (2.36) L	7:42 PM (7.01) H
Mon 6	2:26 AM (1.19) L	8:45 AM (7.13) H	2:21 PM (2.67) L	8:02 PM (6.73) H
Tue 7	2:53 AM (1.44) L	9:13 AM (6.83) H	2:43 PM (3.02) L	8:24 PM (6.35) H
Wed 8	3:23 AM (1.82) L	9:43 AM (6.46) H	3:06 PM (3.40) L	8:45 PM (5.90) H
Thu 9	3:57 AM (2.28) L	10:19 AM (6.02) H	3:33 PM (3.82) L	9:02 PM (5.42) H
Fri 10	4:40 AM (2.76) L	11:07 AM (5.58) H	4:29 PM (4.24) L	9:19 PM (4.94) H
Sat 11	5:41 AM (3.18) L	12:21 PM (5.24) H	7:22 PM (4.42) L	11:04 PM (4.47) H
Sun 12	7:12 AM (3.39) L	2:39 PM (5.29) H	10:00 PM (3.96) L	
Mon 13	3:06 AM (4.75) H	9:05 AM (3.23) L	3:55 PM (5.73) H	10:29 PM (3.41) L
Tue 14	4:01 AM (5.37) H	10:15 AM (2.83) L	4:33 PM (6.19) H	11:00 PM (2.79) L
Wed 15	4:46 AM (6.03) H	11:02 AM (2.44) L	5:06 PM (6.62) H	11:32 PM (2.13) L
Thu 16	5:30 AM (6.68) H	11:42 AM (2.14) L	5:37 PM (6.98) H	
Fri 17	12:06 AM (1.48) L	6:14 AM (7.24) H	12:16 PM (1.97) L	6:05 PM (7.23) H
Sat 18	12:41 AM (0.92) L	6:55 AM (7.66) H	12:49 PM (1.94) L	6:31 PM (7.37) H
Sun 19	1:15 AM (0.53) L	7:35 AM (7.86) H	1:21 PM (2.04) L	7:00 PM (7.38) H
Mon 20	1:50 AM (0.38) L	8:14 AM (7.84) H	1:54 PM (2.28) L	7:30 PM (7.24) H
Tue 21	2:29 AM (0.49) L	8:54 AM (7.59) H	2:30 PM (2.63) L	8:03 PM (6.91) H
Wed 22	3:09 AM (0.87) L	9:36 AM (7.16) H	3:11 PM (3.06) L	8:40 PM (6.42) H
Thu 23	3:53 AM (1.46) L	10:24 AM (6.62) H	4:01 PM (3.53) L	9:23 PM (5.80) H
Fri 24	4:46 AM (2.14) L	11:23 AM (6.09) H	5:27 PM (3.90) L	10:32 PM (5.14) H
Sat 25	5:59 AM (2.75) L	12:42 PM (5.73) H	7:35 PM (3.83) L	
Sun 26	1:15 AM (4.88) H	7:36 AM (3.08) L	2:15 PM (5.73) H	9:15 PM (3.31) L
Mon 27	3:01 AM (5.31) H	9:13 AM (3.05) L	3:29 PM (5.97) H	10:14 PM (2.72) L
Tue 28	4:05 AM (5.85) H	10:19 AM (2.86) L	4:19 PM (6.25) H	10:57 PM (2.20) L
Wed 29	4:57 AM (6.34) H	11:06 AM (2.68) L	4:57 PM (6.47) H	11:32 PM (1.78) L
Thu 30	5:41 AM (6.75) H	11:45 AM (2.56) L	5:27 PM (6.61) H	

Fremantle - WA

DAY/DATE	TIDE 5
Sun 5	11:48 PM (0.73) L
Mon 6	10:50 PM (0.71) H

DAY/DATE	TIDE 1	TIDE 2	TIDE 3	TIDE 4
Wed 1	3:36 AM (0.75) L	10:24 AM (1.00) H	4:03 PM (0.78) L	9:56 PM (0.95) H
Thu 2	2:55 AM (0.77) L	10:24 AM (1.06) H	4:45 PM (0.76) L	10:47 PM (0.88) H
Fri 3	2:51 AM (0.76) L	10:14 AM (1.11) H	5:24 PM (0.75) L	11:38 PM (0.83) H
Sat 4	3:04 AM (0.76) L	10:15 AM (1.15) H	7:55 PM (0.73) L	10:29 PM (0.77) H
Sun 5*	3:03 AM (0.75) L	10:30 AM (1.18) H	8:49 PM (0.72) L	10:36 PM (0.74) H
Mon 6*	1:09 AM (0.74) H	2:35 AM (0.73) L	10:55 AM (1.20) H	9:39 PM (0.70) L
Tue 7	12:26 AM (0.70) L	1:59 AM (0.71) H	2:36 AM (0.71) L	11:23 AM (1.19) H
Wed 8	1:01 AM (0.68) L	11:54 AM (1.18) H		
Thu 9	1:31 AM (0.66) L	12:28 PM (1.15) H		
Fri 10	1:59 AM (0.65) L	1:07 PM (1.12) H		
Sat 11	2:21 AM (0.65) L	3:45 PM (1.10) H		
Sun 12	2:36 AM (0.66) L	5:15 PM (1.09) H		
Mon 13	2:42 AM (0.68) L	10:54 AM (0.95) H	12:04 PM (0.95) L	6:49 PM (1.08) H
Tue 14	2:45 AM (0.71) L	9:27 AM (0.97) H	1:31 PM (0.90) L	7:53 PM (1.06) H
Wed 15	2:48 AM (0.75) L	9:16 AM (1.03) H	2:55 PM (0.83) L	9:00 PM (1.01) H
Thu 16	2:47 AM (0.79) L	9:24 AM (1.10) H	3:59 PM (0.76) L	10:23 PM (0.95) H
Fri 17	2:33 AM (0.82) L	9:36 AM (1.17) H	5:00 PM (0.70) L	11:31 PM (0.89) H
Sat 18	2:20 AM (0.83) L	9:52 AM (1.24) H	6:40 PM (0.65) L	
Sun 19	12:37 AM (0.82) H	1:57 AM (0.81) L	10:12 AM (1.29) H	8:09 PM (0.60) L
Mon 20	10:37 AM (1.31) H	9:15 PM (0.58) L		
Tue 21	11:05 AM (1.30) H	11:56 PM (0.56) L		
Wed 22	11:34 AM (1.27) H			
Thu 23	12:45 AM (0.56) L	12:04 PM (1.21) H		
Fri 24	1:28 AM (0.59) L	12:35 PM (1.14) H	1:28 PM (1.14) L	2:56 PM (1.15) H
Sat 25	2:03 AM (0.65) L	3:56 PM (1.09) H		
Sun 26	2:30 AM (0.71) L	10:33 AM (1.00) H	11:56 AM (0.99) L	6:14 PM (1.03) H
Mon 27	2:30 AM (0.78) L	9:07 AM (1.01) H	2:24 PM (0.93) L	7:30 PM (0.99) H
Tue 28	2:04 AM (0.83) L	8:55 AM (1.06) H	3:04 PM (0.88) L	8:44 PM (0.95) H
Wed 29	1:41 AM (0.85) L	8:53 AM (1.12) H	3:46 PM (0.83) L	9:53 PM (0.91) H
Thu 30	1:05 AM (0.85) L	8:46 AM (1.18) H	4:32 PM (0.78) L	10:45 PM (0.88) H

* Additional Tide 5 - See Additional Tide 5

Sun Rise & Sun Set Times:

Darwin, NT: Rise: 06:50am Set: 06:40pm

***Melbourne, VIC:** Rise: 06:40am Set: 05:50pm

***Adelaide, SA:** Rise: 06:30am Set: 05:50pm

Perth, WA: Rise: 06:30am Set: 05:50pm

***Sydney, NSW:** Rise: 06:17am Set: 05:32pm

Brisbane, QLD: Rise: 06:00am Set: 05:30pm

Hobart, TAS: Rise: 06:40am Set: 05:30pm

(Note: These times are averages for the month)

*Note: Daylight Savings ends (clocks turn backward 1 hour) on Sunday, April 7th at 3:00 AM for states marked * Add 1 hour to rise/set time for days before April 7th*

Hobart - TAS

DAY/DATE	TIDE 1	TIDE 2	TIDE 3	TIDE 4
Wed 1	2:34 AM (0.73) L	8:29 AM (1.19) H	2:50 PM (0.64) L	9:10 PM (1.20) H
Thu 2	3:47 AM (0.68) L	9:36 AM (1.10) H	3:21 PM (0.74) L	9:45 PM (1.23) H
Fri 3	4:53 AM (0.62) L	10:58 AM (1.05) H	3:45 PM (0.84) L	10:16 PM (1.26) H
Sat 4	5:48 AM (0.57) L	12:09 PM (1.03) H	4:03 PM (0.92) L	10:48 PM (1.29) H
Sun 5	5:35 AM (0.53) L	12:12 PM (1.04) H	3:17 PM (0.98) L	10:19 PM (1.31) H
Mon 6	6:18 AM (0.50) L	1:11 PM (1.05) H	3:38 PM (1.03) L	10:54 PM (1.31) H
Tue 7	7:00 AM (0.49) L	2:21 PM (1.06) H	5:14 PM (1.06) L	11:35 PM (1.32) H
Wed 8	7:41 AM (0.48) L	3:40 PM (1.07) H	6:41 PM (1.06) L	
Thu 9	12:20 AM (1.31) H	8:23 AM (0.49) L	4:15 PM (1.08) H	7:32 PM (1.04) L
Fri 10	1:09 AM (1.30) H	9:05 AM (0.49) L	4:38 PM (1.08) H	8:18 PM (1.01) L
Sat 11	2:00 AM (1.30) H	9:45 AM (0.49) L	5:00 PM (1.08) H	9:02 PM (0.97) L
Sun 12	2:52 AM (1.30) H	10:21 AM (0.49) L	5:21 PM (1.10) H	9:47 PM (0.93) L
Mon 13	3:47 AM (1.29) H	10:55 AM (0.50) L	5:45 PM (1.13) H	10:37 PM (0.87) L
Tue 14	4:43 AM (1.28) H	11:27 AM (0.53) L	6:11 PM (1.17) H	11:33 PM (0.80) L
Wed 15	5:38 AM (1.25) H	12:00 PM (0.58) L	6:40 PM (1.24) H	
Thu 16	12:36 AM (0.72) L	6:38 AM (1.21) H	12:33 PM (0.66) L	7:13 PM (1.31) H
Fri 17	1:47 AM (0.61) L	7:48 AM (1.16) H	1:10 PM (0.76) L	7:50 PM (1.39) H
Sat 18	2:59 AM (0.49) L	9:18 AM (1.12) H	1:53 PM (0.86) L	8:33 PM (1.47) H
Sun 19	4:05 AM (0.37) L	10:44 AM (1.13) H	2:49 PM (0.96) L	9:23 PM (1.52) H
Mon 20	5:07 AM (0.27) L	11:58 AM (1.15) H	4:10 PM (1.03) L	10:18 PM (1.55) H
Tue 21	6:06 AM (0.21) L	1:08 PM (1.17) H	5:28 PM (1.05) L	11:17 PM (1.56) H
Wed 22	7:03 AM (0.19) L	2:17 PM (1.18) H	6:32 PM (1.04) L	
Thu 23	12:16 AM (1.53) H	8:00 AM (0.22) L	3:15 PM (1.18) H	7:32 PM (1.01) L
Fri 24	1:17 AM (1.48) H	8:55 AM (0.27) L	4:00 PM (1.18) H	8:33 PM (0.96) L
Sat 25	2:23 AM (1.42) H	9:45 AM (0.35) L	4:38 PM (1.18) H	9:36 PM (0.90) L
Sun 26	3:31 AM (1.34) H	10:30 AM (0.43) L	5:13 PM (1.20) H	10:42 PM (0.83) L
Mon 27	4:36 AM (1.27) H	11:09 AM (0.53) L	5:45 PM (1.23) H	11:48 PM (0.77) L
Tue 28	5:34 AM (1.19) H	11:40 AM (0.63) L	6:16 PM (1.27) H	
Wed 29	12:52 AM (0.71) L	6:33 AM (1.11) H	12:02 PM (0.73) L	6:46 PM (1.31) H
Thu 30	1:53 AM (0.65) L	7:40 AM (1.05) H	12:17 PM (0.83) L	7:14 PM (1.34) H

Port Phillip Heads - VIC

DAY/DATE	TIDE 1	TIDE 2	TIDE 3	TIDE 4
Wed 1	5:46 AM (0.69) L	12:21 PM (1.35) H	6:09 PM (0.64) L	
Thu 2	12:51 AM (1.42) H	6:51 AM (0.57) L	1:29 PM (1.46) H	7:15 PM (0.64) L
Fri 3	1:40 AM (1.46) H	7:40 AM (0.46) L	2:24 PM (1.57) H	8:05 PM (0.63) L
Sat 4	2:20 AM (1.49) H	8:20 AM (0.38) L	3:10 PM (1.65) H	8:46 PM (0.63) L
Sun 5	2:56 AM (1.51) H	7:56 AM (0.33) L	2:48 PM (1.69) H	8:21 PM (0.64) L
Mon 6	2:28 AM (1.51) H	8:30 AM (0.31) L	3:22 PM (1.70) H	8:54 PM (0.65) L
Tue 7	2:58 AM (1.51) H	9:04 AM (0.30) L	3:53 PM (1.69) H	9:27 PM (0.66) L
Wed 8	3:29 AM (1.50) H	9:38 AM (0.32) L	4:23 PM (1.65) H	10:00 PM (0.68) L
Thu 9	4:01 AM (1.47) H	10:12 AM (0.35) L	4:56 PM (1.60) H	10:32 PM (0.71) L
Fri 10	4:35 AM (1.44) H	10:45 AM (0.38) L	5:32 PM (1.53) H	11:06 PM (0.75) L
Sat 11	5:10 AM (1.39) H	11:16 AM (0.43) L	6:13 PM (1.47) H	11:41 PM (0.79) L
Sun 12	5:49 AM (1.33) H	11:49 AM (0.49) L	7:00 PM (1.41) H	
Mon 13	12:19 AM (0.82) L	6:38 AM (1.27) H	12:30 PM (0.56) L	7:55 PM (1.36) H
Tue 14	1:07 AM (0.84) L	7:43 AM (1.23) H	1:21 PM (0.64) L	8:56 PM (1.34) H
Wed 15	2:10 AM (0.82) L	9:05 AM (1.24) H	2:29 PM (0.72) L	9:57 PM (1.34) H
Thu 16	3:25 AM (0.74) L	10:32 AM (1.32) H	3:49 PM (0.77) L	10:55 PM (1.38) H
Fri 17	4:40 AM (0.62) L	11:45 AM (1.46) H	5:15 PM (0.78) L	11:47 PM (1.42) H
Sat 18	5:39 AM (0.48) L	12:45 PM (1.61) H	6:21 PM (0.76) L	
Sun 19	12:36 AM (1.48) H	6:29 AM (0.34) L	1:37 PM (1.74) H	7:11 PM (0.74) L
Mon 20	1:21 AM (1.52) H	7:16 AM (0.24) L	2:26 PM (1.82) H	7:56 PM (0.72) L
Tue 21	2:05 AM (1.56) H	8:04 AM (0.19) L	3:12 PM (1.84) H	8:39 PM (0.70) L
Wed 22	2:48 AM (1.58) H	8:51 AM (0.17) L	3:58 PM (1.81) H	9:22 PM (0.70) L
Thu 23	3:31 AM (1.57) H	9:39 AM (0.20) L	4:45 PM (1.74) H	10:06 PM (0.70) L
Fri 24	4:17 AM (1.54) H	10:27 AM (0.27) L	5:33 PM (1.66) H	10:51 PM (0.71) L
Sat 25	5:06 AM (1.49) H	11:15 AM (0.36) L	6:26 PM (1.57) H	11:41 PM (0.73) L
Sun 26	6:03 AM (1.41) H	12:04 PM (0.48) L	7:23 PM (1.50) H	
Mon 27	12:37 AM (0.74) L	7:16 AM (1.35) H	1:00 PM (0.60) L	8:21 PM (1.44) H
Tue 28	1:49 AM (0.73) L	8:45 AM (1.33) H	2:04 PM (0.71) L	9:18 PM (1.41) H
Wed 29	3:08 AM (0.69) L	10:04 AM (1.37) H	3:20 PM (0.80) L	10:15 PM (1.40) H
Thu 30	4:18 AM (0.62) L	11:14 AM (1.45) H	4:39 PM (0.84) L	11:07 PM (1.41) H

Fort Denison - NSW

DAY/DATE	TIDE 1	TIDE 2	TIDE 3	TIDE 4
Wed 1	2:35 AM (0.48) L	8:44 AM (1.71) H	3:00 PM (0.42) L	9:12 PM (1.68) H
Thu 2	3:17 AM (0.46) L	9:23 AM (1.64) H	3:30 PM (0.45) L	9:45 PM (1.72) H
Fri 3	3:59 AM (0.47) L	10:00 AM (1.57) H	3:58 PM (0.50) L	10:18 PM (1.74) H
Sat 4	4:38 AM (0.49) L	10:37 AM (1.49) H	4:25 PM (0.56) L	10:51 PM (1.74) H
Sun 5	4:18 AM (0.53) L	10:15 AM (1.41) H	3:53 PM (0.62) L	10:24 PM (1.72) H
Mon 6	5:00 AM (0.57) L	10:53 AM (1.33) H	4:23 PM (0.68) L	10:59 PM (1.68) H
Tue 7	5:44 AM (0.62) L	11:35 AM (1.26) H	4:59 PM (0.75) L	11:39 PM (1.62) H
Wed 8	6:35 AM (0.68) L	12:24 PM (1.21) H	5:42 PM (0.81) L	
Thu 9	12:28 AM (1.56) H	7:35 AM (0.72) L	1:24 PM (1.17) H	6:39 PM (0.86) L
Fri 10	1:28 AM (1.51) H	8:45 AM (0.72) L	2:39 PM (1.16) H	7:54 PM (0.88) L
Sat 11	2:40 AM (1.50) H	9:50 AM (0.69) L	3:55 PM (1.21) H	9:15 PM (0.86) L
Sun 12	3:49 AM (1.53) H	10:44 AM (0.63) L	4:52 PM (1.29) H	10:23 PM (0.79) L
Mon 13	4:45 AM (1.59) H	11:27 AM (0.55) L	5:36 PM (1.40) H	11:19 PM (0.70) L
Tue 14	5:34 AM (1.66) H	12:05 PM (0.48) L	6:15 PM (1.53) H	
Wed 15	12:09 AM (0.59) L	6:18 AM (1.70) H	12:42 PM (0.42) L	6:54 PM (1.67) H

DAY/DATE	TIDE 1	TIDE 2	TIDE 3	TIDE 4
Thu 16	12:57 AM (0.49) L	7:03 AM (1.73) H	1:17 PM (0.38) L	7:33 PM (1.80) H
Fri 17	1:45 AM (0.40) L	7:50 AM (1.71) H	1:56 PM (0.38) L	8:15 PM (1.91) H
Sat 18	2:34 AM (0.34) L	8:39 AM (1.66) H	2:35 PM (0.41) L	8:59 PM (1.98) H
Sun 19	3:27 AM (0.32) L	9:30 AM (1.59) H	3:17 PM (0.46) L	9:45 PM (2.01) H
Mon 20	4:22 AM (0.33) L	10:25 AM (1.49) H	4:03 PM (0.54) L	10:35 PM (1.99) H
Tue 21	5:22 AM (0.37) L	11:23 AM (1.40) H	4:55 PM (0.63) L	11:29 PM (1.93) H
Wed 22	6:27 AM (0.44) L	12:28 PM (1.32) H	5:53 PM (0.71) L	
Thu 23	12:30 AM (1.84) H	7:37 AM (0.49) L	1:40 PM (1.28) H	7:01 PM (0.77) L
Fri 24	1:39 AM (1.75) H	8:48 AM (0.52) L	2:56 PM (1.29) H	8:19 PM (0.79) L
Sat 25	2:53 AM (1.69) H	9:51 AM (0.53) L	4:03 PM (1.35) H	9:37 PM (0.76) L
Sun 26	4:01 AM (1.66) H	10:45 AM (0.53) L	4:59 PM (1.44) H	10:45 PM (0.71) L
Mon 27	5:00 AM (1.64) H	11:30 AM (0.52) L	5:46 PM (1.54) H	11:45 PM (0.65) L
Tue 28	5:49 AM (1.61) H	12:08 PM (0.51) L	6:28 PM (1.63) H	
Wed 29	12:36 AM (0.60) L	6:34 AM (1.58) H	12:43 PM (0.52) L	7:05 PM (1.70) H
Thu 30	1:20 AM (0.56) L	7:15 AM (1.53) H	1:14 PM (0.54) L	7:40 PM (1.76) H

BITE TIMES

Apogee moon phase on Tuesday 7th
Perigee moon phase on Sunday 19th

New moon on Friday 17th
First quarter moon on Friday 24th
Full moon on Thursday 2nd
Last quarter moon phase on Friday 10th

DAY	MINOR BITE	MAJOR BITE	MINOR BITE	MAJOR BITE	SALT WATER RATING	FRESH WATER RATING
WED 1	4:39 PM	10:58 PM	4:26 AM	10:37 AM	3	8
THUR 2	5:02 PM	11:41 PM	5:28 AM	11:19 AM	5	7
FRI 3	5:26 PM		6:30 AM	12:02 PM	7	6
SAT 4	5:53 PM	12:24 AM	7:33 AM	12:46 PM	7	6
SUN 5	6:25 PM	1:09 AM	8:35 AM	1:33 PM	5	5
MON 6	7:01 PM	1:57 AM	9:37 AM	2:21 PM	5	5
TUE 7	7:44 PM	2:46 AM	10:36 AM	3:11 PM	4	4
WED 8	8:34 PM	3:37 AM	11:31 AM	4:02 PM	3	6
THUR 9	9:30 PM	4:28 AM	12:20 PM	4:53 PM	4	4
FRI 10	10:31 PM	5:20 AM	1:03 PM	5:44 PM	5	5
SAT 11	11:35 PM	6:09 AM	1:39 PM	6:33 PM	6	6
SUN 12		6:58 AM	2:10 PM	7:21 PM	7	7
MON 13	12:40 AM	7:44 AM	2:38 PM	8:07 PM	7	8
TUE 14	1:46 AM	8:30 AM	3:03 PM	8:52 PM	5	8
WED 15	2:53 AM	9:16 AM	3:28 PM	9:39 PM	6	7

DAY	MINOR BITE	MAJOR BITE	MINOR BITE	MAJOR BITE	SALT WATER RATING	FRESH WATER RATING
THUR 16	4:02 AM	10:03 AM	3:54 PM	10:27 PM	8	8
FRI 17	5:14 AM	10:53 AM	4:22 PM	11:19 PM	8	8
SAT 18	6:29 AM	11:47 AM	4:55 PM		8	6
SUN 19	7:47 AM	12:45 PM	5:35 PM	12:16 AM	7	6
MON 20	9:06 AM	1:47 PM	6:25 PM	1:15 AM	6	7
TUE 21	10:19 AM	2:52 PM	7:24 PM	2:19 AM	5	5
WED 22	11:23 AM	3:56 PM	8:33 PM	3:23 AM	4	6
THUR 23	12:14 PM	4:57 PM	9:46 PM	4:26 AM	3	5
FRI 24	12:56 PM	5:53 PM	10:58 PM	5:25 AM	4	6
SAT 25	1:29 PM	6:44 PM		6:18 AM	5	6
SUN 26	1:56 PM	7:31 PM	12:08 AM	7:07 AM	4	5
MON 27	2:21 PM	8:14 PM	1:14 AM	7:52 AM	3	5
TUE 28	2:44 PM	8:57 PM	2:18 AM	8:35 AM	6	6
WED 29	3:06 PM	9:38 PM	3:20 AM	9:17 AM	5	7
THUR 30	3:30 PM	10:21 PM	4:21 AM	9:59 AM	5	7

TIDE TIMES

Adelaide Outer Harbour - SA

DAY/DATE	TIDE 1	TIDE 2	TIDE 3	TIDE 4
Fri 1	4:26 AM (2.11) H	10:06 AM (0.61) L	4:23 PM (2.70) H	10:55 PM (0.39) L
Sat 2	4:45 AM (2.10) H	10:21 AM (0.59) L	4:43 PM (2.79) H	11:17 PM (0.37) L
Sun 3	5:06 AM (2.07) H	10:41 AM (0.58) L	5:06 PM (2.84) H	11:44 PM (0.38) L
Mon 4	5:31 AM (2.03) H	11:03 AM (0.60) L	5:32 PM (2.83) H	
Tue 5	12:11 AM (0.42) L	5:57 AM (1.97) H	11:26 AM (0.64) L	5:59 PM (2.78) H
Wed 6	12:37 AM (0.50) L	6:21 AM (1.91) H	11:47 AM (0.68) L	6:22 PM (2.71) H
Thu 7	1:00 AM (0.58) L	6:42 AM (1.85) H	12:08 PM (0.73) L	6:45 PM (2.62) H
Fri 8	1:25 AM (0.66) L	7:05 AM (1.80) H	12:31 PM (0.81) L	7:10 PM (2.50) H
Sat 9	1:55 AM (0.77) L	7:35 AM (1.71) H	12:58 PM (0.95) L	7:41 PM (2.31) H
Sun 10	2:41 AM (0.92) L	8:27 AM (1.57) H	1:29 PM (1.18) L	8:28 PM (2.03) H
Mon 11	4:28 AM (1.09) L	12:30 PM (1.51) H	2:20 PM (1.50) L	11:23 PM (1.74) H
Tue 12	7:19 AM (1.03) L	2:25 PM (1.85) H	8:26 PM (1.22) L	
Wed 13	2:06 AM (1.86) H	8:26 AM (0.86) L	2:58 PM (2.18) H	9:16 PM (0.85) L
Thu 14	3:11 AM (2.01) H	9:04 AM (0.77) L	3:25 PM (2.44) H	9:55 PM (0.58) L
Fri 15	3:54 AM (2.07) H	9:32 AM (0.75) L	3:49 PM (2.64) H	10:30 PM (0.41) L
Sat 16	4:27 AM (2.03) H	9:54 AM (0.77) L	4:13 PM (2.78) H	11:02 PM (0.34) L
Sun 17	4:55 AM (1.93) H	10:13 AM (0.79) L	4:39 PM (2.88) H	11:36 PM (0.35) L
Mon 18	5:21 AM (1.81) H	10:32 AM (0.80) L	5:07 PM (2.91) H	
Tue 19	12:10 AM (0.42) L	5:46 AM (1.71) H	10:52 AM (0.81) L	5:37 PM (2.87) H
Wed 20	12:42 AM (0.55) L	6:08 AM (1.63) H	11:11 AM (0.81) L	6:05 PM (2.77) H
Thu 21	1:07 AM (0.70) L	6:26 AM (1.60) H	11:31 AM (0.82) L	6:30 PM (2.63) H
Fri 22	1:25 AM (0.82) L	6:46 AM (1.62) H	11:58 AM (0.85) L	6:56 PM (2.47) H
Sat 23	1:42 AM (0.90) L	7:16 AM (1.66) H	12:34 PM (0.95) L	7:26 PM (2.27) H
Sun 24	2:09 AM (0.97) L	8:07 AM (1.67) H	1:22 PM (1.15) L	8:05 PM (2.01) H
Mon 25	3:00 AM (1.07) L	9:56 AM (1.66) H	3:01 PM (1.42) L	9:30 PM (1.70) H
Tue 26	5:04 AM (1.15) L	12:44 PM (1.86) H	7:57 PM (1.30) L	
Wed 27	12:56 AM (1.60) H	7:11 AM (1.09) L	2:00 PM (2.16) H	9:00 PM (0.99) L
Thu 28	2:33 AM (1.73) H	8:13 AM (0.97) L	2:47 PM (2.42) H	9:38 PM (0.74) L
Fri 29	3:25 AM (1.86) H	8:55 AM (0.89) L	3:23 PM (2.62) H	10:11 PM (0.57) L
Sat 30	4:02 AM (1.93) H	9:27 AM (0.84) L	3:54 PM (2.74) H	10:41 PM (0.48) L
Sun 31	4:33 AM (1.96) H	9:56 AM (0.81) L	4:23 PM (2.81) H	11:10 PM (0.45) L

Brisbane Bar - QLD

DAY/DATE	TIDE 1	TIDE 2	TIDE 3	TIDE 4
Fri 1	3:25 AM (0.64) L	9:01 AM (2.06) H	3:15 PM (0.46) L	9:38 PM (2.45) H
Sat 2	4:03 AM (0.66) L	9:35 AM (1.98) H	3:43 PM (0.46) L	10:11 PM (2.46) H
Sun 3	4:40 AM (0.68) L	10:07 AM (1.91) H	4:11 PM (0.49) L	10:43 PM (2.45) H
Mon 4	5:15 AM (0.73) L	10:41 AM (1.83) H	4:40 PM (0.53) L	11:15 PM (2.41) H
Tue 5	5:50 AM (0.78) L	11:15 AM (1.76) H	5:11 PM (0.60) L	11:50 PM (2.34) H
Wed 6	6:28 AM (0.84) L	11:52 AM (1.69) H	5:45 PM (0.68) L	
Thu 7	12:29 AM (2.27) H	7:11 AM (0.89) L	12:36 PM (1.63) H	6:25 PM (0.77) L
Fri 8	1:13 AM (2.20) H	8:05 AM (0.92) L	1:31 PM (1.59) H	7:15 PM (0.85) L
Sat 9	2:06 AM (2.14) H	9:08 AM (0.91) L	2:44 PM (1.60) H	8:22 PM (0.91) L
Sun 10	3:09 AM (2.12) H	10:12 AM (0.85) L	4:01 PM (1.68) H	9:41 PM (0.92) L
Mon 11	4:15 AM (2.14) H	11:10 AM (0.75) L	5:11 PM (1.83) H	10:57 PM (0.87) L
Tue 12	5:15 AM (2.18) H	12:01 PM (0.63) L	6:08 PM (2.02) H	
Wed 13	12:06 AM (0.79) L	6:09 AM (2.20) H	12:49 PM (0.52) L	7:00 PM (2.22) H
Thu 14	1:10 AM (0.70) L	7:00 AM (2.20) H	1:35 PM (0.43) L	7:49 PM (2.40) H
Fri 15	2:09 AM (0.62) L	7:49 AM (2.17) H	2:18 PM (0.36) L	8:37 PM (2.56) H
Sat 16	3:05 AM (0.56) L	8:38 AM (2.10) H	3:00 PM (0.32) L	9:24 PM (2.68) H
Sun 17	4:00 AM (0.52) L	9:29 AM (2.02) H	3:43 PM (0.32) L	10:13 PM (2.75) H
Mon 18	4:55 AM (0.52) L	10:20 AM (1.93) H	4:25 PM (0.35) L	11:01 PM (2.75) H
Tue 19	5:50 AM (0.54) L	11:15 AM (1.85) H	5:10 PM (0.41) L	11:52 PM (2.70) H
Wed 20	6:47 AM (0.59) L	12:12 PM (1.77) H	5:59 PM (0.51) L	
Thu 21	12:44 AM (2.61) H	7:46 AM (0.64) L	1:14 PM (1.72) H	6:54 PM (0.63) L
Fri 22	1:38 AM (2.49) H	8:45 AM (0.67) L	2:20 PM (1.72) H	7:59 PM (0.74) L
Sat 23	2:36 AM (2.36) H	9:41 AM (0.67) L	3:30 PM (1.77) H	9:12 PM (0.82) L
Sun 24	3:37 AM (2.25) H	10:33 AM (0.66) L	4:39 PM (1.87) H	10:27 PM (0.86) L
Mon 25	4:36 AM (2.16) H	11:24 AM (0.62) L	5:40 PM (2.01) H	11:38 PM (0.85) L
Tue 26	5:32 AM (2.09) H	12:10 PM (0.57) L	6:32 PM (2.14) H	
Wed 27	12:40 AM (0.82) L	6:23 AM (2.02) H	12:52 PM (0.53) L	7:18 PM (2.27) H
Thu 28	1:35 AM (0.79) L	7:09 AM (1.96) H	1:30 PM (0.50) L	8:00 PM (2.36) H
Fri 29	2:23 AM (0.75) L	7:51 AM (1.91) H	2:04 PM (0.48) L	8:38 PM (2.43) H
Sat 30	3:07 AM (0.72) L	8:30 AM (1.86) H	2:37 PM (0.48) L	9:14 PM (2.47) H
Sun 31	3:48 AM (0.70) L	9:09 AM (1.82) H	3:10 PM (0.48) L	9:48 PM (2.47) H

Darwin - NT

DAY/DATE	TIDE 1	TIDE 2	TIDE 3	TIDE 4
Fri 1	12:02 AM (1.46) L	6:20 AM (7.04) H	12:16 PM (2.49) L	5:52 PM (6.69) H
Sat 2	12:30 AM (1.24) L	6:56 AM (7.21) H	12:45 PM (2.49) L	6:16 PM (6.72) H
Sun 3	12:58 AM (1.12) L	7:28 AM (7.26) H	1:11 PM (2.55) L	6:42 PM (6.67) H
Mon 4	1:26 AM (1.11) L	7:58 AM (7.19) H	1:36 PM (2.66) L	7:08 PM (6.56) H
Tue 5	1:55 AM (1.23) L	8:26 AM (7.03) H	2:01 PM (2.83) L	7:36 PM (6.36) H
Wed 6	2:26 AM (1.46) L	8:55 AM (6.79) H	2:30 PM (3.04) L	8:05 PM (6.08) H
Thu 7	3:00 AM (1.79) L	9:27 AM (6.50) H	3:01 PM (3.30) L	8:35 PM (5.74) H
Fri 8	3:36 AM (2.18) L	10:03 AM (6.18) H	3:40 PM (3.59) L	9:10 PM (5.36) H
Sat 9	4:18 AM (2.59) L	10:47 AM (5.86) H	4:42 PM (3.86) L	10:01 PM (4.98) H
Sun 10	5:13 AM (2.95) L	11:45 AM (5.61) H	6:30 PM (3.91) L	11:41 PM (4.72) H
Mon 11	6:23 AM (3.20) L	12:58 PM (5.52) H	8:11 PM (3.60) L	
Tue 12	1:45 AM (4.88) H	7:47 AM (3.26) L	2:14 PM (5.64) H	9:14 PM (3.06) L
Wed 13	3:08 AM (5.40) H	9:07 AM (3.13) L	3:15 PM (5.91) H	10:02 PM (2.43) L
Thu 14	4:09 AM (6.03) H	10:10 AM (2.91) L	4:00 PM (6.22) H	10:45 PM (1.77) L
Fri 15	5:01 AM (6.65) H	11:00 AM (2.69) L	4:40 PM (6.52) H	11:27 PM (1.16) L
Sat 16	5:51 AM (7.19) H	11:44 AM (2.53) L	5:16 PM (6.76) H	
Sun 17	12:07 AM (0.68) L	6:39 AM (7.56) H	12:23 PM (2.45) L	5:52 PM (6.92) H
Mon 18	12:48 AM (0.39) L	7:23 AM (7.73) H	1:02 PM (2.46) L	6:30 PM (6.97) H
Tue 19	1:30 AM (0.33) L	8:06 AM (7.69) H	1:43 PM (2.55) L	7:11 PM (6.87) H
Wed 20	2:13 AM (0.52) L	8:50 AM (7.48) H	2:27 PM (2.72) L	7:54 PM (6.60) H
Thu 21	2:59 AM (0.92) L	9:34 AM (7.14) H	3:17 PM (2.94) L	8:43 PM (6.19) H
Fri 22	3:48 AM (1.48) L	10:21 AM (6.75) H	4:20 PM (3.15) L	9:44 PM (5.70) H
Sat 23	4:43 AM (2.10) L	11:13 AM (6.35) H	5:39 PM (3.25) L	11:09 PM (5.29) H
Sun 24	5:45 AM (2.67) L	12:09 PM (6.03) H	7:01 PM (3.12) L	
Mon 25	12:51 AM (5.17) H	6:57 AM (3.10) L	1:11 PM (5.81) H	8:16 PM (2.82) L
Tue 26	2:17 AM (5.36) H	8:12 AM (3.33) L	2:15 PM (5.74) H	9:19 PM (2.46) L
Wed 27	3:30 AM (5.69) H	9:25 AM (3.37) L	3:12 PM (5.76) H	10:09 PM (2.12) L
Thu 28	4:29 AM (6.07) H	10:26 AM (3.29) L	3:59 PM (5.84) H	10:50 PM (1.83) L
Fri 29	5:17 AM (6.42) H	11:13 AM (3.16) L	4:37 PM (5.93) H	11:25 PM (1.60) L
Sat 30	6:00 AM (6.70) H	11:51 AM (3.02) L	5:10 PM (6.03) H	11:57 PM (1.42) L
Sun 31	6:38 AM (6.87) H	12:23 PM (2.92) L	5:42 PM (6.11) H	

Fremantle - WA

DAY/DATE	TIDE 1	TIDE 2	TIDE 3	TIDE 4
Fri 1	1:22 AM (0.84) L	8:54 AM (1.23) H	5:36 PM (0.74) L	11:32 PM (0.85) H
Sat 2	1:40 AM (0.83) L	9:10 AM (1.26) H	6:50 PM (0.71) L	
Sun 3	12:21 AM (0.83) H	1:34 AM (0.83) L	9:30 AM (1.29) H	7:35 PM (0.70) L
Mon 4	9:56 AM (1.29) H	8:17 PM (0.69) L		
Tue 5	10:25 AM (1.29) H	9:00 PM (0.70) L		
Wed 6	10:56 AM (1.27) H	9:45 PM (0.71) L		
Thu 7	11:29 AM (1.25) H	10:36 PM (0.73) L	11:30 PM (0.73) L	
Fri 8	12:31 AM (0.73) L	12:01 PM (1.22) H		
Sat 9	1:00 AM (0.74) L	12:38 PM (1.18) H		
Sun 10	1:14 AM (0.75) L	1:20 PM (1.13) H		
Mon 11	12:51 AM (0.78) L	3:42 PM (1.07) H		
Tue 12	12:55 AM (0.80) L	8:02 AM (1.05) H	12:51 PM (0.98) L	5:45 PM (1.01) H
Wed 13	1:03 AM (0.84) L	7:50 AM (1.12) H	2:38 PM (0.89) L	8:06 PM (0.96) H
Thu 14	1:06 AM (0.88) L	7:59 AM (1.20) H	3:43 PM (0.79) L	10:00 PM (0.93) H
Fri 15	12:51 AM (0.90) L	8:17 AM (1.28) H	4:51 PM (0.70) L	11:25 PM (0.90) H
Sat 16	12:02 AM (0.90) L	8:43 AM (1.35) H	6:11 PM (0.62) L	
Sun 17	9:13 AM (1.40) H	7:11 PM (0.57) L		
Mon 18	9:45 AM (1.41) H	8:06 PM (0.55) L		
Tue 19	10:22 AM (1.39) H	9:07 PM (0.57) L		
Wed 20	11:00 AM (1.35) H	11:09 PM (0.60) L		
Thu 21	11:28 AM (1.28) H			
Fri 22	12:08 AM (0.65) L	11:43 AM (1.20) H	12:42 PM (1.20) L	1:38 PM (1.20) L
Sat 23	12:52 AM (0.72) L	12:00 PM (1.12) H	1:31 PM (1.11) L	2:19 PM (1.12) H
Sun 24	1:24 AM (0.80) L	9:43 AM (1.06) H	11:07 AM (1.05) L	12:10 PM (1.06) H
Mon 25	1:08 AM (0.87) L	7:56 AM (1.07) H	9:34 PM (0.90) L	
Tue 26	7:36 AM (1.13) H	6:54 PM (0.89) L	8:34 PM (0.89) L	9:46 PM (0.89) L
Wed 27	7:35 AM (1.19) H	5:14 PM (0.83) L		
Thu 28	7:37 AM (1.24) H	5:34 PM (0.78) L		
Fri 29	7:51 AM (1.29) H	5:52 PM (0.74) L		
Sat 30	8:11 AM (1.32) H	6:13 PM (0.71) L		
Sun 31	8:35 AM (1.34) H	6:41 PM (0.69) L		

Sun Rise & Sun Set Times:

Darwin, NT: Rise: 06:50am Set: 06:20pm

Melbourne, VIC: Rise: 07:10am Set: 05:20pm

Adelaide, SA: Rise: 07:00am Set: 05:20pm

Perth, WA: Rise: 06:50am Set: 05:20pm

Sydney, NSW: Rise: 06:40am Set: 05:03pm

Brisbane, QLD: Rise: 06:20am Set: 05:00pm

Hobart, TAS: Rise: 07:10am Set: 04:50pm

(Note: These times are averages for the month)

Hobart - TAS

DAY/DATE	TIDE 1	TIDE 2	TIDE 3	TIDE 4
Fri 1	2:47 AM (0.59) L	8:59 AM (1.02) H	12:30 PM (0.92) L	7:40 PM (1.37) H
Sat 2	3:34 AM (0.54) L	10:15 AM (1.03) H	12:44 PM (0.99) L	8:06 PM (1.39) H
Sun 3	4:15 AM (0.51) L	11:24 AM (1.06) H	1:00 PM (1.05) L	8:35 PM (1.40) H
Mon 4	4:56 AM (0.49) L	12:34 PM (1.09) H	1:16 PM (1.09) L	9:09 PM (1.40) H
Tue 5	5:35 AM (0.48) L	9:49 PM (1.39) H		
Wed 6	6:16 AM (0.48) L	10:35 PM (1.37) H		
Thu 7	6:59 AM (0.49) L	3:05 PM (1.13) H	5:52 PM (1.11) L	11:25 PM (1.35) H
Fri 8	7:41 AM (0.50) L	3:20 PM (1.13) H	6:52 PM (1.09) L	
Sat 9	12:17 AM (1.32) H	8:20 AM (0.51) L	3:37 PM (1.14) H	7:47 PM (1.05) L
Sun 10	1:12 AM (1.29) H	8:57 AM (0.52) L	3:58 PM (1.16) H	8:44 PM (1.00) L
Mon 11	2:10 AM (1.26) H	9:30 AM (0.54) L	4:21 PM (1.20) H	9:42 PM (0.94) L
Tue 12	3:13 AM (1.23) H	9:59 AM (0.57) L	4:45 PM (1.26) H	10:41 PM (0.84) L
Wed 13	4:19 AM (1.19) H	10:28 AM (0.63) L	5:15 PM (1.34) H	11:41 PM (0.73) L
Thu 14	5:28 AM (1.16) H	10:58 AM (0.71) L	5:47 PM (1.43) H	
Fri 15	12:44 AM (0.60) L	6:42 AM (1.13) H	11:30 AM (0.81) L	6:24 PM (1.51) H
Sat 16	1:46 AM (0.46) L	8:05 AM (1.11) H	12:06 PM (0.91) L	7:07 PM (1.59) H
Sun 17	2:49 AM (0.33) L	9:31 AM (1.13) H	12:50 PM (1.01) L	7:57 PM (1.65) H
Mon 18	3:50 AM (0.23) L	10:48 AM (1.16) H	1:52 PM (1.08) L	8:52 PM (1.68) H
Tue 19	4:48 AM (0.17) L	12:00 PM (1.19) H	3:43 PM (1.11) L	9:52 PM (1.67) H
Wed 20	5:46 AM (0.16) L	1:03 PM (1.21) H	5:09 PM (1.10) L	10:54 PM (1.63) H
Thu 21	6:44 AM (0.20) L	1:57 PM (1.22) H	6:17 PM (1.05) L	11:58 PM (1.55) H
Fri 22	7:39 AM (0.27) L	2:41 PM (1.24) H	7:24 PM (1.00) L	
Sat 23	1:04 AM (1.45) H	8:30 AM (0.36) L	3:20 PM (1.25) H	8:35 PM (0.93) L
Sun 24	2:15 AM (1.33) H	9:16 AM (0.47) L	3:56 PM (1.28) H	9:49 PM (0.86) L
Mon 25	3:24 AM (1.23) H	9:54 AM (0.58) L	4:29 PM (1.32) H	11:00 PM (0.78) L
Tue 26	4:30 AM (1.13) H	10:22 AM (0.69) L	5:00 PM (1.36) H	
Wed 27	12:03 AM (0.71) L	5:37 AM (1.06) H	10:40 AM (0.79) L	5:30 PM (1.40) H
Thu 28	12:58 AM (0.64) L	6:45 AM (1.02) H	10:48 AM (0.88) L	5:56 PM (1.43) H
Fri 29	1:45 AM (0.59) L	7:58 AM (1.01) H	10:56 AM (0.95) L	6:22 PM (1.45) H
Sat 30	2:26 AM (0.55) L	9:09 AM (1.03) H	11:08 AM (1.00) L	6:49 PM (1.47) H
Sun 31	3:02 AM (0.52) L	10:18 AM (1.05) H	11:21 AM (1.05) L	7:20 PM (1.48) H

Port Phillip Heads - VIC

DAY/DATE	TIDE 1	TIDE 2	TIDE 3	TIDE 4
Fri 1	5:15 AM (0.54) L	12:15 PM (1.55) H	5:47 PM (0.84) L	11:55 PM (1.42) H
Sat 2	6:00 AM (0.47) L	1:04 PM (1.64) H	6:38 PM (0.82) L	
Sun 3	12:36 AM (1.44) H	6:41 AM (0.41) L	1:45 PM (1.70) H	7:17 PM (0.80) L
Mon 4	1:14 AM (1.46) H	7:18 AM (0.38) L	2:21 PM (1.73) H	7:52 PM (0.78) L
Tue 5	1:48 AM (1.47) H	7:55 AM (0.37) L	2:53 PM (1.74) H	8:26 PM (0.77) L
Wed 6	2:23 AM (1.48) H	8:30 AM (0.37) L	3:24 PM (1.72) H	9:00 PM (0.76) L
Thu 7	2:58 AM (1.48) H	9:05 AM (0.39) L	3:56 PM (1.69) H	9:33 PM (0.77) L
Fri 8	3:33 AM (1.46) H	9:39 AM (0.42) L	4:30 PM (1.65) H	10:08 PM (0.78) L
Sat 9	4:10 AM (1.43) H	10:10 AM (0.46) L	5:06 PM (1.60) H	10:42 PM (0.79) L
Sun 10	4:48 AM (1.39) H	10:41 AM (0.51) L	5:45 PM (1.55) H	11:15 PM (0.80) L
Mon 11	5:31 AM (1.35) H	11:15 AM (0.57) L	6:26 PM (1.51) H	11:54 PM (0.79) L
Tue 12	6:23 AM (1.32) H	11:56 AM (0.65) L	7:11 PM (1.46) H	
Wed 13	12:40 AM (0.76) L	7:30 AM (1.31) H	12:48 PM (0.75) L	8:01 PM (1.43) H
Thu 14	1:35 AM (0.71) L	8:48 AM (1.36) H	1:54 PM (0.85) L	8:57 PM (1.41) H
Fri 15	2:39 AM (0.63) L	10:08 AM (1.45) H	3:10 PM (0.92) L	9:54 PM (1.42) H
Sat 16	3:45 AM (0.52) L	11:18 AM (1.58) H	4:31 PM (0.95) L	10:52 PM (1.44) H
Sun 17	4:50 AM (0.41) L	12:19 PM (1.71) H	5:44 PM (0.93) L	11:50 PM (1.48) H
Mon 18	5:49 AM (0.31) L	1:15 PM (1.80) H	6:40 PM (0.89) L	
Tue 19	12:45 AM (1.53) H	6:45 AM (0.24) L	2:07 PM (1.86) H	7:30 PM (0.84) L
Wed 20	1:37 AM (1.57) H	7:39 AM (0.22) L	2:57 PM (1.86) H	8:18 PM (0.80) L
Thu 21	2:28 AM (1.59) H	8:31 AM (0.23) L	3:45 PM (1.83) H	9:06 PM (0.76) L
Fri 22	3:17 AM (1.58) H	9:23 AM (0.29) L	4:33 PM (1.78) H	9:55 PM (0.72) L
Sat 23	4:09 AM (1.55) H	10:14 AM (0.38) L	5:22 PM (1.71) H	10:46 PM (0.70) L
Sun 24	5:04 AM (1.50) H	11:03 AM (0.48) L	6:10 PM (1.65) H	11:41 PM (0.68) L
Mon 25	6:11 AM (1.44) H	11:52 AM (0.60) L	6:59 PM (1.58) H	
Tue 26	12:38 AM (0.66) L	7:30 AM (1.41) H	12:43 PM (0.73) L	7:47 PM (1.52) H
Wed 27	1:37 AM (0.64) L	8:43 AM (1.42) H	1:37 PM (0.84) L	8:36 PM (1.47) H
Thu 28	2:37 AM (0.62) L	9:48 AM (1.45) H	2:41 PM (0.93) L	9:25 PM (1.43) H
Fri 29	3:36 AM (0.58) L	10:51 AM (1.51) H	3:52 PM (0.98) L	10:15 PM (1.41) H
Sat 30	4:30 AM (0.54) L	11:47 AM (1.58) H	5:02 PM (0.99) L	11:03 PM (1.40) H
Sun 31	5:18 AM (0.50) L	12:36 PM (1.64) H	5:59 PM (0.97) L	11:49 PM (1.40) H

Fort Denison - NSW

DAY/DATE	TIDE 1	TIDE 2	TIDE 3	TIDE 4
Fri 1	2:01 AM (0.53) L	7:55 AM (1.49) H	1:44 PM (0.57) L	8:13 PM (1.80) H
Sat 2	2:41 AM (0.52) L	8:33 AM (1.44) H	2:14 PM (0.61) L	8:45 PM (1.81) H
Sun 3	3:19 AM (0.52) L	9:13 AM (1.40) H	2:45 PM (0.65) L	9:18 PM (1.81) H
Mon 4	3:58 AM (0.54) L	9:52 AM (1.36) H	3:17 PM (0.69) L	9:53 PM (1.79) H
Tue 5	4:38 AM (0.57) L	10:32 AM (1.32) H	3:53 PM (0.74) L	10:30 PM (1.75) H
Wed 6	5:21 AM (0.61) L	11:15 AM (1.28) H	4:31 PM (0.78) L	11:10 PM (1.70) H
Thu 7	6:09 AM (0.65) L	12:03 PM (1.25) H	5:17 PM (0.82) L	11:56 PM (1.64) H
Fri 8	7:02 AM (0.68) L	12:58 PM (1.23) H	6:11 PM (0.86) L	
Sat 9	12:49 AM (1.59) H	8:00 AM (0.68) L	2:00 PM (1.24) H	7:16 PM (0.88) L
Sun 10	1:49 AM (1.56) H	8:55 AM (0.65) L	3:03 PM (1.29) H	8:29 PM (0.87) L
Mon 11	2:54 AM (1.56) H	9:45 AM (0.60) L	4:00 PM (1.39) H	9:39 PM (0.81) L
Tue 12	3:54 AM (1.58) H	10:29 AM (0.55) L	4:47 PM (1.51) H	10:44 PM (0.73) L
Wed 13	4:49 AM (1.60) H	11:11 AM (0.50) L	5:32 PM (1.65) H	11:42 PM (0.61) L
Thu 14	5:42 AM (1.62) H	11:52 AM (0.46) L	6:16 PM (1.80) H	
Fri 15	12:36 AM (0.50) L	6:34 AM (1.61) H	12:34 PM (0.45) L	7:01 PM (1.93) H
Sat 16	1:30 AM (0.40) L	7:28 AM (1.59) H	1:18 PM (0.46) L	7:48 PM (2.04) H

DAY/DATE	TIDE 1	TIDE 2	TIDE 3	TIDE 4
Sun 17	2:24 AM (0.32) L	8:23 AM (1.55) H	2:05 PM (0.49) L	8:37 PM (2.10) H
Mon 18	3:19 AM (0.29) L	9:20 AM (1.50) H	2:55 PM (0.53) L	9:29 PM (2.11) H
Tue 19	4:16 AM (0.30) L	10:18 AM (1.45) H	3:48 PM (0.58) L	10:22 PM (2.08) H
Wed 20	5:16 AM (0.33) L	11:18 AM (1.40) H	4:45 PM (0.64) L	11:17 PM (2.00) H
Thu 21	6:17 AM (0.39) L	12:20 PM (1.37) H	5:45 PM (0.70) L	
Fri 22	12:16 AM (1.89) H	7:19 AM (0.45) L	1:25 PM (1.36) H	6:51 PM (0.75) L
Sat 23	1:19 AM (1.77) H	8:18 AM (0.51) L	2:29 PM (1.39) H	8:02 PM (0.78) L
Sun 24	2:24 AM (1.67) H	9:11 AM (0.55) L	3:28 PM (1.44) H	9:15 PM (0.78) L
Mon 25	3:27 AM (1.58) H	9:59 AM (0.57) L	4:22 PM (1.52) H	10:24 PM (0.76) L
Tue 26	4:24 AM (1.50) H	10:41 AM (0.59) L	5:10 PM (1.60) H	11:26 PM (0.72) L
Wed 27	5:15 AM (1.45) H	11:18 AM (0.61) L	5:53 PM (1.67) H	
Thu 28	12:19 AM (0.67) L	6:03 AM (1.41) H	11:55 AM (0.62) L	6:32 PM (1.73) H
Fri 29	1:05 AM (0.62) L	6:47 AM (1.39) H	12:30 PM (0.64) L	7:08 PM (1.78) H
Sat 30	1:45 AM (0.58) L	7:30 AM (1.37) H	1:04 PM (0.65) L	7:44 PM (1.82) H
Sun 31	2:24 AM (0.55) L	8:11 AM (1.36) H	1:39 PM (0.67) L	8:18 PM (1.84) H

BITE TIMES

Apogee moon phase on Tuesday 5th
Perigee moon phase on Sunday 17th

● New moon on Sunday 17th
First quarter moon on Saturday 23rd
○ Full moon on Saturday 2nd and Sunday 31st
Last quarter moon phase on Sunday 10th

DAY	MINOR BITE	MAJOR BITE	MINOR BITE	MAJOR BITE	SALT WATER RATING	FRESH WATER RATING
FRI 1	3:56 PM	11:05 PM	5:23 AM	10:43 AM	3	8
SAT 2	4:25 PM	11:52 PM	6:25 AM	11:28 AM	5 ○	7
SUN 3	5:00 PM		7:27 AM	12:16 PM	7	6
MON 4	5:41 PM	12:40 AM	8:27 AM	1:05 PM	7	6
TUE 5	6:28 PM	1:31 AM	9:24 AM	1:56 PM	5	5
WED 6	7:22 PM	2:22 AM	10:15 AM	2:47 PM	4	4
THUR 7	8:21 PM	3:13 AM	10:59 AM	3:37 PM	3	6
FRI 8	9:23 PM	4:03 AM	11:37 AM	4:26 PM	3	6
SAT 9	10:26 PM	4:51 AM	12:09 PM	5:14 PM	4	4
SUN 10	11:30 PM	5:37 AM	12:38 PM	5:59 PM	5	5
MON 11		6:22 AM	1:03 PM	6:44 PM	6	6
TUE 12	12:34 AM	7:06 AM	1:28 PM	7:29 PM	7	7
WED 13	1:41 AM	7:52 AM	1:52 PM	8:15 PM	7	8
THUR 14	2:49 AM	8:39 AM	2:19 PM	9:04 PM	5	8
FRI 15	4:02 AM	9:30 AM	2:49 PM	9:57 PM	6	7

DAY	MINOR BITE	MAJOR BITE	MINOR BITE	MAJOR BITE	SALT WATER RATING	FRESH WATER RATING
SAT 16	5:19 AM	10:26 AM	3:26 PM	10:56 PM	8	8
SUN 17	6:39 AM	11:28 AM	4:11 PM		8 ●	8
MON 18	7:57 AM	12:33 PM	5:08 PM	12:00 AM	8	6
TUE 19	9:07 AM	1:41 PM	6:16 PM	1:07 AM	7	6
WED 20	10:06 AM	2:46 PM	7:30 PM	2:13 AM	6	7
THUR 21	10:53 AM	3:46 PM	8:45 PM	3:15 AM	5	5
FRI 22	11:30 AM	4:40 PM	9:58 PM	4:13 AM	3	5
SAT 23	12:00 PM	5:28 PM	11:06 PM	5:03 AM	4	6
SUN 24	12:25 PM	6:13 PM		5:50 AM	5	6
MON 25	12:49 PM	6:56 PM	12:11 AM	6:34 AM	5	6
TUE 26	1:11 PM	7:38 PM	1:14 AM	7:16 AM	4	5
WED 27	1:34 PM	8:20 PM	2:15 AM	7:59 AM	3	5
THUR 28	1:59 PM	9:03 PM	3:16 AM	8:41 AM	6	6
FRI 29	2:28 PM	9:49 PM	4:17 AM	9:26 AM	5	7
SAT 30	3:00 PM	10:36 PM	5:19 AM	10:12 AM	3	8
SUN 31	3:39 PM	11:26 PM	6:20 AM	11:01 AM	5 ○	7

TIDE TIMES

Adelaide Outer Harbour - SA

DAY/DATE	TIDE 1	TIDE 2	TIDE 3	TIDE 4
Mon 1	5:01 AM (1.97) H	10:23 AM (0.78) L	4:53 PM (2.84) H	11:38 PM (0.45) L
Tue 2	5:30 AM (1.96) H	10:52 AM (0.77) L	5:23 PM (2.83) H	
Wed 3	12:08 AM (0.47) L	5:58 AM (1.94) H	11:20 AM (0.78) L	5:52 PM (2.79) H
Thu 4	12:36 AM (0.52) L	6:26 AM (1.92) H	11:49 AM (0.81) L	6:20 PM (2.73) H
Fri 5	1:04 AM (0.57) L	6:54 AM (1.90) H	12:17 PM (0.85) L	6:47 PM (2.64) H
Sat 6	1:32 AM (0.62) L	7:24 AM (1.89) H	12:49 PM (0.92) L	7:17 PM (2.54) H
Sun 7	2:04 AM (0.67) L	8:04 AM (1.89) H	1:30 PM (1.01) L	7:54 PM (2.38) H
Mon 8	2:45 AM (0.74) L	9:00 AM (1.89) H	2:30 PM (1.15) L	8:45 PM (2.16) H
Tue 9	3:41 AM (0.86) L	10:18 AM (1.91) H	4:12 PM (1.28) L	10:09 PM (1.91) H
Wed 10	4:58 AM (0.98) L	11:58 AM (2.03) H	6:41 PM (1.21) L	
Thu 11	12:16 AM (1.73) H	6:33 AM (1.05) L	1:24 PM (2.23) H	8:28 PM (0.95) L
Fri 12	2:16 AM (1.73) H	7:49 AM (1.06) L	2:27 PM (2.45) H	9:33 PM (0.68) L
Sat 13	3:36 AM (1.77) H	8:44 AM (1.07) L	3:15 PM (2.62) H	10:24 PM (0.50) L
Sun 14	4:30 AM (1.76) H	9:24 AM (1.07) L	3:56 PM (2.75) H	11:07 PM (0.42) L
Mon 15	5:09 AM (1.72) H	9:57 AM (1.05) L	4:32 PM (2.82) H	11:45 PM (0.42) L
Tue 16	5:38 AM (1.67) H	10:27 AM (1.00) L	5:07 PM (2.84) H	
Wed 17	12:20 AM (0.48) L	6:01 AM (1.65) H	10:57 AM (0.95) L	5:40 PM (2.81) H
Thu 18	12:49 AM (0.57) L	6:23 AM (1.67) H	11:28 AM (0.91) L	6:11 PM (2.72) H
Fri 19	1:12 AM (0.66) L	6:45 AM (1.74) H	12:00 PM (0.89) L	6:38 PM (2.60) H
Sat 20	1:28 AM (0.72) L	7:11 AM (1.84) H	12:36 PM (0.91) L	7:06 PM (2.46) H
Sun 21	1:44 AM (0.73) L	7:45 AM (1.97) H	1:19 PM (0.96) L	7:36 PM (2.31) H
Mon 22	2:06 AM (0.73) L	8:30 AM (2.07) H	2:13 PM (1.06) L	8:14 PM (2.12) H
Tue 23	2:39 AM (0.76) L	9:26 AM (2.13) H	3:23 PM (1.19) L	9:04 PM (1.89) H
Wed 24	3:24 AM (0.86) L	10:36 AM (2.15) H	5:10 PM (1.28) L	10:24 PM (1.63) H
Thu 25	4:28 AM (1.02) L	12:09 PM (2.20) H	7:48 PM (1.17) L	
Fri 26	12:51 AM (1.50) H	6:18 AM (1.15) L	1:45 PM (2.31) H	9:15 PM (0.93) L
Sat 27	3:00 AM (1.60) H	8:03 AM (1.15) L	2:53 PM (2.47) H	10:05 PM (0.72) L
Sun 28	4:02 AM (1.74) H	9:06 AM (1.08) L	3:42 PM (2.60) H	10:44 PM (0.58) L
Mon 29	4:42 AM (1.84) H	9:50 AM (1.00) L	4:20 PM (2.69) H	11:15 PM (0.51) L
Tue 30	5:12 AM (1.89) H	10:24 AM (0.92) L	4:52 PM (2.75) H	11:43 PM (0.48) L

Brisbane Bar - QLD

DAY/DATE	TIDE 1	TIDE 2	TIDE 3	TIDE 4
Mon 1	4:26 AM (0.70) L	9:45 AM (1.79) H	3:42 PM (0.50) L	10:23 PM (2.46) H
Tue 2	5:02 AM (0.72) L	10:20 AM (1.77) H	4:15 PM (0.53) L	10:57 PM (2.43) H
Wed 3	5:37 AM (0.75) L	10:58 AM (1.75) H	4:50 PM (0.57) L	11:31 PM (2.39) H
Thu 4	6:14 AM (0.78) L	11:37 AM (1.73) H	5:27 PM (0.62) L	
Fri 5	12:09 AM (2.34) H	6:54 AM (0.79) L	12:21 PM (1.71) H	6:08 PM (0.69) L
Sat 6	12:48 AM (2.29) H	7:38 AM (0.80) L	1:12 PM (1.70) H	6:56 PM (0.76) L
Sun 7	1:32 AM (2.25) H	8:27 AM (0.77) L	2:11 PM (1.72) H	7:54 PM (0.83) L
Mon 8	2:23 AM (2.20) H	9:19 AM (0.72) L	3:17 PM (1.79) H	9:02 PM (0.88) L
Tue 9	3:20 AM (2.15) H	10:14 AM (0.65) L	4:27 PM (1.92) H	10:17 PM (0.88) L
Wed 10	4:22 AM (2.10) H	11:07 AM (0.56) L	5:31 PM (2.09) H	11:32 PM (0.84) L
Thu 11	5:23 AM (2.05) H	12:00 PM (0.48) L	6:30 PM (2.28) H	
Fri 12	12:45 AM (0.77) L	6:23 AM (2.01) H	12:53 PM (0.41) L	7:25 PM (2.47) H
Sat 13	1:54 AM (0.68) L	7:21 AM (1.96) H	1:44 PM (0.36) L	8:18 PM (2.62) H
Sun 14	2:57 AM (0.59) L	8:20 AM (1.91) H	2:34 PM (0.32) L	9:10 PM (2.73) H
Mon 15	3:55 AM (0.52) L	9:17 AM (1.88) H	3:23 PM (0.31) L	10:00 PM (2.79) H
Tue 16	4:51 AM (0.49) L	10:15 AM (1.86) H	4:13 PM (0.32) L	10:50 PM (2.79) H
Wed 17	5:45 AM (0.48) L	11:10 AM (1.85) H	5:01 PM (0.37) L	11:39 PM (2.74) H
Thu 18	6:36 AM (0.51) L	12:03 PM (1.84) H	5:52 PM (0.45) L	
Fri 19	12:27 AM (2.63) H	7:24 AM (0.54) L	12:57 PM (1.83) H	6:44 PM (0.57) L
Sat 20	1:14 AM (2.49) H	8:10 AM (0.58) L	1:52 PM (1.84) H	7:39 PM (0.70) L
Sun 21	2:00 AM (2.33) H	8:55 AM (0.60) L	2:52 PM (1.87) H	8:40 PM (0.82) L
Mon 22	2:50 AM (2.16) H	9:40 AM (0.61) L	3:56 PM (1.92) H	9:47 PM (0.92) L
Tue 23	3:43 AM (2.00) H	10:26 AM (0.61) L	4:59 PM (2.01) H	11:00 PM (0.96) L
Wed 24	4:40 AM (1.87) H	11:13 AM (0.59) L	5:57 PM (2.12) H	
Thu 25	12:13 AM (0.93) L	5:38 AM (1.79) H	12:00 PM (0.57) L	6:48 PM (2.23) H
Fri 26	1:15 AM (0.87) L	6:34 AM (1.74) H	12:46 PM (0.55) L	7:34 PM (2.32) H
Sat 27	2:07 AM (0.79) L	7:25 AM (1.73) H	1:30 PM (0.52) L	8:15 PM (2.39) H
Sun 28	2:53 AM (0.73) L	8:11 AM (1.73) H	2:10 PM (0.50) L	8:54 PM (2.43) H
Mon 29	3:34 AM (0.69) L	8:51 AM (1.74) H	2:47 PM (0.49) L	9:31 PM (2.44) H
Tue 30	4:12 AM (0.68) L	9:29 AM (1.76) H	3:24 PM (0.48) L	10:06 PM (2.45) H

Darwin - NT

DAY/DATE	TIDE 1	TIDE 2	TIDE 3	TIDE 4
Mon 1	12:29 AM (1.31) L	7:12 AM (6.94) H	12:51 PM (2.86) L	6:15 PM (6.17) H
Tue 2	1:00 AM (1.28) L	7:44 AM (6.93) H	1:18 PM (2.84) L	6:46 PM (6.18) H
Wed 3	1:33 AM (1.34) L	8:14 AM (6.85) H	1:47 PM (2.86) L	7:20 PM (6.13) H
Thu 4	2:07 AM (1.48) L	8:44 AM (6.72) H	2:20 PM (2.93) L	7:55 PM (6.00) H
Fri 5	2:43 AM (1.69) L	9:15 AM (6.57) H	2:57 PM (3.04) L	8:32 PM (5.79) H
Sat 6	3:18 AM (1.97) L	9:49 AM (6.39) H	3:42 PM (3.16) L	9:15 PM (5.55) H
Sun 7	3:57 AM (2.28) L	10:26 AM (6.20) H	4:39 PM (3.24) L	10:10 PM (5.31) H
Mon 8	4:42 AM (2.62) L	11:07 AM (6.01) H	5:46 PM (3.20) L	11:23 PM (5.16) H
Tue 9	5:37 AM (2.95) L	11:55 AM (5.83) H	6:56 PM (2.99) L	
Wed 10	12:45 AM (5.20) H	6:44 AM (3.22) L	12:51 PM (5.71) H	8:02 PM (2.62) L
Thu 11	2:08 AM (5.48) H	8:00 AM (3.36) L	1:53 PM (5.69) H	9:04 PM (2.14) L
Fri 12	3:28 AM (5.93) H	9:16 AM (3.35) L	2:56 PM (5.79) H	10:00 PM (1.62) L
Sat 13	4:35 AM (6.45) H	10:22 AM (3.21) L	3:51 PM (5.99) H	10:53 PM (1.13) L
Sun 14	5:34 AM (6.92) H	11:17 AM (3.02) L	4:42 PM (6.23) H	11:43 PM (0.75) L
Mon 15	6:28 AM (7.28) H	12:07 PM (2.83) L	5:30 PM (6.46) H	
Tue 16	12:31 AM (0.51) L	7:16 AM (7.49) H	12:53 PM (2.66) L	6:16 PM (6.61) H
Wed 17	1:19 AM (0.45) L	8:02 AM (7.55) H	1:41 PM (2.53) L	7:05 PM (6.64) H
Thu 18	2:06 AM (0.59) L	8:46 AM (7.47) H	2:30 PM (2.46) L	7:57 PM (6.53) H
Fri 19	2:54 AM (0.91) L	9:28 AM (7.28) H	3:24 PM (2.44) L	8:53 PM (6.30) H
Sat 20	3:40 AM (1.39) L	10:07 AM (7.00) H	4:20 PM (2.46) L	9:53 PM (5.98) H
Sun 21	4:27 AM (1.98) L	10:45 AM (6.66) H	5:16 PM (2.49) L	10:59 PM (5.66) H
Mon 22	5:14 AM (2.58) L	11:24 AM (6.26) H	6:15 PM (2.50) L	
Tue 23	12:06 AM (5.41) H	6:04 AM (3.14) L	12:04 PM (5.87) H	7:14 PM (2.49) L
Wed 24	1:20 AM (5.29) H	7:05 AM (3.57) L	12:52 PM (5.51) H	8:15 PM (2.42) L
Thu 25	2:42 AM (5.38) H	8:20 AM (3.80) L	1:56 PM (5.26) H	9:15 PM (2.29) L
Fri 26	3:59 AM (5.66) H	9:45 AM (3.78) L	3:05 PM (5.19) H	10:07 PM (2.11) L
Sat 27	4:58 AM (6.00) H	10:55 AM (3.59) L	4:01 PM (5.28) H	10:53 PM (1.91) L
Sun 28	5:45 AM (6.30) H	11:42 AM (3.36) L	4:45 PM (5.45) H	11:33 PM (1.72) L
Mon 29	6:25 AM (6.53) H	12:16 PM (3.15) L	5:24 PM (5.66) H	
Tue 30	12:12 AM (1.55) L	7:00 AM (6.67) H	12:45 PM (2.98) L	6:00 PM (5.87) H

Fremantle - WA

DAY/DATE	TIDE 1	TIDE 2	TIDE 3	TIDE 4
Mon 1	9:04 AM (1.34) H	7:15 PM (0.68) L		
Tue 2	9:35 AM (1.34) H	7:50 PM (0.68) L		
Wed 3	10:09 AM (1.32) H	8:27 PM (0.70) L		
Thu 4	10:42 AM (1.30) H	9:02 PM (0.72) L		
Fri 5	11:15 AM (1.26) H	9:37 PM (0.75) L		
Sat 6	11:46 AM (1.22) H	10:08 PM (0.78) L		
Sun 7	12:17 PM (1.17) H	10:32 PM (0.81) L		
Mon 8	12:47 PM (1.11) H	10:42 PM (0.85) L		
Tue 9	6:51 AM (1.07) H	12:00 PM (1.02) L	1:08 PM (1.02) L	9:30 PM (0.88) L
Wed 10	6:33 AM (1.13) H	8:55 PM (0.89) L		
Thu 11	6:40 AM (1.22) H	4:16 PM (0.80) L		
Fri 12	7:05 AM (1.30) H	4:51 PM (0.70) L		
Sat 13	7:38 AM (1.37) H	5:35 PM (0.60) L		
Sun 14	8:16 AM (1.42) H	6:22 PM (0.54) L		
Mon 15	9:00 AM (1.44) H	7:10 PM (0.52) L		
Tue 16	9:47 AM (1.43) H	7:58 PM (0.54) L		
Wed 17	10:42 AM (1.38) H	8:47 PM (0.59) L		
Thu 18	11:43 AM (1.31) H	9:38 PM (0.67) L		
Fri 19	12:31 PM (1.22) H	10:07 PM (0.76) L		
Sat 20	11:17 AM (1.13) H	9:54 PM (0.83) L		
Sun 21	9:19 AM (1.06) H	10:02 AM (1.06) L	11:17 AM (1.06) L	7:31 PM (0.86) L
Mon 22	8:37 AM (1.05) H	7:29 PM (0.84) L		
Tue 23	6:20 AM (1.11) H	7:04 PM (0.82) L		
Wed 24	6:25 AM (1.17) H	6:17 PM (0.79) L		
Thu 25	6:32 AM (1.22) H	5:25 PM (0.75) L		
Fri 26	6:52 AM (1.26) H	5:27 PM (0.72) L		
Sat 27	7:18 AM (1.29) H	5:41 PM (0.69) L		
Sun 28	7:47 AM (1.31) H	5:59 PM (0.67) L		
Mon 29	8:20 AM (1.32) H	6:24 PM (0.66) L		
Tue 30	8:55 AM (1.32) H	6:53 PM (0.66) L		

Sun Rise & Sun Set Times:

Darwin, NT: Rise: 07:00am Set: 06:20pm

Melbourne, VIC: Rise: 07:30am Set: 05:00pm

Adelaide, SA: Rise: 07:20am Set: 05:10pm

Perth, WA: Rise: 07:10am Set: 05:10pm

Sydney, NSW: Rise: 05:50am Set: 04:50pm

Brisbane, QLD: Rise: 06:30am Set: 05:00pm

Hobart, TAS: Rise: 07:40am Set: 04:40pm

(Note: These times are averages for the month)

Hobart - TAS

DAY/DATE	TIDE 1	TIDE 2	TIDE 3	TIDE 4
Mon 1	3:40 AM (0.50) L	7:56 PM (1.49) H		
Tue 2	4:18 AM (0.49) L	8:34 PM (1.48) H		
Wed 3	4:58 AM (0.49) L	9:16 PM (1.46) H		
Thu 4	5:39 AM (0.50) L	10:00 PM (1.43) H		
Fri 5	6:19 AM (0.51) L	2:06 PM (1.15) H	4:52 PM (1.13) L	10:45 PM (1.39) H
Sat 6	6:59 AM (0.53) L	2:19 PM (1.17) H	6:11 PM (1.10) L	11:35 PM (1.33) H
Sun 7	7:35 AM (0.55) L	2:38 PM (1.20) H	7:24 PM (1.06) L	
Mon 8	12:33 AM (1.27) H	8:08 AM (0.58) L	3:00 PM (1.25) H	8:35 PM (0.99) L
Tue 9	1:41 AM (1.21) H	8:38 AM (0.62) L	3:24 PM (1.32) H	9:41 PM (0.89) L
Wed 10	2:56 AM (1.16) H	9:07 AM (0.68) L	3:52 PM (1.40) H	10:40 PM (0.76) L
Thu 11	4:12 AM (1.12) H	9:37 AM (0.75) L	4:25 PM (1.49) H	11:38 PM (0.62) L
Fri 12	5:31 AM (1.10) H	10:09 AM (0.84) L	5:03 PM (1.58) H	
Sat 13	12:36 AM (0.47) L	6:54 AM (1.10) H	10:45 AM (0.92) L	5:48 PM (1.67) H
Sun 14	1:35 AM (0.34) L	8:12 AM (1.11) H	11:24 AM (1.00) L	6:39 PM (1.73) H
Mon 15	2:34 AM (0.24) L	9:23 AM (1.13) H	12:13 PM (1.06) L	7:35 PM (1.76) H
Tue 16	3:31 AM (0.18) L	10:32 AM (1.15) H	1:20 PM (1.10) L	8:33 PM (1.76) H
Wed 17	4:29 AM (0.17) L	11:37 AM (1.18) H	3:15 PM (1.10) L	9:34 PM (1.71) H
Thu 18	5:25 AM (0.21) L	12:32 PM (1.20) H	4:48 PM (1.06) L	10:37 PM (1.62) H
Fri 19	6:20 AM (0.28) L	1:18 PM (1.24) H	6:04 PM (1.01) L	11:45 PM (1.50) H
Sat 20	7:13 AM (0.38) L	1:59 PM (1.28) H	7:20 PM (0.95) L	
Sun 21	12:54 AM (1.36) H	8:00 AM (0.49) L	2:35 PM (1.33) H	8:38 PM (0.87) L
Mon 22	2:04 AM (1.22) H	8:41 AM (0.61) L	3:10 PM (1.37) H	9:52 PM (0.79) L
Tue 23	3:15 AM (1.11) H	9:13 AM (0.73) L	3:42 PM (1.42) H	10:58 PM (0.71) L
Wed 24	4:30 AM (1.04) H	9:34 AM (0.83) L	4:13 PM (1.45) H	11:53 PM (0.65) L
Thu 25	5:49 AM (1.01) H	9:45 AM (0.90) L	4:41 PM (1.48) H	
Fri 26	12:39 AM (0.60) L	6:59 AM (1.01) H	9:53 AM (0.96) L	5:10 PM (1.50) H
Sat 27	1:17 AM (0.56) L	7:56 AM (1.03) H	10:09 AM (1.00) L	5:41 PM (1.51) H
Sun 28	1:53 AM (0.54) L	8:45 AM (1.05) H	10:32 AM (1.03) L	6:15 PM (1.52) H
Mon 29	2:30 AM (0.52) L	9:37 AM (1.06) H	11:00 AM (1.05) L	6:54 PM (1.53) H
Tue 30	3:07 AM (0.51) L	10:37 AM (1.07) H	11:26 AM (1.07) L	7:33 PM (1.53) H

Port Phillip Heads - VIC

DAY/DATE	TIDE 1	TIDE 2	TIDE 3	TIDE 4
Mon 1	6:02 AM (0.46) L	1:17 PM (1.69) H	6:43 PM (0.93) L	
Tue 2	12:32 AM (1.42) H	6:45 AM (0.44) L	1:54 PM (1.71) H	7:22 PM (0.90) L
Wed 3	1:14 AM (1.44) H	7:24 AM (0.43) L	2:28 PM (1.72) H	8:00 PM (0.86) L
Thu 4	1:53 AM (1.46) H	8:02 AM (0.43) L	3:00 PM (1.72) H	8:36 PM (0.84) L
Fri 5	2:32 AM (1.46) H	8:37 AM (0.45) L	3:34 PM (1.71) H	9:13 PM (0.82) L
Sat 6	3:12 AM (1.45) H	9:10 AM (0.48) L	4:08 PM (1.69) H	9:47 PM (0.80) L
Sun 7	3:51 AM (1.44) H	9:40 AM (0.52) L	4:43 PM (1.66) H	10:22 PM (0.78) L
Mon 8	4:32 AM (1.42) H	10:12 AM (0.58) L	5:17 PM (1.63) H	10:57 PM (0.75) L
Tue 9	5:18 AM (1.40) H	10:49 AM (0.64) L	5:53 PM (1.59) H	11:34 PM (0.70) L
Wed 10	6:12 AM (1.40) H	11:34 AM (0.73) L	6:32 PM (1.55) H	
Thu 11	12:17 AM (0.64) L	7:16 AM (1.42) H	12:28 PM (0.83) L	7:15 PM (1.51) H
Fri 12	1:06 AM (0.58) L	8:28 AM (1.47) H	1:28 PM (0.93) L	8:05 PM (1.48) H
Sat 13	2:02 AM (0.51) L	9:40 AM (1.54) H	2:36 PM (1.01) L	9:01 PM (1.46) H
Sun 14	3:06 AM (0.44) L	10:48 AM (1.62) H	3:52 PM (1.05) L	10:03 PM (1.46) H
Mon 15	4:15 AM (0.37) L	11:54 AM (1.71) H	5:07 PM (1.03) L	11:10 PM (1.48) H
Tue 16	5:21 AM (0.31) L	12:54 PM (1.77) H	6:11 PM (0.97) L	
Wed 17	12:16 AM (1.52) H	6:24 AM (0.27) L	1:50 PM (1.81) H	7:08 PM (0.90) L
Thu 18	1:18 AM (1.56) H	7:22 AM (0.27) L	2:42 PM (1.83) H	8:02 PM (0.81) L
Fri 19	2:15 AM (1.59) H	8:17 AM (0.30) L	3:31 PM (1.82) H	8:56 PM (0.74) L
Sat 20	3:10 AM (1.59) H	9:11 AM (0.37) L	4:17 PM (1.79) H	9:50 PM (0.67) L
Sun 21	4:05 AM (1.57) H	10:00 AM (0.46) L	5:01 PM (1.75) H	10:43 PM (0.61) L
Mon 22	5:05 AM (1.54) H	10:48 AM (0.56) L	5:43 PM (1.69) H	11:32 PM (0.57) L
Tue 23	6:12 AM (1.50) H	11:32 AM (0.68) L	6:23 PM (1.63) H	
Wed 24	12:20 AM (0.55) L	7:17 AM (1.48) H	12:17 PM (0.79) L	7:03 PM (1.56) H
Thu 25	1:06 AM (0.55) L	8:18 AM (1.48) H	1:03 PM (0.89) L	7:45 PM (1.50) H
Fri 26	1:54 AM (0.55) L	9:15 AM (1.48) H	1:56 PM (0.98) L	8:28 PM (1.44) H
Sat 27	2:45 AM (0.56) L	10:13 AM (1.50) H	2:58 PM (1.04) L	9:16 PM (1.39) H
Sun 28	3:40 AM (0.55) L	11:08 AM (1.53) H	4:06 PM (1.06) L	10:08 PM (1.37) H
Mon 29	4:36 AM (0.53) L	12:00 PM (1.57) H	5:13 PM (1.04) L	11:02 PM (1.36) H
Tue 30	5:28 AM (0.50) L	12:46 PM (1.60) H	6:08 PM (1.00) L	11:55 PM (1.38) H

Fort Denison - NSW

DAY/DATE	TIDE 1	TIDE 2	TIDE 3	TIDE 4
Mon 1	3:00 AM (0.53) L	8:51 AM (1.35) H	2:15 PM (0.69) L	8:54 PM (1.84) H
Tue 2	3:39 AM (0.53) L	9:31 AM (1.33) H	2:52 PM (0.70) L	9:30 PM (1.83) H
Wed 3	4:18 AM (0.55) L	10:12 AM (1.32) H	3:31 PM (0.72) L	10:08 PM (1.80) H
Thu 4	4:59 AM (0.57) L	10:54 AM (1.30) H	4:13 PM (0.75) L	10:47 PM (1.76) H
Fri 5	5:42 AM (0.59) L	11:38 AM (1.29) H	4:57 PM (0.78) L	11:30 PM (1.71) H
Sat 6	6:27 AM (0.60) L	12:27 PM (1.30) H	5:47 PM (0.80) L	
Sun 7	12:15 AM (1.66) H	7:13 AM (0.60) L	1:20 PM (1.33) H	6:45 PM (0.83) L
Mon 8	1:06 AM (1.60) H	8:00 AM (0.59) L	2:15 PM (1.39) H	7:50 PM (0.83) L
Tue 9	2:03 AM (1.56) H	8:46 AM (0.57) L	3:10 PM (1.48) H	9:01 PM (0.79) L
Wed 10	3:06 AM (1.52) H	9:33 AM (0.55) L	4:02 PM (1.60) H	10:13 PM (0.72) L
Thu 11	4:10 AM (1.50) H	10:21 AM (0.53) L	4:54 PM (1.73) H	11:20 PM (0.61) L
Fri 12	5:13 AM (1.48) H	11:09 AM (0.51) L	5:45 PM (1.87) H	
Sat 13	12:22 AM (0.49) L	6:14 AM (1.48) H	12:00 PM (0.51) L	6:36 PM (1.99) H
Sun 14	1:20 AM (0.38) L	7:14 AM (1.47) H	12:52 PM (0.51) L	7:30 PM (2.08) H
Mon 15	2:16 AM (0.29) L	8:13 AM (1.46) H	1:45 PM (0.51) L	8:23 PM (2.14) H

DAY/DATE	TIDE 1	TIDE 2	TIDE 3	TIDE 4
Tue 16	3:12 AM (0.25) L	9:10 AM (1.45) H	2:41 PM (0.52) L	9:16 PM (2.15) H
Wed 17	4:06 AM (0.25) L	10:06 AM (1.44) H	3:37 PM (0.54) L	10:10 PM (2.10) H
Thu 18	5:00 AM (0.29) L	11:02 AM (1.43) H	4:33 PM (0.57) L	11:02 PM (2.01) H
Fri 19	5:54 AM (0.35) L	11:58 AM (1.43) H	5:31 PM (0.63) L	11:55 PM (1.87) H
Sat 20	6:45 AM (0.43) L	12:54 PM (1.44) H	6:31 PM (0.69) L	
Sun 21	12:49 AM (1.72) H	7:34 AM (0.50) L	1:49 PM (1.46) H	7:35 PM (0.75) L
Mon 22	1:45 AM (1.57) H	8:19 AM (0.57) L	2:45 PM (1.49) H	8:45 PM (0.78) L
Tue 23	2:42 AM (1.43) H	9:03 AM (0.62) L	3:38 PM (1.54) H	9:57 PM (0.78) L
Wed 24	3:42 AM (1.34) H	9:46 AM (0.65) L	4:29 PM (1.59) H	11:04 PM (0.75) L
Thu 25	4:41 AM (1.28) H	10:30 AM (0.67) L	5:16 PM (1.65) H	
Fri 26	12:01 AM (0.69) L	5:36 AM (1.27) H	11:13 AM (0.68) L	6:00 PM (1.70) H
Sat 27	12:48 AM (0.63) L	6:27 AM (1.27) H	11:55 AM (0.68) L	6:41 PM (1.75) H
Sun 28	1:29 AM (0.57) L	7:12 AM (1.29) H	12:36 PM (0.67) L	7:19 PM (1.79) H
Mon 29	2:07 AM (0.53) L	7:53 AM (1.31) H	1:16 PM (0.66) L	7:58 PM (1.82) H
Tue 30	2:43 AM (0.50) L	8:32 AM (1.32) H	1:56 PM (0.65) L	8:34 PM (1.83) H

BITE TIMES

Apogee moon phase on Monday 1st and Sunday 28th
Perigee moon phase on Monday 15th

New moon on Monday 15th
First quarter moon on Monday 22nd
Full moon on Tuesday 30th
Last quarter moon phase on Monday 8th

DAY	MINOR BITE	MAJOR BITE	MINOR BITE	MAJOR BITE	SALT WATER RATING	FRESH WATER RATING
MON 1	4:25 PM		7:17 AM	11:51 AM	7	6
TUE 2	5:17 PM	12:17 AM	8:10 AM	12:43 PM	7	6
WED 3	6:14 PM	1:09 AM	8:57 AM	1:33 PM	7	6
THUR 4	7:15 PM	1:59 AM	9:36 AM	2:22 PM	5	5
FRI 5	8:17 PM	2:47 AM	10:10 AM	3:09 PM	4	4
SAT 6	9:20 PM	3:33 AM	10:39 AM	3:55 PM	3	6
SUN 7	10:22 PM	4:18 AM	11:05 AM	4:39 PM	4	4
MON 8	11:26 PM	5:01 AM	11:29 AM	5:22 PM	5	5
TUE 9		5:44 AM	11:53 AM	6:06 PM	6	6
WED 10	12:31 AM	6:29 AM	12:18 PM	6:52 PM	7	7
THUR 11	1:40 AM	7:17 AM	12:45 PM	7:42 PM	7	8
FRI 12	2:52 AM	8:09 AM	1:18 PM	8:37 PM	5	8
SAT 13	4:09 AM	9:07 AM	1:58 PM	9:38 PM	6	7
SUN 14	5:28 AM	10:10 AM	2:49 PM	10:44 PM	8	8
MON 15	6:44 AM	11:18 AM	3:52 PM	11:52 PM	8	8

DAY	MINOR BITE	MAJOR BITE	MINOR BITE	MAJOR BITE	SALT WATER RATING	FRESH WATER RATING
TUE 16	7:49 AM	12:26 PM	5:05 PM		8	6
WED 17	8:43 AM	1:30 PM	6:23 PM	12:58 AM	7	6
THUR 18	9:25 AM	2:28 PM	7:40 PM	1:59 AM	6	7
FRI 19	9:59 AM	3:21 PM	8:52 PM	2:54 AM	5	5
SAT 20	10:27 AM	4:09 PM	10:00 PM	3:45 AM	4	6
SUN 21	10:52 AM	4:54 PM	11:05 PM	4:31 AM	3	5
MON 22	11:15 AM	5:36 PM		5:15 AM	4	6
TUE 23	11:38 AM	6:19 PM	12:08 AM	5:57 AM	5	6
WED 24	12:03 PM	7:02 PM	1:09 AM	6:40 AM	4	5
THUR 25	12:30 PM	7:46 PM	2:11 AM	7:24 AM	3	5
FRI 26	1:01 PM	8:33 PM	3:12 AM	8:09 AM	6	6
SAT 27	1:38 PM	9:22 PM	4:13 AM	8:57 AM	6	6
SUN 28	2:21 PM	10:13 PM	5:12 AM	9:47 AM	5	7
MON 29	3:12 PM	11:05 PM	6:06 AM	10:39 AM	3	8
TUE 30	4:08 PM	11:55 PM	6:55 AM	11:30 AM	5	7

TIDE TIMES

Adelaide Outer Harbour - SA

DAY/DATE	TIDE 1	TIDE 2	TIDE 3	TIDE 4
Wed 1	5:36 AM (1.93) H	10:54 AM (0.85) L	5:21 PM (2.78) H	
Thu 2	12:08 AM (0.47) L	6:00 AM (1.96) H	11:24 AM (0.80) L	5:49 PM (2.78) H
Fri 3	12:33 AM (0.47) L	6:27 AM (1.99) H	11:55 AM (0.78) L	6:17 PM (2.74) H
Sat 4	12:59 AM (0.48) L	6:55 AM (2.03) H	12:28 PM (0.80) L	6:45 PM (2.67) H
Sun 5	1:24 AM (0.50) L	7:26 AM (2.08) H	1:02 PM (0.83) L	7:15 PM (2.57) H
Mon 6	1:50 AM (0.52) L	7:59 AM (2.15) H	1:43 PM (0.88) L	7:46 PM (2.43) H
Tue 7	2:17 AM (0.57) L	8:36 AM (2.21) H	2:30 PM (0.95) L	8:24 PM (2.23) H
Wed 8	2:48 AM (0.67) L	9:21 AM (2.25) H	3:30 PM (1.05) L	9:10 PM (1.96) H
Thu 9	3:23 AM (0.83) L	10:15 AM (2.24) H	4:58 PM (1.16) L	10:15 PM (1.63) H
Fri 10	4:03 AM (1.05) L	11:33 AM (2.21) H	7:51 PM (1.10) L	
Sat 11	1:20 AM (1.36) H	5:07 AM (1.29) L	1:37 PM (2.26) H	9:51 PM (0.81) L
Sun 12	4:40 AM (1.51) H	8:14 AM (1.37) L	3:10 PM (2.43) H	10:47 PM (0.56) L
Mon 13	5:20 AM (1.64) H	9:30 AM (1.28) L	4:07 PM (2.59) H	11:28 PM (0.43) L
Tue 14	5:45 AM (1.69) H	10:16 AM (1.15) L	4:47 PM (2.70) H	11:59 PM (0.40) L
Wed 15*	6:01 AM (1.71) H	10:49 AM (1.02) L	5:19 PM (2.74) H	
Thu 16	12:22 AM (0.45) L	6:11 AM (1.76) H	11:17 AM (0.90) L	5:45 PM (2.72) H
Fri 17	12:39 AM (0.51) L	6:23 AM (1.86) H	11:47 AM (0.81) L	6:09 PM (2.65) H
Sat 18	12:52 AM (0.56) L	6:39 AM (1.99) H	12:17 PM (0.77) L	6:32 PM (2.55) H
Sun 19	1:03 AM (0.56) L	7:02 AM (2.15) H	12:49 PM (0.77) L	6:55 PM (2.44) H
Mon 20	1:15 AM (0.54) L	7:30 AM (2.28) H	1:24 PM (0.80) L	7:19 PM (2.32) H
Tue 21	1:33 AM (0.51) L	8:02 AM (2.38) H	2:01 PM (0.87) L	7:46 PM (2.17) H
Wed 22	1:57 AM (0.53) L	8:40 AM (2.41) H	2:45 PM (0.98) L	8:17 PM (1.98) H
Thu 23	2:24 AM (0.63) L	9:22 AM (2.34) H	3:39 PM (1.14) L	8:51 PM (1.72) H
Fri 24	2:53 AM (0.84) L	10:17 AM (2.20) H	5:26 PM (1.31) L	9:31 PM (1.41) H
Sat 25	3:17 AM (1.11) L	12:15 PM (2.05) H	9:52 PM (1.08) L	
Sun 26	5:20 AM (1.41) H	7:22 AM (1.39) L	2:49 PM (2.19) H	10:27 PM (0.80) L
Mon 27	4:43 AM (1.65) H	9:21 AM (1.23) L	3:51 PM (2.40) H	10:57 PM (0.59) L
Tue 28	5:04 AM (1.81) H	10:08 AM (1.05) L	4:29 PM (2.56) H	11:21 PM (0.47) L
Wed 29	5:24 AM (1.91) H	10:37 AM (0.91) L	4:57 PM (2.66) H	11:41 PM (0.43) L
Thu 30	5:39 AM (1.97) H	11:00 AM (0.80) L	5:20 PM (2.71) H	11:59 PM (0.41) L
Fri 31	5:55 AM (2.03) H	11:24 AM (0.71) L	5:42 PM (2.73) H	

Brisbane Bar - QLD

DAY/DATE	TIDE 1	TIDE 2	TIDE 3	TIDE 4
Wed 1	4:47 AM (0.68) L	10:05 AM (1.78) H	4:00 PM (0.48) L	10:40 PM (2.44) H
Thu 2	5:22 AM (0.68) L	10:43 AM (1.80) H	4:37 PM (0.50) L	11:14 PM (2.43) H
Fri 3	5:56 AM (0.67) L	11:23 AM (1.81) H	5:15 PM (0.53) L	11:47 PM (2.40) H
Sat 4	6:31 AM (0.66) L	12:05 PM (1.82) H	5:55 PM (0.59) L	
Sun 5	12:22 AM (2.35) H	7:08 AM (0.65) L	12:50 PM (1.83) H	6:39 PM (0.67) L
Mon 6	1:00 AM (2.28) H	7:47 AM (0.63) L	1:41 PM (1.85) H	7:30 PM (0.77) L
Tue 7	1:42 AM (2.18) H	8:30 AM (0.60) L	2:40 PM (1.90) H	8:31 PM (0.85) L
Wed 8	2:33 AM (2.06) H	9:21 AM (0.57) L	3:47 PM (1.99) H	9:46 PM (0.90) L
Thu 9	3:37 AM (1.94) H	10:18 AM (0.54) L	4:59 PM (2.13) H	11:11 PM (0.88) L
Fri 10	4:49 AM (1.84) H	11:20 AM (0.49) L	6:06 PM (2.29) H	
Sat 11	12:34 AM (0.80) L	6:01 AM (1.79) H	12:22 PM (0.44) L	7:09 PM (2.46) H
Sun 12	1:49 AM (0.68) L	7:10 AM (1.78) H	1:22 PM (0.38) L	8:06 PM (2.61) H
Mon 13	2:54 AM (0.57) L	8:15 AM (1.80) H	2:20 PM (0.32) L	9:00 PM (2.71) H
Tue 14	3:50 AM (0.48) L	9:14 AM (1.84) H	3:15 PM (0.28) L	9:49 PM (2.77) H
Wed 15	4:41 AM (0.43) L	10:07 AM (1.88) H	4:05 PM (0.27) L	10:36 PM (2.76) H
Thu 16	5:28 AM (0.42) L	10:57 AM (1.92) H	4:54 PM (0.31) L	11:20 PM (2.69) H
Fri 17	6:10 AM (0.43) L	11:44 AM (1.95) H	5:40 PM (0.39) L	
Sat 18	12:01 AM (2.57) H	6:48 AM (0.46) L	12:30 PM (1.96) H	6:25 PM (0.52) L
Sun 19	12:41 AM (2.41) H	7:25 AM (0.50) L	1:16 PM (1.95) H	7:12 PM (0.68) L
Mon 20	1:19 AM (2.21) H	8:00 AM (0.54) L	2:07 PM (1.94) H	8:03 PM (0.84) L
Tue 21	1:59 AM (2.01) H	8:38 AM (0.58) L	3:03 PM (1.94) H	9:05 PM (0.96) L
Wed 22	2:45 AM (1.81) H	9:21 AM (0.62) L	4:10 PM (1.97) H	10:23 PM (1.03) L
Thu 23	3:45 AM (1.66) H	10:14 AM (0.65) L	5:18 PM (2.04) H	11:48 PM (0.99) L
Fri 24	5:00 AM (1.57) H	11:12 AM (0.65) L	6:18 PM (2.13) H	
Sat 25	12:59 AM (0.90) L	6:11 AM (1.57) H	12:11 PM (0.63) L	7:10 PM (2.23) H
Sun 26	1:51 AM (0.79) L	7:09 AM (1.62) H	1:04 PM (0.58) L	7:54 PM (2.31) H
Mon 27	2:35 AM (0.71) L	7:56 AM (1.68) H	1:50 PM (0.52) L	8:34 PM (2.37) H
Tue 28	3:15 AM (0.65) L	8:36 AM (1.74) H	2:32 PM (0.47) L	9:12 PM (2.41) H
Wed 29	3:50 AM (0.62) L	9:13 AM (1.79) H	3:11 PM (0.43) L	9:46 PM (2.44) H
Thu 30	4:24 AM (0.59) L	9:49 AM (1.85) H	3:48 PM (0.42) L	10:19 PM (2.46) H
Fri 31	4:58 AM (0.56) L	10:27 AM (1.89) H	4:26 PM (0.42) L	10:51 PM (2.45) H

Darwin - NT

DAY/DATE	TIDE 1	TIDE 2	TIDE 3	TIDE 4
Wed 1	12:47 AM (1.42) L	7:34 AM (6.77) H	1:12 PM (2.83) L	6:36 PM (6.04) H
Thu 2	1:22 AM (1.36) L	8:04 AM (6.82) H	1:43 PM (2.71) L	7:13 PM (6.14) H
Fri 3	1:55 AM (1.38) L	8:33 AM (6.83) H	2:17 PM (2.62) L	7:50 PM (6.15) H
Sat 4	2:28 AM (1.48) L	9:01 AM (6.80) H	2:56 PM (2.56) L	8:30 PM (6.09) H
Sun 5	2:59 AM (1.68) L	9:29 AM (6.72) H	3:37 PM (2.51) L	9:13 PM (5.98) H
Mon 6	3:31 AM (1.97) L	9:56 AM (6.58) H	4:21 PM (2.47) L	10:02 PM (5.82) H
Tue 7	4:08 AM (2.34) L	10:25 AM (6.36) H	5:08 PM (2.41) L	11:00 PM (5.67) H
Wed 8	4:52 AM (2.78) L	10:58 AM (6.09) H	6:00 PM (2.34) L	
Thu 9	12:03 AM (5.56) H	5:49 AM (3.24) L	11:38 AM (5.79) H	6:58 PM (2.22) L
Fri 10	1:20 AM (5.54) H	7:03 AM (3.62) L	12:33 PM (5.50) H	8:08 PM (2.03) L
Sat 11	2:54 AM (5.74) H	8:36 AM (3.77) L	1:53 PM (5.34) H	9:26 PM (1.73) L
Sun 12	4:20 AM (6.16) H	10:01 AM (3.63) L	3:22 PM (5.47) H	10:34 PM (1.35) L
Mon 13	5:27 AM (6.63) H	11:09 AM (3.31) L	4:30 PM (5.80) H	11:33 PM (0.97) L
Tue 14	6:22 AM (7.05) H	12:06 PM (2.92) L	5:25 PM (6.18) H	
Wed 15	12:27 AM (0.69) L	7:11 AM (7.37) H	12:57 PM (2.54) L	6:17 PM (6.51) H
Thu 16	1:15 AM (0.56) L	7:55 AM (7.56) H	1:44 PM (2.19) L	7:10 PM (6.71) H
Fri 17	2:00 AM (0.62) L	8:32 AM (7.61) H	2:30 PM (1.91) L	8:02 PM (6.76) H
Sat 18	2:42 AM (0.90) L	9:06 AM (7.49) H	3:15 PM (1.76) L	8:54 PM (6.64) H
Sun 19	3:19 AM (1.36) L	9:37 AM (7.23) H	3:57 PM (1.74) L	9:42 PM (6.38) H
Mon 20	3:55 AM (1.95) L	10:04 AM (6.86) H	4:39 PM (1.85) L	10:30 PM (6.02) H
Tue 21	4:27 AM (2.59) L	10:28 AM (6.40) H	5:20 PM (2.05) L	11:19 PM (5.63) H
Wed 22	5:00 AM (3.20) L	10:51 AM (5.90) H	6:05 PM (2.29) L	
Thu 23	12:16 AM (5.29) H	5:50 AM (3.74) L	11:22 AM (5.37) H	6:58 PM (2.49) L
Fri 24	1:35 AM (5.10) H	7:14 AM (4.10) L	12:18 PM (4.87) H	8:06 PM (2.59) L
Sat 25	3:33 AM (5.25) H	9:23 AM (4.12) L	2:19 PM (4.62) H	9:27 PM (2.51) L
Sun 26	4:48 AM (5.64) H	11:15 AM (3.78) L	3:48 PM (4.80) H	10:34 PM (2.27) L
Mon 27	5:34 AM (6.01) H	11:54 AM (3.43) L	4:39 PM (5.14) H	11:24 PM (1.98) L
Tue 28	6:13 AM (6.32) H	12:22 PM (3.14) L	5:19 PM (5.51) H	
Wed 29	12:04 AM (1.69) L	6:46 AM (6.59) H	12:46 PM (2.87) L	5:56 PM (5.87) H
Thu 30	12:40 AM (1.45) L	7:17 AM (6.81) H	1:11 PM (2.60) L	6:32 PM (6.17) H
Fri 31	1:13 AM (1.29) L	7:46 AM (6.99) H	1:40 PM (2.33) L	7:09 PM (6.39) H

Fremantle - WA

DAY/DATE	TIDE 1	TIDE 2	TIDE 3	TIDE 4
Wed 1	9:30 AM (1.31) H	7:22 PM (0.67) L		
Thu 2	10:05 AM (1.29) H	7:46 PM (0.69) L		
Fri 3	10:38 AM (1.26) H	7:57 PM (0.72) L		
Sat 4	11:07 AM (1.21) H	7:45 PM (0.75) L		
Sun 5	11:34 AM (1.15) H	7:41 PM (0.78) L		
Mon 6	11:58 AM (1.08) H	7:37 PM (0.80) L		
Tue 7	3:55 AM (1.01) H	7:42 AM (0.99) L	9:30 AM (1.00) H	7:30 PM (0.82) L
Wed 8	4:25 AM (1.08) H	6:58 PM (0.82) L		
Thu 9	5:01 AM (1.16) H	3:51 PM (0.76) L		
Fri 10	5:43 AM (1.23) H	4:13 PM (0.66) L		
Sat 11	6:30 AM (1.30) H	4:48 PM (0.58) L		
Sun 12	7:19 AM (1.36) H	5:30 PM (0.52) L		
Mon 13	8:12 AM (1.39) H	6:14 PM (0.50) L		
Tue 14	9:04 AM (1.38) H	6:57 PM (0.51) L		
Wed 15	9:57 AM (1.35) H	7:37 PM (0.56) L		
Thu 16	10:48 AM (1.28) H	8:10 PM (0.64) L		
Fri 17	11:32 AM (1.19) H	8:18 PM (0.73) L		
Sat 18	2:46 AM (0.86) H	3:34 AM (0.86) L	11:18 AM (1.09) H	7:20 PM (0.80) L
Sun 19	2:57 AM (0.91) H	4:39 AM (0.91) L	10:47 AM (1.00) H	6:17 PM (0.80) L
Mon 20	2:46 AM (0.98) H	6:06 AM (0.95) L	8:29 AM (0.97) H	6:16 PM (0.77) L
Tue 21	3:14 AM (1.03) H	6:08 PM (0.75) L		
Wed 22	3:54 AM (1.08) H	5:31 PM (0.72) L		
Thu 23	4:40 AM (1.12) H	5:26 PM (0.69) L		
Fri 24	5:30 AM (1.15) H	4:50 PM (0.67) L		
Sat 25	6:18 AM (1.18) H	4:56 PM (0.65) L		
Sun 26	7:01 AM (1.21) H	5:11 PM (0.63) L		
Mon 27	7:42 AM (1.22) H	5:30 PM (0.62) L		
Tue 28	8:20 AM (1.24) H	5:53 PM (0.62) L		
Wed 29	8:56 AM (1.24) H	6:13 PM (0.63) L		
Thu 30	12:50 AM (0.81) H	1:39 AM (0.81) L	9:30 AM (1.22) H	6:19 PM (0.65) L
Fri 31	12:28 AM (0.82) H	2:34 AM (0.81) L	10:01 AM (1.19) H	6:21 PM (0.68) L

Sun Rise & Sun Set Times:

Adelaide, SA: Rise: 07:20am Set: 05:20pm

Brisbane, QLD: Rise: 06:30am Set: 05:10pm

Darwin, NT: Rise: 07:00am Set: 06:30pm

Perth, WA: Rise: 07:10am Set: 05:30pm

Hobart, TAS: Rise: 07:30am Set: 04:50pm

Melbourne, VIC: Rise: 07:30am Set: 05:20pm

Sydney, NSW: Rise: 06:50am Set: 05:00pm

(Note: These times are averages for the month)

Hobart - TAS

DAY/DATE	TIDE 1	TIDE 2	TIDE 3	TIDE 4
Wed 1	3:45 AM (0.50) L	8:14 PM (1.52) H		
Thu 2	4:24 AM (0.51) L	12:28 PM (1.09) H	1:04 PM (1.09) L	8:54 PM (1.49) H
Fri 3	5:00 AM (0.52) L	12:42 PM (1.11) H	2:49 PM (1.10) L	9:35 PM (1.44) H
Sat 4	5:36 AM (0.54) L	1:00 PM (1.15) H	4:26 PM (1.08) L	10:19 PM (1.37) H
Sun 5	6:11 AM (0.57) L	1:20 PM (1.20) H	5:58 PM (1.05) L	11:14 PM (1.29) H
Mon 6	6:44 AM (0.61) L	1:44 PM (1.26) H	7:21 PM (0.99) L	
Tue 7	12:24 AM (1.21) H	7:16 AM (0.66) L	2:09 PM (1.34) H	8:32 PM (0.89) L
Wed 8	1:42 AM (1.14) H	7:50 AM (0.73) L	2:37 PM (1.42) H	9:33 PM (0.77) L
Thu 9	2:59 AM (1.09) H	8:24 AM (0.80) L	3:09 PM (1.50) H	10:30 PM (0.63) L
Fri 10	4:21 AM (1.07) H	9:00 AM (0.87) L	3:46 PM (1.59) H	11:25 PM (0.50) L
Sat 11	5:48 AM (1.07) H	9:40 AM (0.92) L	4:32 PM (1.67) H	
Sun 12	12:22 AM (0.37) L	7:00 AM (1.09) H	10:21 AM (0.97) L	5:26 PM (1.73) H
Mon 13	1:19 AM (0.28) L	8:00 AM (1.10) H	11:07 AM (0.99) L	6:24 PM (1.77) H
Tue 14	2:16 AM (0.23) L	8:57 AM (1.11) H	12:00 PM (1.01) L	7:23 PM (1.78) H
Wed 15	3:13 AM (0.21) L	9:57 AM (1.12) H	1:14 PM (1.02) L	8:21 PM (1.74) H
Thu 16	4:07 AM (0.24) L	10:56 AM (1.15) H	3:00 PM (1.01) L	9:21 PM (1.65) H
Fri 17	5:00 AM (0.31) L	11:47 AM (1.19) H	4:37 PM (0.97) L	10:26 PM (1.51) H
Sat 18	5:51 AM (0.41) L	12:32 PM (1.25) H	6:00 PM (0.91) L	11:37 PM (1.37) H
Sun 19	6:39 AM (0.52) L	1:12 PM (1.31) H	7:18 PM (0.84) L	
Mon 20	12:48 AM (1.23) H	7:22 AM (0.64) L	1:47 PM (1.37) H	8:30 PM (0.77) L
Tue 21	1:56 AM (1.11) H	8:00 AM (0.76) L	2:21 PM (1.42) H	9:34 PM (0.70) L
Wed 22	3:09 AM (1.03) H	8:30 AM (0.85) L	2:53 PM (1.45) H	10:31 PM (0.64) L
Thu 23	4:39 AM (1.00) H	8:50 AM (0.92) L	3:24 PM (1.47) H	11:20 PM (0.60) L
Fri 24	5:59 AM (1.01) H	9:07 AM (0.97) L	3:56 PM (1.48) H	
Sat 25	12:01 AM (0.58) L	6:48 AM (1.03) H	9:29 AM (0.99) L	4:31 PM (1.49) H
Sun 26	12:39 AM (0.55) L	7:25 AM (1.04) H	9:57 AM (1.00) L	5:11 PM (1.51) H
Mon 27	1:16 AM (0.54) L	8:00 AM (1.05) H	10:29 AM (1.00) L	5:53 PM (1.52) H
Tue 28	1:55 AM (0.52) L	8:38 AM (1.04) H	11:02 AM (1.00) L	6:34 PM (1.53) H
Wed 29	2:32 AM (0.51) L	9:20 AM (1.04) H	11:41 AM (1.00) L	7:14 PM (1.52) H
Thu 30	3:09 AM (0.51) L	10:05 AM (1.04) H	12:30 PM (1.01) L	7:54 PM (1.49) H
Fri 31	3:44 AM (0.52) L	10:46 AM (1.06) H	1:39 PM (1.01) L	8:34 PM (1.45) H

Port Phillip Heads - VIC

DAY/DATE	TIDE 1	TIDE 2	TIDE 3	TIDE 4
Wed 1	6:15 AM (0.48) L	1:28 PM (1.63) H	6:56 PM (0.95) L	
Thu 2	12:44 AM (1.40) H	7:00 AM (0.46) L	2:04 PM (1.66) H	7:38 PM (0.90) L
Fri 3	1:30 AM (1.42) H	7:38 AM (0.46) L	2:39 PM (1.68) H	8:18 PM (0.84) L
Sat 4	2:14 AM (1.44) H	8:14 AM (0.48) L	3:13 PM (1.69) H	8:56 PM (0.79) L
Sun 5	2:56 AM (1.46) H	8:46 AM (0.51) L	3:45 PM (1.69) H	9:31 PM (0.74) L
Mon 6	3:37 AM (1.47) H	9:19 AM (0.55) L	4:17 PM (1.68) H	10:05 PM (0.68) L
Tue 7	4:20 AM (1.47) H	9:56 AM (0.61) L	4:49 PM (1.66) H	10:40 PM (0.62) L
Wed 8	5:07 AM (1.48) H	10:38 AM (0.68) L	5:22 PM (1.62) H	11:15 PM (0.56) L
Thu 9	6:00 AM (1.49) H	11:23 AM (0.77) L	5:58 PM (1.58) H	11:56 PM (0.50) L
Fri 10	6:58 AM (1.51) H	12:11 PM (0.86) L	6:37 PM (1.54) H	
Sat 11	12:42 AM (0.45) L	8:03 AM (1.52) H	1:03 PM (0.95) L	7:23 PM (1.51) H
Sun 12	1:33 AM (0.41) L	9:11 AM (1.54) H	2:04 PM (1.02) L	8:19 PM (1.47) H
Mon 13	2:36 AM (0.39) L	10:22 AM (1.57) H	3:16 PM (1.06) L	9:27 PM (1.45) H
Tue 14	3:49 AM (0.36) L	11:31 AM (1.62) H	4:35 PM (1.03) L	10:45 PM (1.46) H
Wed 15	5:04 AM (0.33) L	12:35 PM (1.67) H	5:49 PM (0.96) L	
Thu 16	12:01 AM (1.49) H	6:12 AM (0.31) L	1:32 PM (1.72) H	6:54 PM (0.85) L
Fri 17	1:07 AM (1.54) H	7:12 AM (0.32) L	2:24 PM (1.76) H	7:53 PM (0.73) L
Sat 18	2:08 AM (1.58) H	8:07 AM (0.36) L	3:10 PM (1.78) H	8:48 PM (0.62) L
Sun 19	3:05 AM (1.61) H	8:57 AM (0.42) L	3:52 PM (1.77) H	9:39 PM (0.53) L
Mon 20	4:01 AM (1.61) H	9:44 AM (0.50) L	4:30 PM (1.74) H	10:25 PM (0.48) L
Tue 21	4:58 AM (1.59) H	10:27 AM (0.60) L	5:06 PM (1.69) H	11:07 PM (0.45) L
Wed 22	5:53 AM (1.55) H	11:07 AM (0.69) L	5:41 PM (1.62) H	11:46 PM (0.45) L
Thu 23	6:45 AM (1.52) H	11:46 AM (0.78) L	6:14 PM (1.55) H	
Fri 24	12:25 AM (0.47) L	7:38 AM (1.48) H	12:27 PM (0.86) L	6:49 PM (1.49) H
Sat 25	1:05 AM (0.50) L	8:30 AM (1.45) H	1:11 PM (0.94) L	7:29 PM (1.42) H
Sun 26	1:51 AM (0.52) L	9:23 AM (1.43) H	2:03 PM (1.01) L	8:16 PM (1.37) H
Mon 27	2:46 AM (0.54) L	10:20 AM (1.43) H	3:08 PM (1.05) L	9:14 PM (1.32) H
Tue 28	3:50 AM (0.55) L	11:18 AM (1.44) H	4:24 PM (1.05) L	10:18 PM (1.30) H
Wed 29	4:54 AM (0.53) L	12:13 PM (1.48) H	5:36 PM (1.00) L	11:22 PM (1.31) H
Thu 30	5:50 AM (0.51) L	12:59 PM (1.53) H	6:34 PM (0.93) L	
Fri 31	12:20 AM (1.35) H	6:38 AM (0.49) L	1:38 PM (1.58) H	7:20 PM (0.84) L

Fort Denison - NSW

DAY/DATE	TIDE 1	TIDE 2	TIDE 3	TIDE 4
Wed 1	3:19 AM (0.48) L	9:10 AM (1.33) H	2:34 PM (0.64) L	9:11 PM (1.84) H
Thu 2	3:56 AM (0.48) L	9:48 AM (1.33) H	3:14 PM (0.64) L	9:47 PM (1.82) H
Fri 3	4:32 AM (0.48) L	10:28 AM (1.34) H	3:55 PM (0.65) L	10:25 PM (1.79) H
Sat 4	5:09 AM (0.49) L	11:10 AM (1.36) H	4:38 PM (0.68) L	11:03 PM (1.73) H
Sun 5	5:47 AM (0.50) L	11:54 AM (1.38) H	5:26 PM (0.70) L	11:44 PM (1.66) H
Mon 6	6:27 AM (0.51) L	12:41 PM (1.42) H	6:20 PM (0.73) L	
Tue 7	12:30 AM (1.58) H	7:09 AM (0.52) L	1:31 PM (1.48) H	7:22 PM (0.75) L
Wed 8	1:24 AM (1.48) H	7:55 AM (0.54) L	2:26 PM (1.55) H	8:34 PM (0.73) L
Thu 9	2:30 AM (1.40) H	8:45 AM (0.56) L	3:24 PM (1.64) H	9:53 PM (0.67) L
Fri 10	3:44 AM (1.35) H	9:41 AM (0.57) L	4:23 PM (1.74) H	11:08 PM (0.57) L
Sat 11	4:57 AM (1.33) H	10:40 AM (0.56) L	5:23 PM (1.86) H	
Sun 12	12:15 AM (0.45) L	6:05 AM (1.35) H	11:40 AM (0.54) L	6:21 PM (1.97) H
Mon 13	1:14 AM (0.33) L	7:06 AM (1.38) H	12:39 PM (0.50) L	7:17 PM (2.06) H
Tue 14	2:08 AM (0.25) L	8:03 AM (1.42) H	1:35 PM (0.46) L	8:12 PM (2.11) H
Wed 15	2:59 AM (0.21) L	8:56 AM (1.45) H	2:30 PM (0.44) L	9:03 PM (2.11) H
Thu 16	3:47 AM (0.21) L	9:47 AM (1.47) H	3:24 PM (0.44) L	9:53 PM (2.05) H
Fri 17	4:34 AM (0.25) L	10:37 AM (1.49) H	4:17 PM (0.48) L	10:40 PM (1.93) H
Sat 18	5:18 AM (0.32) L	11:26 AM (1.49) H	5:11 PM (0.54) L	11:27 PM (1.77) H
Sun 19	6:00 AM (0.41) L	12:15 PM (1.50) H	6:05 PM (0.62) L	
Mon 20	12:13 AM (1.59) H	6:41 AM (0.50) L	1:03 PM (1.50) H	7:04 PM (0.70) L
Tue 21	1:00 AM (1.42) H	7:20 AM (0.58) L	1:55 PM (1.50) H	8:11 PM (0.76) L
Wed 22	1:54 AM (1.28) H	8:02 AM (0.65) L	2:48 PM (1.52) H	9:24 PM (0.77) L
Thu 23	2:58 AM (1.19) H	8:50 AM (0.69) L	3:44 PM (1.54) H	10:38 PM (0.74) L
Fri 24	4:09 AM (1.15) H	9:45 AM (0.71) L	4:40 PM (1.57) H	11:39 PM (0.68) L
Sat 25	5:15 AM (1.16) H	10:40 AM (0.71) L	5:31 PM (1.62) H	
Sun 26	12:29 AM (0.61) L	6:10 AM (1.20) H	11:31 AM (0.69) L	6:17 PM (1.68) H
Mon 27	1:10 AM (0.54) L	6:55 AM (1.24) H	12:18 PM (0.65) L	7:00 PM (1.73) H
Tue 28	1:46 AM (0.48) L	7:34 AM (1.28) H	1:00 PM (0.61) L	7:38 PM (1.78) H
Wed 29	2:21 AM (0.44) L	8:11 AM (1.32) H	1:39 PM (0.57) L	8:14 PM (1.81) H
Thu 30	2:54 AM (0.40) L	8:45 AM (1.35) H	2:17 PM (0.54) L	8:49 PM (1.83) H
Fri 31	3:27 AM (0.38) L	9:22 AM (1.39) H	2:57 PM (0.53) L	9:24 PM (1.81) H

BITE TIMES

Apogee moon phase on Sunday 26th
Perigee moon phase on Monday 13th

● **New moon on Tuesday 14th**
First quarter moon on Tuesday 21st
○ **Full moon on Thursday 30th**
Last quarter moon phase on Wednesday 8th

DAY	MINOR BITE	MAJOR BITE	MINOR BITE	MAJOR BITE	SALT WATER RATING	FRESH WATER RATING
WED 1	5:09 PM		7:36 AM	12:20 PM	7	6
THUR 2	6:10 PM	12:45 AM	8:12 AM	1:07 PM	7	6
FRI 3	7:13 PM	1:31 AM	8:42 AM	1:53 PM	5	5
SAT 4	8:15 PM	2:16 AM	9:09 AM	2:37 PM	4	4
SUN 5	9:18 PM	2:59 AM	9:33 AM	3:20 PM	3	6
MON 6	10:21 PM	3:42 AM	9:56 AM	4:03 PM	3	6
TUE 7	11:26 PM	4:25 AM	10:20 AM	4:48 PM	4	4
WED 8		5:11 AM	10:45 AM	5:34 PM	5	5
THUR 9	12:35 AM	5:59 AM	11:15 AM	6:26 PM	6	6
FRI 10	1:48 AM	6:53 AM	11:50 AM	7:22 PM	7	7
SAT 11	3:04 AM	7:52 AM	12:34 PM	8:23 PM	7	8
SUN 12	4:19 AM	8:56 AM	1:30 PM	9:29 PM	6	7
MON 13	5:29 AM	10:03 AM	2:38 PM	10:36 PM	8	8
TUE 14	6:29 AM	11:09 AM	3:54 PM	11:40 PM	8 ●	8
WED 15	7:16 AM	12:11 PM	5:13 PM		8	6
THUR 16	7:54 AM	1:08 PM	6:30 PM	12:39 AM	7	6
FRI 17	8:26 AM	1:59 PM	7:42 PM	1:33 AM	6	7
SAT 18	8:52 AM	2:46 PM	8:50 PM	2:22 AM	5	5
SUN 19	9:17 AM	3:31 PM	9:55 PM	3:08 AM	4	6
MON 20	9:41 AM	4:14 PM	10:59 PM	3:52 AM	3	5
TUE 21	10:05 AM	4:58 PM		4:35 AM	4	6
WED 22	10:32 AM	5:43 PM	12:01 AM	5:20 AM	5	6
THUR 23	11:02 AM	6:29 PM	1:04 AM	6:05 AM	5	6
FRI 24	11:37 AM	7:18 PM	2:05 AM	6:53 AM	4	5
SAT 25	12:18 PM	8:08 PM	3:05 AM	7:43 AM	3	5
SUN 26	1:06 PM	8:59 PM	4:01 AM	8:33 AM	6	6
MON 27	2:00 PM	9:51 PM	4:52 AM	9:24 AM	5	7
TUE 28	3:00 PM	10:41 PM	5:36 AM	10:16 AM	3	8
WED 29	4:02 PM	11:29 PM	6:13 AM	11:05 AM	5	7
THUR 30	5:05 PM		6:45 AM	11:52 AM	5 ○	7
FRI 31	6:09 PM	12:15 AM	7:13 AM	12:37 PM	7	6

TIDE TIMES

Adelaide Outer Harbour - SA

DAY/DATE	TIDE 1	TIDE 2	TIDE 3	TIDE 4
Sat 1	12:15 AM (0.39) L	6:13 AM (2.11) H	11:52 AM (0.65) L	6:05 PM (2.69) H
Sun 2	12:35 AM (0.38) L	6:36 AM (2.20) H	12:23 PM (0.64) L	6:30 PM (2.61) H
Mon 3	12:56 AM (0.40) L	7:02 AM (2.28) H	12:55 PM (0.66) L	6:55 PM (2.49) H
Tue 4	1:15 AM (0.44) L	7:28 AM (2.36) H	1:28 PM (0.70) L	7:19 PM (2.34) H
Wed 5	1:31 AM (0.48) L	7:54 AM (2.43) H	2:01 PM (0.77) L	7:44 PM (2.14) H
Thu 6	1:48 AM (0.56) L	8:23 AM (2.44) H	2:40 PM (0.89) L	8:08 PM (1.89) H
Fri 7	2:02 AM (0.68) L	8:57 AM (2.37) H	3:30 PM (1.10) L	8:22 PM (1.57) H
Sat 8	2:03 AM (0.86) L	9:40 AM (2.17) H		
Sun 9	12:43 AM (0.98) L	1:48 PM (1.93) H	11:04 PM (0.75) L	
Mon 10	6:13 AM (1.63) H	9:26 AM (1.50) L	3:49 PM (2.24) H	11:11 PM (0.48) L
Tue 11	5:46 AM (1.75) H	10:19 AM (1.21) L	4:32 PM (2.49) H	11:31 PM (0.34) L
Wed 12	5:48 AM (1.84) H	10:47 AM (0.98) L	5:01 PM (2.62) H	11:49 PM (0.34) L
Thu 13	5:51 AM (1.89) H	11:08 AM (0.81) L	5:22 PM (2.64) H	
Fri 14	12:00 AM (0.40) L	5:53 AM (1.96) H	11:26 AM (0.69) L	5:38 PM (2.60) H
Sat 15	12:08 AM (0.46) L	5:59 AM (2.10) H	11:45 AM (0.61) L	5:53 PM (2.53) H
Sun 16	12:14 AM (0.47) L	6:12 AM (2.25) H	12:09 PM (0.58) L	6:10 PM (2.44) H
Mon 17	12:23 AM (0.45) L	6:32 AM (2.39) H	12:36 PM (0.59) L	6:29 PM (2.33) H
Tue 18	12:35 AM (0.42) L	6:57 AM (2.49) H	1:03 PM (0.64) L	6:49 PM (2.23) H
Wed 19	12:50 AM (0.41) L	7:23 AM (2.53) H	1:30 PM (0.71) L	7:10 PM (2.11) H
Thu 20	1:09 AM (0.43) L	7:49 AM (2.51) H	2:00 PM (0.82) L	7:30 PM (1.96) H
Fri 21	1:29 AM (0.53) L	8:17 AM (2.40) H	2:32 PM (0.99) L	7:46 PM (1.76) H
Sat 22	1:45 AM (0.71) L	8:48 AM (2.18) H	3:15 PM (1.25) L	7:32 PM (1.51) H
Sun 23	1:34 AM (0.95) L	9:30 AM (1.88) H	11:29 PM (1.01) L	
Mon 24	6:31 AM (1.56) H	9:06 AM (1.53) L	3:21 PM (1.95) H	10:42 PM (0.76) L
Tue 25	5:07 AM (1.71) H	9:55 AM (1.20) L	4:03 PM (2.26) H	10:52 PM (0.53) L
Wed 26	5:04 AM (1.89) H	10:21 AM (0.94) L	4:31 PM (2.47) H	11:08 PM (0.40) L
Thu 27	5:14 AM (2.01) H	10:42 AM (0.76) L	4:53 PM (2.58) H	11:22 PM (0.36) L
Fri 28	5:23 AM (2.09) H	10:59 AM (0.64) L	5:09 PM (2.61) H	11:33 PM (0.35) L
Sat 29*	5:31 AM (2.17) H	11:17 AM (0.54) L	5:26 PM (2.60) H	11:45 PM (0.35) L
Sun 30	5:45 AM (2.29) H	11:41 AM (0.48) L	5:45 PM (2.55) H	
Mon 31	12:00 AM (0.35) L	6:03 AM (2.39) H	12:09 PM (0.46) L	6:06 PM (2.44) H

Brisbane Bar - QLD

DAY/DATE	TIDE 1	TIDE 2	TIDE 3	TIDE 4
Sat 1	5:30 AM (0.53) L	11:05 AM (1.93) H	5:04 PM (0.46) L	11:22 PM (2.41) H
Sun 2	6:02 AM (0.51) L	11:45 AM (1.96) H	5:44 PM (0.53) L	11:54 PM (2.33) H
Mon 3	6:34 AM (0.50) L	12:28 PM (1.98) H	6:25 PM (0.63) L	
Tue 4	12:29 AM (2.21) H	7:07 AM (0.51) L	1:15 PM (1.99) H	7:13 PM (0.74) L
Wed 5	1:07 AM (2.06) H	7:45 AM (0.52) L	2:08 PM (2.01) H	8:12 PM (0.85) L
Thu 6	1:57 AM (1.88) H	8:34 AM (0.54) L	3:15 PM (2.05) H	9:30 PM (0.92) L
Fri 7	3:06 AM (1.72) H	9:38 AM (0.56) L	4:34 PM (2.13) H	11:06 PM (0.90) L
Sat 8	4:35 AM (1.62) H	10:52 AM (0.55) L	5:51 PM (2.27) H	
Sun 9	12:38 AM (0.78) L	6:00 AM (1.63) H	12:06 PM (0.49) L	6:59 PM (2.43) H
Mon 10	1:50 AM (0.63) L	7:14 AM (1.71) H	1:15 PM (0.40) L	7:57 PM (2.57) H
Tue 11	2:47 AM (0.50) L	8:14 AM (1.81) H	2:15 PM (0.31) L	8:47 PM (2.66) H
Wed 12	3:36 AM (0.41) L	9:06 AM (1.90) H	3:09 PM (0.26) L	9:33 PM (2.69) H
Thu 13	4:19 AM (0.37) L	9:53 AM (1.98) H	3:57 PM (0.25) L	10:15 PM (2.66) H
Fri 14	4:59 AM (0.36) L	10:37 AM (2.03) H	4:41 PM (0.30) L	10:53 PM (2.57) H
Sat 15	5:33 AM (0.37) L	11:18 AM (2.07) H	5:22 PM (0.39) L	11:30 PM (2.42) H
Sun 16	6:04 AM (0.40) L	11:59 AM (2.08) H	6:03 PM (0.53) L	
Mon 17	12:03 AM (2.24) H	6:33 AM (0.44) L	12:39 PM (2.06) H	6:44 PM (0.69) L
Tue 18	12:35 AM (2.04) H	7:02 AM (0.49) L	1:22 PM (2.02) H	7:30 PM (0.84) L
Wed 19	1:10 AM (1.84) H	7:34 AM (0.56) L	2:10 PM (1.98) H	8:25 PM (0.97) L
Thu 20	1:51 AM (1.64) H	8:15 AM (0.65) L	3:12 PM (1.94) H	9:45 PM (1.04) L
Fri 21	2:54 AM (1.48) H	9:11 AM (0.73) L	4:30 PM (1.94) H	11:26 PM (1.00) L
Sat 22	4:28 AM (1.42) H	10:25 AM (0.76) L	5:45 PM (2.01) H	
Sun 23	12:38 AM (0.89) L	5:54 AM (1.47) H	11:39 AM (0.72) L	6:41 PM (2.12) H
Mon 24	1:28 AM (0.77) L	6:51 AM (1.58) H	12:41 PM (0.63) L	7:28 PM (2.22) H
Tue 25	2:08 AM (0.67) L	7:35 AM (1.69) H	1:30 PM (0.54) L	8:07 PM (2.31) H
Wed 26	2:45 AM (0.59) L	8:14 AM (1.79) H	2:15 PM (0.46) L	8:44 PM (2.38) H
Thu 27	3:19 AM (0.53) L	8:51 AM (1.88) H	2:55 PM (0.40) L	9:18 PM (2.42) H
Fri 28	3:53 AM (0.47) L	9:29 AM (1.96) H	3:34 PM (0.38) L	9:50 PM (2.43) H
Sat 29	4:26 AM (0.42) L	10:07 AM (2.04) H	4:14 PM (0.39) L	10:22 PM (2.40) H
Sun 30	4:58 AM (0.39) L	10:45 AM (2.10) H	4:53 PM (0.43) L	10:54 PM (2.32) H
Mon 31	5:28 AM (0.38) L	11:26 AM (2.14) H	5:33 PM (0.51) L	11:27 PM (2.20) H

Darwin - NT

DAY/DATE	TIDE 1	TIDE 2	TIDE 3	TIDE 4
Sat 1	1:42 AM (1.24) L	8:13 AM (7.10) H	2:11 PM (2.08) L	7:46 PM (6.53) H
Sun 2	2:09 AM (1.31) L	8:35 AM (7.12) H	2:44 PM (1.87) L	8:24 PM (6.57) H
Mon 3	2:36 AM (1.51) L	8:57 AM (7.05) H	3:18 PM (1.74) L	9:04 PM (6.51) H
Tue 4	3:04 AM (1.83) L	9:17 AM (6.88) H	3:55 PM (1.69) L	9:47 PM (6.37) H
Wed 5	3:36 AM (2.27) L	9:40 AM (6.60) H	4:32 PM (1.74) L	10:36 PM (6.12) H
Thu 6	4:13 AM (2.81) L	10:04 AM (6.23) H	5:15 PM (1.87) L	11:32 PM (5.81) H
Fri 7	5:03 AM (3.40) L	10:36 AM (5.79) H	6:08 PM (2.05) L	
Sat 8	12:45 AM (5.53) H	6:21 AM (3.92) L	11:24 AM (5.30) H	7:28 PM (2.19) L
Sun 9	2:38 AM (5.52) H	8:21 AM (4.11) L	1:10 PM (4.91) H	9:12 PM (2.05) L
Mon 10	4:19 AM (5.96) H	10:13 AM (3.78) L	3:30 PM (5.13) H	10:33 PM (1.65) L
Tue 11	5:23 AM (6.52) H	11:23 AM (3.22) L	4:40 PM (5.69) H	11:34 PM (1.21) L
Wed 12	6:14 AM (7.01) H	12:14 PM (2.63) L	5:36 PM (6.25) H	
Thu 13	12:24 AM (0.88) L	6:57 AM (7.40) H	12:57 PM (2.08) L	6:28 PM (6.71) H
Fri 14	1:07 AM (0.72) L	7:33 AM (7.63) H	1:36 PM (1.62) L	7:15 PM (7.01) H
Sat 15	1:45 AM (0.80) L	8:05 AM (7.68) H	2:13 PM (1.31) L	8:00 PM (7.10) H
Sun 16	2:18 AM (1.08) L	8:31 AM (7.56) H	2:48 PM (1.17) L	8:41 PM (7.00) H
Mon 17	2:48 AM (1.54) L	8:54 AM (7.28) H	3:23 PM (1.22) L	9:19 PM (6.72) H
Tue 18	3:15 AM (2.10) L	9:14 AM (6.90) H	3:55 PM (1.43) L	9:57 PM (6.34) H
Wed 19	3:34 AM (2.69) L	9:30 AM (6.43) H	4:26 PM (1.76) L	10:35 PM (5.89) H
Thu 20	3:52 AM (3.25) L	9:46 AM (5.89) H	5:00 PM (2.16) L	11:21 PM (5.45) H
Fri 21	4:30 AM (3.80) L	10:04 AM (5.30) H	5:47 PM (2.58) L	
Sat 22	12:24 AM (5.06) H	6:08 AM (4.26) L	10:11 AM (4.72) H	7:00 PM (2.89) L
Sun 23	3:06 AM (4.97) H	11:26 AM (4.17) L	1:49 PM (4.24) H	8:48 PM (2.92) L
Mon 24	4:40 AM (5.42) H	11:30 AM (3.72) L	3:59 PM (4.63) H	10:21 PM (2.60) L
Tue 25	5:17 AM (5.85) H	11:47 AM (3.33) L	4:43 PM (5.13) H	11:12 PM (2.19) L
Wed 26	5:49 AM (6.25) H	12:06 PM (2.97) L	5:18 PM (5.63) H	11:50 PM (1.81) L
Thu 27	6:19 AM (6.61) H	12:28 PM (2.58) L	5:53 PM (6.10) H	
Fri 28	12:24 AM (1.51) L	6:47 AM (6.93) H	12:53 PM (2.17) L	6:29 PM (6.50) H
Sat 29	12:54 AM (1.32) L	7:14 AM (7.18) H	1:20 PM (1.77) L	7:04 PM (6.82) H
Sun 30	1:21 AM (1.27) L	7:37 AM (7.31) H	1:50 PM (1.41) L	7:40 PM (7.03) H
Mon 31	1:46 AM (1.36) L	7:57 AM (7.33) H	2:20 PM (1.15) L	8:15 PM (7.10) H

Fremantle - WA

DAY/DATE	TIDE 5
Mon 17	11:45 PM (1.00) H
Tue 18	4:48 PM (0.69) L

DAY/DATE	TIDE 1	TIDE 2	TIDE 3	TIDE 4
Sat 1	12:37 AM (0.85) H	3:21 AM (0.81) L	10:30 AM (1.14) H	6:24 PM (0.71) L
Sun 2	12:58 AM (0.88) H	4:11 AM (0.83) L	10:56 AM (1.07) H	6:23 PM (0.73) L
Mon 3	1:24 AM (0.93) H	5:08 AM (0.85) L	11:18 AM (0.99) H	6:15 PM (0.75) L
Tue 4	1:55 AM (0.98) H	6:29 AM (0.87) L	11:34 AM (0.91) H	6:09 PM (0.76) L
Wed 5	2:30 AM (1.03) H	5:20 PM (0.74) L		
Thu 6	3:12 AM (1.08) H	2:46 PM (0.69) L	3:51 PM (0.69) L	4:43 PM (0.69) L
Fri 7	4:01 AM (1.13) H	3:13 PM (0.60) L		
Sat 8	5:01 AM (1.18) H	3:47 PM (0.53) L		
Sun 9	6:12 AM (1.22) H	4:26 PM (0.49) L		
Mon 10	7:21 AM (1.26) H	5:06 PM (0.48) L		
Tue 11	8:18 AM (1.27) H	5:45 PM (0.50) L		
Wed 12	9:09 AM (1.25) H	6:19 PM (0.55) L		
Thu 13	12:19 AM (0.78) H	1:25 AM (0.77) L	9:57 AM (1.19) H	6:29 PM (0.62) L
Fri 14	12:16 AM (0.80) H	2:31 AM (0.77) L	10:41 AM (1.11) H	6:08 PM (0.70) L
Sat 15	12:29 AM (0.85) H	3:28 AM (0.78) L	11:15 AM (1.01) H	5:50 PM (0.75) L
Sun 16	12:41 AM (0.90) H	4:28 AM (0.80) L	10:39 AM (0.91) H	4:59 PM (0.74) L
Mon 17*	12:56 AM (0.95) H	5:41 AM (0.82) L	10:27 AM (0.84) H	5:00 PM (0.72) L
Tue 18*	12:29 AM (0.99) L	1:16 AM (1.00) H	6:51 AM (0.84) L	7:57 AM (0.84) L
Wed 19	12:07 AM (1.03) H	4:22 PM (0.66) L		
Thu 20	12:43 AM (1.05) H	4:28 PM (0.63) L		
Fri 21	1:32 AM (1.04) H	2:17 AM (1.04) L	3:15 AM (1.05) H	3:30 PM (0.62) L
Sat 22	4:18 AM (1.05) H	3:45 PM (0.60) L		
Sun 23	5:40 AM (1.06) H	4:02 PM (0.59) L		
Mon 24	6:57 AM (1.09) H	4:20 PM (0.59) L		
Tue 25	7:42 AM (1.11) H	4:34 PM (0.59) L		
Wed 26	8:18 AM (1.12) H	4:45 PM (0.60) L	11:18 PM (0.79) H	
Thu 27	1:24 AM (0.77) L	8:52 AM (1.12) H	4:52 PM (0.62) L	11:08 PM (0.81) H
Fri 28	2:15 AM (0.75) L	9:25 AM (1.09) H	5:00 PM (0.65) L	11:15 PM (0.84) H
Sat 29	3:03 AM (0.73) L	9:57 AM (1.04) H	5:05 PM (0.68) L	11:29 PM (0.88) H
Sun 30	3:54 AM (0.72) L	10:26 AM (0.97) H	4:57 PM (0.70) L	11:39 PM (0.93) H
Mon 31	4:51 AM (0.71) L	10:48 AM (0.88) H	4:45 PM (0.71) L	11:27 PM (0.98) H

* Additional Tide 5 - See Additional Tide 5

Sun Rise & Sun Set Times:

Darwin, NT: Rise: 07:00am Set: 06:40pm

Melbourne, VIC: Rise: 07:00am Set: 05:40pm

Adelaide, SA: Rise: 06:50am Set: 05:40pm

Perth, WA: Rise: 06:50am Set: 05:40pm

Sydney, NSW: Rise: 06:30am Set: 05:20pm

Brisbane, QLD: Rise: 06:10am Set: 05:20pm

Hobart, TAS: Rise: 07:00am Set: 05:20pm

(Note: These times are averages for the month)

Hobart - TAS

DAY/DATE	TIDE 1	TIDE 2	TIDE 3	TIDE 4
Sat 1	4:16 AM (0.54) L	11:20 AM (1.11) H	3:02 PM (1.01) L	9:19 PM (1.38) H
Sun 2	4:47 AM (0.58) L	11:50 AM (1.17) H	4:37 PM (0.97) L	10:15 PM (1.29) H
Mon 3	5:19 AM (0.63) L	12:20 PM (1.24) H	6:06 PM (0.91) L	11:29 PM (1.20) H
Tue 4	5:53 AM (0.70) L	12:50 PM (1.32) H	7:19 PM (0.82) L	
Wed 5	12:47 AM (1.13) H	6:31 AM (0.78) L	1:22 PM (1.40) H	8:21 PM (0.71) L
Thu 6	1:59 AM (1.08) H	7:15 AM (0.85) L	1:57 PM (1.48) H	9:17 PM (0.59) L
Fri 7	3:15 AM (1.06) H	8:00 AM (0.91) L	2:36 PM (1.55) H	10:13 PM (0.48) L
Sat 8	4:46 AM (1.06) H	8:46 AM (0.94) L	3:22 PM (1.61) H	11:08 PM (0.39) L
Sun 9	5:57 AM (1.07) H	9:30 AM (0.95) L	4:15 PM (1.67) H	
Mon 10	12:04 AM (0.32) L	6:47 AM (1.08) H	10:16 AM (0.94) L	5:15 PM (1.70) H
Tue 11	1:00 AM (0.28) L	7:34 AM (1.09) H	11:07 AM (0.93) L	6:15 PM (1.71) H
Wed 12	1:55 AM (0.28) L	8:21 AM (1.09) H	12:07 PM (0.92) L	7:14 PM (1.67) H
Thu 13	2:48 AM (0.31) L	9:13 AM (1.11) H	1:27 PM (0.91) L	8:11 PM (1.59) H
Fri 14	3:39 AM (0.37) L	10:06 AM (1.15) H	3:06 PM (0.89) L	9:13 PM (1.47) H
Sat 15	4:28 AM (0.46) L	10:56 AM (1.20) H	4:39 PM (0.83) L	10:25 PM (1.34) H
Sun 16	5:14 AM (0.57) L	11:41 AM (1.27) H	5:57 PM (0.76) L	11:39 PM (1.22) H
Mon 17	5:58 AM (0.69) L	12:20 PM (1.33) H	7:04 PM (0.70) L	
Tue 18	12:46 AM (1.12) H	6:37 AM (0.80) L	12:55 PM (1.37) H	8:04 PM (0.65) L
Wed 19	1:51 AM (1.05) H	7:13 AM (0.89) L	1:29 PM (1.40) H	8:58 PM (0.61) L
Thu 20	3:08 AM (1.02) H	7:45 AM (0.95) L	2:00 PM (1.42) H	9:45 PM (0.59) L
Fri 21	4:45 AM (1.02) H	8:15 AM (0.98) L	2:34 PM (1.42) H	10:30 PM (0.57) L
Sat 22	5:40 AM (1.03) H	8:47 AM (0.99) L	3:13 PM (1.43) H	11:12 PM (0.56) L
Sun 23	6:13 AM (1.04) H	9:19 AM (0.98) L	3:57 PM (1.44) H	11:51 PM (0.55) L
Mon 24	6:42 AM (1.04) H	9:53 AM (0.97) L	4:44 PM (1.45) H	
Tue 25	12:30 AM (0.54) L	7:11 AM (1.04) H	10:28 AM (0.95) L	5:29 PM (1.46) H
Wed 26	1:09 AM (0.53) L	7:40 AM (1.04) H	11:06 AM (0.93) L	6:11 PM (1.46) H
Thu 27	1:45 AM (0.53) L	8:11 AM (1.04) H	11:52 AM (0.92) L	6:53 PM (1.44) H
Fri 28	2:19 AM (0.54) L	8:43 AM (1.06) H	12:49 PM (0.91) L	7:36 PM (1.40) H
Sat 29	2:51 AM (0.57) L	9:19 AM (1.11) H	2:01 PM (0.89) L	8:24 PM (1.33) H
Sun 30	3:23 AM (0.62) L	9:59 AM (1.17) H	3:30 PM (0.85) L	9:24 PM (1.25) H
Mon 31	3:56 AM (0.68) L	10:39 AM (1.24) H	4:54 PM (0.77) L	10:45 PM (1.18) H

Port Phillip Heads - VIC

DAY/DATE	TIDE 1	TIDE 2	TIDE 3	TIDE 4
Sat 1	1:13 AM (1.39) H	7:18 AM (0.48) L	2:13 PM (1.62) H	8:00 PM (0.75) L
Sun 2	2:00 AM (1.45) H	7:55 AM (0.49) L	2:45 PM (1.65) H	8:35 PM (0.67) L
Mon 3	2:45 AM (1.49) H	8:30 AM (0.52) L	3:17 PM (1.67) H	9:09 PM (0.58) L
Tue 4	3:27 AM (1.53) H	9:07 AM (0.56) L	3:49 PM (1.66) H	9:43 PM (0.51) L
Wed 5	4:10 AM (1.56) H	9:46 AM (0.61) L	4:20 PM (1.64) H	10:17 PM (0.45) L
Thu 6	4:54 AM (1.57) H	10:28 AM (0.68) L	4:52 PM (1.61) H	10:55 PM (0.40) L
Fri 7	5:43 AM (1.56) H	11:10 AM (0.75) L	5:27 PM (1.57) H	11:35 PM (0.36) L
Sat 8	6:37 AM (1.53) H	11:53 AM (0.83) L	6:06 PM (1.53) H	
Sun 9	12:19 AM (0.35) L	7:38 AM (1.50) H	12:41 PM (0.90) L	6:53 PM (1.48) H
Mon 10	1:10 AM (0.36) L	8:47 AM (1.47) H	1:36 PM (0.97) L	7:53 PM (1.43) H
Tue 11	2:14 AM (0.38) L	10:01 AM (1.47) H	2:48 PM (0.99) L	9:09 PM (1.40) H
Wed 12	3:34 AM (0.40) L	11:12 AM (1.50) H	4:17 PM (0.95) L	10:38 PM (1.40) H
Thu 13	4:57 AM (0.39) L	12:15 PM (1.56) H	5:39 PM (0.85) L	11:57 PM (1.45) H
Fri 14	6:05 AM (0.38) L	1:11 PM (1.62) H	6:46 PM (0.71) L	
Sat 15	1:04 AM (1.53) H	7:03 AM (0.38) L	1:59 PM (1.68) H	7:42 PM (0.57) L
Sun 16	2:04 AM (1.60) H	7:55 AM (0.41) L	2:41 PM (1.70) H	8:30 PM (0.46) L
Mon 17	2:59 AM (1.64) H	8:40 AM (0.47) L	3:19 PM (1.70) H	9:15 PM (0.39) L
Tue 18	3:49 AM (1.65) H	9:22 AM (0.53) L	3:54 PM (1.67) H	9:54 PM (0.35) L
Wed 19	4:35 AM (1.63) H	10:00 AM (0.60) L	4:25 PM (1.63) H	10:30 PM (0.35) L
Thu 20	5:19 AM (1.59) H	10:36 AM (0.66) L	4:56 PM (1.57) H	11:07 PM (0.37) L
Fri 21	6:01 AM (1.53) H	11:13 AM (0.73) L	5:28 PM (1.51) H	11:43 PM (0.40) L
Sat 22	6:45 AM (1.46) H	11:50 AM (0.79) L	6:01 PM (1.45) H	
Sun 23	12:20 AM (0.45) L	7:32 AM (1.40) H	12:30 PM (0.86) L	6:40 PM (1.38) H
Mon 24	1:02 AM (0.49) L	8:26 AM (1.35) H	1:15 PM (0.93) L	7:27 PM (1.32) H
Tue 25	1:52 AM (0.53) L	9:26 AM (1.33) H	2:14 PM (0.98) L	8:28 PM (1.26) H
Wed 26	2:55 AM (0.57) L	10:30 AM (1.33) H	3:31 PM (0.99) L	9:41 PM (1.24) H
Thu 27	4:12 AM (0.57) L	11:30 AM (1.37) H	5:05 PM (0.93) L	10:57 PM (1.25) H
Fri 28	5:22 AM (0.56) L	12:19 PM (1.43) H	6:11 PM (0.83) L	
Sat 29	12:03 AM (1.32) H	6:15 AM (0.54) L	1:00 PM (1.49) H	6:54 PM (0.72) L
Sun 30	12:59 AM (1.41) H	6:58 AM (0.53) L	1:36 PM (1.55) H	7:30 PM (0.60) L
Mon 31	1:47 AM (1.50) H	7:36 AM (0.53) L	2:11 PM (1.59) H	8:03 PM (0.49) L

Fort Denison - NSW

DAY/DATE	TIDE 1	TIDE 2	TIDE 3	TIDE 4
Sat 1	4:00 AM (0.38) L	10:00 AM (1.42) H	3:38 PM (0.53) L	10:00 PM (1.77) H
Sun 2	4:32 AM (0.38) L	10:39 AM (1.46) H	4:22 PM (0.55) L	10:38 PM (1.70) H
Mon 3	5:07 AM (0.40) L	11:20 AM (1.50) H	5:10 PM (0.58) L	11:18 PM (1.60) H
Tue 4	5:44 AM (0.44) L	12:05 PM (1.53) H	6:03 PM (0.62) L	
Wed 5	12:05 AM (1.48) H	6:24 AM (0.49) L	12:54 PM (1.56) H	7:06 PM (0.65) L
Thu 6	1:00 AM (1.36) H	7:12 AM (0.55) L	1:50 PM (1.59) H	8:21 PM (0.65) L
Fri 7	2:11 AM (1.26) H	8:09 AM (0.60) L	2:56 PM (1.64) H	9:47 PM (0.61) L
Sat 8	3:35 AM (1.21) H	9:17 AM (0.61) L	4:05 PM (1.71) H	11:05 PM (0.51) L
Sun 9	4:57 AM (1.23) H	10:29 AM (0.59) L	5:13 PM (1.81) H	
Mon 10	12:10 AM (0.39) L	6:03 AM (1.29) H	11:34 AM (0.52) L	6:13 PM (1.91) H
Tue 11	1:05 AM (0.28) L	7:00 AM (1.36) H	12:32 PM (0.45) L	7:08 PM (1.99) H
Wed 12	1:53 AM (0.21) L	7:49 AM (1.43) H	1:28 PM (0.38) L	7:58 PM (2.03) H
Thu 13	2:38 AM (0.18) L	8:37 AM (1.49) H	2:19 PM (0.35) L	8:45 PM (2.00) H
Fri 14	3:20 AM (0.20) L	9:22 AM (1.53) H	3:09 PM (0.36) L	9:30 PM (1.91) H
Sat 15	4:00 AM (0.25) L	10:06 AM (1.56) H	3:59 PM (0.40) L	10:14 PM (1.77) H
Sun 16	4:36 AM (0.33) L	10:49 AM (1.56) H	4:47 PM (0.48) L	10:55 PM (1.61) H
Mon 17	5:11 AM (0.42) L	11:31 AM (1.56) H	5:38 PM (0.56) L	11:36 PM (1.44) H
Tue 18	5:45 AM (0.52) L	12:15 PM (1.53) H	6:32 PM (0.64) L	
Wed 19	12:20 AM (1.29) H	6:19 AM (0.60) L	1:00 PM (1.51) H	7:33 PM (0.70) L
Thu 20	1:11 AM (1.17) H	7:00 AM (0.67) L	1:53 PM (1.48) H	8:45 PM (0.73) L
Fri 21	2:17 AM (1.10) H	7:55 AM (0.73) L	2:55 PM (1.47) H	10:02 PM (0.71) L
Sat 22	3:39 AM (1.08) H	9:04 AM (0.75) L	4:01 PM (1.49) H	11:09 PM (0.65) L
Sun 23	4:54 AM (1.11) H	10:14 AM (0.73) L	5:02 PM (1.54) H	
Mon 24	12:00 AM (0.58) L	5:49 AM (1.17) H	11:12 AM (0.68) L	5:52 PM (1.60) H
Tue 25	12:42 AM (0.50) L	6:32 AM (1.24) H	12:00 PM (0.61) L	6:34 PM (1.67) H
Wed 26	1:16 AM (0.43) L	7:09 AM (1.30) H	12:42 PM (0.55) L	7:12 PM (1.73) H
Thu 27	1:49 AM (0.38) L	7:43 AM (1.37) H	1:21 PM (0.49) L	7:47 PM (1.77) H
Fri 28	2:19 AM (0.33) L	8:16 AM (1.43) H	2:00 PM (0.44) L	8:22 PM (1.78) H
Sat 29	2:50 AM (0.31) L	8:52 AM (1.50) H	2:41 PM (0.42) L	8:59 PM (1.76) H
Sun 30	3:21 AM (0.30) L	9:29 AM (1.56) H	3:23 PM (0.41) L	9:37 PM (1.70) H
Mon 31	3:54 AM (0.32) L	10:07 AM (1.61) H	4:09 PM (0.42) L	10:17 PM (1.61) H

BITE TIMES

Apogee moon phase on Saturday 22nd
Perigee moon phase on Monday 10th

New moon on Thursday 13th
First quarter moon on Thursday 20th
Full moon on Friday 28th
Last quarter moon phase on Thursday 6th

DAY	MINOR BITE	MAJOR BITE	MINOR BITE	MAJOR BITE	SALT WATER RATING	FRESH WATER RATING
SAT 1	7:12 PM	12:59 AM	7:38 AM	1:20 PM	7	6
SUN 2	8:14 PM	1:42 AM	8:02 AM	2:03 PM	5	5
MON 3	9:19 PM	2:25 AM	8:25 AM	2:46 PM	4	4
TUE 4	10:26 PM	3:09 AM	8:49 AM	3:31 PM	3	6
WED 5	11:35 PM	3:55 AM	9:17 AM	4:20 PM	4	4
THUR 6		4:46 AM	9:49 AM	5:13 PM	5	5
FRI 7	12:48 AM	5:41 AM	10:28 AM	6:11 PM	6	6
SAT 8	2:02 AM	6:41 AM	11:17 AM	7:12 PM	7	7
SUN 9	3:12 AM	7:45 AM	12:18 PM	8:17 PM	7	8
10	4:15 AM	8:50 AM	1:29 PM	9:21 PM	5	8
TUE 11	5:07 AM	9:53 AM	2:46 PM	10:22 PM	6	7
WED 12	5:48 AM	10:52 AM	4:04 PM	11:18 PM	8	8
THUR 13	6:22 AM	11:46 AM	5:18 PM		8	8
FRI 14	6:51 AM	12:35 PM	6:29 PM	12:10 AM	8	6
SAT 15	7:17 AM	1:22 PM	7:37 PM	12:58 AM	7	6

DAY	MINOR BITE	MAJOR BITE	MINOR BITE	MAJOR BITE	SALT WATER RATING	FRESH WATER RATING
SUN 16	7:41 AM	2:07 PM	8:43 PM	1:44 AM	6	7
MON 17	8:06 AM	2:51 PM	9:47 PM	2:29 AM	5	5
TUE 18	8:32 AM	3:36 PM	10:51 PM	3:13 AM	4	6
WED 19	9:01 AM	4:23 PM	11:54 PM	3:59 AM	3	5
THUR 20	9:34 AM	5:11 PM		4:46 AM	4	6
FRI 21	10:13 AM	6:01 PM	12:55 AM	5:35 AM	5	6
SAT 22	10:59 AM	6:52 PM	1:53 AM	6:26 AM	4	5
SUN 23	11:51 AM	7:44 PM	2:46 AM	7:17 AM	3	5
MON 24	12:49 PM	8:34 PM	3:32 AM	8:09 AM	3	5
TUE 25	1:51 PM	9:23 PM	4:12 AM	8:58 AM	6	6
WED 26	2:54 PM	10:10 PM	4:46 AM	9:46 AM	5	7
THUR 27	3:58 PM	10:55 PM	5:16 AM	10:32 AM	3	8
FRI 28	5:02 PM	11:39 PM	5:42 AM	11:16 AM	5	7
SAT 29	6:06 PM		6:06 AM	12:01 PM	7	6
SUN 30	7:11 PM	12:23 AM	6:30 AM	12:45 PM	7	6
MON 31	8:17 PM	1:07 AM	6:54 AM	1:30 PM	5	5

TIDE TIMES

* Additional Tide 5 - See Additional Tide 5

Adelaide Outer Harbour - SA

DAY/DATE	TIDE 5
Mon 7	11:05 PM (0.63) L
Mon 21	11:15 PM (0.97) L

DAY/DATE	TIDE 1	TIDE 2	TIDE 3	TIDE 4
Tue 1	12:15 AM (0.39) L	6:26 AM (2.47) H	12:37 PM (0.50) L	6:28 PM (2.28) H
Wed 2	12:29 AM (0.44) L	6:47 AM (2.53) H	1:03 PM (0.57) L	6:45 PM (2.12) H
Thu 3	12:38 AM (0.47) L	7:07 AM (2.55) H	1:27 PM (0.67) L	7:00 PM (1.95) H
Fri 4	12:45 AM (0.50) L	7:28 AM (2.52) H	1:49 PM (0.82) L	7:10 PM (1.77) H
Sat 5	12:53 AM (0.57) L	7:49 AM (2.39) H	2:12 PM (1.06) L	7:01 PM (1.56) H
Sun 6	12:47 AM (0.68) L	8:03 AM (2.12) H	2:15 PM (1.39) L	5:19 PM (1.48) H
Mon 7*	12:00 AM (0.76) L	7:10 AM (1.80) H	11:47 AM (1.59) L	3:55 PM (1.81) H
Tue 8	5:41 AM (1.75) H	10:19 AM (1.29) L	4:11 PM (2.17) H	10:56 PM (0.44) L
Wed 9	5:16 AM (1.89) H	10:29 AM (0.94) L	4:34 PM (2.41) H	11:06 PM (0.34) L
Thu 10	5:15 AM (2.02) H	10:45 AM (0.70) L	4:54 PM (2.50) H	11:16 PM (0.35) L
Fri 11	5:15 AM (2.11) H	11:00 AM (0.55) L	5:07 PM (2.48) H	11:21 PM (0.41) L
Sat 12	5:17 AM (2.22) H	11:15 AM (0.47) L	5:16 PM (2.41) H	11:23 PM (0.44) L
Sun 13	5:22 AM (2.36) H	11:30 AM (0.42) L	5:27 PM (2.34) H	11:29 PM (0.42) L
Mon 14	5:36 AM (2.50) H	11:51 AM (0.41) L	5:42 PM (2.26) H	11:39 PM (0.40) L
Tue 15	5:57 AM (2.58) H	12:15 PM (0.45) L	6:00 PM (2.17) H	11:53 PM (0.39) L
Wed 16	6:20 AM (2.61) H	12:38 PM (0.52) L	6:20 PM (2.08) H	
Thu 17	12:09 AM (0.41) L	6:43 AM (2.58) H	1:00 PM (0.61) L	6:39 PM (1.98) H
Fri 18	12:26 AM (0.45) L	7:04 AM (2.51) H	1:21 PM (0.71) L	6:55 PM (1.88) H
Sat 19	12:44 AM (0.54) L	7:25 AM (2.38) H	1:44 PM (0.87) L	7:07 PM (1.73) H
Sun 20	12:56 AM (0.69) L	7:45 AM (2.17) H	2:07 PM (1.10) L	6:58 PM (1.53) H
Mon 21*	12:45 AM (0.89) L	7:49 AM (1.87) H	2:00 PM (1.42) L	4:39 PM (1.46) H
Tue 22	5:56 AM (1.62) H	10:08 AM (1.45) L	3:28 PM (1.80) H	10:17 PM (0.76) L
Wed 23	4:40 AM (1.76) H	9:51 AM (1.10) L	3:50 PM (2.12) H	10:21 PM (0.53) L
Thu 24	4:32 AM (1.98) H	10:08 AM (0.80) L	4:14 PM (2.35) H	10:34 PM (0.40) L
Fri 25	4:41 AM (2.14) H	10:28 AM (0.59) L	4:33 PM (2.44) H	10:46 PM (0.36) L
Sat 26	4:49 AM (2.26) H	10:45 AM (0.45) L	4:50 PM (2.45) H	10:56 PM (0.37) L
Sun 27	4:58 AM (2.38) H	11:04 AM (0.36) L	5:05 PM (2.40) H	11:06 PM (0.38) L
Mon 28	5:10 AM (2.50) H	11:28 AM (0.30) L	5:23 PM (2.31) H	11:19 PM (0.40) L
Tue 29	5:29 AM (2.60) H	11:54 AM (0.31) L	5:44 PM (2.18) H	11:32 PM (0.45) L
Wed 30	5:50 AM (2.65) H	12:21 PM (0.39) L	6:03 PM (2.01) H	11:43 PM (0.50) L

Brisbane Bar - QLD

DAY/DATE	TIDE 1	TIDE 2	TIDE 3	TIDE 4
Tue 1	5:58 AM (0.39) L	12:07 PM (2.15) H	6:15 PM (0.62) L	
Wed 2	12:02 AM (2.05) H	6:30 AM (0.43) L	12:52 PM (2.15) H	7:04 PM (0.73) L
Thu 3	12:43 AM (1.86) H	7:08 AM (0.49) L	1:45 PM (2.12) H	8:07 PM (0.84) L
Fri 4	1:37 AM (1.67) H	8:00 AM (0.57) L	2:55 PM (2.11) H	9:35 PM (0.90) L
Sat 5	3:00 AM (1.52) H	9:13 AM (0.63) L	4:18 PM (2.15) H	11:17 PM (0.84) L
Sun 6	4:44 AM (1.50) H	10:40 AM (0.61) L	5:39 PM (2.26) H	
Mon 7	12:39 AM (0.69) L	6:09 AM (1.61) H	12:01 PM (0.53) L	6:45 PM (2.39) H
Tue 8	1:39 AM (0.53) L	7:13 AM (1.77) H	1:11 PM (0.41) L	7:41 PM (2.50) H
Wed 9	2:28 AM (0.42) L	8:05 AM (1.91) H	2:08 PM (0.33) L	8:28 PM (2.55) H
Thu 10	3:10 AM (0.35) L	8:51 AM (2.02) H	2:58 PM (0.29) L	9:09 PM (2.53) H
Fri 11	3:47 AM (0.32) L	9:33 AM (2.11) H	3:43 PM (0.30) L	9:46 PM (2.47) H
Sat 12	4:20 AM (0.31) L	10:13 AM (2.17) H	4:24 PM (0.36) L	10:21 PM (2.35) H
Sun 13	4:50 AM (0.32) L	10:50 AM (2.20) H	5:02 PM (0.45) L	10:54 PM (2.21) H
Mon 14	5:16 AM (0.35) L	11:27 AM (2.21) H	5:41 PM (0.57) L	11:25 PM (2.04) H
Tue 15	5:43 AM (0.39) L	12:03 PM (2.18) H	6:19 PM (0.70) L	11:56 PM (1.86) H
Wed 16	6:09 AM (0.46) L	12:41 PM (2.12) H	7:00 PM (0.82) L	
Thu 17	12:29 AM (1.69) H	6:39 AM (0.56) L	1:23 PM (2.03) H	7:51 PM (0.93) L
Fri 18	1:09 AM (1.53) H	7:18 AM (0.68) L	2:16 PM (1.95) H	9:05 PM (1.00) L
Sat 19	2:11 AM (1.40) H	8:13 AM (0.79) L	3:30 PM (1.90) H	10:47 PM (0.98) L
Sun 20	3:54 AM (1.36) H	9:33 AM (0.84) L	4:54 PM (1.93) H	
Mon 21	12:00 AM (0.87) L	5:26 AM (1.45) H	11:00 AM (0.80) L	5:59 PM (2.03) H
Tue 22	12:48 AM (0.76) L	6:22 AM (1.59) H	12:08 PM (0.69) L	6:47 PM (2.14) H
Wed 23	1:30 AM (0.64) L	7:06 AM (1.74) H	1:01 PM (0.58) L	7:29 PM (2.24) H
Thu 24	2:06 AM (0.53) L	7:46 AM (1.88) H	1:48 PM (0.49) L	8:07 PM (2.31) H
Fri 25	2:42 AM (0.44) L	8:25 AM (2.01) H	2:33 PM (0.43) L	8:42 PM (2.34) H
Sat 26	3:15 AM (0.37) L	9:04 AM (2.12) H	3:16 PM (0.40) L	9:16 PM (2.32) H
Sun 27	3:49 AM (0.31) L	9:45 AM (2.22) H	4:00 PM (0.41) L	9:52 PM (2.27) H
Mon 28	4:21 AM (0.28) L	10:25 AM (2.30) H	4:43 PM (0.44) L	10:28 PM (2.17) H
Tue 29	4:53 AM (0.29) L	11:06 AM (2.34) H	5:27 PM (0.51) L	11:05 PM (2.03) H
Wed 30	5:25 AM (0.33) L	11:49 AM (2.34) H	6:14 PM (0.61) L	11:46 PM (1.86) H

Darwin - NT

DAY/DATE	TIDE 1	TIDE 2	TIDE 3	TIDE 4
Tue 1	2:12 AM (1.58) L	8:15 AM (7.23) H	2:52 PM (1.03) L	8:52 PM (7.04) H
Wed 2	2:40 AM (1.95) L	8:36 AM (7.01) H	3:25 PM (1.09) L	9:31 PM (6.81) H
Thu 3	3:11 AM (2.44) L	8:59 AM (6.67) H	4:01 PM (1.33) L	10:16 PM (6.43) H
Fri 4	3:47 AM (3.03) L	9:23 AM (6.20) H	4:43 PM (1.72) L	11:11 PM (5.94) H
Sat 5	4:35 AM (3.65) L	9:51 AM (5.63) H	5:38 PM (2.18) L	
Sun 6	12:27 AM (5.49) H	6:08 AM (4.18) L	10:37 AM (5.00) H	7:14 PM (2.53) L
Mon 7	2:37 AM (5.46) H	8:56 AM (4.13) L	2:11 PM (4.61) H	9:15 PM (2.39) L
Tue 8	4:14 AM (5.97) H	10:38 AM (3.47) L	3:57 PM (5.24) H	10:34 PM (1.94) L
Wed 9	5:08 AM (6.52) H	11:25 AM (2.77) L	4:55 PM (5.96) H	11:28 PM (1.52) L
Thu 10	5:51 AM (7.00) H	12:04 PM (2.11) L	5:44 PM (6.58) H	
Fri 11	12:11 AM (1.24) L	6:28 AM (7.34) H	12:40 PM (1.55) L	6:29 PM (7.04) H
Sat 12	12:46 AM (1.15) L	6:59 AM (7.52) H	1:13 PM (1.12) L	7:10 PM (7.31) H
Sun 13	1:19 AM (1.26) L	7:24 AM (7.53) H	1:45 PM (0.87) L	7:47 PM (7.37) H
Mon 14	1:48 AM (1.52) L	7:45 AM (7.40) H	2:15 PM (0.81) L	8:22 PM (7.25) H
Tue 15	2:14 AM (1.91) L	8:04 AM (7.14) H	2:43 PM (0.94) L	8:55 PM (6.98) H
Wed 16	2:36 AM (2.36) L	8:23 AM (6.79) H	3:11 PM (1.23) L	9:27 PM (6.61) H
Thu 17	2:56 AM (2.84) L	8:41 AM (6.34) H	3:38 PM (1.65) L	10:00 PM (6.17) H
Fri 18	3:15 AM (3.31) L	8:59 AM (5.80) H	4:10 PM (2.15) L	10:40 PM (5.70) H
Sat 19	3:43 AM (3.80) L	9:12 AM (5.23) H	4:57 PM (2.68) L	11:33 PM (5.24) H
Sun 20	5:11 AM (4.27) L	9:03 AM (4.69) H	6:10 PM (3.12) L	
Mon 21	1:08 AM (4.96) H	11:38 AM (4.08) L	2:40 PM (4.10) H	8:02 PM (3.25) L
Tue 22	4:04 AM (5.28) H	11:01 AM (3.66) L	3:57 PM (4.67) H	9:50 PM (2.93) L
Wed 23	4:38 AM (5.73) H	11:12 AM (3.21) L	4:31 PM (5.26) H	10:43 PM (2.50) L
Thu 24	5:07 AM (6.16) H	11:30 AM (2.74) L	5:05 PM (5.84) H	11:21 PM (2.11) L
Fri 25	5:35 AM (6.57) H	11:54 AM (2.23) L	5:40 PM (6.39) H	11:55 PM (1.81) L
Sat 26	6:03 AM (6.92) H	12:21 PM (1.70) L	6:15 PM (6.87) H	
Sun 27	12:26 AM (1.63) L	6:29 AM (7.17) H	12:50 PM (1.21) L	6:52 PM (7.25) H
Mon 28	12:54 AM (1.59) L	6:51 AM (7.30) H	1:20 PM (0.82) L	7:28 PM (7.49) H
Tue 29	1:21 AM (1.69) L	7:13 AM (7.32) H	1:51 PM (0.59) L	8:03 PM (7.54) H
Wed 30	1:50 AM (1.91) L	7:36 AM (7.21) H	2:23 PM (0.57) L	8:40 PM (7.41) H

Fremantle - WA

DAY/DATE	TIDE 5
Wed 2	3:47 PM (0.68) L

DAY/DATE	TIDE 1	TIDE 2	TIDE 3	TIDE 4
Tue 1	5:57 AM (0.72) L	11:04 AM (0.79) H	4:37 PM (0.71) L	11:41 PM (1.02) H
Wed 2*	10:00 AM (0.69) L	11:11 AM (0.70) H	12:58 PM (0.68) L	2:14 PM (0.69) H
Thu 3	12:05 AM (1.06) H	1:29 PM (0.60) L		
Fri 4	12:37 AM (1.07) H	2:03 PM (0.53) L		
Sat 5	3:21 AM (1.07) H	2:39 PM (0.48) L		
Sun 6	4:31 AM (1.08) H	3:15 PM (0.46) L		
Mon 7	6:15 AM (1.10) H	3:50 PM (0.47) L		
Tue 8	7:31 AM (1.11) H	4:20 PM (0.51) L		
Wed 9	8:24 AM (1.10) H	4:30 PM (0.56) L	10:46 PM (0.78) H	
Thu 10	1:39 AM (0.74) L	9:12 AM (1.06) H	4:27 PM (0.62) L	10:49 PM (0.82) H
Fri 11	3:16 AM (0.71) L	10:00 AM (0.99) H	4:32 PM (0.68) L	11:00 PM (0.87) H
Sat 12	4:14 AM (0.69) L	10:49 AM (0.91) H	4:09 PM (0.71) L	11:03 PM (0.92) H
Sun 13	4:58 AM (0.68) L	11:37 AM (0.82) H	3:32 PM (0.70) L	10:36 PM (0.97) H
Mon 14	5:37 AM (0.68) L	12:21 PM (0.74) H	3:41 PM (0.68) L	10:37 PM (1.01) H
Tue 15	12:05 PM (0.67) L	1:03 PM (0.68) H	3:20 PM (0.65) L	10:58 PM (1.04) H
Wed 16	12:45 PM (0.63) L	1:47 PM (0.63) H	3:05 PM (0.62) L	11:26 PM (1.05) H
Thu 17	1:23 PM (0.59) L	2:42 PM (0.60) H	3:10 PM (0.60) L	11:59 PM (1.03) H
Fri 18	1:56 PM (0.58) L			
Sat 19	12:35 AM (1.01) H	2:23 PM (0.57) L		
Sun 20	1:21 AM (0.97) H	2:46 PM (0.56) L		
Mon 21	4:32 AM (0.96) H	3:05 PM (0.56) L		
Tue 22	6:32 AM (0.97) H	3:18 PM (0.57) L		
Wed 23	7:26 AM (0.99) H	3:25 PM (0.59) L	10:02 PM (0.79) H	
Thu 24	1:00 AM (0.76) L	8:08 AM (0.99) H	3:31 PM (0.61) L	9:42 PM (0.82) H
Fri 25	1:57 AM (0.72) L	8:48 AM (0.97) H	3:37 PM (0.64) L	9:42 PM (0.87) H
Sat 26	2:54 AM (0.67) L	9:34 AM (0.93) H	3:33 PM (0.67) L	9:46 PM (0.92) H
Sun 27	3:54 AM (0.63) L	10:40 AM (0.86) H	3:20 PM (0.69) L	9:56 PM (0.98) H
Mon 28	4:51 AM (0.60) L	11:49 AM (0.79) H	3:15 PM (0.70) L	10:11 PM (1.03) H
Tue 29	5:53 AM (0.58) L	12:50 PM (0.71) H	3:00 PM (0.69) L	10:31 PM (1.07) H
Wed 30	8:36 AM (0.55) L	10:58 PM (1.09) H		

* Additional Tide 5 - See Additional Tide 5

Sun Rise & Sun Set Times:

Adelaide, SA: Rise: 06:10am Set: 06:00pm

Brisbane, QLD: Rise: 05:40am Set: 05:40pm

Darwin, NT: Rise: 06:40am Set: 06:40pm

Perth, WA: Rise: 06:50am Set: 05:40pm

Hobart, TAS: Rise: 06:10am Set: 05:50pm

Melbourne, VIC: Rise: 06:20am Set: 06:10pm

Sydney, NSW: Rise: 05:50am Set: 05:40pm

(Note: These times are averages for the month)

Hobart - TAS

DAY/DATE	TIDE 1	TIDE 2	TIDE 3	TIDE 4
Tue 1	4:32 AM (0.75) L	11:19 AM (1.32) H	6:04 PM (0.67) L	
Wed 2	12:02 AM (1.14) H	5:15 AM (0.83) L	12:00 PM (1.39) H	7:05 PM (0.58) L
Thu 3	1:09 AM (1.11) H	6:09 AM (0.90) L	12:41 PM (1.45) H	8:02 PM (0.49) L
Fri 4	2:18 AM (1.08) H	7:06 AM (0.95) L	1:25 PM (1.50) H	8:58 PM (0.42) L
Sat 5	3:42 AM (1.08) H	7:59 AM (0.96) L	2:12 PM (1.54) H	9:53 PM (0.37) L
Sun 6	4:54 AM (1.08) H	8:46 AM (0.95) L	3:06 PM (1.57) H	10:48 PM (0.33) L
Mon 7	5:41 AM (1.08) H	9:34 AM (0.92) L	4:08 PM (1.58) H	11:42 PM (0.33) L
Tue 8	6:21 AM (1.09) H	10:24 AM (0.88) L	5:11 PM (1.58) H	
Wed 9	12:34 AM (0.35) L	7:00 AM (1.10) H	11:21 AM (0.84) L	6:10 PM (1.54) H
Thu 10	1:25 AM (0.39) L	7:42 AM (1.12) H	12:30 PM (0.82) L	7:07 PM (1.47) H
Fri 11	2:13 AM (0.47) L	8:26 AM (1.16) H	1:54 PM (0.78) L	8:07 PM (1.36) H
Sat 12	2:59 AM (0.56) L	9:11 AM (1.20) H	3:22 PM (0.73) L	9:18 PM (1.25) H
Sun 13	3:42 AM (0.67) L	9:57 AM (1.26) H	4:39 PM (0.66) L	10:36 PM (1.16) H
Mon 14	4:23 AM (0.77) L	10:40 AM (1.30) H	5:42 PM (0.60) L	11:45 PM (1.11) H
Tue 15	5:03 AM (0.87) L	11:18 AM (1.34) H	6:36 PM (0.56) L	
Wed 16	12:47 AM (1.08) H	5:43 AM (0.94) L	11:54 AM (1.35) H	7:24 PM (0.53) L
Thu 17	1:50 AM (1.06) H	6:24 AM (0.99) L	12:28 PM (1.36) H	8:09 PM (0.53) L
Fri 18	3:06 AM (1.05) H	7:07 AM (1.01) L	1:03 PM (1.36) H	8:52 PM (0.53) L
Sat 19	4:16 AM (1.06) H	7:48 AM (1.01) L	1:43 PM (1.36) H	9:34 PM (0.54) L
Sun 20	4:55 AM (1.06) H	8:29 AM (0.99) L	2:28 PM (1.35) H	10:15 PM (0.54) L
Mon 21	5:24 AM (1.06) H	9:06 AM (0.96) L	3:17 PM (1.36) H	10:55 PM (0.54) L
Tue 22	5:50 AM (1.06) H	9:45 AM (0.93) L	4:09 PM (1.36) H	11:32 PM (0.54) L
Wed 23	6:15 AM (1.07) H	10:26 AM (0.90) L	4:59 PM (1.35) H	
Thu 24	12:07 AM (0.55) L	6:41 AM (1.09) H	11:12 AM (0.87) L	5:45 PM (1.34) H
Fri 25	12:40 AM (0.57) L	7:08 AM (1.12) H	12:07 PM (0.83) L	6:33 PM (1.30) H
Sat 26	1:12 AM (0.61) L	7:38 AM (1.17) H	1:12 PM (0.78) L	7:27 PM (1.25) H
Sun 27	1:45 AM (0.67) L	8:11 AM (1.23) H	2:28 PM (0.71) L	8:31 PM (1.19) H
Mon 28	2:20 AM (0.75) L	8:49 AM (1.30) H	3:44 PM (0.61) L	9:56 PM (1.15) H
Tue 29	3:00 AM (0.83) L	9:33 AM (1.37) H	4:50 PM (0.51) L	11:15 PM (1.13) H
Wed 30	3:51 AM (0.90) L	10:22 AM (1.42) H	5:50 PM (0.41) L	

Port Phillip Heads - VIC

DAY/DATE	TIDE 1	TIDE 2	TIDE 3	TIDE 4
Tue 1	2:32 AM (1.58) H	8:14 AM (0.54) L	2:45 PM (1.61) H	8:38 PM (0.40) L
Wed 2	3:15 AM (1.64) H	8:52 AM (0.57) L	3:17 PM (1.61) H	9:14 PM (0.33) L
Thu 3	3:56 AM (1.66) H	9:32 AM (0.60) L	3:51 PM (1.59) H	9:52 PM (0.29) L
Fri 4	4:39 AM (1.64) H	10:13 AM (0.65) L	4:25 PM (1.56) H	10:32 PM (0.27) L
Sat 5	5:25 AM (1.59) H	10:53 AM (0.71) L	5:02 PM (1.53) H	11:15 PM (0.28) L
Sun 6	6:16 AM (1.52) H	11:34 AM (0.77) L	5:45 PM (1.48) H	
Mon 7	12:00 AM (0.32) L	7:17 AM (1.45) H	12:20 PM (0.83) L	6:36 PM (1.42) H
Tue 8	12:52 AM (0.37) L	8:28 AM (1.39) H	1:16 PM (0.88) L	7:45 PM (1.36) H
Wed 9	2:00 AM (0.44) L	9:42 AM (1.38) H	2:35 PM (0.88) L	9:14 PM (1.32) H
Thu 10	3:26 AM (0.48) L	10:49 AM (1.41) H	4:13 PM (0.81) L	10:44 PM (1.36) H
Fri 11	4:49 AM (0.49) L	11:48 AM (1.47) H	5:32 PM (0.68) L	11:59 PM (1.45) H
Sat 12	5:58 AM (0.48) L	12:41 PM (1.53) H	6:31 PM (0.53) L	
Sun 13	1:02 AM (1.56) H	6:52 AM (0.48) L	1:27 PM (1.58) H	7:19 PM (0.41) L
Mon 14	1:58 AM (1.64) H	7:39 AM (0.50) L	2:06 PM (1.60) H	8:01 PM (0.33) L
Tue 15	2:45 AM (1.69) H	8:19 AM (0.53) L	2:42 PM (1.60) H	8:40 PM (0.29) L
Wed 16	3:27 AM (1.70) H	8:57 AM (0.56) L	3:14 PM (1.58) H	9:16 PM (0.28) L
Thu 17	4:05 AM (1.67) H	9:31 AM (0.60) L	3:45 PM (1.55) H	9:52 PM (0.29) L
Fri 18	4:40 AM (1.61) H	10:06 AM (0.64) L	4:16 PM (1.51) H	10:27 PM (0.33) L
Sat 19	5:15 AM (1.54) H	10:42 AM (0.68) L	4:49 PM (1.46) H	11:02 PM (0.37) L
Sun 20	5:52 AM (1.47) H	11:17 AM (0.73) L	5:24 PM (1.40) H	11:39 PM (0.42) L
Mon 21	6:34 AM (1.39) H	11:54 AM (0.79) L	6:02 PM (1.33) H	
Tue 22	12:17 AM (0.48) L	7:27 AM (1.33) H	12:35 PM (0.84) L	6:50 PM (1.27) H
Wed 23	1:01 AM (0.54) L	8:28 AM (1.28) H	1:28 PM (0.88) L	7:53 PM (1.21) H
Thu 24	1:57 AM (0.60) L	9:33 AM (1.27) H	2:38 PM (0.89) L	9:15 PM (1.19) H
Fri 25	3:09 AM (0.65) L	10:34 AM (1.30) H	4:15 PM (0.83) L	10:38 PM (1.24) H
Sat 26	4:37 AM (0.66) L	11:27 AM (1.35) H	5:29 PM (0.71) L	11:46 PM (1.35) H
Sun 27	5:45 AM (0.64) L	12:13 PM (1.41) H	6:12 PM (0.57) L	
Mon 28	12:43 AM (1.48) H	6:33 AM (0.62) L	12:54 PM (1.47) H	6:48 PM (0.44) L
Tue 29	1:31 AM (1.60) H	7:15 AM (0.60) L	1:32 PM (1.51) H	7:25 PM (0.33) L
Wed 30	2:15 AM (1.69) H	7:54 AM (0.59) L	2:11 PM (1.54) H	8:03 PM (0.25) L

Fort Denison - NSW

DAY/DATE	TIDE 1	TIDE 2	TIDE 3	TIDE 4
Tue 1	4:29 AM (0.37) L	10:49 AM (1.64) H	4:59 PM (0.46) L	11:01 PM (1.49) H
Wed 2	5:07 AM (0.44) L	11:34 AM (1.65) H	5:55 PM (0.51) L	11:52 PM (1.36) H
Thu 3	5:50 AM (0.52) L	12:26 PM (1.63) H	7:00 PM (0.55) L	
Fri 4	12:54 AM (1.24) H	6:44 AM (0.60) L	1:27 PM (1.62) H	8:21 PM (0.57) L
Sat 5	2:12 AM (1.16) H	7:51 AM (0.65) L	2:40 PM (1.62) H	9:47 PM (0.53) L
Sun 6	3:43 AM (1.15) H	9:11 AM (0.65) L	3:57 PM (1.67) H	11:00 PM (0.44) L
Mon 7	4:59 AM (1.22) H	10:27 AM (0.59) L	5:05 PM (1.75) H	11:58 PM (0.35) L
Tue 8	5:57 AM (1.31) H	11:31 AM (0.50) L	6:02 PM (1.83) H	
Wed 9	12:46 AM (0.27) L	6:45 AM (1.41) H	12:28 PM (0.41) L	6:53 PM (1.88) H
Thu 10	1:29 AM (0.22) L	7:30 AM (1.50) H	1:18 PM (0.35) L	7:40 PM (1.87) H
Fri 11	2:08 AM (0.22) L	8:13 AM (1.58) H	2:07 PM (0.32) L	8:23 PM (1.81) H
Sat 12	2:45 AM (0.25) L	8:53 AM (1.62) H	2:54 PM (0.33) L	9:05 PM (1.71) H
Sun 13	3:18 AM (0.31) L	9:32 AM (1.65) H	3:40 PM (0.37) L	9:45 PM (1.59) H
Mon 14	3:50 AM (0.38) L	10:10 AM (1.65) H	4:25 PM (0.43) L	10:25 PM (1.45) H
Tue 15	4:20 AM (0.47) L	10:48 AM (1.63) H	5:11 PM (0.51) L	11:05 PM (1.33) H

DAY/DATE	TIDE 1	TIDE 2	TIDE 3	TIDE 4
Wed 16	4:51 AM (0.56) L	11:27 AM (1.58) H	6:00 PM (0.58) L	11:47 PM (1.22) H
Thu 17	5:25 AM (0.64) L	12:08 PM (1.53) H	6:56 PM (0.64) L	
Fri 18	12:38 AM (1.13) H	6:08 AM (0.71) L	12:59 PM (1.47) H	8:02 PM (0.68) L
Sat 19	1:44 AM (1.08) H	7:08 AM (0.76) L	2:01 PM (1.43) H	9:17 PM (0.68) L
Sun 20	3:06 AM (1.07) H	8:26 AM (0.78) L	3:16 PM (1.43) H	10:26 PM (0.63) L
Mon 21	4:23 AM (1.12) H	9:42 AM (0.75) L	4:23 PM (1.47) H	11:18 PM (0.56) L
Tue 22	5:16 AM (1.19) H	10:45 AM (0.69) L	5:16 PM (1.54) H	
Wed 23	12:00 AM (0.49) L	5:59 AM (1.28) H	11:35 AM (0.61) L	6:00 PM (1.61) H
Thu 24	12:35 AM (0.42) L	6:35 AM (1.37) H	12:19 PM (0.52) L	6:38 PM (1.66) H
Fri 25	1:06 AM (0.36) L	7:09 AM (1.47) H	1:00 PM (0.45) L	7:15 PM (1.69) H
Sat 26	1:37 AM (0.31) L	7:44 AM (1.57) H	1:42 PM (0.38) L	7:54 PM (1.70) H
Sun 27	2:09 AM (0.29) L	8:19 AM (1.66) H	2:25 PM (0.34) L	8:33 PM (1.66) H
Mon 28	2:42 AM (0.30) L	8:58 AM (1.73) H	3:11 PM (0.32) L	9:16 PM (1.60) H
Tue 29	3:17 AM (0.34) L	9:39 AM (1.78) H	4:00 PM (0.32) L	10:03 PM (1.50) H
Wed 30	3:57 AM (0.40) L	10:23 AM (1.79) H	4:53 PM (0.36) L	10:54 PM (1.39) H

BITE TIMES

Apogee moon phase on Saturday 19th
Perigee moon phase on Monday 7th

New moon on Friday 11th
First quarter moon on Saturday 19th
Full moon on Sunday 27th
Last quarter moon phase on Friday 4th

DAY	MINOR BITE	MAJOR BITE	MINOR BITE	MAJOR BITE	SALT WATER RATING	FRESH WATER RATING
TUE 1	9:27 PM	1:53 AM	7:20 AM	2:18 PM	4	4
WED 2	10:39 PM	2:43 AM	7:51 AM	3:09 PM	3	6
THUR 3	11:52 PM	3:37 AM	8:28 AM	4:06 PM	4	4
FRI 4		4:35 AM	9:13 AM	5:05 PM	5	5
SAT 5	1:02 AM	5:36 AM	10:09 AM	6:07 PM	6	6
SUN 6	2:06 AM	6:39 AM	11:15 AM	7:10 PM	7	7
MON 7	3:00 AM	7:41 AM	12:28 PM	8:10 PM	7	8
TUE 8	3:44 AM	8:40 AM	1:43 PM	9:07 PM	5	8
WED 9	4:20 AM	9:34 AM	2:57 PM	9:59 PM	6	7
THUR 10	4:50 AM	10:25 AM	4:08 PM	10:48 PM	8	8
FRI 11	5:17 AM	11:12 AM	5:17 PM	11:34 PM	8	8
SAT 12	5:42 AM	11:58 AM	6:24 PM		8	6
SUN 13	6:07 AM	12:43 PM	7:29 PM	12:20 AM	7	6
MON 14	6:32 AM	1:28 PM	8:34 PM	1:05 AM	6	7
TUE 15	7:00 AM	2:15 PM	9:39 PM	1:51 AM	5	5

DAY	MINOR BITE	MAJOR BITE	MINOR BITE	MAJOR BITE	SALT WATER RATING	FRESH WATER RATING
WED 16	7:32 AM	3:03 PM	10:42 PM	2:38 AM	5	5
THUR 17	8:09 AM	3:53 PM	11:42 PM	3:28 AM	4	6
FRI 18	8:52 AM	4:44 PM		4:18 AM	3	5
SAT 19	9:42 AM	5:35 PM	12:37 AM	5:09 AM	4	6
SUN 20	10:38 AM	6:26 PM	1:26 AM	6:00 AM	5	6
MON 21	11:37 AM	7:15 PM	2:09 AM	6:50 AM	4	5
TUE 22	12:40 PM	8:03 PM	2:45 AM	7:39 AM	3	5
WED 23	1:43 PM	8:48 PM	3:16 AM	8:25 AM	6	6
THUR 24	2:47 PM	9:33 PM	3:43 AM	9:10 AM	5	7
FRI 25	3:51 PM	10:17 PM	4:08 AM	9:54 AM	3	8
SAT 26	4:57 PM	11:02 PM	4:32 AM	10:39 AM	3	8
SUN 27	6:04 PM	11:48 PM	4:57 AM	11:24 AM	5	7
MON 28	7:14 PM		5:23 AM	12:13 PM	7	6
TUE 29	8:27 PM	12:38 AM	5:53 AM	1:04 PM	7	6
WED 30	9:41 PM	1:31 AM	6:28 AM	2:00 PM	5	5

TIDE TIMES

* Additional Tide 5 - See Additional Tide 5

Adelaide Outer Harbour - SA

DAY/DATE	TIDE 5
Tue 6	11:25 PM (0.75) L
Tue 20	11:34 PM (1.14) L

DAY/DATE	TIDE 1	TIDE 2	TIDE 3	TIDE 4
Thu 1	6:11 AM (2.64) H	12:45 PM (0.52) L	6:16 PM (1.85) H	11:49 PM (0.52) L
Fri 2	6:29 AM (2.59) H	1:00 PM (0.66) L	6:25 PM (1.72) H	11:56 PM (0.52) L
Sat 3	6:46 AM (2.50) H	1:13 PM (0.82) L	6:29 PM (1.62) H	
Sun 4	12:04 AM (0.56) L	8:02 AM (2.32) H	2:23 PM (1.03) L	7:15 PM (1.52) H
Mon 5	1:02 AM (0.68) L	8:05 AM (2.03) H	2:10 PM (1.29) L	6:01 PM (1.49) H
Tue 6*	12:22 AM (0.80) L	7:03 AM (1.75) H	12:16 PM (1.40) L	4:53 PM (1.72) H
Wed 7	5:49 AM (1.76) H	11:00 AM (1.10) L	4:53 PM (2.01) H	11:12 PM (0.59) L
Thu 8	5:25 AM (1.96) H	11:07 AM (0.75) L	5:11 PM (2.20) H	11:20 PM (0.49) L
Fri 9	5:25 AM (2.17) H	11:24 AM (0.51) L	5:28 PM (2.27) H	11:29 PM (0.46) L
Sat 10	5:30 AM (2.33) H	11:41 AM (0.38) L	5:41 PM (2.25) H	11:33 PM (0.47) L
Sun 11	5:37 AM (2.47) H	11:56 AM (0.32) L	5:51 PM (2.20) H	11:39 PM (0.46) L
Mon 12	5:47 AM (2.59) H	12:13 PM (0.29) L	6:04 PM (2.14) H	11:48 PM (0.44) L
Tue 13	6:05 AM (2.68) H	12:34 PM (0.30) L	6:22 PM (2.09) H	
Wed 14	12:04 AM (0.43) L	6:29 AM (2.70) H	12:59 PM (0.36) L	6:44 PM (2.01) H
Thu 15	12:23 AM (0.46) L	6:53 AM (2.66) H	1:23 PM (0.45) L	7:05 PM (1.93) H
Fri 16	12:42 AM (0.51) L	7:15 AM (2.58) H	1:44 PM (0.55) L	7:24 PM (1.85) H
Sat 17	1:00 AM (0.56) L	7:37 AM (2.48) H	2:03 PM (0.65) L	7:41 PM (1.77) H
Sun 18	1:18 AM (0.64) L	7:58 AM (2.34) H	2:26 PM (0.78) L	7:58 PM (1.66) H
Mon 19	1:35 AM (0.78) L	8:19 AM (2.14) H	2:54 PM (0.98) L	8:09 PM (1.48) H
Tue 20*	1:37 AM (0.99) L	8:35 AM (1.85) H	3:45 PM (1.26) L	6:20 PM (1.28) H
Wed 21	6:33 AM (1.55) H	10:35 AM (1.46) L	3:25 PM (1.60) H	10:13 PM (0.91) L
Thu 22	4:40 AM (1.74) H	10:15 AM (1.08) L	4:08 PM (1.91) H	10:25 PM (0.68) L
Fri 23	4:40 AM (2.03) H	10:37 AM (0.74) L	4:40 PM (2.13) H	10:44 PM (0.53) L
Sat 24	4:54 AM (2.26) H	11:02 AM (0.48) L	5:06 PM (2.22) H	11:00 PM (0.49) L
Sun 25	5:08 AM (2.43) H	11:27 AM (0.31) L	5:29 PM (2.22) H	11:15 PM (0.49) L
Mon 26	5:22 AM (2.57) H	11:51 AM (0.22) L	5:49 PM (2.14) H	11:29 PM (0.51) L
Tue 27	5:40 AM (2.68) H	12:18 PM (0.20) L	6:10 PM (2.03) H	11:44 PM (0.54) L
Wed 28	6:02 AM (2.75) H	12:47 PM (0.24) L	6:33 PM (1.89) H	
Thu 29	12:00 AM (0.58) L	6:28 AM (2.74) H	1:17 PM (0.36) L	6:54 PM (1.74) H
Fri 30	12:13 AM (0.62) L	6:52 AM (2.66) H	1:43 PM (0.52) L	7:08 PM (1.61) H
Sat 31	12:22 AM (0.64) L	7:13 AM (2.55) H	2:00 PM (0.69) L	7:18 PM (1.54) H

Brisbane Bar - QLD

DAY/DATE	TIDE 1	TIDE 2	TIDE 3	TIDE 4
Thu 1	6:00 AM (0.40) L	12:37 PM (2.30) H	7:09 PM (0.72) L	
Fri 2	12:35 AM (1.68) H	6:44 AM (0.50) L	1:33 PM (2.24) H	8:19 PM (0.80) L
Sat 3	1:41 AM (1.53) H	7:42 AM (0.61) L	2:44 PM (2.19) H	9:49 PM (0.80) L
Sun 4	3:16 AM (1.47) H	9:03 AM (0.68) L	4:03 PM (2.19) H	11:13 PM (0.72) L
Mon 5	4:51 AM (1.55) H	10:34 AM (0.66) L	5:18 PM (2.25) H	
Tue 6	12:19 AM (0.59) L	6:03 AM (1.72) H	11:53 AM (0.57) L	6:22 PM (2.33) H
Wed 7	1:12 AM (0.47) L	7:00 AM (1.89) H	12:59 PM (0.47) L	7:15 PM (2.37) H
Thu 8	1:57 AM (0.38) L	7:47 AM (2.05) H	1:53 PM (0.41) L	8:00 PM (2.36) H
Fri 9	2:35 AM (0.33) L	8:30 AM (2.16) H	2:41 PM (0.40) L	8:39 PM (2.31) H
Sat 10	3:09 AM (0.30) L	9:10 AM (2.25) H	3:25 PM (0.42) L	9:15 PM (2.22) H
Sun 11	3:39 AM (0.30) L	9:46 AM (2.30) H	4:06 PM (0.47) L	9:48 PM (2.11) H
Mon 12	4:06 AM (0.30) L	10:22 AM (2.33) H	4:45 PM (0.54) L	10:20 PM (1.99) H
Tue 13	4:32 AM (0.33) L	10:57 AM (2.32) H	5:22 PM (0.62) L	10:52 PM (1.86) H
Wed 14	4:59 AM (0.39) L	11:30 AM (2.28) H	5:59 PM (0.70) L	11:24 PM (1.73) H
Thu 15	5:27 AM (0.47) L	12:07 PM (2.20) H	6:38 PM (0.79) L	11:59 PM (1.61) H
Fri 16	5:59 AM (0.57) L	12:46 PM (2.11) H	7:23 PM (0.87) L	
Sat 17	12:41 AM (1.50) H	6:37 AM (0.68) L	1:34 PM (2.02) H	8:26 PM (0.93) L
Sun 18	1:38 AM (1.42) H	7:29 AM (0.79) L	2:35 PM (1.95) H	9:47 PM (0.92) L
Mon 19	3:05 AM (1.40) H	8:42 AM (0.86) L	3:48 PM (1.94) H	10:59 PM (0.85) L
Tue 20	4:37 AM (1.48) H	10:09 AM (0.85) L	4:57 PM (2.00) H	11:53 PM (0.74) L
Wed 21	5:41 AM (1.64) H	11:22 AM (0.77) L	5:52 PM (2.08) H	
Thu 22	12:39 AM (0.61) L	6:30 AM (1.81) H	12:23 PM (0.67) L	6:39 PM (2.16) H
Fri 23	1:19 AM (0.49) L	7:15 AM (1.99) H	1:17 PM (0.58) L	7:21 PM (2.20) H
Sat 24	1:58 AM (0.38) L	7:57 AM (2.15) H	2:09 PM (0.52) L	8:02 PM (2.20) H
Sun 25	2:35 AM (0.31) L	8:39 AM (2.29) H	2:59 PM (0.47) L	8:43 PM (2.16) H
Mon 26	3:11 AM (0.25) L	9:22 AM (2.41) H	3:46 PM (0.45) L	9:24 PM (2.09) H
Tue 27	3:46 AM (0.23) L	10:05 AM (2.50) H	4:35 PM (0.47) L	10:07 PM (1.99) H
Wed 28	4:23 AM (0.25) L	10:50 AM (2.53) H	5:25 PM (0.51) L	10:52 PM (1.87) H
Thu 29	5:00 AM (0.30) L	11:37 AM (2.52) H	6:19 PM (0.57) L	11:43 PM (1.74) H
Fri 30	5:43 AM (0.39) L	12:29 PM (2.46) H	7:19 PM (0.64) L	
Sat 31	12:41 AM (1.62) H	6:32 AM (0.51) L	1:26 PM (2.38) H	8:29 PM (0.69) L

Darwin - NT

DAY/DATE	TIDE 1	TIDE 2	TIDE 3	TIDE 4
Thu 1	2:21 AM (2.27) L	8:01 AM (6.96) H	2:59 PM (0.78) L	9:19 PM (7.09) H
Fri 2	2:57 AM (2.74) L	8:29 AM (6.55) H	3:37 PM (1.22) L	10:05 PM (6.61) H
Sat 3	3:38 AM (3.29) L	8:59 AM (6.00) H	4:23 PM (1.81) L	11:00 PM (6.05) H
Sun 4	4:36 AM (3.84) L	9:36 AM (5.34) H	5:28 PM (2.44) L	
Mon 5	12:20 AM (5.61) H	6:40 AM (4.14) L	11:02 AM (4.65) H	7:13 PM (2.84) L
Tue 6	2:15 AM (5.60) H	9:15 AM (3.70) L	2:50 PM (4.85) H	9:07 PM (2.71) L
Wed 7	3:40 AM (6.01) H	10:20 AM (2.96) L	4:00 PM (5.59) H	10:17 PM (2.37) L
Thu 8	4:32 AM (6.44) H	11:02 AM (2.27) L	4:51 PM (6.27) H	11:07 PM (2.07) L
Fri 9	5:13 AM (6.80) H	11:39 AM (1.67) L	5:37 PM (6.83) H	11:46 PM (1.90) L
Sat 10	5:45 AM (7.04) H	12:12 PM (1.20) L	6:17 PM (7.22) H	
Sun 11	12:20 AM (1.86) L	6:13 AM (7.15) H	12:42 PM (0.88) L	6:55 PM (7.43) H
Mon 12	12:50 AM (1.94) L	6:36 AM (7.15) H	1:11 PM (0.72) L	7:30 PM (7.47) H
Tue 13	1:18 AM (2.11) L	6:58 AM (7.05) H	1:38 PM (0.73) L	8:01 PM (7.35) H
Wed 14	1:45 AM (2.36) L	7:21 AM (6.85) H	2:05 PM (0.91) L	8:31 PM (7.12) H
Thu 15	2:10 AM (2.67) L	7:45 AM (6.55) H	2:32 PM (1.23) L	9:01 PM (6.80) H
Fri 16	2:34 AM (3.00) L	8:08 AM (6.16) H	3:00 PM (1.66) L	9:33 PM (6.41) H
Sat 17	3:00 AM (3.36) L	8:32 AM (5.69) H	3:34 PM (2.17) L	10:11 PM (5.98) H
Sun 18	3:36 AM (3.75) L	8:55 AM (5.19) H	4:18 PM (2.71) L	10:59 PM (5.57) H
Mon 19	4:46 AM (4.12) L	9:16 AM (4.68) H	5:25 PM (3.18) L	
Tue 20	12:09 AM (5.27) H	7:55 AM (4.16) L	11:52 AM (4.22) H	7:01 PM (3.42) L
Wed 21	1:57 AM (5.27) H	9:47 AM (3.66) L	3:19 PM (4.66) H	8:45 PM (3.29) L
Thu 22	3:22 AM (5.60) H	10:14 AM (3.13) L	4:00 PM (5.28) H	9:53 PM (2.97) L
Fri 23	4:04 AM (5.99) H	10:43 AM (2.55) L	4:38 PM (5.92) H	10:40 PM (2.64) L
Sat 24	4:38 AM (6.36) H	11:13 AM (1.94) L	5:16 PM (6.54) H	11:18 PM (2.38) L
Sun 25	5:09 AM (6.68) H	11:45 AM (1.35) L	5:56 PM (7.09) H	11:54 PM (2.21) L
Mon 26	5:38 AM (6.92) H	12:17 PM (0.83) L	6:35 PM (7.51) H	
Tue 27	12:28 AM (2.15) L	6:05 AM (7.08) H	12:50 PM (0.47) L	7:15 PM (7.74) H
Wed 28	1:00 AM (2.20) L	6:34 AM (7.12) H	1:24 PM (0.31) L	7:52 PM (7.77) H
Thu 29	1:33 AM (2.36) L	7:05 AM (7.03) H	2:00 PM (0.40) L	8:31 PM (7.59) H
Fri 30	2:11 AM (2.62) L	7:39 AM (6.78) H	2:39 PM (0.73) L	9:14 PM (7.25) H
Sat 31	2:52 AM (2.97) L	8:16 AM (6.37) H	3:23 PM (1.27) L	10:01 PM (6.79) H

Fremantle - WA

DAY/DATE	TIDE 1	TIDE 2	TIDE 3	TIDE 4
Thu 1	9:46 AM (0.52) L	10:55 AM (0.53) H	12:00 PM (0.52) L	11:27 PM (1.09) H
Fri 2	12:47 PM (0.47) L			
Sat 3	12:00 AM (1.06) H	1:29 PM (0.45) L		
Sun 4	12:39 AM (1.01) H	1:38 AM (1.01) L	2:53 AM (1.02) H	2:06 PM (0.45) L
Mon 5	4:03 AM (0.98) H	2:40 PM (0.48) L		
Tue 6	6:28 AM (0.96) H	3:05 PM (0.53) L	10:30 PM (0.79) H	
Wed 7	12:35 AM (0.78) L	7:35 AM (0.95) H	3:09 PM (0.60) L	9:21 PM (0.81) H
Thu 8	2:09 AM (0.72) L	8:33 AM (0.91) H	3:00 PM (0.65) L	9:20 PM (0.86) H
Fri 9	3:07 AM (0.66) L	9:33 AM (0.86) H	2:59 PM (0.69) L	9:16 PM (0.92) H
Sat 10	3:55 AM (0.62) L	10:29 AM (0.81) H	2:05 PM (0.70) L	9:12 PM (0.98) H
Sun 11	4:41 AM (0.59) L	11:17 AM (0.75) H	2:11 PM (0.69) L	9:20 PM (1.03) H
Mon 12	5:29 AM (0.57) L	12:02 PM (0.70) H	2:22 PM (0.67) L	9:35 PM (1.06) H
Tue 13	7:25 AM (0.56) L	12:46 PM (0.65) H	1:58 PM (0.65) L	9:56 PM (1.08) H
Wed 14	8:21 AM (0.55) L	10:21 PM (1.08) H		
Thu 15	9:07 AM (0.55) L	10:52 AM (0.57) H	11:45 AM (0.57) L	10:51 PM (1.06) H
Fri 16	9:55 AM (0.56) L	11:04 AM (0.57) H	12:28 PM (0.56) L	11:24 PM (1.03) H
Sat 17*	1:03 PM (0.56) L	11:58 PM (1.00) H		
Sun 18*	1:32 PM (0.56) L			
Mon 19	12:34 AM (0.95) H	1:54 PM (0.57) L		
Tue 20	1:18 AM (0.91) H	2:06 PM (0.58) L	10:49 PM (0.84) H	11:16 PM (0.84) L
Wed 21	4:42 AM (0.88) H	2:05 PM (0.60) L	8:52 PM (0.83) H	
Thu 22	12:36 AM (0.79) L	6:48 AM (0.86) H	2:01 PM (0.63) L	8:21 PM (0.87) H
Fri 23	1:50 AM (0.72) L	8:00 AM (0.85) H	2:01 PM (0.66) L	8:20 PM (0.92) H
Sat 24	2:55 AM (0.65) L	9:15 AM (0.82) H	1:58 PM (0.69) L	8:30 PM (0.99) H
Sun 25	3:48 AM (0.58) L	10:26 AM (0.78) H	1:53 PM (0.71) L	8:46 PM (1.06) H
Mon 26	4:43 AM (0.51) L	11:27 AM (0.74) H	1:44 PM (0.71) L	9:07 PM (1.11) H
Tue 27	5:50 AM (0.46) L	12:38 PM (0.69) H	1:08 PM (0.69) L	9:31 PM (1.15) H
Wed 28	7:21 AM (0.42) L	10:00 PM (1.16) H		
Thu 29	8:26 AM (0.41) L	10:30 PM (1.15) H		
Fri 30	9:29 AM (0.42) L	11:02 PM (1.10) H		
Sat 31	12:05 PM (0.43) L	11:33 PM (1.04) H		

Sun Rise & Sun Set Times:

Darwin, NT: Rise: 06:20am Set: 06:40pm

***Melbourne, VIC**: Rise: 06:30am Set: 07:30pm

***Adelaide, SA**: Rise: 06:30am Set: 07:20pm

Perth, WA: Rise: 06:50am Set: 05:40pm

***Sydney, NSW**: Rise: 06:13am Set: 07:08pm

Brisbane, QLD: Rise: 05:10am Set: 05:50pm

Hobart, TAS: Rise: 06:20am Set: 07:30pm

(Note: These times are averages for the month)

*Note: Daylight Savings start (clocks turn forward 1 hour) on Sunday, October 1st at 2:00 AM for states marked * Subtract1 hour from rise/set time for days before Oct 1st*

Hobart - TAS

DAY/DATE	TIDE 1	TIDE 2	TIDE 3	TIDE 4
Thu 1	12:21 AM (1.13) H	4:58 AM (0.97) L	11:14 AM (1.47) H	6:46 PM (0.34) L
Fri 2	1:27 AM (1.13) H	6:06 AM (1.00) L	12:06 PM (1.50) H	7:42 PM (0.31) L
Sat 3	2:37 AM (1.13) H	7:05 AM (0.99) L	12:59 PM (1.50) H	8:36 PM (0.29) L
Sun 4	4:42 AM (1.12) H	8:59 AM (0.97) L	2:55 PM (1.50) H	10:30 PM (0.31) L
Mon 5	5:30 AM (1.12) H	9:51 AM (0.92) L	3:57 PM (1.47) H	11:22 PM (0.34) L
Tue 6	6:10 AM (1.13) H	10:45 AM (0.86) L	5:03 PM (1.43) H	
Wed 7	12:11 AM (0.39) L	6:46 AM (1.15) H	11:45 AM (0.81) L	6:07 PM (1.38) H
Thu 8	12:56 AM (0.47) L	7:22 AM (1.18) H	12:52 PM (0.75) L	7:07 PM (1.30) H
Fri 9	1:37 AM (0.56) L	7:59 AM (1.22) H	2:06 PM (0.69) L	8:08 PM (1.22) H
Sat 10	2:15 AM (0.66) L	8:35 AM (1.26) H	3:20 PM (0.63) L	9:19 PM (1.14) H
Sun 11	2:49 AM (0.77) L	9:12 AM (1.30) H	4:28 PM (0.56) L	10:40 PM (1.09) H
Mon 12	3:21 AM (0.87) L	9:48 AM (1.33) H	5:25 PM (0.51) L	11:52 PM (1.07) H
Tue 13	3:49 AM (0.95) L	10:25 AM (1.35) H	6:13 PM (0.47) L	
Wed 14	12:55 AM (1.08) H	4:20 AM (1.02) L	11:01 AM (1.35) H	6:57 PM (0.45) L
Thu 15	1:54 AM (1.08) H	5:18 AM (1.05) L	11:39 AM (1.35) H	7:38 PM (0.46) L
Fri 16	2:52 AM (1.09) H	6:37 AM (1.07) L	12:19 PM (1.34) H	8:18 PM (0.47) L
Sat 17	3:46 AM (1.09) H	7:31 AM (1.05) L	1:02 PM (1.32) H	9:00 PM (0.49) L
Sun 18	4:27 AM (1.09) H	8:18 AM (1.03) L	1:50 PM (1.30) H	9:41 PM (0.50) L
Mon 19	4:58 AM (1.09) H	9:04 AM (0.99) L	2:40 PM (1.28) H	10:21 PM (0.51) L
Tue 20	5:25 AM (1.10) H	9:50 AM (0.95) L	3:32 PM (1.26) H	10:57 PM (0.53) L
Wed 21	5:50 AM (1.12) H	10:38 AM (0.91) L	4:29 PM (1.24) H	11:30 PM (0.55) L
Thu 22	6:15 AM (1.15) H	11:28 AM (0.85) L	5:26 PM (1.22) H	
Fri 23	12:00 AM (0.58) L	6:42 AM (1.19) H	12:23 PM (0.79) L	6:23 PM (1.18) H
Sat 24	12:29 AM (0.63) L	7:10 AM (1.25) H	1:23 PM (0.70) L	7:23 PM (1.15) H
Sun 25	12:58 AM (0.71) L	7:41 AM (1.32) H	2:28 PM (0.60) L	8:32 PM (1.11) H
Mon 26	1:30 AM (0.79) L	8:16 AM (1.39) H	3:34 PM (0.49) L	9:56 PM (1.10) H
Tue 27	2:09 AM (0.89) L	8:57 AM (1.46) H	4:36 PM (0.37) L	11:17 PM (1.11) H
Wed 28	2:58 AM (0.97) L	9:45 AM (1.51) H	5:34 PM (0.27) L	
Thu 29	12:28 AM (1.14) H	4:13 AM (1.03) L	10:40 AM (1.54) H	6:30 PM (0.21) L
Fri 30	1:31 AM (1.16) H	5:47 AM (1.05) L	11:40 AM (1.55) H	7:26 PM (0.19) L
Sat 31	2:32 AM (1.17) H	6:57 AM (1.03) L	12:40 PM (1.53) H	8:21 PM (0.20) L

Port Phillip Heads - VIC

DAY/DATE	TIDE 1	TIDE 2	TIDE 3	TIDE 4
Thu 1	2:59 AM (1.74) H	8:33 AM (0.60) L	2:47 PM (1.55) H	8:45 PM (0.20) L
Fri 2	3:41 AM (1.74) H	9:14 AM (0.61) L	3:25 PM (1.55) H	9:27 PM (0.19) L
Sat 3	4:24 AM (1.69) H	9:54 AM (0.64) L	4:03 PM (1.52) H	10:11 PM (0.21) L
Sun 4	6:10 AM (1.61) H	11:35 AM (0.67) L	5:45 PM (1.48) H	11:56 PM (0.26) L
Mon 5	7:00 AM (1.51) H	12:19 PM (0.71) L	6:34 PM (1.42) H	
Tue 6	12:44 AM (0.34) L	8:00 AM (1.43) H	1:08 PM (0.74) L	7:34 PM (1.35) H
Wed 7	1:39 AM (0.44) L	9:08 AM (1.37) H	2:10 PM (0.76) L	8:54 PM (1.30) H
Thu 8	2:48 AM (0.54) L	10:15 AM (1.35) H	3:36 PM (0.73) L	10:30 PM (1.30) H
Fri 9	4:13 AM (0.61) L	11:17 AM (1.36) H	5:05 PM (0.64) L	11:50 PM (1.38) H
Sat 10	5:34 AM (0.63) L	12:15 PM (1.40) H	6:14 PM (0.52) L	
Sun 11	12:58 AM (1.49) H	6:43 AM (0.63) L	1:05 PM (1.44) H	7:05 PM (0.40) L
Mon 12	1:55 AM (1.61) H	7:36 AM (0.62) L	1:50 PM (1.48) H	7:48 PM (0.32) L
Tue 13	2:43 AM (1.69) H	8:18 AM (0.61) L	2:29 PM (1.50) H	8:27 PM (0.27) L
Wed 14	3:24 AM (1.73) H	8:56 AM (0.60) L	3:04 PM (1.50) H	9:04 PM (0.25) L
Thu 15	4:00 AM (1.72) H	9:30 AM (0.61) L	3:37 PM (1.50) H	9:40 PM (0.26) L
Fri 16	4:33 AM (1.69) H	10:04 AM (0.61) L	4:10 PM (1.48) H	10:15 PM (0.28) L
Sat 17	5:04 AM (1.64) H	10:39 AM (0.63) L	4:44 PM (1.45) H	10:51 PM (0.32) L
Sun 18	5:37 AM (1.57) H	11:14 AM (0.66) L	5:18 PM (1.41) H	11:26 PM (0.37) L
Mon 19	6:13 AM (1.50) H	11:48 AM (0.69) L	5:55 PM (1.35) H	
Tue 20	12:00 AM (0.43) L	6:52 AM (1.43) H	12:24 PM (0.73) L	6:35 PM (1.29) H
Wed 21	12:35 AM (0.49) L	7:38 AM (1.36) H	1:03 PM (0.76) L	7:25 PM (1.23) H
Thu 22	1:15 AM (0.57) L	8:31 AM (1.31) H	1:51 PM (0.77) L	8:30 PM (1.19) H
Fri 23	2:07 AM (0.66) L	9:30 AM (1.29) H	2:52 PM (0.75) L	9:53 PM (1.21) H
Sat 24	3:14 AM (0.73) L	10:30 AM (1.28) H	4:05 PM (0.69) L	11:15 PM (1.29) H
Sun 25	4:35 AM (0.78) L	11:26 AM (1.31) H	5:19 PM (0.57) L	
Mon 26	12:24 AM (1.42) H	6:01 AM (0.78) L	12:18 PM (1.35) H	6:15 PM (0.44) L
Tue 27	1:20 AM (1.56) H	7:01 AM (0.75) L	1:07 PM (1.40) H	7:02 PM (0.32) L
Wed 28	2:11 AM (1.69) H	7:47 AM (0.71) L	1:54 PM (1.45) H	7:48 PM (0.21) L
Thu 29	2:57 AM (1.77) H	8:30 AM (0.68) L	2:38 PM (1.49) H	8:33 PM (0.15) L
Fri 30	3:42 AM (1.80) H	9:13 AM (0.65) L	3:22 PM (1.52) H	9:19 PM (0.13) L
Sat 31	4:27 AM (1.77) H	9:55 AM (0.63) L	4:05 PM (1.52) H	10:06 PM (0.15) L

Fort Denison - NSW

DAY/DATE	TIDE 1	TIDE 2	TIDE 3	TIDE 4
Thu 1	4:40 AM (0.48) L	11:12 AM (1.77) H	5:52 PM (0.41) L	11:51 PM (1.28) H
Fri 2	5:30 AM (0.57) L	12:07 PM (1.72) H	7:01 PM (0.46) L	
Sat 3	1:00 AM (1.19) H	6:32 AM (0.65) L	1:13 PM (1.66) H	8:20 PM (0.48) L
Sun 4	3:22 AM (1.16) H	8:48 AM (0.68) L	3:29 PM (1.64) H	10:37 PM (0.46) L
Mon 5	4:44 AM (1.20) H	10:10 AM (0.66) L	4:45 PM (1.65) H	11:41 PM (0.41) L
Tue 6	5:47 AM (1.29) H	11:23 AM (0.59) L	5:50 PM (1.69) H	
Wed 7	12:32 AM (0.36) L	6:39 AM (1.40) H	12:25 PM (0.50) L	6:45 PM (1.71) H
Thu 8	1:16 AM (0.32) L	7:24 AM (1.51) H	1:20 PM (0.43) L	7:33 PM (1.71) H
Fri 9	1:55 AM (0.30) L	8:06 AM (1.60) H	2:10 PM (0.37) L	8:17 PM (1.67) H
Sat 10	2:30 AM (0.32) L	8:45 AM (1.67) H	2:56 PM (0.35) L	9:00 PM (1.60) H
Sun 11	3:03 AM (0.35) L	9:22 AM (1.72) H	3:40 PM (0.35) L	9:40 PM (1.52) H
Mon 12	3:34 AM (0.41) L	9:59 AM (1.74) H	4:22 PM (0.38) L	10:19 PM (1.43) H
Tue 13	4:05 AM (0.47) L	10:33 AM (1.73) H	5:03 PM (0.42) L	11:00 PM (1.34) H
Wed 14	4:35 AM (0.54) L	11:09 AM (1.70) H	5:46 PM (0.47) L	11:40 PM (1.27) H
Thu 15	5:08 AM (0.61) L	11:45 AM (1.65) H	6:30 PM (0.53) L	
Fri 16	12:23 AM (1.20) H	5:45 AM (0.68) L	12:27 PM (1.58) H	7:21 PM (0.59) L
Sat 17	1:13 AM (1.15) H	6:31 AM (0.73) L	1:14 PM (1.51) H	8:19 PM (0.63) L
Sun 18	2:12 AM (1.11) H	7:30 AM (0.78) L	2:12 PM (1.46) H	9:26 PM (0.64) L
Mon 19	3:25 AM (1.12) H	8:43 AM (0.80) L	3:21 PM (1.43) H	10:30 PM (0.61) L
Tue 20	4:36 AM (1.16) H	10:00 AM (0.78) L	4:30 PM (1.45) H	11:23 PM (0.56) L
Wed 21	5:31 AM (1.25) H	11:06 AM (0.72) L	5:28 PM (1.49) H	
Thu 22	12:06 AM (0.49) L	6:15 AM (1.35) H	12:03 PM (0.64) L	6:15 PM (1.53) H
Fri 23	12:43 AM (0.43) L	6:54 AM (1.47) H	12:52 PM (0.55) L	7:00 PM (1.57) H
Sat 24	1:17 AM (0.38) L	7:31 AM (1.59) H	1:38 PM (0.45) L	7:43 PM (1.59) H
Sun 25	1:51 AM (0.35) L	8:09 AM (1.71) H	2:25 PM (0.36) L	8:26 PM (1.59) H
Mon 26	2:28 AM (0.34) L	8:48 AM (1.82) H	3:12 PM (0.29) L	9:13 PM (1.55) H
Tue 27	3:06 AM (0.36) L	9:31 AM (1.90) H	4:00 PM (0.25) L	10:02 PM (1.50) H
Wed 28	3:47 AM (0.40) L	10:16 AM (1.94) H	4:53 PM (0.25) L	10:55 PM (1.43) H
Thu 29	4:33 AM (0.46) L	11:05 AM (1.93) H	5:49 PM (0.28) L	11:51 PM (1.35) H
Fri 30	5:24 AM (0.53) L	11:58 AM (1.89) H	6:50 PM (0.33) L	
Sat 31	12:53 AM (1.28) H	6:22 AM (0.60) L	12:56 PM (1.81) H	7:57 PM (0.38) L

BITE TIMES

Apogee moon phase on Saturday 17th
Perigee moon phase on Friday 2nd and Thursday 29th

New moon on Sunday 11th
First quarter moon on Monday 19th
Full moon on Monday 26th
Last quarter moon phase on Saturday 3rd

DAY	MINOR BITE	MAJOR BITE	MINOR BITE	MAJOR BITE	SALT WATER RATING	FRESH WATER RATING
THUR 1	10:54 PM	2:29 AM	7:11 AM	2:59 PM	4	4
FRI 2		3:30 AM	8:04 AM	4:01 PM	3	6
SAT 3		4:33 AM	9:07 AM	5:03 PM	5	5
SUN 4	12:57 AM	5:35 AM	10:17 AM	6:04 PM	6	6
MON 5	1:43 AM	6:34 AM	11:31 AM	7:00 PM	7	7
TUE 6	2:20 AM	7:28 AM	12:44 PM	7:52 PM	7	7
WED 7	2:52 AM	8:18 AM	1:54 PM	8:41 PM	7	8
THUR 8	3:19 AM	9:06 AM	3:02 PM	9:28 PM	5	8
FRI 9	3:44 AM	9:51 AM	4:08 PM	10:13 PM	6	7
SAT 10	4:08 AM	10:36 AM	5:13 PM	10:57 PM	8	8
SUN 11	4:33 AM	11:20 AM	6:18 PM	11:42 PM	8	8
MON 12	5:00 AM	12:06 PM	7:23 PM		8	6
TUE 13	5:30 AM	12:54 PM	8:27 PM	12:30 AM	7	6
WED 14	6:05 AM	1:44 PM	9:29 PM	1:19 AM	6	7
THUR 15	6:46 AM	2:35 PM	10:27 PM	2:09 AM	5	5

DAY	MINOR BITE	MAJOR BITE	MINOR BITE	MAJOR BITE	SALT WATER RATING	FRESH WATER RATING
FRI 16	7:34 AM	3:26 PM	11:19 PM	3:00 AM	4	6
SAT 17	8:27 AM	4:17 PM		3:51 AM	3	5
SUN 18	9:25 AM	5:07 PM	12:03 AM	4:42 AM	3	5
MON 19	10:26 AM	5:55 PM	12:42 AM	5:30 AM	4	6
TUE 20	11:28 AM	6:40 PM	1:14 AM	6:17 AM	5	6
WED 21	12:30 PM	7:25 PM	1:43 AM	7:02 AM	4	5
THUR 22	1:34 PM	8:08 PM	2:08 AM	7:46 AM	3	5
FRI 23	2:38 PM	8:52 PM	2:32 AM	8:30 AM	6	6
SAT 24	3:44 PM	9:38 PM	2:57 AM	9:15 AM	5	7
SUN 25	4:54 PM	10:27 PM	3:22 AM	10:02 AM	3	8
MON 26	6:07 PM	11:20 PM	3:51 AM	10:53 AM	5	7
TUE 27	7:23 PM		4:25 AM	11:48 AM	7	6
WED 28	8:39 PM	12:17 AM	5:06 AM	12:48 PM	7	6
THUR 29	9:50 PM	1:20 AM	5:57 AM	1:52 PM	5	5
FRI 30	10:51 PM	2:24 AM	6:58 AM	2:56 PM	4	4
SAT 31	11:41 PM	3:28 AM	8:08 AM	3:58 PM	3	6

TIDE TIMES

* Additional Tide 5 - See Additional Tide 5

Adelaide Outer Harbour - SA

DAY/DATE	TIDE 5
Wed 4	10:00 PM (1.08) L

DAY/DATE	TIDE 1	TIDE 2	TIDE 3	TIDE 4
Sun 1	12:33 AM (0.65) L	7:32 AM (2.39) H	2:11 PM (0.84) L	7:28 PM (1.50) H
Mon 2	12:50 AM (0.72) L	7:52 AM (2.18) H	2:23 PM (0.99) L	7:36 PM (1.44) H
Tue 3	1:03 AM (0.88) L	8:05 AM (1.89) H	2:37 PM (1.18) L	6:55 PM (1.34) H
Wed 4*	12:15 AM (1.12) L	6:53 AM (1.58) H	12:47 PM (1.38) L	4:09 PM (1.43) H
Thu 5	4:32 AM (1.66) H	10:17 AM (1.10) L	4:08 PM (1.66) H	10:00 PM (0.89) L
Fri 6	4:13 AM (1.97) H	10:32 AM (0.75) L	4:31 PM (1.85) H	10:16 PM (0.75) L
Sat 7	4:26 AM (2.25) H	10:56 AM (0.50) L	4:55 PM (1.95) H	10:33 PM (0.66) L
Sun 8	4:44 AM (2.46) H	11:18 AM (0.35) L	5:15 PM (1.98) H	10:49 PM (0.61) L
Mon 9	5:02 AM (2.60) H	11:40 AM (0.28) L	5:34 PM (1.98) H	11:04 PM (0.58) L
Tue 10	5:22 AM (2.69) H	12:02 PM (0.25) L	5:54 PM (1.96) H	11:24 PM (0.55) L
Wed 11	5:46 AM (2.73) H	12:27 PM (0.26) L	6:17 PM (1.94) H	11:46 PM (0.55) L
Thu 12	6:14 AM (2.72) H	12:54 PM (0.31) L	6:43 PM (1.90) H	
Fri 13	12:12 AM (0.57) L	6:42 AM (2.66) H	1:20 PM (0.39) L	7:09 PM (1.85) H
Sat 14	12:36 AM (0.62) L	7:08 AM (2.56) H	1:45 PM (0.48) L	7:32 PM (1.79) H
Sun 15	1:00 AM (0.68) L	7:32 AM (2.45) H	2:09 PM (0.57) L	7:55 PM (1.74) H
Mon 16	1:23 AM (0.76) L	7:58 AM (2.32) H	2:36 PM (0.67) L	8:24 PM (1.67) H
Tue 17	1:52 AM (0.88) L	8:27 AM (2.14) H	3:14 PM (0.80) L	9:09 PM (1.57) H
Wed 18	2:30 AM (1.07) L	9:09 AM (1.90) H	4:22 PM (0.97) L	11:15 PM (1.48) H
Thu 19	4:19 AM (1.33) L	11:06 AM (1.60) H	7:09 PM (1.04) L	
Fri 20	2:27 AM (1.69) H	8:53 AM (1.14) L	2:35 PM (1.63) H	8:50 PM (0.91) L
Sat 21	3:22 AM (2.01) H	9:55 AM (0.79) L	3:54 PM (1.80) H	9:39 PM (0.79) L
Sun 22	3:58 AM (2.28) H	10:36 AM (0.49) L	4:41 PM (1.90) H	10:13 PM (0.74) L
Mon 23	4:28 AM (2.48) H	11:13 AM (0.29) L	5:17 PM (1.91) H	10:40 PM (0.73) L
Tue 24	4:55 AM (2.63) H	11:46 AM (0.19) L	5:48 PM (1.85) H	11:03 PM (0.74) L
Wed 25	5:22 AM (2.72) H	12:20 PM (0.18) L	6:15 PM (1.77) H	11:26 PM (0.74) L
Thu 26	5:52 AM (2.76) H	12:55 PM (0.23) L	6:43 PM (1.67) H	11:49 PM (0.74) L
Fri 27	6:24 AM (2.72) H	1:29 PM (0.34) L	7:07 PM (1.59) H	
Sat 28	12:12 AM (0.75) L	6:54 AM (2.62) H	1:58 PM (0.49) L	7:28 PM (1.54) H
Sun 29	12:33 AM (0.76) L	7:21 AM (2.48) H	2:18 PM (0.63) L	7:46 PM (1.55) H
Mon 30	12:57 AM (0.79) L	7:46 AM (2.31) H	2:32 PM (0.73) L	8:12 PM (1.59) H

Brisbane Bar - QLD

DAY/DATE	TIDE 1	TIDE 2	TIDE 3	TIDE 4
Sun 1	1:52 AM (1.55) H	7:36 AM (0.62) L	2:30 PM (2.30) H	9:39 PM (0.68) L
Mon 2	3:16 AM (1.56) H	8:56 AM (0.69) L	3:38 PM (2.25) H	10:44 PM (0.62) L
Tue 3	4:35 AM (1.68) H	10:18 AM (0.69) L	4:45 PM (2.23) H	11:42 PM (0.54) L
Wed 4	5:42 AM (1.84) H	11:33 AM (0.65) L	5:46 PM (2.21) H	
Thu 5	12:32 AM (0.46) L	6:37 AM (2.01) H	12:37 PM (0.61) L	6:38 PM (2.18) H
Fri 6	1:15 AM (0.39) L	7:24 AM (2.16) H	1:33 PM (0.57) L	7:24 PM (2.12) H
Sat 7	1:54 AM (0.35) L	8:07 AM (2.27) H	2:23 PM (0.56) L	8:05 PM (2.05) H
Sun 8	2:28 AM (0.33) L	8:45 AM (2.35) H	3:09 PM (0.56) L	8:44 PM (1.98) H
Mon 9	2:59 AM (0.32) L	9:23 AM (2.40) H	3:51 PM (0.58) L	9:19 PM (1.90) H
Tue 10	3:28 AM (0.33) L	9:58 AM (2.41) H	4:30 PM (0.61) L	9:54 PM (1.82) H
Wed 11	3:56 AM (0.36) L	10:32 AM (2.39) H	5:08 PM (0.65) L	10:28 PM (1.75) H
Thu 12	4:26 AM (0.41) L	11:06 AM (2.35) H	5:44 PM (0.70) L	11:02 PM (1.69) H
Fri 13	4:57 AM (0.48) L	11:42 AM (2.28) H	6:20 PM (0.76) L	11:39 PM (1.62) H
Sat 14	5:31 AM (0.56) L	12:19 PM (2.21) H	7:01 PM (0.81) L	
Sun 15	12:21 AM (1.57) H	6:11 AM (0.65) L	1:01 PM (2.14) H	7:51 PM (0.84) L
Mon 16	1:14 AM (1.53) H	7:00 AM (0.75) L	1:51 PM (2.08) H	8:49 PM (0.84) L
Tue 17	2:19 AM (1.52) H	8:00 AM (0.83) L	2:47 PM (2.04) H	9:50 PM (0.79) L
Wed 18	3:38 AM (1.57) H	9:15 AM (0.87) L	3:48 PM (2.03) H	10:47 PM (0.71) L
Thu 19	4:49 AM (1.70) H	10:30 AM (0.85) L	4:47 PM (2.04) H	11:39 PM (0.60) L
Fri 20	5:48 AM (1.88) H	11:41 AM (0.79) L	5:43 PM (2.05) H	
Sat 21	12:27 AM (0.48) L	6:40 AM (2.08) H	12:45 PM (0.71) L	6:34 PM (2.05) H
Sun 22	1:12 AM (0.38) L	7:29 AM (2.27) H	1:45 PM (0.63) L	7:25 PM (2.03) H
Mon 23	1:55 AM (0.31) L	8:15 AM (2.43) H	2:43 PM (0.56) L	8:14 PM (1.99) H
Tue 24	2:37 AM (0.26) L	9:02 AM (2.56) H	3:37 PM (0.51) L	9:04 PM (1.94) H
Wed 25	3:19 AM (0.23) L	9:50 AM (2.65) H	4:31 PM (0.48) L	9:55 PM (1.88) H
Thu 26	4:02 AM (0.24) L	10:39 AM (2.68) H	5:26 PM (0.48) L	10:48 PM (1.82) H
Fri 27	4:47 AM (0.29) L	11:29 AM (2.67) H	6:21 PM (0.51) L	11:44 PM (1.76) H
Sat 28	5:35 AM (0.36) L	12:19 PM (2.61) H	7:17 PM (0.54) L	
Sun 29	12:42 AM (1.72) H	6:29 AM (0.47) L	1:12 PM (2.51) H	8:13 PM (0.57) L
Mon 30	1:44 AM (1.70) H	7:29 AM (0.58) L	2:06 PM (2.39) H	9:07 PM (0.58) L

Darwin - NT

DAY/DATE	TIDE 1	TIDE 2	TIDE 3	TIDE 4
Sun 1	3:44 AM (3.36) L	9:00 AM (5.81) H	4:14 PM (1.94) L	10:58 PM (6.32) H
Mon 2	5:00 AM (3.68) L	10:02 AM (5.18) H	5:22 PM (2.59) L	
Tue 3	12:07 AM (5.96) H	6:52 AM (3.65) L	12:19 PM (4.78) H	6:54 PM (3.03) L
Wed 4	1:27 AM (5.86) H	8:32 AM (3.19) L	2:29 PM (5.14) H	8:30 PM (3.12) L
Thu 5	2:41 AM (5.99) H	9:39 AM (2.57) L	3:40 PM (5.74) H	9:42 PM (3.00) L
Fri 6	3:38 AM (6.20) H	10:28 AM (1.99) L	4:34 PM (6.31) H	10:36 PM (2.85) L
Sat 7	4:21 AM (6.39) H	11:07 AM (1.53) L	5:21 PM (6.78) H	11:19 PM (2.74) L
Sun 8	4:56 AM (6.53) H	11:41 AM (1.18) L	6:02 PM (7.13) H	11:55 PM (2.67) L
Mon 9	5:25 AM (6.61) H	12:11 PM (0.97) L	6:40 PM (7.33) H	
Tue 10	12:27 AM (2.65) L	5:53 AM (6.63) H	12:39 PM (0.87) L	7:14 PM (7.38) H
Wed 11	12:56 AM (2.69) L	6:22 AM (6.59) H	1:07 PM (0.90) L	7:45 PM (7.31) H
Thu 12	1:24 AM (2.78) L	6:51 AM (6.49) H	1:36 PM (1.06) L	8:15 PM (7.14) H
Fri 13	1:52 AM (2.91) L	7:21 AM (6.31) H	2:05 PM (1.32) L	8:45 PM (6.90) H
Sat 14	2:21 AM (3.09) L	7:52 AM (6.04) H	2:36 PM (1.68) L	9:16 PM (6.62) H
Sun 15	2:54 AM (3.32) L	8:24 AM (5.71) H	3:10 PM (2.11) L	9:51 PM (6.32) H
Mon 16	3:35 AM (3.56) L	8:59 AM (5.32) H	3:48 PM (2.57) L	10:32 PM (6.03) H
Tue 17	4:39 AM (3.77) L	9:46 AM (4.92) H	4:40 PM (3.02) L	11:23 PM (5.78) H
Wed 18	6:16 AM (3.79) L	11:16 AM (4.60) H	5:53 PM (3.37) L	
Thu 19	12:25 AM (5.63) H	7:49 AM (3.52) L	1:28 PM (4.69) H	7:19 PM (3.54) L
Fri 20	1:34 AM (5.64) H	8:56 AM (3.03) L	3:03 PM (5.19) H	8:41 PM (3.49) L
Sat 21	2:38 AM (5.79) H	9:45 AM (2.44) L	4:01 PM (5.84) H	9:46 PM (3.31) L
Sun 22	3:30 AM (6.03) H	10:27 AM (1.83) L	4:50 PM (6.49) H	10:38 PM (3.10) L
Mon 23	4:13 AM (6.29) H	11:07 AM (1.25) L	5:36 PM (7.06) H	11:23 PM (2.92) L
Tue 24	4:51 AM (6.53) H	11:46 AM (0.76) L	6:20 PM (7.50) H	
Wed 25	12:04 AM (2.78) L	5:29 AM (6.73) H	12:26 PM (0.44) L	7:04 PM (7.75) H
Thu 26	12:44 AM (2.72) L	6:08 AM (6.84) H	1:05 PM (0.31) L	7:47 PM (7.81) H
Fri 27	1:24 AM (2.72) L	6:48 AM (6.83) H	1:46 PM (0.42) L	8:30 PM (7.70) H
Sat 28	2:08 AM (2.78) L	7:32 AM (6.67) H	2:30 PM (0.75) L	9:14 PM (7.46) H
Sun 29	2:59 AM (2.90) L	8:20 AM (6.36) H	3:16 PM (1.27) L	9:59 PM (7.14) H
Mon 30	3:58 AM (3.03) L	9:15 AM (5.92) H	4:07 PM (1.91) L	10:45 PM (6.79) H

Fremantle - WA

DAY/DATE	TIDE 5
Tue 3	9:27 PM (0.84) H

DAY/DATE	TIDE 1	TIDE 2	TIDE 3	TIDE 4
Sun 1	12:03 AM (0.46) H			
Mon 2	12:03 AM (0.96) L	1:25 AM (0.96) L	2:25 AM (0.96) L	1:30 PM (0.51) L
Tue 3*	12:30 AM (0.88) H	1:49 AM (0.88) L	3:27 AM (0.89) H	1:58 PM (0.58) L
Wed 4	2:20 AM (0.79) L	4:56 AM (0.82) H	1:56 PM (0.65) L	8:04 PM (0.87) H
Thu 5	2:53 AM (0.72) L	7:50 AM (0.78) H	1:15 PM (0.69) L	8:03 PM (0.93) H
Fri 6	3:24 AM (0.65) L	9:20 AM (0.75) H	12:28 PM (0.71) L	8:00 PM (1.00) H
Sat 7	4:00 AM (0.59) L	10:17 AM (0.72) H	12:12 PM (0.70) L	8:04 PM (1.05) H
Sun 8	4:49 AM (0.54) L	11:08 AM (0.70) H	12:31 PM (0.69) L	8:20 PM (1.10) H
Mon 9	5:44 AM (0.50) L	8:39 PM (1.12) H		
Tue 10	6:26 AM (0.48) L	9:00 PM (1.14) H		
Wed 11	7:06 AM (0.47) L	9:26 PM (1.13) H		
Thu 12	7:45 AM (0.48) L	9:55 PM (1.11) H		
Fri 13	8:24 AM (0.50) L	10:26 PM (1.08) H		
Sat 14	9:05 AM (0.52) L	10:58 PM (1.05) H		
Sun 15	9:46 AM (0.55) L	11:30 PM (1.01) H		
Mon 16	12:09 AM (0.58) H			
Tue 17	12:00 AM (0.96) L	11:08 AM (0.61) L		
Wed 18	12:28 AM (0.90) H	11:38 AM (0.63) L	8:42 PM (0.87) H	
Thu 19	11:58 AM (0.66) L	7:19 PM (0.90) H		
Fri 20	12:06 PM (0.69) L	7:15 PM (0.97) H		
Sat 21	3:18 AM (0.66) L	9:16 AM (0.72) H	11:57 AM (0.72) L	7:24 PM (1.04) H
Sun 22	3:50 AM (0.57) L	7:44 PM (1.12) H		
Mon 23	4:39 AM (0.47) L	8:10 PM (1.18) H		
Tue 24	5:34 AM (0.39) L	8:40 PM (1.22) H		
Wed 25	6:30 AM (0.34) L	9:13 PM (1.24) H		
Thu 26	7:22 AM (0.33) L	9:48 PM (1.22) H		
Fri 27	8:12 AM (0.35) L	10:24 PM (1.17) H		
Sat 28	9:03 AM (0.40) L	10:54 PM (1.09) H		
Sun 29	9:59 AM (0.47) L	11:13 PM (1.00) H		
Mon 30	12:05 PM (0.55) L	11:24 PM (0.92) H		

* Additional Tide 5 - See Additional Tide 5

Sun Rise & Sun Set Times:

Darwin, NT: Rise: 06:10am Set: 06:50pm

Melbourne, VIC: Rise: 06:00am Set: 08:10pm

Adelaide, SA: Rise: 06:00am Set: 07:50pm

Perth, WA: Rise: 06:50am Set: 05:40pm

Sydney, NSW: Rise: 05:40am Set: 07:30pm

Brisbane, QLD: Rise: 04:40am Set: 06:10pm

Hobart, TAS: Rise: 05:30am Set: 08:10pm

(Note: These times are averages for the month.

Hobart - TAS

DAY/DATE	TIDE 1	TIDE 2	TIDE 3	TIDE 4
Sun 1	3:29 AM (1.17) H	7:58 AM (0.99) L	1:40 PM (1.48) H	9:15 PM (0.25) L
Mon 2	4:15 AM (1.18) H	8:58 AM (0.93) L	2:43 PM (1.41) H	10:06 PM (0.32) L
Tue 3	4:55 AM (1.19) H	10:01 AM (0.86) L	3:51 PM (1.33) H	10:52 PM (0.41) L
Wed 4	5:31 AM (1.21) H	11:08 AM (0.79) L	5:00 PM (1.24) H	11:32 PM (0.51) L
Thu 5	6:06 AM (1.25) H	12:17 PM (0.71) L	6:07 PM (1.16) H	
Fri 6	12:06 AM (0.61) L	6:40 AM (1.30) H	1:25 PM (0.63) L	7:14 PM (1.08) H
Sat 7	12:31 AM (0.72) L	7:13 AM (1.34) H	2:29 PM (0.56) L	8:27 PM (1.03) H
Sun 8	12:51 AM (0.82) L	7:44 AM (1.37) H	3:26 PM (0.50) L	9:46 PM (1.01) H
Mon 9	1:06 AM (0.91) L	8:15 AM (1.39) H	4:15 PM (0.45) L	11:01 PM (1.02) H
Tue 10	1:22 AM (0.98) L	8:45 AM (1.40) H	4:58 PM (0.42) L	
Wed 11	12:10 AM (1.05) H	1:41 AM (1.04) L	9:18 AM (1.40) H	5:37 PM (0.40) L
Thu 12	1:15 AM (1.08) H	2:06 AM (1.07) L	9:55 AM (1.39) H	6:15 PM (0.40) L
Fri 13	10:35 AM (1.37) H	6:55 PM (0.42) L		
Sat 14	2:47 AM (1.11) H	5:33 AM (1.09) L	11:20 AM (1.34) H	7:34 PM (0.44) L
Sun 15	3:15 AM (1.11) H	6:48 AM (1.07) L	12:08 PM (1.31) H	8:15 PM (0.46) L
Mon 16	3:40 AM (1.11) H	7:44 AM (1.04) L	12:58 PM (1.27) H	8:53 PM (0.48) L
Tue 17	4:02 AM (1.13) H	8:40 AM (0.99) L	1:50 PM (1.22) H	9:29 PM (0.51) L
Wed 18	4:27 AM (1.15) H	9:37 AM (0.94) L	2:47 PM (1.18) H	10:00 PM (0.54) L
Thu 19	4:51 AM (1.20) H	10:35 AM (0.88) L	3:51 PM (1.13) H	10:30 PM (0.58) L
Fri 20	5:16 AM (1.25) H	11:31 AM (0.79) L	4:59 PM (1.08) H	10:56 PM (0.64) L
Sat 21	5:44 AM (1.32) H	12:28 PM (0.68) L	6:10 PM (1.05) H	11:23 PM (0.71) L
Sun 22	6:15 AM (1.40) H	1:25 PM (0.56) L	7:25 PM (1.03) H	11:53 PM (0.80) L
Mon 23	6:51 AM (1.48) H	2:24 PM (0.43) L	8:46 PM (1.04) H	
Tue 24	12:28 AM (0.88) L	7:32 AM (1.55) H	3:23 PM (0.30) L	10:07 PM (1.06) H
Wed 25	1:09 AM (0.97) L	8:21 AM (1.60) H	4:20 PM (0.20) L	11:19 PM (1.10) H
Thu 26	2:03 AM (1.03) L	9:16 AM (1.63) H	5:16 PM (0.13) L	
Fri 27	12:24 AM (1.13) H	3:36 AM (1.07) L	10:15 AM (1.63) H	6:11 PM (0.11) L
Sat 28	1:24 AM (1.16) H	5:29 AM (1.05) L	11:18 AM (1.59) H	7:06 PM (0.13) L
Sun 29	2:15 AM (1.18) H	6:43 AM (1.00) L	12:22 PM (1.52) H	8:00 PM (0.19) L
Mon 30	3:00 AM (1.20) H	7:51 AM (0.93) L	1:28 PM (1.41) H	8:51 PM (0.28) L

Port Phillip Heads - VIC

DAY/DATE	TIDE 1	TIDE 2	TIDE 3	TIDE 4
Sun 1	5:12 AM (1.71) H	10:38 AM (0.62) L	4:50 PM (1.50) H	10:54 PM (0.21) L
Mon 2	5:58 AM (1.63) H	11:23 AM (0.62) L	5:39 PM (1.45) H	11:42 PM (0.30) L
Tue 3	6:47 AM (1.54) H	12:12 PM (0.62) L	6:33 PM (1.39) H	
Wed 4	12:32 AM (0.41) L	7:43 AM (1.47) H	1:06 PM (0.63) L	7:43 PM (1.33) H
Thu 5	1:28 AM (0.53) L	8:42 AM (1.41) H	2:12 PM (0.61) L	9:13 PM (1.31) H
Fri 6	2:31 AM (0.65) L	9:41 AM (1.37) H	3:27 PM (0.57) L	10:33 PM (1.35) H
Sat 7	3:45 AM (0.74) L	10:38 AM (1.35) H	4:40 PM (0.51) L	11:44 PM (1.43) H
Sun 8	5:05 AM (0.78) L	11:33 AM (1.36) H	5:41 PM (0.43) L	
Mon 9	12:45 AM (1.53) H	6:17 AM (0.78) L	12:24 PM (1.37) H	6:31 PM (0.35) L
Tue 10	1:37 AM (1.62) H	7:12 AM (0.75) L	1:10 PM (1.39) H	7:15 PM (0.30) L
Wed 11	2:22 AM (1.68) H	7:55 AM (0.72) L	1:51 PM (1.40) H	7:55 PM (0.27) L
Thu 12	3:00 AM (1.71) H	8:31 AM (0.69) L	2:30 PM (1.42) H	8:33 PM (0.26) L
Fri 13	3:34 AM (1.71) H	9:06 AM (0.67) L	3:06 PM (1.43) H	9:10 PM (0.27) L
Sat 14	4:06 AM (1.68) H	9:41 AM (0.65) L	3:42 PM (1.42) H	9:46 PM (0.29) L
Sun 15	4:37 AM (1.64) H	10:16 AM (0.65) L	4:18 PM (1.40) H	10:21 PM (0.33) L
Mon 16	5:10 AM (1.60) H	10:51 AM (0.65) L	4:55 PM (1.37) H	10:53 PM (0.38) L
Tue 17	5:45 AM (1.55) H	11:26 AM (0.66) L	5:33 PM (1.33) H	11:25 PM (0.45) L
Wed 18	6:21 AM (1.49) H	12:00 PM (0.66) L	6:16 PM (1.29) H	11:59 PM (0.52) L
Thu 19	7:00 AM (1.44) H	12:39 PM (0.66) L	7:07 PM (1.25) H	
Fri 20	12:39 AM (0.60) L	7:43 AM (1.39) H	1:22 PM (0.64) L	8:10 PM (1.24) H
Sat 21	1:29 AM (0.70) L	8:31 AM (1.35) H	2:13 PM (0.60) L	9:27 PM (1.27) H
Sun 22	2:31 AM (0.80) L	9:25 AM (1.32) H	3:13 PM (0.53) L	10:44 PM (1.36) H
Mon 23	3:45 AM (0.87) L	10:22 AM (1.31) H	4:17 PM (0.44) L	11:52 PM (1.47) H
Tue 24	5:07 AM (0.90) L	11:21 AM (1.32) H	5:22 PM (0.34) L	
Wed 25	12:53 AM (1.60) H	6:20 AM (0.87) L	12:20 PM (1.36) H	6:22 PM (0.24) L
Thu 26	1:48 AM (1.70) H	7:17 AM (0.82) L	1:17 PM (1.41) H	7:18 PM (0.16) L
Fri 27	2:39 AM (1.77) H	8:07 AM (0.75) L	2:12 PM (1.46) H	8:11 PM (0.12) L
Sat 28	3:28 AM (1.79) H	8:54 AM (0.69) L	3:03 PM (1.50) H	9:02 PM (0.12) L
Sun 29	4:15 AM (1.77) H	9:41 AM (0.63) L	3:53 PM (1.51) H	9:53 PM (0.16) L
Mon 30	5:01 AM (1.73) H	10:29 AM (0.58) L	4:45 PM (1.50) H	10:43 PM (0.24) L

Fort Denison - NSW

DAY/DATE	TIDE 1	TIDE 2	TIDE 3	TIDE 4
Sun 1	2:01 AM (1.24) H	7:29 AM (0.66) L	2:00 PM (1.72) H	9:06 PM (0.42) L
Mon 2	3:15 AM (1.25) H	8:43 AM (0.68) L	3:12 PM (1.65) H	10:11 PM (0.43) L
Tue 3	4:24 AM (1.31) H	10:00 AM (0.66) L	4:23 PM (1.61) H	11:07 PM (0.42) L
Wed 4	5:22 AM (1.39) H	11:11 AM (0.62) L	5:26 PM (1.58) H	11:56 PM (0.42) L
Thu 5	6:13 AM (1.50) H	12:15 PM (0.55) L	6:21 PM (1.55) H	
Fri 6	12:38 AM (0.41) L	6:58 AM (1.59) H	1:11 PM (0.49) L	7:10 PM (1.51) H
Sat 7	1:15 AM (0.42) L	7:39 AM (1.68) H	2:00 PM (0.45) L	7:55 PM (1.46) H
Sun 8	1:49 AM (0.45) L	8:17 AM (1.74) H	2:45 PM (0.41) L	8:37 PM (1.42) H
Mon 9	2:23 AM (0.48) L	8:53 AM (1.77) H	3:26 PM (0.40) L	9:18 PM (1.37) H
Tue 10	2:55 AM (0.52) L	9:29 AM (1.79) H	4:06 PM (0.40) L	9:59 PM (1.33) H
Wed 11	3:28 AM (0.56) L	10:03 AM (1.78) H	4:45 PM (0.42) L	10:38 PM (1.29) H
Thu 12	4:02 AM (0.60) L	10:39 AM (1.75) H	5:24 PM (0.45) L	11:18 PM (1.26) H
Fri 13	4:39 AM (0.64) L	11:16 AM (1.71) H	6:05 PM (0.50) L	
Sat 14	12:00 AM (1.22) H	5:19 AM (0.69) L	11:56 AM (1.65) H	6:50 PM (0.54) L
Sun 15	12:47 AM (1.20) H	6:05 AM (0.73) L	12:40 PM (1.59) H	7:40 PM (0.57) L
Mon 16	1:39 AM (1.18) H	6:58 AM (0.77) L	1:30 PM (1.53) H	8:33 PM (0.59) L
Tue 17	2:39 AM (1.19) H	8:00 AM (0.79) L	2:26 PM (1.48) H	9:28 PM (0.58) L
Wed 18	3:41 AM (1.24) H	9:10 AM (0.79) L	3:28 PM (1.45) H	10:18 PM (0.55) L
Thu 19	4:37 AM (1.32) H	10:20 AM (0.76) L	4:30 PM (1.44) H	11:04 PM (0.51) L
Fri 20	5:26 AM (1.43) H	11:25 AM (0.68) L	5:27 PM (1.45) H	11:46 PM (0.47) L
Sat 21	6:10 AM (1.56) H	12:23 PM (0.58) L	6:20 PM (1.46) H	
Sun 22	12:27 AM (0.44) L	6:53 AM (1.70) H	1:17 PM (0.47) L	7:13 PM (1.47) H
Mon 23	1:08 AM (0.42) L	7:37 AM (1.83) H	2:10 PM (0.36) L	8:04 PM (1.47) H
Tue 24	1:52 AM (0.41) L	8:22 AM (1.94) H	3:01 PM (0.27) L	8:58 PM (1.46) H
Wed 25	2:38 AM (0.42) L	9:11 AM (2.01) H	3:54 PM (0.21) L	9:52 PM (1.43) H
Thu 26	3:27 AM (0.44) L	10:01 AM (2.05) H	4:47 PM (0.19) L	10:48 PM (1.40) H
Fri 27	4:19 AM (0.47) L	10:54 AM (2.04) H	5:44 PM (0.21) L	11:45 PM (1.37) H
Sat 28	5:15 AM (0.52) L	11:47 AM (1.98) H	6:41 PM (0.26) L	
Sun 29	12:45 AM (1.34) H	6:15 AM (0.56) L	12:44 PM (1.89) H	7:39 PM (0.32) L
Mon 30	1:46 AM (1.34) H	7:18 AM (0.61) L	1:43 PM (1.77) H	8:37 PM (0.38) L

BITE TIMES

Apogee moon phase on Saturday 14th
Perigee moon phase on Thursday 26th

New moon on Monday 9th
First quarter moon on Tuesday 17th
Full moon on Wednesday 25th
Last quarter moon phase on Monday 2nd

DAY	MINOR BITE	MAJOR BITE	MINOR BITE	MAJOR BITE	SALT WATER RATING	FRESH WATER RATING
SUN 1		4:29 AM	9:22 AM	4:56 PM	4	4
MON 2	12:22 AM	5:25 AM	10:35 AM	5:50 PM	5	5
TUE 3	12:54 AM	6:16 AM	11:46 AM	6:39 PM	6	6
WED 4	1:23 AM	7:03 AM	12:54 PM	7:25 PM	7	7
THUR 5	1:48 AM	7:48 AM	1:59 PM	8:10 PM	7	8
FRI 6	2:12 AM	8:32 AM	3:03 PM	8:53 PM	5	8
SAT 7	2:36 AM	9:16 AM	4:07 PM	9:38 PM	6	7
SUN 8	3:02 AM	10:01 AM	5:11 PM	10:24 PM	8	8
MON 9	3:31 AM	10:48 AM	6:15 PM	11:12 PM	8	8
TUE 10	4:04 AM	11:37 AM	7:17 PM		8	6
WED 11	4:43 AM	12:27 PM	8:17 PM	12:02 AM	7	6
THUR 12	5:28 AM	1:19 PM	9:11 PM	12:53 AM	7	6
FRI 13	6:19 AM	2:10 PM	9:58 PM	1:44 AM	6	7
SAT 14	7:15 AM	3:00 PM	10:38 PM	2:35 AM	5	5
SUN 15	8:15 AM	3:48 PM	11:13 PM	3:23 AM	4	6

DAY	MINOR BITE	MAJOR BITE	MINOR BITE	MAJOR BITE	SALT WATER RATING	FRESH WATER RATING
MON 16	9:16 AM	4:34 PM	11:42 PM	4:11 AM	3	5
TUE 17	10:17 AM	5:18 PM		4:56 AM	4	6
WED 18	11:18 AM	6:00 PM	12:08 AM	5:39 AM	5	6
THUR 19	12:20 PM	6:43 PM	12:32 AM	6:21 AM	4	5
FRI 20	1:24 PM	7:27 PM	12:56 AM	7:04 AM	3	5
SAT 21	2:30 PM	8:13 PM	1:20 AM	7:49 AM	6	6
SUN 22	3:41 PM	9:04 PM	1:47 AM	8:38 AM	5	7
MON 23	4:55 PM	9:59 PM	2:18 AM	9:31 AM	5	7
TUE 24	6:13 PM	11:00 PM	2:55 AM	10:29 AM	3	8
WED 25	7:29 PM		3:43 AM	11:33 AM	5	7
THUR 26	8:37 PM	12:06 AM	4:41 AM	12:39 PM	7	6
FRI 27	9:34 PM	1:13 AM	5:51 AM	1:45 PM	5	5
SAT 28	10:19 PM	2:18 AM	7:06 AM	2:47 PM	4	4
SUN 29	10:56 PM	3:17 AM	8:23 AM	3:44 PM	3	6
MON 30	11:26 PM	4:12 AM	9:36 AM	4:36 PM	4	4

TIDE TIMES

Adelaide Outer Harbour - SA

DAY/DATE	TIDE 1	TIDE 2	TIDE 3	TIDE 4
Tue 1	1:29 AM (0.86) L	8:13 AM (2.12) H	2:50 PM (0.80) L	8:51 PM (1.62) H
Wed 2	2:15 AM (1.01) L	8:45 AM (1.88) H	3:20 PM (0.88) L	10:04 PM (1.64) H
Thu 3	3:37 AM (1.21) L	9:36 AM (1.59) H	4:18 PM (1.00) L	
Fri 4	12:23 AM (1.71) H	8:13 AM (1.23) L	12:35 PM (1.34) H	6:49 PM (1.09) L
Sat 5	2:18 AM (1.94) H	9:50 AM (0.92) L	3:28 PM (1.43) H	8:41 PM (1.02) L
Sun 6	3:21 AM (2.19) H	10:31 AM (0.65) L	4:27 PM (1.59) H	9:37 PM (0.92) L
Mon 7	4:05 AM (2.39) H	11:06 AM (0.45) L	5:04 PM (1.71) H	10:17 PM (0.84) L
Tue 8	4:41 AM (2.53) H	11:36 AM (0.34) L	5:35 PM (1.79) H	10:49 PM (0.77) L
Wed 9	5:13 AM (2.61) H	12:04 PM (0.28) L	6:02 PM (1.83) H	11:19 PM (0.72) L
Thu 10	5:44 AM (2.65) H	12:31 PM (0.27) L	6:28 PM (1.85) H	11:48 PM (0.67) L
Fri 11	6:14 AM (2.66) H	12:59 PM (0.28) L	6:53 PM (1.87) H	
Sat 12	12:17 AM (0.65) L	6:43 AM (2.63) H	1:25 PM (0.32) L	7:19 PM (1.87) H
Sun 13	12:46 AM (0.65) L	7:11 AM (2.57) H	1:51 PM (0.37) L	7:45 PM (1.86) H
Mon 14	1:15 AM (0.68) L	7:38 AM (2.48) H	2:15 PM (0.42) L	8:13 PM (1.86) H
Tue 15	1:45 AM (0.74) L	8:04 AM (2.37) H	2:42 PM (0.47) L	8:45 PM (1.87) H
Wed 16	2:22 AM (0.81) L	8:35 AM (2.23) H	3:12 PM (0.54) L	9:27 PM (1.88) H
Thu 17	3:10 AM (0.92) L	9:15 AM (2.03) H	3:49 PM (0.65) L	10:23 PM (1.88) H
Fri 18	4:23 AM (1.05) L	10:11 AM (1.78) H	4:40 PM (0.81) L	11:41 PM (1.89) H
Sat 19	6:22 AM (1.11) L	11:49 AM (1.50) H	5:58 PM (0.99) L	
Sun 20	1:22 AM (1.97) H	8:56 AM (0.93) L	2:48 PM (1.41) H	8:01 PM (1.09) L
Mon 21	2:54 AM (2.15) H	10:22 AM (0.63) L	4:45 PM (1.53) H	9:28 PM (1.08) L
Tue 22	3:59 AM (2.34) H	11:16 AM (0.38) L	5:39 PM (1.62) H	10:22 PM (1.04) L
Wed 23	4:46 AM (2.50) H	12:00 PM (0.23) L	6:17 PM (1.65) H	11:02 PM (0.97) L
Thu 24	5:27 AM (2.60) H	12:39 PM (0.18) L	6:46 PM (1.64) H	11:35 PM (0.90) L
Fri 25	6:02 AM (2.66) H	1:12 PM (0.20) L	7:08 PM (1.63) H	
Sat 26	12:06 AM (0.82) L	6:35 AM (2.65) H	1:40 PM (0.28) L	7:28 PM (1.64) H
Sun 27	12:37 AM (0.76) L	7:05 AM (2.57) H	2:02 PM (0.38) L	7:45 PM (1.70) H
Mon 28	1:06 AM (0.73) L	7:32 AM (2.45) H	2:17 PM (0.47) L	8:05 PM (1.79) H
Tue 29	1:37 AM (0.73) L	7:56 AM (2.30) H	2:27 PM (0.51) L	8:30 PM (1.92) H
Wed 30	2:12 AM (0.76) L	8:19 AM (2.15) H	2:40 PM (0.51) L	9:00 PM (2.04) H
Thu 31	2:53 AM (0.83) L	8:45 AM (1.98) H	2:59 PM (0.51) L	9:42 PM (2.10) H

Brisbane Bar - QLD

DAY/DATE	TIDE 1	TIDE 2	TIDE 3	TIDE 4
Tue 1	2:52 AM (1.73) H	8:37 AM (0.69) L	3:03 PM (2.27) H	10:00 PM (0.57) L
Wed 2	4:02 AM (1.81) H	9:50 AM (0.76) L	4:01 PM (2.15) H	10:52 PM (0.55) L
Thu 3	5:09 AM (1.93) H	11:03 AM (0.79) L	5:00 PM (2.05) H	11:43 PM (0.51) L
Fri 4	6:07 AM (2.07) H	12:13 PM (0.79) L	5:56 PM (1.96) H	
Sat 5	12:29 AM (0.47) L	6:59 AM (2.20) H	1:14 PM (0.75) L	6:47 PM (1.89) H
Sun 6	1:11 AM (0.43) L	7:44 AM (2.31) H	2:08 PM (0.71) L	7:35 PM (1.83) H
Mon 7	1:49 AM (0.41) L	8:25 AM (2.38) H	2:56 PM (0.68) L	8:19 PM (1.80) H
Tue 8	2:26 AM (0.40) L	9:03 AM (2.42) H	3:40 PM (0.66) L	9:00 PM (1.77) H
Wed 9	3:00 AM (0.40) L	9:40 AM (2.43) H	4:19 PM (0.66) L	9:37 PM (1.75) H
Thu 10	3:32 AM (0.42) L	10:15 AM (2.42) H	4:56 PM (0.67) L	10:13 PM (1.74) H
Fri 11	4:05 AM (0.44) L	10:49 AM (2.40) H	5:30 PM (0.69) L	10:47 PM (1.73) H
Sat 12	4:39 AM (0.47) L	11:23 AM (2.36) H	6:04 PM (0.72) L	11:24 PM (1.72) H
Sun 13	5:15 AM (0.53) L	11:58 AM (2.32) H	6:40 PM (0.73) L	
Mon 14	12:04 AM (1.70) H	5:54 AM (0.60) L	12:34 PM (2.27) H	7:18 PM (0.74) L
Tue 15	12:49 AM (1.69) H	6:37 AM (0.68) L	1:14 PM (2.21) H	8:01 PM (0.74) L
Wed 16	1:43 AM (1.68) H	7:29 AM (0.78) L	1:57 PM (2.14) H	8:49 PM (0.71) L
Thu 17	2:45 AM (1.71) H	8:30 AM (0.86) L	2:47 PM (2.07) H	9:41 PM (0.67) L
Fri 18	3:55 AM (1.80) H	9:43 AM (0.91) L	3:46 PM (1.99) H	10:37 PM (0.60) L
Sat 19	5:04 AM (1.95) H	11:00 AM (0.90) L	4:50 PM (1.93) H	11:33 PM (0.53) L
Sun 20	6:06 AM (2.13) H	12:16 PM (0.83) L	5:55 PM (1.89) H	
Mon 21	12:28 AM (0.45) L	7:03 AM (2.33) H	1:29 PM (0.74) L	6:56 PM (1.86) H
Tue 22	1:21 AM (0.37) L	7:57 AM (2.50) H	2:33 PM (0.63) L	7:56 PM (1.86) H
Wed 23	2:13 AM (0.31) L	8:48 AM (2.64) H	3:32 PM (0.54) L	8:54 PM (1.86) H
Thu 24	3:02 AM (0.26) L	9:39 AM (2.73) H	4:28 PM (0.48) L	9:50 PM (1.87) H
Fri 25	3:52 AM (0.24) L	10:29 AM (2.78) H	5:20 PM (0.44) L	10:45 PM (1.88) H
Sat 26	4:41 AM (0.25) L	11:17 AM (2.77) H	6:10 PM (0.44) L	11:36 PM (1.89) H
Sun 27	5:30 AM (0.31) L	12:04 PM (2.70) H	6:57 PM (0.46) L	
Mon 28	12:28 AM (1.89) H	6:21 AM (0.42) L	12:50 PM (2.58) H	7:41 PM (0.50) L
Tue 29	1:20 AM (1.89) H	7:13 AM (0.56) L	1:35 PM (2.41) H	8:24 PM (0.53) L
Wed 30	2:16 AM (1.90) H	8:10 AM (0.71) L	2:21 PM (2.22) H	9:08 PM (0.56) L
Thu 31	3:19 AM (1.92) H	9:15 AM (0.85) L	3:12 PM (2.03) H	9:54 PM (0.59) L

Darwin - NT

DAY/DATE	TIDE 1	TIDE 2	TIDE 3	TIDE 4
Tue 1	5:08 AM (3.09) L	10:29 AM (5.47) H	5:05 PM (2.57) L	11:36 PM (6.44) H
Wed 2	6:23 AM (3.00) L	12:03 PM (5.20) H	6:13 PM (3.15) L	
Thu 3	12:30 AM (6.15) H	7:38 AM (2.76) L	1:40 PM (5.26) H	7:30 PM (3.54) L
Fri 4	1:30 AM (5.94) H	8:46 AM (2.42) L	3:04 PM (5.59) H	8:48 PM (3.70) L
Sat 5	2:30 AM (5.85) H	9:45 AM (2.07) L	4:12 PM (6.04) H	9:59 PM (3.66) L
Sun 6	3:25 AM (5.85) H	10:32 AM (1.76) L	5:05 PM (6.47) H	10:55 PM (3.53) L
Mon 7	4:11 AM (5.91) H	11:12 AM (1.52) L	5:49 PM (6.82) H	11:39 PM (3.37) L
Tue 8	4:50 AM (6.00) H	11:45 AM (1.34) L	6:29 PM (7.06) H	
Wed 9	12:15 AM (3.22) L	5:26 AM (6.10) H	12:17 PM (1.23) L	7:04 PM (7.17) H
Thu 10	12:45 AM (3.11) L	6:00 AM (6.19) H	12:48 PM (1.20) L	7:36 PM (7.18) H
Fri 11	1:15 AM (3.05) L	6:34 AM (6.23) H	1:19 PM (1.25) L	8:07 PM (7.13) H
Sat 12	1:44 AM (3.03) L	7:09 AM (6.22) H	1:50 PM (1.38) L	8:35 PM (7.03) H
Sun 13	2:16 AM (3.04) L	7:44 AM (6.12) H	2:21 PM (1.61) L	9:05 PM (6.90) H
Mon 14	2:52 AM (3.09) L	8:20 AM (5.94) H	2:52 PM (1.91) L	9:35 PM (6.74) H
Tue 15	3:35 AM (3.16) L	9:00 AM (5.70) H	3:23 PM (2.27) L	10:06 PM (6.56) H
Wed 16	4:25 AM (3.21) L	9:46 AM (5.43) H	3:58 PM (2.68) L	10:40 PM (6.35) H
Thu 17	5:22 AM (3.19) L	10:48 AM (5.19) H	4:45 PM (3.12) L	11:18 PM (6.12) H
Fri 18	6:24 AM (3.07) L	12:07 PM (5.08) H	5:53 PM (3.55) L	
Sat 19	12:06 AM (5.90) H	7:29 AM (2.81) L	1:36 PM (5.22) H	7:15 PM (3.84) L
Sun 20	1:03 AM (5.73) H	8:36 AM (2.43) L	3:12 PM (5.65) H	8:44 PM (3.92) L
Mon 21	2:11 AM (5.70) H	9:40 AM (1.95) L	4:24 PM (6.24) H	10:00 PM (3.79) L
Tue 22	3:19 AM (5.83) H	10:35 AM (1.45) L	5:20 PM (6.83) H	11:00 PM (3.55) L
Wed 23	4:17 AM (6.08) H	11:26 AM (0.98) L	6:12 PM (7.31) H	11:51 PM (3.28) L
Thu 24	5:08 AM (6.37) H	12:14 PM (0.63) L	7:00 PM (7.65) H	
Fri 25	12:39 AM (3.02) L	5:57 AM (6.63) H	12:59 PM (0.45) L	7:45 PM (7.84) H
Sat 26	1:26 AM (2.78) L	6:45 AM (6.79) H	1:43 PM (0.48) L	8:27 PM (7.89) H
Sun 27	2:15 AM (2.58) L	7:36 AM (6.80) H	2:27 PM (0.73) L	9:06 PM (7.80) H
Mon 28	3:04 AM (2.43) L	8:29 AM (6.66) H	3:10 PM (1.18) L	9:44 PM (7.58) H
Tue 29	3:56 AM (2.36) L	9:25 AM (6.39) H	3:51 PM (1.80) L	10:19 PM (7.26) H
Wed 30	4:47 AM (2.34) L	10:24 AM (6.02) H	4:32 PM (2.50) L	10:54 PM (6.85) H
Thu 31	5:41 AM (2.39) L	11:27 AM (5.64) H	5:15 PM (3.21) L	11:28 PM (6.39) H

Fremantle - WA

DAY/DATE	TIDE 1	TIDE 2	TIDE 3	TIDE 4
Tue 1	10:48 AM (0.63) L	11:45 AM (0.63) L	12:42 PM (0.63) L	8:49 PM (0.88) H
Wed 2	8:11 AM (0.68) L	9:57 AM (0.69) H	10:43 AM (0.69) L	7:03 PM (0.90) H
Thu 3	7:48 AM (0.67) L	7:02 PM (0.97) H		
Fri 4	5:30 AM (0.62) L	7:05 PM (1.04) H		
Sat 5	4:54 AM (0.56) L	7:11 PM (1.09) H		
Sun 6	5:17 AM (0.51) L	7:28 PM (1.13) H		
Mon 7	5:39 AM (0.47) L	7:50 PM (1.16) H		
Tue 8	5:58 AM (0.45) L	8:15 PM (1.17) H		
Wed 9	6:18 AM (0.44) L	8:42 PM (1.17) H		
Thu 10	6:45 AM (0.44) L	9:12 PM (1.15) H		
Fri 11	7:15 AM (0.45) L	9:44 PM (1.13) H		
Sat 12	7:43 AM (0.48) L	10:15 PM (1.10) H		
Sun 13	8:04 AM (0.51) L	10:45 PM (1.06) H		
Mon 14	8:01 AM (0.55) L	11:11 PM (1.01) H		
Tue 15	7:58 AM (0.58) L	11:31 PM (0.95) H		
Wed 16	8:00 AM (0.61) L	9:42 PM (0.89) H		
Thu 17	7:59 AM (0.63) L	6:21 PM (0.90) H		
Fri 18	7:51 AM (0.65) L	6:05 PM (0.97) H		
Sat 19	6:32 AM (0.64) L	6:14 PM (1.05) H		
Sun 20	4:28 AM (0.57) L	6:40 PM (1.13) H		
Mon 21	4:43 AM (0.47) L	7:14 PM (1.20) H		
Tue 22	5:13 AM (0.38) L	7:52 PM (1.25) H		
Wed 23	5:50 AM (0.32) L	8:34 PM (1.27) H		
Thu 24	6:31 AM (0.29) L	9:18 PM (1.26) H		
Fri 25	7:13 AM (0.31) L	10:04 PM (1.22) H		
Sat 26	7:52 AM (0.37) L	10:46 PM (1.14) H		
Sun 27	8:26 AM (0.45) L	11:06 PM (1.04) H		
Mon 28	8:44 AM (0.54) L	10:51 PM (0.94) H		
Tue 29	8:10 AM (0.62) L	8:33 PM (0.88) H		
Wed 30	6:52 AM (0.63) L	5:45 PM (0.89) H		
Thu 31	6:45 AM (0.61) L	5:52 PM (0.96) H		

Sun Rise & Sun Set Times:

Darwin, NT: Rise: 06:10am Set: 07:00pm

Melbourne, VIC: Rise: 05:50am Set: 08:30pm

Adelaide, SA: Rise: 05:50am Set: 08:20pm

Perth, WA: Rise: 06:50am Set: 05:40pm

Sydney, NSW: Rise: 05:30am Set: 08:00pm

Brisbane, QLD: Rise: 04:40am Set: 06:30pm

Hobart, TAS: Rise: 05:20am Set: 08:40pm

(Note: These times are averages for the month

Hobart - TAS

DAY/DATE	TIDE 1	TIDE 2	TIDE 3	TIDE 4
Tue 1	3:39 AM (1.23) H	9:02 AM (0.86) L	2:37 PM (1.29) H	9:38 PM (0.39) L
Wed 2	4:16 AM (1.27) H	10:15 AM (0.78) L	3:48 PM (1.17) H	10:18 PM (0.51) L
Thu 3	4:51 AM (1.31) H	11:28 AM (0.68) L	5:01 PM (1.06) H	10:50 PM (0.63) L
Fri 4	5:25 AM (1.36) H	12:34 PM (0.60) L	6:16 PM (0.99) H	11:12 PM (0.74) L
Sat 5	5:57 AM (1.40) H	1:33 PM (0.52) L	7:36 PM (0.95) H	11:24 PM (0.83) L
Sun 6	6:28 AM (1.42) H	2:25 PM (0.47) L	8:52 PM (0.95) H	11:33 PM (0.90) L
Mon 7	6:59 AM (1.44) H	3:10 PM (0.43) L	10:01 PM (0.97) H	11:45 PM (0.96) L
Tue 8	7:30 AM (1.44) H	3:49 PM (0.41) L		
Wed 9	8:03 AM (1.44) H	4:26 PM (0.39) L		
Thu 10	8:40 AM (1.43) H	5:03 PM (0.39) L		
Fri 11	9:20 AM (1.41) H	5:41 PM (0.40) L		
Sat 12	10:01 AM (1.39) H	6:18 PM (0.41) L		
Sun 13	2:16 AM (1.08) H	4:12 AM (1.07) L	10:45 AM (1.35) H	6:56 PM (0.43) L
Mon 14	2:33 AM (1.09) H	5:55 AM (1.05) L	11:30 AM (1.30) H	7:30 PM (0.46) L
Tue 15	2:52 AM (1.12) H	7:11 AM (1.02) L	12:17 PM (1.23) H	8:04 PM (0.49) L
Wed 16	3:13 AM (1.16) H	8:23 AM (0.97) L	1:14 PM (1.16) H	8:36 PM (0.54) L
Thu 17	3:35 AM (1.21) H	9:30 AM (0.90) L	2:19 PM (1.09) H	9:04 PM (0.59) L
Fri 18	3:59 AM (1.27) H	10:30 AM (0.80) L	3:32 PM (1.03) H	9:32 PM (0.65) L
Sat 19	4:25 AM (1.35) H	11:25 AM (0.69) L	4:48 PM (0.99) H	10:00 PM (0.72) L
Sun 20	4:55 AM (1.43) H	12:17 PM (0.56) L	6:11 PM (0.97) H	10:33 PM (0.79) L
Mon 21	5:30 AM (1.51) H	1:12 PM (0.42) L	7:35 PM (0.99) H	11:10 PM (0.86) L
Tue 22	6:15 AM (1.58) H	2:08 PM (0.30) L	8:48 PM (1.01) H	11:51 PM (0.92) L
Wed 23	7:05 AM (1.64) H	3:05 PM (0.19) L	9:54 PM (1.04) H	
Thu 24	12:39 AM (0.96) L	8:01 AM (1.68) H	4:01 PM (0.12) L	10:57 PM (1.06) H
Fri 25	1:41 AM (1.00) L	9:00 AM (1.69) H	4:57 PM (0.09) L	11:58 PM (1.09) H
Sat 26	3:16 AM (1.01) L	10:01 AM (1.65) H	5:51 PM (0.11) L	
Sun 27	12:52 AM (1.12) H	5:09 AM (0.97) L	11:05 AM (1.56) H	6:45 PM (0.17) L
Mon 28	1:40 AM (1.17) H	6:32 AM (0.91) L	12:14 PM (1.44) H	7:36 PM (0.27) L
Tue 29	2:21 AM (1.22) H	7:50 AM (0.83) L	1:25 PM (1.30) H	8:24 PM (0.39) L
Wed 30	3:00 AM (1.28) H	9:07 AM (0.74) L	2:35 PM (1.16) H	9:07 PM (0.52) L
Thu 31	3:36 AM (1.34) H	10:20 AM (0.65) L	3:47 PM (1.04) H	9:44 PM (0.64) L

Port Phillip Heads - VIC

DAY/DATE	TIDE 1	TIDE 2	TIDE 3	TIDE 4
Tue 1	5:46 AM (1.67) H	11:18 AM (0.53) L	5:38 PM (1.46) H	11:32 PM (0.34) L
Wed 2	6:32 AM (1.60) H	12:11 PM (0.50) L	6:39 PM (1.41) H	
Thu 3	12:22 AM (0.47) L	7:19 AM (1.54) H	1:05 PM (0.48) L	7:54 PM (1.37) H
Fri 4	1:13 AM (0.60) L	8:07 AM (1.47) H	2:00 PM (0.46) L	9:10 PM (1.37) H
Sat 5	2:07 AM (0.72) L	8:58 AM (1.41) H	2:59 PM (0.44) L	10:17 PM (1.40) H
Sun 6	3:08 AM (0.82) L	9:49 AM (1.36) H	3:59 PM (0.43) L	11:20 PM (1.45) H
Mon 7	4:18 AM (0.88) L	10:44 AM (1.32) H	4:58 PM (0.40) L	
Tue 8	12:19 AM (1.51) H	5:32 AM (0.89) L	11:37 AM (1.30) H	5:53 PM (0.37) L
Wed 9	1:12 AM (1.56) H	6:35 AM (0.86) L	12:28 PM (1.30) H	6:42 PM (0.34) L
Thu 10	1:58 AM (1.61) H	7:25 AM (0.82) L	1:15 PM (1.32) H	7:27 PM (0.31) L
Fri 11	2:37 AM (1.63) H	8:07 AM (0.77) L	1:59 PM (1.34) H	8:08 PM (0.30) L
Sat 12	3:13 AM (1.64) H	8:46 AM (0.73) L	2:40 PM (1.36) H	8:48 PM (0.30) L
Sun 13	3:45 AM (1.64) H	9:24 AM (0.69) L	3:20 PM (1.37) H	9:25 PM (0.32) L
Mon 14	4:18 AM (1.63) H	10:00 AM (0.65) L	4:00 PM (1.37) H	9:58 PM (0.35) L
Tue 15	4:50 AM (1.61) H	10:36 AM (0.63) L	4:38 PM (1.36) H	10:30 PM (0.40) L
Wed 16	5:22 AM (1.59) H	11:10 AM (0.60) L	5:18 PM (1.35) H	11:00 PM (0.46) L
Thu 17	5:55 AM (1.56) H	11:45 AM (0.57) L	6:02 PM (1.33) H	11:35 PM (0.54) L
Fri 18	6:29 AM (1.51) H	12:19 PM (0.53) L	6:51 PM (1.32) H	
Sat 19	12:16 AM (0.62) L	7:04 AM (1.47) H	12:57 PM (0.49) L	7:49 PM (1.33) H
Sun 20	1:04 AM (0.72) L	7:45 AM (1.42) H	1:41 PM (0.44) L	8:56 PM (1.36) H
Mon 21	2:00 AM (0.82) L	8:31 AM (1.37) H	2:31 PM (0.39) L	10:06 PM (1.41) H
Tue 22	3:03 AM (0.91) L	9:26 AM (1.34) H	3:30 PM (0.34) L	11:16 PM (1.47) H
Wed 23	4:17 AM (0.95) L	10:28 AM (1.32) H	4:39 PM (0.28) L	
Thu 24	12:25 AM (1.55) H	5:36 AM (0.94) L	11:37 AM (1.34) H	5:50 PM (0.22) L
Fri 25	1:27 AM (1.63) H	6:45 AM (0.88) L	12:48 PM (1.38) H	6:57 PM (0.17) L
Sat 26	2:22 AM (1.69) H	7:45 AM (0.78) L	1:54 PM (1.43) H	7:57 PM (0.14) L
Sun 27	3:15 AM (1.73) H	8:40 AM (0.68) L	2:52 PM (1.49) H	8:52 PM (0.15) L
Mon 28	4:02 AM (1.74) H	9:32 AM (0.57) L	3:47 PM (1.52) H	9:45 PM (0.20) L
Tue 29	4:47 AM (1.73) H	10:25 AM (0.47) L	4:43 PM (1.53) H	10:34 PM (0.28) L
Wed 30	5:30 AM (1.70) H	11:15 AM (0.40) L	5:40 PM (1.51) H	11:22 PM (0.38) L
Thu 31	6:10 AM (1.65) H	12:03 PM (0.35) L	6:41 PM (1.48) H	

Fort Denison - NSW

DAY/DATE	TIDE 1	TIDE 2	TIDE 3	TIDE 4
Tue 1	2:49 AM (1.36) H	8:27 AM (0.65) L	2:45 PM (1.64) H	9:32 PM (0.44) L
Wed 2	3:50 AM (1.41) H	9:39 AM (0.67) L	3:49 PM (1.52) H	10:23 PM (0.48) L
Thu 3	4:48 AM (1.48) H	10:52 AM (0.66) L	4:52 PM (1.43) H	11:10 PM (0.51) L
Fri 4	5:40 AM (1.55) H	12:00 PM (0.63) L	5:52 PM (1.36) H	11:53 PM (0.53) L
Sat 5	6:28 AM (1.63) H	1:00 PM (0.58) L	6:45 PM (1.32) H	
Sun 6	12:34 AM (0.55) L	7:12 AM (1.69) H	1:51 PM (0.52) L	7:35 PM (1.30) H
Mon 7	1:13 AM (0.56) L	7:51 AM (1.74) H	2:34 PM (0.48) L	8:20 PM (1.29) H
Tue 8	1:50 AM (0.58) L	8:30 AM (1.77) H	3:14 PM (0.44) L	9:01 PM (1.29) H
Wed 9	2:27 AM (0.59) L	9:06 AM (1.79) H	3:51 PM (0.42) L	9:41 PM (1.29) H
Thu 10	3:04 AM (0.60) L	9:43 AM (1.79) H	4:28 PM (0.42) L	10:19 PM (1.29) H
Fri 11	3:42 AM (0.61) L	10:19 AM (1.78) H	5:04 PM (0.43) L	10:58 PM (1.28) H
Sat 12	4:20 AM (0.63) L	10:56 AM (1.76) H	5:42 PM (0.46) L	11:37 PM (1.27) H
Sun 13	5:00 AM (0.65) L	11:33 AM (1.72) H	6:20 PM (0.48) L	
Mon 14	12:19 AM (1.26) H	5:43 AM (0.68) L	12:12 PM (1.66) H	7:01 PM (0.51) L
Tue 15	1:04 AM (1.27) H	6:30 AM (0.71) L	12:53 PM (1.59) H	7:44 PM (0.52) L
Wed 16	1:54 AM (1.29) H	7:23 AM (0.75) L	1:39 PM (1.52) H	8:28 PM (0.53) L
Thu 17	2:47 AM (1.33) H	8:25 AM (0.77) L	2:31 PM (1.45) H	9:14 PM (0.54) L
Fri 18	3:42 AM (1.40) H	9:33 AM (0.76) L	3:32 PM (1.39) H	10:01 PM (0.53) L
Sat 19	4:35 AM (1.50) H	10:46 AM (0.70) L	4:40 PM (1.35) H	10:51 PM (0.53) L
Sun 20	5:28 AM (1.61) H	11:57 AM (0.61) L	5:47 PM (1.34) H	11:43 PM (0.51) L
Mon 21	6:19 AM (1.74) H	1:00 PM (0.49) L	6:50 PM (1.35) H	
Tue 22	12:34 AM (0.49) L	7:12 AM (1.87) H	1:59 PM (0.36) L	7:51 PM (1.37) H
Wed 23	1:28 AM (0.47) L	8:04 AM (1.98) H	2:53 PM (0.25) L	8:48 PM (1.40) H
Thu 24	2:21 AM (0.44) L	8:58 AM (2.07) H	3:46 PM (0.18) L	9:44 PM (1.42) H
Fri 25	3:15 AM (0.43) L	9:51 AM (2.11) H	4:38 PM (0.15) L	10:37 PM (1.43) H
Sat 26	4:10 AM (0.42) L	10:44 AM (2.10) H	5:30 PM (0.17) L	11:30 PM (1.44) H
Sun 27	5:06 AM (0.44) L	11:35 AM (2.03) H	6:20 PM (0.22) L	
Mon 28	12:24 AM (1.44) H	6:03 AM (0.49) L	12:27 PM (1.90) H	7:09 PM (0.30) L
Tue 29	1:18 AM (1.45) H	7:02 AM (0.55) L	1:18 PM (1.74) H	7:57 PM (0.38) L
Wed 30	2:14 AM (1.46) H	8:04 AM (0.62) L	2:12 PM (1.56) H	8:44 PM (0.47) L
Thu 31	3:10 AM (1.48) H	9:13 AM (0.68) L	3:10 PM (1.40) H	9:30 PM (0.55) L

BITE TIMES

Apogee moon phase on Friday 11th

Perigee moon phase on Thursday 24th

New moon on Wednesday 9th

First quarter moon on Thursday 17th

Full moon on Thursday 24th

Last quarter moon phase on Tuesday 1st and Thursday 31st

DAY	MINOR BITE	MAJOR BITE	MINOR BITE	MAJOR BITE	SALT WATER RATING	FRESH WATER RATING
TUE 1	11:52 PM	5:01 AM	10:46 AM	5:23 PM	5	5
WED 2		5:47 AM	11:52 AM	6:08 PM	6	6
THUR 3	12:16 AM	6:31 AM	12:57 PM	6:52 PM	7	7
FRI 4	12:40 AM	7:15 AM	2:00 PM	7:37 PM	7	8
SAT 5	1:05 AM	7:59 AM	3:03 PM	8:22 PM	7	8
SUN 6	1:33 AM	8:45 AM	4:06 PM	9:08 PM	5	8
MON 7	2:04 AM	9:32 AM	5:08 PM	9:56 PM	6	7
TUE 8	2:41 AM	10:22 AM	6:09 PM	10:47 PM	8	8
WED 9	3:24 AM	11:13 AM	7:04 PM	11:38 PM	8	8
THUR 10	4:13 AM	12:05 PM	7:54 PM		8	6
FRI 11	5:08 AM	12:55 PM	8:37 PM	12:30 AM	7	6
SAT 12	6:07 AM	1:44 PM	9:13 PM	1:19 AM	6	7
SUN 13	7:07 AM	2:30 PM	9:43 PM	2:07 AM	6	7
MON 14	8:08 AM	3:14 PM	10:10 PM	2:52 AM	5	5
TUE 15	9:08 AM	3:56 PM	10:34 PM	3:35 AM	4	6
WED 16	10:08 AM	4:38 PM	10:57 PM	4:16 AM	3	5
THUR 17	11:09 AM	5:20 PM	11:21 PM	4:59 AM	4	6
FRI 18	12:12 PM	6:03 PM	11:45 PM	5:41 AM	5	6
SAT 19	1:18 PM	6:50 PM		6:26 AM	4	5
SUN 20	2:29 PM	7:41 PM	12:13 AM	7:15 AM	3	5
MON 21	3:43 PM	8:38 PM	12:46 AM	8:09 AM	6	6
TUE 22	4:59 PM	9:41 PM	1:27 AM	9:09 AM	5	7
WED 23	6:12 PM	10:48 PM	2:19 AM	10:14 AM	3	8
THUR 24	7:17 PM	11:56 PM	3:24 AM	11:22 AM	5	7
FRI 25	8:09 PM		4:39 AM	12:28 PM	7	6
SAT 26	8:51 PM	1:00 AM	5:58 AM	1:29 PM	7	6
SUN 27	9:25 PM	1:59 AM	7:16 AM	2:26 PM	5	5
MON 28	9:53 PM	2:53 AM	8:31 AM	3:17 PM	4	4
TUE 29	10:19 PM	3:42 AM	9:41 AM	4:04 PM	3	6
WED 30	10:44 PM	4:28 AM	10:48 AM	4:50 PM	4	4
THUR 31	11:09 PM	5:13 AM	11:52 AM	5:34 PM	5	5

FISHING JOURNAL

LOCATION

DATE: **DAY:** **SEASON:** **FISHING COMPANIONS:**

LOCATION:

GPS WAY POINT:

ARRIVAL: **DEPARTURE:** **ACCESS NOTES:**

WEATHER CONDITIONS

WIND STRENGTH:
Morn:
Mid:
Noon:
A/noon:
Even:
Night:

WIND DIRECTION:
Morn:
Mid:
Noon:
A/noon:
Even:
Night:

ATMOSPHERIC PRESSURE:
FALLING
STEADY
RISING

LOW
MODERATE
HIGH

Morning:
Noon:
Evening:

AIR TEMPERATURE:
Morn:
Mid:
Noon:
A/noon:
Even:
Night:

WIND NOTES:

ATMOSPHERE & TEMPERATURE NOTES:

WEATHER CONDITIONS:

SUNNY CLOUDY OVERCAST RAIN
Morning

SUNNY CLOUDY OVERCAST RAIN
Noon

SUNNY CLOUDY OVERCAST RAIN
Afternoon

NOTES:

WATER CONDITIONS

WATER TEMPERATURE:
Min: Surface: 10m:
Max: 1m: 20m:

WATER CLARITY:
CRYSTAL CLEAR STAINED CLOUDY DIRTY MUDDY

NOTES:

WATER LEVELS:
DRY LOW NORMAL HIGH FLOOD

Rising
Falling
Steady

NOTES:

MOON PHASE:

NEW FIRST QTR. FULL LAST QTR. NEW

NOTES: ______

PRIME TIME CAPTURES

12 am 6 am 12 pm 6 pm 12 am

SPECIES	ANGLER	SIZE	LENGTH	TACKLE: BAIT/LURE/FLY

TACTICS:

GENERAL:

FISHING JOURNAL

LOCATION

DATE: ______ **DAY:** ______ **SEASON:** ______ **FISHING COMPANIONS:** ______

LOCATION: ______

______

______

______ **GPS WAY POINT:** ______

ARRIVAL: **DEPARTURE:** **ACCESS NOTES:**

WEATHER CONDITIONS

WIND STRENGTH:
Morn: ______
Mid: ______
Noon: ______
A/noon: ______
Even: ______
Night: ______

WIND DIRECTION:
Morn: ______
Mid: ______
Noon: ______
A/noon: ______
Even: ______
Night: ______

ATMOSPHERIC PRESSURE:
FALLING
STEADY
RISING
LOW
MODERATE
HIGH
Morning: ______
Noon: ______
Evening: ______

AIR TEMPERATURE:
Morn: ______
Mid: ______
Noon: ______
A/noon: ______
Even: ______
Night: ______

WIND NOTES: ______

ATMOSPHERE & TEMPERATURE NOTES: ______

WEATHER CONDITIONS:

SUNNY	CLOUDY	OVERCAST	RAIN
Morning			
Noon			
Afternoon			

NOTES: ______

WATER CONDITIONS

WATER TEMPERATURE:
Min: ______ Surface: ______ 10m: ______
Max: ______ 1m: ______ 20m: ______

WATER CLARITY:
CRYSTAL CLEAR STAINED CLOUDY DIRTY MUDDY

NOTES: ______

WATER LEVELS:
DRY LOW NORMAL HIGH FLOOD

Rising ☐
Falling ☐
Steady ☐

NOTES: ______

MOON PHASE: NEW — FIRST QTR. — FULL — LAST QTR. — NEW

NOTES: ______________________________

PRIME TIME CAPTURES

12 am — 6 am — 12 pm — 6 pm — 12 am

SPECIES	ANGLER	SIZE	LENGTH	TACKLE: BAIT/LURE/FLY

TACTICS:

GENERAL:

FISHING JOURNAL

LOCATION

DATE: ____ DAY: ____ SEASON: ____ FISHING COMPANIONS: ____

LOCATION: ____

GPS WAY POINT: ____

ARRIVAL: DEPARTURE: ACCESS NOTES:

WEATHER CONDITIONS

WIND STRENGTH:
Morn: ____
Mid: ____
Noon: ____
A/noon: ____
Even: ____
Night: ____

WIND DIRECTION:
Morn: ____
Mid: ____
Noon: ____
A/noon: ____
Even: ____
Night: ____

ATMOSPHERIC PRESSURE:
FALLING
STEADY
RISING
LOW
MODERATE
HIGH
Morning: ____
Noon: ____
Evening: ____

AIR TEMPERATURE:
Morn: ____
Mid: ____
Noon: ____
A/noon: ____
Even: ____
Night: ____

WIND NOTES: ____

ATMOSPHERE & TEMPERATURE NOTES: ____

WEATHER CONDITIONS:

SUNNY CLOUDY OVERCAST RAIN
Morning

SUNNY CLOUDY OVERCAST RAIN
Noon

SUNNY CLOUDY OVERCAST RAIN
Afternoon

NOTES: ____

WATER CONDITIONS

WATER TEMPERATURE:
Min: ____ Surface: ____ 10m: ____
Max: ____ 1m: ____ 20m: ____

WATER CLARITY:
CRYSTAL CLEAR STAINED CLOUDY DIRTY MUDDY

NOTES: ____

WATER LEVELS:
DRY LOW NORMAL HIGH FLOOD

Rising ☐
Falling ☐
Steady ☐

NOTES: ____

MOON PHASE: NEW — FIRST QTR. — FULL — LAST QTR. — NEW

NOTES:

PRIME TIME CAPTURES

12 am — 6 am — 12 pm — 6 pm — 12 am

SPECIES	ANGLER	SIZE	LENGTH	TACKLE: BAIT/LURE/FLY

TACTICS:

GENERAL:

MOON

FISH CAUGHT

NOTES

FISHING JOURNAL

LOCATION

DATE: ______ **DAY:** ______ **SEASON:** ______ **FISHING COMPANIONS:** ______

LOCATION: ______

GPS WAY POINT: ______

ARRIVAL: **DEPARTURE:** **ACCESS NOTES:**

WEATHER CONDITIONS

WIND STRENGTH:
Morn: ______
Mid: ______
Noon: ______
A/noon: ______
Even: ______
Night: ______

WIND DIRECTION:
Morn: ______
Mid: ______
Noon: ______
A/noon: ______
Even: ______
Night: ______

ATMOSPHERIC PRESSURE:
FALLING
STEADY
RISING

LOW
MODERATE
HIGH

Morning: ______
Noon: ______
Evening: ______

AIR TEMPERATURE:
Morn: ______
Mid: ______
Noon: ______
A/noon: ______
Even: ______
Night: ______

WIND NOTES:

ATMOSPHERE & TEMPERATURE NOTES:

WEATHER CONDITIONS:

SUNNY CLOUDY OVERCAST RAIN
Morning

SUNNY CLOUDY OVERCAST RAIN
Noon

SUNNY CLOUDY OVERCAST RAIN
Afternoon

NOTES: ______

WATER CONDITIONS

WATER TEMPERATURE:
Min: ______ Surface: ______ 10m: ______
Max: ______ 1m: ______ 20m: ______

WATER CLARITY:
CRYSTAL CLEAR STAINED CLOUDY DIRTY MUDDY

NOTES: ______

WATER LEVELS:
DRY LOW NORMAL HIGH FLOOD

Rising ☐
Falling ☐
Steady ☐

NOTES: ______

MOON PHASE: NEW — FIRST QTR. — FULL — LAST QTR. — NEW

NOTES: ______________________________

____

PRIME TIME CAPTURES

12 am — 6 am — 12 pm — 6 pm — 12 am

SPECIES	ANGLER	SIZE	LENGTH	TACKLE: BAIT/LURE/FLY

TACTICS:

____

____

____

____

GENERAL:

____

____

____

____

MOON

FISH CAUGHT

NOTES

FISHING JOURNAL

LOCATION

DATE: ____ **DAY:** ____ **SEASON:** ____ **FISHING COMPANIONS:** ____

LOCATION: ____

GPS WAY POINT: ____

ARRIVAL: **DEPARTURE:** **ACCESS NOTES:**

WEATHER CONDITIONS

WIND STRENGTH:
Morn: ____
Mid: ____
Noon: ____
A/noon: ____
Even: ____
Night: ____

WIND DIRECTION:
Morn: ____
Mid: ____
Noon: ____
A/noon: ____
Even: ____
Night: ____

ATMOSPHERIC PRESSURE:
FALLING
STEADY
RISING
LOW
MODERATE
HIGH
Morning: ____
Noon: ____
Evening: ____

AIR TEMPERATURE:
Morn: ____
Mid: ____
Noon: ____
A/noon: ____
Even: ____
Night: ____

WIND NOTES:

ATMOSPHERE & TEMPERATURE NOTES:

WEATHER CONDITIONS:

SUNNY CLOUDY OVERCAST RAIN — Morning

SUNNY CLOUDY OVERCAST RAIN — Noon

SUNNY CLOUDY OVERCAST RAIN — Afternoon

NOTES: ____

WATER CONDITIONS

WATER TEMPERATURE:
Min: ____ Surface: ____ 10m: ____
Max: ____ 1m: ____ 20m: ____

WATER CLARITY:
CRYSTAL CLEAR STAINED CLOUDY DIRTY MUDDY

NOTES: ____

WATER LEVELS:
DRY LOW NORMAL HIGH FLOOD

Rising ☐
Falling ☐
Steady ☐

NOTES: ____

MOON PHASE: NEW — FIRST QTR. — FULL — LAST QTR. — NEW

NOTES:

PRIME TIME CAPTURES

12 am — 6 am — 12 pm — 6 pm — 12 am

SPECIES	ANGLER	SIZE	LENGTH	TACKLE: BAIT/LURE/FLY

TACTICS:

GENERAL:

MOON

FISH CAUGHT

NOTES

FISHING JOURNAL

LOCATION

DATE: ______ DAY: ______ SEASON: ______ FISHING COMPANIONS: ______

LOCATION: ______

GPS WAY POINT: ______

ARRIVAL: DEPARTURE: ACCESS NOTES:

WEATHER CONDITIONS

WIND STRENGTH:
Morn: ______
Mid: ______
Noon: ______
A/noon: ______
Even: ______
Night: ______

WIND DIRECTION:
Morn: ______
Mid: ______
Noon: ______
A/noon: ______
Even: ______
Night: ______

ATMOSPHERIC PRESSURE:
FALLING
STEADY
RISING
LOW
MODERATE
HIGH

Morning: ______
Noon: ______
Evening: ______

AIR TEMPERATURE:
Morn: ______
Mid: ______
Noon: ______
A/noon: ______
Even: ______
Night: ______

WIND NOTES: ______

ATMOSPHERE & TEMPERATURE NOTES: ______

WEATHER CONDITIONS:

Morning: SUNNY CLOUDY OVERCAST RAIN

Noon: SUNNY CLOUDY OVERCAST RAIN

Afternoon: SUNNY CLOUDY OVERCAST RAIN

NOTES: ______

WATER CONDITIONS

WATER TEMPERATURE:
Min: ______ Surface: ______ 10m: ______
Max: ______ 1m: ______ 20m: ______

WATER CLARITY:
CRYSTAL CLEAR STAINED CLOUDY DIRTY MUDDY

NOTES: ______

WATER LEVELS:
DRY LOW NORMAL HIGH FLOOD

Rising ☐
Falling ☐
Steady ☐

NOTES: ______

FISH COOLER DELUXE RANGE

Keep your catch
ICE COOL for LONGER

Small	750 mm x 400 mm x 330 mm	AC1679
Midi	915 mm x 460 mm x 330 mm	AC1136
Medium	1220 mm x 510 mm x 330 mm	AC1143
Large	1520 mm x 510 mm x 330 mm	AC1150
Extra Large	1830 mm x 510 mm x 330 mm	AC1167

Small

Midi

Medium

Large

Extra Large

KAYAK COOLER DELUXE RANGE

Medium	610 mm length - Top width 180mm - Bottom width x 400 mm	AC1112-11000
Large	910 mm length - Top width 250mm - Bottom width x 510 mm	AC1129-13700

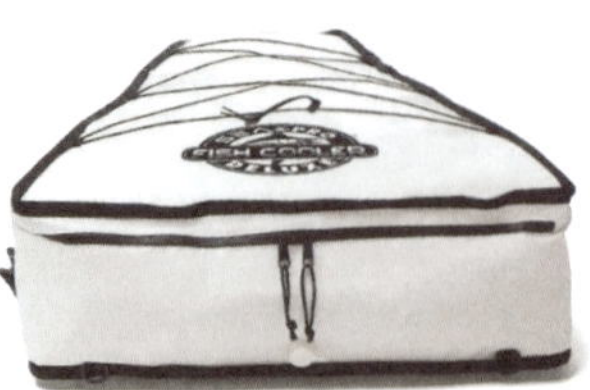

Medium
With rubber handle

Large
With 3 rubber handles

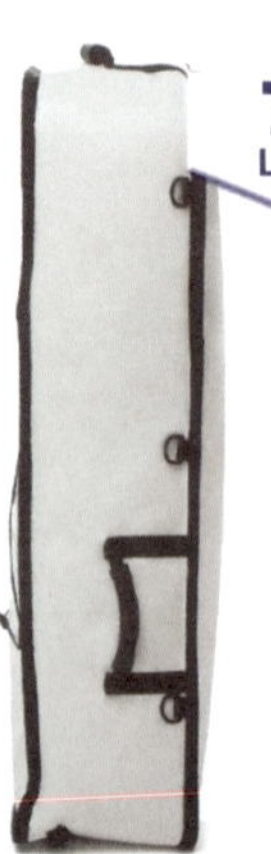